DATE DUE

			PRINTED IN U.S.A.

Authors & Artists for Young Adults

ISSN 1040-5682

R

Authors & Artists for Young Adults

VOLUME 27

Thomas McMahon
Editor

GALE

DETROIT • LONDON

Thomas McMahon, *Editor*

Joyce Nakamura, *Managing Editor*
Hal May, *Publisher*

Diane Andreassi, Joanna Brod, Ken Cuthbertson, R. Garcia-Johnson, Kevin S. Hile,
J. Sydney Jones, Sharon Malinowski, Susan Reicha, Peggy Saari, Gerard J. Senick,
Pamela L. Shelton, Tracy J. Sukraw, *Sketchwriters/Contributing Editors*

Victoria B. Cariappa, *Research Manager*
Cheryl L. Warnock, *Project Coordinator*
Gary P. Oudersluys, *Research Specialist*
Jeffrey D. Daniels, Norma Sawaya, *Research Associates*
Patricia Tsune Ballard, Phyllis Blackman, Wendy K. Festerling, Corrine A. Stocker,
Research Assistants

Susan M. Trosky, *Permissions Manager*
Maria L. Franklin, *Permissions Specialist*
Sarah Chesney, Edna Hedblad, Michele Lonoconus, *Permissions Associates*

Mary Beth Trimper, *Production Director*
Cindy Range, *Production Assistant*

Randy Bassett, *Image Database Supervisor*
Gary Leach, *Graphic Artist*
Robert Duncan, Michael Logusz, *Imaging Specialists*
Pamela A. Reed, *Photography Coordinator*

The paper used in this publication meets the minimum requirements of
American National Standard for Information Sciences—Permanence Paper
for Printed Library Materials, ANSI Z39.48-1984.

Library of Congress Catalog Card Number 89-641100
ISBN 0-7876-2070-X
ISSN 1040-5682

10 9 8 7 6 5 4 3 2 1

Printed in the United States of America

Authors and Artists for Young Adults

TEEN BOARD

―――――

The staff of *Authors and Artists for Young Adults* wishes to thank the following young adult readers for their teen board participation:

Contents

Introduction

Authors and Artists for Young Adults is a reference series designed to serve the needs of middle school, junior high, and high school students interested in creative artists. Originally inspired by the need to bridge the gap between Gale's *Something about the Author,* created for children, and *Contemporary Authors,* intended for older students and adults, *Authors and Artists for Young Adults* has been expanded to cover not only an international scope of authors, but also a wide variety of other artists.

Although the emphasis of the series remains on the writer for young adults, we recognize that these readers have diverse interests covering a wide range of reading levels. The series therefore contains not only those creative artists who are of high interest to young adults, including cartoonists, photographers, music composers, bestselling authors of adult novels, media directors, producers, and performers, but also literary and artistic figures studied in academic curricula, such as influential novelists, playwrights, poets, and painters. The goal of *Authors and Artists for Young Adults* is to present this great diversity of creative artists in a format that is entertaining, informative, and understandable to the young adult reader.

Entry Format

Each volume of *Authors and Artists for Young Adults* will furnish in-depth coverage of twenty to twenty-five authors and artists. The typical entry consists of:

—A detailed biographical section that includes date of birth, marriage, children, education, and addresses.

—A comprehensive bibliography or filmography including publishers, producers, and years.

—Adaptations into other media forms.

—Works in progress.

—A distinctive essay featuring comments on an artist's life, career, artistic intentions, world views, and controversies.

—References for further reading.

—Extensive illustrations, photographs, movie stills, cartoons, book covers, and other relevant visual material.

A cumulative index to featured authors and artists appears in each volume.

Compilation Methods

The editors of *Authors and Artists for Young Adults* make every effort to secure information directly from the authors and artists through personal correspondence and interviews. Sketches on living authors and artists are sent to the biographee for review prior to publication. Any sketches not personally reviewed by biographees or their representatives are marked with an asterisk (*).

Highlights of Forthcoming Volumes

Among the authors and artists planned for future volumes are:

Sherman Alexie	Barbara Hambly	Edvard Munch
Jennifer Armstrong	John Hersey	Phyllis Reynolds Naylor
Lilian Jackson Braun	Victor Hugo	Han Nolan
Melvin Burgess	Paul Jennings	Robert B. Parker
Chuck Close	Sebastian Junger	Elizabeth Ann Scarborough
Edwidge Danticat	Laurie R. King	Mary Stewart
Julie Dash	Jackie French Koller	Sue Townsend
Sharon M. Draper	Nancy Kress	Paul Theroux
T. S. Eliot	Jonathan Larson	Joan D. Vinge
Harlan Ellison	Spike Lee	Will Weaver
Philip Jose Farmer	Morgan Llywelyn	Michael Whelan
Charles Ferry	Jess Mowry	Tad Williams

Contact the Editor

We encourage our readers to examine the entire *AAYA* series. Please write and tell us if we can make AAYA even more helpful to you. Give your comments and suggestions to the editor:

BY MAIL: The Editor, *Authors and Artists for Young Adults*, 27500 Drake Rd., Farmington Hills, MI 48331-3535.

BY TELEPHONE: (800) 347-GALE

Authors & Artists for Young Adults

Nathan Aaseng

■ Personal

Born July 7, 1953, in Park Rapids, MN; son of Rolf E. (a minister) and Viola (a librarian; maiden name, Anderson) Aaseng; married Linda Jansen, December 20, 1975; children: Jay, Maury, Mikhaila, Evan. *Education:* Luther College, B.A., 1975.

■ Addresses

Home and office—109 West Grant Ave., Eau Claire, WI 54701.

■ Career

Bio-Tech Resources, Manitowoc, WI, microbiologist-biochemist, 1975-79; writer, 1979—.

■ Awards, Honors

Children's Choice awards, International Reading Association/Children's Book Council, 1984, for *Baseball: You Are the Manager* and *Football: You Are the Coach,* and 1986, for *Baseball: It's Your Team* and *Football: It's Your Team;* Children's Books of the Year citation, Child Study Association of America, 1985, for *Carl Lewis: Legend Chaser;* Outstanding Science Trade Book citation, *Children and Science,* 1986, for *More with Less: The Future World of Buckminster Fuller,* 1987, for *The Disease Fighters: The Nobel Prize in Medicine,* and 1988, for *The Inventors: Nobel Prizes in Chemistry, Physics, and Medicine;* Notable Children's Trade Book in the Field of Social Studies citation, Children's Book Council of the National Council for the Social Studies, 1989, for *Better Mousetraps: Product Improvements That Led to Success, The Fortunate Fortunes: Business Successes That Began with a Lucky Break, The Problem Solvers: People Who Turned Problems into Products, The Rejects: People and Products That Outsmarted the Experts,* and *The Unsung Heroes: Unheralded People Who Invented Famous Products;* Notable Children's Trade Book in the Field of Social Studies, National Council for the Social Studies, 1992, for *Robert E. Lee;* Junior Library Guild selection, 1992, Young Hoosier Book of the Year finalist, 1993, and International Reading Association CBC Young Adult Choices selection, 1994, all for *Navajo Code Talkers;* Gold Medallion Award finalist, Christian Publishers Association, 1993, for *Ben Carson,* 1994, for *Billy Graham;* Young Hoosier Book of the Year finalist, 1995, for *True Champions;* Curriculum Administrator's "Top 100 Products" list, 1995, for "American Indian Lives" series.

■ Writings

"SPORTS ACHIEVERS" SERIES

Bruce Jenner: Decathlon Winner, Lerner, 1979.
Eric Heiden: Winner in Gold, Lerner, 1980.
Pete Rose: Baseball's Charlie Hustle, Lerner, 1981.

"SPORTS ACHIEVERS" SERIES; UNDER NAME NATE AASENG

Steve Carlton: Baseball's Silent Strongman, Lerner, 1984.
Carl Lewis: Legend Chaser, Lerner, 1985.
Dwight Gooden: Strikeout King, Lerner, 1988.
Florence Griffith Joyner: Dazzling Olympian, Lerner, 1989.
Jose Canseco: Baseball's Forty-Forty Man, Lerner, 1989.

"SPORTS HEROES LIBRARY" SERIES

Baseball's Finest Pitchers, Lerner, 1980.
(And photographer) *Basketball's High Flyers,* Lerner, 1980.
Football's Breakaway Backs, Lerner, 1980.
(And photographer) *Football's Fierce Defenses,* Lerner, 1980.
Football's Sure-Handed Receivers, Lerner, 1980.
Football's Winning Quarterbacks, Lerner, 1980.
Little Giants of Pro Sports, Lerner, 1980.
Winners Never Quit: Athletes Who Beat the Odds, Lerner, 1980.
Football's Cunning Coaches, Lerner, 1981.
Football's Steadiest Kickers, Lerner, 1981.
Football's Toughest Tight Ends, Lerner, 1981.
Track's Magnificent Milers, Lerner, 1981.
Winning Men of Tennis, Lerner, 1981.
Winning Women of Tennis, Lerner, 1981.

"SPORTS HEROES LIBRARY" SERIES; UNDER NAME NATE AASENG

Baseball's Brilliant Managers, Lerner, 1982.
Football's Crushing Blockers, Lerner, 1982.
Football's Super Bowl Champions: I-VIII, Lerner, 1982.
Football's Super Bowl Champions: IX-XVI, Lerner, 1982.
Memorable World Series Moments, Lerner, 1982.
Superstars Stopped Short, Lerner, 1982.
World-Class Marathoners, Lerner, 1982.
Baseball's Hottest Hitters, Lerner, 1983.
Baseball's Power Hitters, Lerner, 1983.
Basketball's Playmakers, Lerner, 1983.
Basketball's Sharpshooters, Lerner, 1983.

Comeback Stars of Pro Sports, Lerner, 1983.
Football's Hard-hitting Linebackers, Lerner, 1983.
Supersubs of Pro Sports, Lerner, 1983.
Baseball's Ace Relief Pitchers, Lerner, 1984.
Football's Daring Defensive Backs, Lerner, 1984.
Football's Punishing Pass Rushers, Lerner, 1984.
Hockey's Fearless Goalies, Lerner, 1984.
Hockey's Super Scorers, Lerner, 1984.
Basketball's Power Players, Lerner, 1985.
A Decade of Champions: Super Bowls XV to XXIV, Lerner, 1991.

"YOU ARE THE COACH" SERIES; UNDER NAME NATE AASENG

Baseball: You Are the Manager, Lerner, 1983, published as *You Are the Manager: Baseball,* Dell, 1984.
Basketball: You Are the Coach, Lerner, 1983, published as *You Are the Coach: Basketball,* Dell, 1983.
Football: You Are the Coach, Lerner, 1983, published as *You Are the Coach: Football,* Dell, 1983.
Hockey: You Are the Coach, Lerner, 1983, published as *You Are the Coach: Hockey,* Dell, 1984.
College Basketball: You Are the Coach, Lerner, 1984, published as *You Are the Coach: College Basketball,* Dell, 1986.
College Football: You Are the Coach, Lerner, 1984, published as *You Are the Coach: College Football,* Dell, 1985.
Baseball: It's Your Team, Lerner, 1985, published as *It's Your Team: Baseball,* Dell, 1985.
Football: It's Your Team, Lerner, 1985, published as *It's Your Team: Football,* Dell, 1985.

"SPORTS TALK" SERIES; UNDER NAME NATE AASENG

Baseball's Greatest Teams, Lerner, 1986.
Baseball's Worst Teams, Lerner, 1986.
Football's Most Controversial Calls, Lerner, 1986.
Football's Most Shocking Upsets, Lerner, 1986.
Pro Sports' Greatest Rivalries, Lerner, 1986.
College Football's Hottest Rivalries, Lerner, 1987.
Football's Incredible Bulks, Lerner, 1987.
Record Breakers of Pro Sports, Lerner, 1987.
Ultramarathons: The World's Most Punishing Races, Lerner, 1987.
Great Summer Olympic Moments, Lerner, 1990.
Great Winter Olympics Moments, Lerner, 1990.

"NOBEL PRIZE WINNERS" SERIES

The Disease Fighters: The Nobel Prize in Medicine, Lerner, 1987.

The Inventors: Nobel Prizes in Chemistry, Physics, and Medicine, Lerner, 1987.

The Peace Seekers: The Nobel Peace Prize, Lerner, 1987.

"INSIDE BUSINESS" SERIES

Better Mousetraps: Product Improvements That Led to Success, Lerner, 1989.

The Fortunate Fortunes: Business Successes That Began with a Lucky Break, Lerner, 1989.

The Problem Solvers: People Who Turned Problems into Products, Lerner, 1989.

The Rejects: People and Products That Outsmarted the Experts, Lerner, 1989.

The Unsung Heroes: Unheralded People Who Invented Famous Products, Lerner, 1989.

Close Calls: From the Brink of Ruin to Business Success, Lerner, 1990.

From Rags to Riches: People Who Started Businesses from Scratch, Lerner, 1990.

Midstream Changes: People Who Started Over and Made It Work, Lerner, 1990.

"EARLY NATURE" PICTURE BOOK; ILLUSTRATED BY A. C. DORNISCH

Animal Specialists, Lerner, 1987.

Horned Animals, Lerner 1987.

Meat-Eating Animals, Lerner, 1987.

Prey Animals, Lerner, 1987.

"SPORTS GREAT" SERIES

Sports Great Michael Jordan, Enslow, 1992.

Sports Great David Robinson, Enslow, 1992.

Sports Great Kirby Puckett, Enslow, 1993.

Sports Great John Stockton, Enslow, 1995.

"GREAT DECISIONS" SERIES

You Are the Supreme Court Justice, Oliver Press, 1994.

You Are the President, Oliver Press, 1994.

You Are the President II: 1800-1899, Oliver Press, 1994.

You Are the General, Oliver Press, 1994.

You Are the General II: 1800-1899, Oliver Press, 1995.

You Are the Senator, Oliver Press, 1996.

You Are a Juror, Oliver Press, 1997.

You Are the Corporate Executive, Oliver Press, 1997.

OTHER NONFICTION

Bob Geldof: The Man behind Live Aid, Lerner, 1986.

More with Less: The Future World of Buckminster Fuller, Lerner, 1986.

Playing for Life: Sports Stories for Teens, Augsburg, 1987.

Bob Dylan: Spellbinding Songwriter, Lerner, 1987.

Jim Henson: Muppet Master, Lerner, 1988.

Robert E. Lee, Lerner, 1991.

Overpopulation: Crisis or Challenge?, F. Watts, 1991.

Ending World Hunger, F. Watts, 1991.

Cerebral Palsy, F. Watts, 1991.

Twentieth-Century Inventors, Facts on File, 1991.

Paris, Simon & Schuster, 1992.

Breaking the Sound Barrier, Silver Burdett, 1992.

(With Cecil Murphey) *Ben Carson*, Zondervan, 1992.

The Common Cold and the Flu, F. Watts, 1992.

Navajo Code Talkers, Walker & Co., 1992.

Great Justices of the Supreme Court, Oliver Press, 1992.

True Champions: Great Athletes and Their Off-the-Field Heroics, Walker & Co., 1993.

The Locker Room Mirror: How Sports Reflect Society, Walker & Co., 1993.

Vertebrates, F. Watts, 1993.

Invertebrates, F. Watts, 1993.

Charles Darwin: Revolutionary Biologist, Lerner, 1993.

Billy Graham, Zondervan, 1993.

Jobs vs. the Environment: Can We Save Both?, Enslow, 1994.

Barry Sanders: Star Running Back, Enslow, 1994.

Science vs. Pseudoscience, F. Watts, 1994.

The O. J. Simpson Trial: What It Shows Us about Our Legal System, Walker & Co., 1995.

Autoimmune Diseases, F. Watts, 1995.

Athletes ("American Indian Lives" series), Facts on File, 1995.

Yearbooks in Science: 1940-1949, Twenty-First Century Books, 1995.

Yearbooks in Science: 1930-1939, Twenty-First Century Books, 1995.

America's Third-Party Presidential Candidates, Oliver Press, 1995.

Genetics: Unlocking the Secret Code, Oliver Press, 1996.

Head Injuries, F. Watts, 1996.

Meat-Eating Plants, Enslow, 1996.

American Dinosaur Hunters, Enslow, 1996.

Black Inventors ("American Profiles" series), Facts on File, 1997.

Treacherous Traitor, Oliver Press, 1997.

Poisonous Creatures, Twenty-First Century Books, 1997.

FICTION; UNDER NAME NATE AASENG

Batting Ninth for the Braves, Cook, 1982, published as *A Winning Season for the Braves*, 1988.

Forty-two Red on Four, Cook, 1983, published as
   At Left Linebacker: Chip Demory, 1988.
(With Mike Sherer) *Night of Wonder: Service-Story
   for Christmas Eve* (short story), CSS, 1985.
Batter Up!, Cook, 1990.
Full Court Press, Cook, 1990.
All-Star Line-Up, Cook, 1994.
Aliens! ("Grubstake Adventures" series), Augsburg,
   1995.
Swamped! ("Grubstake Adventures" series), Augs-
   burg, 1995.
Sneak Attack! ("Grubstake Adventures" series),
   Augsburg, 1995.
Lost in the Forest! ("Grubstake Adventures" series),
   Augsburg, 1996.

DEVOTIONALS

*I'm Learning, Lord, but I Still Need Help: Story De-
   votions for Boys,* Augsburg, 1981.
I'm Searching, Lord, but I Need Your Light, Augs-
   burg, 1983.
*Which Way Are You Leading Me, Lord?: Bible Devo-
   tions for Boys,* Augsburg, 1984.
Explorers for God, illustrated by Douglas Oudekerk,
   Augsberg, 1998.

■ Sidelights

Nathan Aaseng is a prolific writer of juvenile
nonfiction and fiction with over 130 titles to his
credit. While much of his early work was done
in the field of sports, writing several popular series such as "You Are the Coach" for the Minne-
apolis-based Lerner Publications, he has branched
out into a broad range of themes that include
general science, biography, business innovation,
and Nobel Prize winners. His varied interests have
taken him from a study of invertebrates to Navajo code talkers in World War II; from a profile
of the Olympian Bruce Jenner to an account of
the O. J. Simpson murder trial. Yet for Aaseng, a
self-described "Norwegian Lutheran" with a wry
sense of humor, this is only the beginning. "At
this point in my career, I must admit that I have
not reached a single goal that I set for myself
when I decided to enter the business of writing,"
he wrote in an essay for *Something about the Author Autobiography Series* (*SAAS*). "I suppose there
are very few 'failures' who get so many books
published this early in their lives, and I am certain this gives me a perspective that is different
from that of most 'successful' writers."

Like so many other writers for young readers,
Aaseng had no intention of writing for a juvenile
audience when he set out on a writing career, but
he quickly found that he had a unique perspective from which to write to youth. "If a writer's
gift is being able to see things that others do not
see or can no longer see, and to speak in ways
that do not occur to others," he commented in
SAAS, "it must be to his or her advantage to live
an abnormal life. The evidence shows that I had
this advantage." One of five children of a
Lutheran minister, Aaseng was born in Park Rapids, Minnesota, a world not far removed from that
described by Garrison Keillor in his humorous
Lake Wobegon tales. His father was a well-re-
spected minister, noted for a quiet nature that
bordered on the taciturn—a trait Aaseng claims
to have inherited, and which also led to his bare-
bones writing approach, one well fitted to younger
readers. "To this day, I nearly always have to go
back and *add* material after my first draft," Aaseng
wrote in *SAAS.*

A small child during elementary and junior high
schools, Aaseng also had a stutter, two features
that set him apart from the rest of the children
in St. Louis Park, Minnesota, and that made for
a somewhat lonely schooling. His home environment provided the nurturing that he missed in
school, however, and family camping trips were
an integral part of his early years. Books were
also important to Aaseng. "It is rare to meet an
author who has not loved to read since early
childhood," Aaseng noted in *SAAS,* "and I am no
exception there. I was fortunate to have an older
brother and sister to scout out a path through the
library wilderness." Some of his earliest favorites
were *Big Red* and *Wild Trek* by the outdoor writer
Jim Kjelgaard, sports biographies by Milton
Shapiro, and the "Freddy the Pig" books of Walter
R. Brooks. Later, Aaseng's father introduced him
to the "Chronicles of Narnia" by C. S. Lewis, a
series of books that he rereads periodically even
now. "I do not think of my childhood in terms
of happy or unhappy—there were many times
when it was one or the other, or neither," Aaseng
recalled in *SAAS.* "But when I think of pleasurable times as a child, reading jumps to mind immediately."

Aaseng had an early love for writing, as well.
"My writing assignments almost always came back
with the world *clever* scrawled across the top. I
saw *clever* on my papers so often that I began to

Martin Luther King, Jr., shown here receiving the 1964 Nobel Peace Prize, is one of nine prizewinners profiled in Aaseng's 1987 work, *The Peace Seekers*.

think there was a conspiracy among teachers that I was to be so labeled." But it wasn't until high school that Aaseng began to find a place for himself in the give and take of adolescent society. It was then that—through the model of his brother—he discovered sports, specifically track and distance running. And this proved to be his niche, something that he was not only good at, but also something that won him friends and developed his own sense of self-worth. It helped that he also grew eight inches in one year and slowly began

to control his stuttering. "One of the sweetest ironies of my life was the fact that there were only three boys in my high school class of more than seven hundred who earned athletic letters as first-semester sophomores, and one of them was me . . . ," Aaseng noted in *SAAS*. "There is unquestionably much to be desired in the way we emphasize sports in our society. But I cannot ignore the debt that I owe to sports. They gave me at least a measure of respect. Respect is one of those trace elements of human interaction that we simply must have in order to function. Sports also provided a support group."

When it came time to picking a college, Aaseng chose Luther College in Decorah, Iowa, not the least reason for this selection being the fine wooded trails around the school on which he could continue to run. Aaseng studied English and biology, appreciating the scientific rigor of the one and the creative outlet provided by the other, and also met the young woman whom he would later marry, Linda Jansen. His interest in writing continued to grow, as well, partly fueled by a term paper on the *Iliad* that he wrote in rhyme and meter reminiscent of Homer himself, and for which he received an A+. At this time he read

Aaseng describes the work of a group of Navajo soldiers who created a special code during World War II, which enabled the U.S. to send messages that could not be deciphered by the enemy.

the works of George Orwell, whose essay, "The Politics of the English Language," particularly affected his writing style. He also wrote a weekly column for the school newspaper, in which he let his humor loose in print for the first time. "Nothing that I have written since has brought me as much favorable comment as the year-and-a-half run of 'The Armchair Norseman,'" Aaseng noted in *SAAS*.

The Accidental Profession

After graduating from college, Aaseng followed Jansen to Wisconsin, where she was teaching fourth grade. They soon were married and he took work first in a canning company and then as a microbiologist in a biotech company. But writing was what he really wanted to do, so he decided to take a shot at a writing career just as he and his wife were expecting their first child. The pragmatic Aaseng figured the way to break into publishing was by working as a journalist or an editor in a publishing house. It was while applying for editorial positions that he stumbled into his first writing assignment. Meeting with a senior editor at Lerner Publications, Aaseng found there were no editorial positions open, but that the house did need someone to put together a short biography on Bruce Jenner, the 1976 Olympic decathlon champ. Lerner had acquired a number of photos of Jenner and was looking for text to accompany them. "No one gets anywhere in the writing world without some luck greasing the wheels," Aaseng wrote in *SAAS*. This was more than luck; this seemed pre-ordained. Not only was Aaseng himself a track man, but he had also once competed at the same meet with Jenner during college and had subsequently followed his career. The resulting book, Aaseng's first, was *Bruce Jenner: Decathlon Winner,* a manuscript with which his wife assisted him in finding the correct reading level for fourth graders, the target audience. On the strength of that book and further contracts with Lerner, Aaseng settled into the life of a full-time author.

There followed a number of books in Lerner's "Sports Achievers" series, including an award-winning title on Carl Lewis. *Florence Griffith Joyner: Dazzling Olympian* is typical of the series. Some sixty pages of text following the course of the athlete's life are combined with photos documenting major athletic achievements. "Aaseng's smooth,

NATHAN AASENG

The Locker Room Mirror

HOW SPORTS REFLECT SOCIETY

In this work, Aaseng discusses scandals in which so-called heroes of the sports world have been involved with drugs, crime, and discrimination.

easy style accurately captures the development of this star athlete's quest," noted Janice C. Hayes in *School Library Journal*, and *Bulletin of the Center for Children's Books* critic Betsy Hearne also commented on Aaseng's "smooth style" as he covered the high points in the life of this determined sprinter, one of eleven children in a family from a Watts housing project. Aaseng also penned the popular "Sports Heroes Library" series for Lerner, which includes titles on outstanding male and female athletes, as well as outstanding teams. "Nutshell" glimpses is how a *School Library Journal* reviewer referred to series titles such as *Basketball's High Flyers*, adding that while the books are necessarily brief, they provide "a good feel for the personalities." Commenting on several of the titles in another *School Library Journal* re-

view, Robert E. Unsworth praised Aaseng as a writer who "respects his readers—never talks down to them—and does this sort of thing—short, eye-catching, easy-to-read profiles—as well as anyone."

Among Aaseng's most popular sports titles are the "You Are the Coach" series, an idea that came to him while riding a Minneapolis city bus. "I overheard some mothers discussing how much their children enjoyed those 'Choose Your Own Adventure' books," Aaseng recalled in *SAAS*. "The reader participation format seemed quite limiting to me as far as fiction was concerned. The thought occurred to me that this type of book was really more suited to nonfiction." By the end of the bus ride, Aaseng had hit upon the format of "You Are the Coach": basically an opportunity to second-guess coaches or managers in do-or-die situations that really happened. Readers are presented with turning-point situations in actual baseball, football, basketball, and hockey games, then given several possible choices—who to pinch-hit, what play to run—from which to choose. Turning the page, the reader sees what choice was actually made with what result and how his or her choice matches up against the pro's. Elaine Fort Weischedel, writing in *School Library Journal*, thought that "the novelty of the format should hold readers," and Joe McKenzie, in another *School Library Journal* review of the series, commented that it was "a marvelous concept."

In writing the stories of athletes, potentially presenting them as modern-day heroes and role models for youth, Aaseng also saw the possible downside of this sort of writing. "I can understand the frustration of seeing much of society enamored of superstars and superteams in sports to the exclusion of more thought-provoking pursuits," Aaseng wrote in *SAAS*. As a result, he explained, "while doing sports books for Lerner, I felt a strong obligation to keep athletics and athletic heroes in perspective." To that end, he wrote three unusual sports books that show more realistic or admirable views of sports: *Superstars Stopped Short, Baseball's Worst Teams,* and *Playing for Life,* the last of which relates several "unheralded act[s] of exceptional compassion or courage on the part of a world-class athlete," as Aaseng described it.

Aaseng has also written sports fiction, including *Batting Ninth for the Braves,* in which he highlighted his own early frustrations in athletics, failing even to make the cuts in Little League try-outs. With *Batting Ninth for the Braves,* Aaseng tried to close a personal "wound that would not heal," as he noted in *SAAS.* "I created my own Little League, coached by a person whom I would have loved to play for." Other sports writing by Aaseng has also been of a more reflective nature, including the 1993 title for Walker, *The Locker Room: How Sports Reflect Society,* demonstrating how athletics has some of the same problems as society as a whole with drugs, violence, racism, and greed. Jack Forman, reviewing the book in *School Library Journal,* concluded that it was a

"provocative overview" that "raises questions that beg to be asked."

Branching Out

Aaseng got a chance to move out of sports writing with a series of overview books on the Nobel Prizes for medicine, physics, chemistry, and peace. His personal favorite is the volume *The Peace Seekers: The Nobel Peace Prize,* a profile of eight winners in a book that makes for "brisk engaging reading," according to Steve Matthews in *School Library Journal.* Especially difficult for Aaseng was his "trial by fire" in compiling the volume on physics and chemistry. As he related in *SAAS,* "After surviving a bout with the most incomprehensible subject I had ever encountered, nothing else looked difficult. Over the next few years, I wrote about subjects ranging from animals to Bob Dylan to Buckminster Fuller."

He also created the award-winning "Inside Business" series for Lerner, another series inspired by Aaseng's own questioning nature. "While sipping a can of Coca-Cola," Aaseng recalled in *SAAS,* "I began thinking about this product's effect on the twentieth century." He began to see how universal the symbol of the red and white can was, and wanted to know how this transformation of a product consumed worldwide had come about. This started the titles on influential products, corporations, inventions, and entrepreneurs that form the core of "Inside Business." Examining everything from Astro-Turf to Kleenex, Aaseng creates "a lively history of the commonplace," according to Margaret A. Bush in a *Horn Book* of *The Fortunate Fortunes, The Problem Solvers, The Rejects.* "The information here is exceptionally well organized to entertain and instruct," noted a critic in *Kirkus Reviews,* adding that "Aaseng tells his stories well." And Zena Sutherland concluded in a *Bulletin of the Center for Children's Books* review that "separately or together, the books provide a good introduction to the business world."

From early books on sports and business, Aaseng has branched out into the sciences in several books published by Watts. Two books of a more urgent social nature appeared in 1991: *Ending World Hunger* and *Overpopulation: Crisis or Challenge?* Again providing an overview and a starting place for further reading, Aaseng compiled the most recent data in a format that "may serve as

The author uses real historical situations to help readers experience what it would be like to be president of the United States.

If you enjoy the works of Nathan Aaseng, you may also want to check out the following books:

Russell Freedman, *The Wright Brothers: How They Invented the Airplane*, 1991.
Nat Hentoff, *The First Freedom: The Tumultuous History of Free Speech in America*, 1980.
Jim Murphy, *The Great Fire*, 1995.

the basis for some very important discussions on the most important issue for our time and for all the future," according to Carol R. Bilge in *Appraisal: Science Books for Young People*. Reviewing *Ending World Hunger* in *School Library Journal*, Jonathan Betz-Zall concluded that "this book can fill an important need for a timely, balanced comprehensive treatment of a critical subject."

With his *Science Versus Pseudoscience*, Aaseng measured ESP, astrology, UFOs and various other so-called pseudosciences against pure science in a book that is "written in an easily accessible and engaging style," according to Carolyn Angus in *School Library Journal*; *Bulletin of the Center for Children's Books* contributor Roger Sutton commented that it was "useful to both science and current events classrooms." Reviewing Aaseng's zoological contribution, *Vertebrates*, in *Science Books and Films*, Eleanor Wenger noted that it "is generally a well-written and well-organized book," but also pointed out several factual errors that she believed readers would later be forced to "unlearn."

Aaseng has also turned his hand to history, combining political, judicial, and military studies with the same participatory approach he devised in the "You Are the Coach" series. The reader assumes an active role as a president of the United States, a general, or a Supreme Court justice, and, presented with the facts of historical crises or cases, must pit her or his judgment against the historical reality. With his *You Are the President*, Aaseng presented eight crises from the Pennsylvania coal strike to missiles in Cuba. Reviewing that book in *Voice of Youth Advocates*, Laura L. Lent concluded that "Aaseng's interactive approach to teaching history to American teenagers is innovative, invigorating, and informative."

A man of varied interests, Aaseng spent many years trying to convince publishers that he could write about more than sports. Now his subject matter ranges far and wide, but threading through most of his books is the persistent theme of overcoming adversity. Hannah Pickworth, reviewing the "Inside Business" series for *Appraisal: Science Books for Young People*, noted that "the main lesson of this series is that these people were successful because they believed in themselves, regardless of their previous failures and the ridicule from those around them." The same could be said for Aaseng himself in overcoming his own youthful insecurities. Humble of his achievements, Aaseng once told *SATA* about the process of writing for children, which he sometimes finds frustrating. "Words are my tools," he noted, "and the younger the reader, the fewer tools (words) I can use. I have to say something within their vocabulary. On the other hand, I have felt comfortable writing for young people because I do not believe in trying to impress people with huge words or intimidating style. I always thought the idea in writing was to communicate, not to show off."

■ Works Cited

Aaseng, Nathan, essay in *Something about the Author Autobiography Series*, Volume 12, Gale, 1991, pp. 19-35.

Angus, Carolyn, review of *Science Versus Pseudoscience*, *School Library Journal*, September, 1994, pp. 243-44.

Review of *Basketball's High Flyers, Football's Fierce Defenses, Little Giants of Pro Sports, Winners Never Quit*, *School Library Journal*, December, 1980, p. 77.

Betz-Zall, Jonathan, review of *Ending World Hunger*, *School Library Journal*, August, 1991, p. 196.

Bilge, Carol R., review of *Ending World Hunger* and *Overpopulation: Crisis or Challenge?*, *Appraisal: Science Books for Young People*, winter, 1992, pp. 88-89.

Bush, Margaret A., review of *The Fortunate Fortunes, The Problem Solvers, The Rejects,* and *The Unsung Heroes, Horn Book*, July-August, 1989, p. 497.

Forman, Jack, review of *The Locker Room Mirror: How Sports Reflect Society*, *School Library Journal*, May, 1993, p. 130.

Review of *The Fortunate Fortunes, The Problem Solvers, The Rejects,* and *The Unsung Heroes, Kirkus Reviews*, February 15, 1989, p. 288.

Hayes, Janice C., review of *Florence Griffith Joyner: Dazzling Olympian, School Library Journal*, March, 1990, p. 222.

Hearne, Betsy, review of *Florence Griffith Joyner: Dazzling Olympian, Bulletin of the Center for Children's Books*, January, 1990, pp. 101-2.

Lent, Laura L., review of *You Are the President, Voice of Youth Advocates*, August, 1994.

Matthews, Steve, review of *The Disease Fighters: The Nobel Prize in Medicine* and *The Peace Seekers: The Nobel Peace Prize, School Library Journal*, March, 1988, p. 202.

McKenzie, Joe, review of *Basketball: You Are the Coach* and *Football: You Are the Coach, School Library Journal*, May, 1983, p. 95.

Pickworth, Hannah, review of *The Rejects, The Unsung Heroes, The Fortunate Fortunes*, and *The Problem Solvers, Appraisal: Science Books for Young People*, summer, 1990, pp. 58-60.

Sutherland, Zena, review of *The Fortunate Fortunes, Bulletin of the Center for Children's Books*, June, 1989, p. 241.

Sutton, Roger, review of *Science Versus Pseudoscience, Bulletin of the Center for Children's Books*, July-August, 1994, pp. 348-49.

Unsworth, Robert E., review of *Football's Daring Defensive Backs, Football's Hard-Hitting Linebackers*, and *Football's Punishing Pass Rushers, School Library Journal*, May, 1984, p. 104.

Weischedel, Elaine Fort, review of *Baseball: You Are the Manager, School Library Journal*, September, 1983, p. 113.

Wenger, Eleanor, review of *Vertebrates, Science Books and Films*, May, 1994, p. 108.

■ For More Information See

PERIODICALS

Appraisal: Science Books for Young People, winter, 1989, p. 7; winter, 1993, p. 5; spring, 1994, p. 78; winter, 1995, p. 98.

Bulletin of the Center for Children's Books, February, 1981, p. 105; July, 1981, p. 205; November, 1985, p. 41; September, 1987, p. 1; April, 1988, p. 149; December, 1992, p. 104; June, 1993, p. 306.

Horn Book, March, 1990, p. 224; September, 1990, p. 628.

School Library Journal, June, 1993, pp. 112-13; February, 1996, pp. 115-16; August, 1998, p. 169.

Voice of Youth Advocates, April, 1984, p. 28; October, 1984, p. 204; October, 1988, p. 186; August, 1991, p. 185; April, 1992, p. 49; February, 1993, p. 362; June, 1993, p. 107.

—Sketch by J. Sydney Jones

Scott Adams

■ Awards, Honors

National Cartoonists Society's Reuben Award, for Outstanding Cartoonist of the Year and Best Newspaper Comic Strip of 1997.

■ Personal

Born June 8, 1957, in Windham, NY; son of Paul (a postal clerk) and Virginia (a homemaker) Adams. *Education:* Hartwick College, Oneonta, NY, B.A. (economics), 1979; University of California at Berkeley, M.B.A., 1986; Clement School of Hypnosis, San Francisco, CA, certified hypnotist, 1981.

■ Addresses

Home—near San Francisco, CA. *Agent*—United Media, 200 Madison Ave., New York, NY 10016-3905. *Electronic mail*—ScottAdams@aol.com.

■ Career

Crocker National Bank, San Francisco, CA, worked as a bank teller, computer programmer, financial analyst, product manager, and commercial lender, 1979-86; Pacific Bell, San Ramon, CA, worked in various positions, 1986-95; creator and author of *Dilbert* comic strip, distributed by United Feature Syndicate, 1989—. Speaker at company meetings and conventions.

■ Writings

HUMOR

The Dilbert Principle: A Cubicle-Eye View of Bosses, Meetings, Management Fads and Other Workplace Afflictions, HarperBusiness, 1996.
Dogbert's Top Secret Management Handbook, HarperBusiness, 1996.
The Dilbert Future: Thriving on Stupidity in the 21st Century, HarperBusiness, 1997.
The Joy of Work, HarperCollins, 1998.

"DILBERT" COMIC STRIP COLLECTIONS

Dogbert's Clues for the Clueless: All-New Original Cartoons Featuring Dogbert from the Nationally Syndicated Dilbert Strip, Andrews & McMeel, 1993.
Always Postpone Meetings with Time-Wasting Morons, Andrews & McMeel, 1994.
Build a Better Life by Stealing Office Supplies, Andrews & McMeel, 1994.
Shave the Whales, Andrews & McMeel, 1994.
It's Obvious You Won't Survive by Your Wits Alone, Andrews & McMeel, 1995.

Bring Me the Head of Willie the Mailboy, Andrews & McMeel, 1995.

Conversations with Dogbert, Andrews & McMeel, 1996.

You Don't Need Experience If You've Got Attitude, Andrews & McMeel, 1996.

Access Denied: Dilbert's Quest for Love in the Nineties, Andrews & McMeel, 1996.

Fugitive from the Cubicle Police, Andrews & McMeel, 1996.

Still Pumped from Using the Mouse, Andrews & McMeel, 1996.

Casual Day Has Gone Too Far, Andrews & McMeel, 1997.

The Boss: Nameless, Blameless & Shameless, Andrews & McMeel, 1997.

The Dilbert Bunch, Andrews & McMeel, 1997.

Work Is a Contact Sport, Andrews & McMeel, 1997.

Don't Feed the Egos, Andrews & McMeel, 1997.

You'd Better Watch Out, Andrews & McMeel, 1997.

Seven Years of Highly Defective People: The Origins and Evolutions of Dilbert, Andrews & McMeel, 1997.

I'm Not Anti-Business, I'm Anti-Idiot, Andrews & McMeel, 1998.

OTHER

(Author of foreword) Guy Kawasaki, *How to Drive Your Competition Crazy: Creating Disruption for Fun and Profit*, Hyperion, 1996.

Telling It Like It Isn't: A Tiptoe Approach to Communications—A Dilbert Little Book, Andrews & McMeel, 1996.

Dilbert Postcard Book, Andrews & McMeel, 1997.

■ Adaptations

Dilbert audio collection was recorded in 1997; a television show based on the comic strip is scheduled to debut on the UPN network in 1999.

■ Sidelights

For anyone who has gone on a job interview not knowing how to tell whether their potential place of employment is a good company for which to work, there is good news. A highly reliable test to measure employee disgruntlement appeared in the 1990s called the "Dilbert" comic strip. All one needs to do is take a peek at the cubicles of the company's staff. If the employees have posted "Dilbert" strips on their walls, computer screens, cabinets, or anything else, it is a good sign that they have some sort of grudge against the management of the company. The more "Dilbert" strips posted, the quantitatively higher the degree of disgruntlement. And if an entire wall or bulletin board has been covered with "Dilbert," it is advisable to flee for one's life. Who is "Dilbert"? He is the meek engineer cartoon character created by Scott Adams, and he is the hero of all those who have ever worked in or near an office cubicle. The strip chronicles the misadventures of the odd-looking, mouthless engineer who works at a nameless company designing products that are equally anonymous. Dilbert struggles to maintain his sanity while managers thwart him at every turn with lunatic policies, pointless meetings, and a morass of meaningless corporate rhetoric involving terms such as "employee empowerment" and "right-sizing."

Adams himself worked in a cubicle for over fifteen years, performing a variety of jobs for Crocker National Bank and, later, Pacific Bell. But he had always wanted to be a comic strip writer. One of three children, Adams was born in a ski resort town in New York's Catskill Mountains. When he was just eleven years old he entered the mail-order "Famous Artists School" drawing competition but was rejected because the minimum age to enter was twelve. Despite the early rejection, Adams nurtured a dream in his heart of being the next Charles Schulz, the creator of "Peanuts." In the meantime, he was practical and studied hard in school. He graduated valedictorian from his high school and went on to get a bachelor's degree in economics.

Having always hated the cold weather of New York, he left soon after earning his degree—and after getting trapped in his car during a blizzard—for the warmer climes of California. He chose San Francisco over the balmier Los Angeles, however, and found a job as a bank teller. It was not a very enjoyable job, as Adams suffered the frightening experience of seeing a gun pointed at him during armed robberies on two separate occasions.

The Origin of Dilbert

Though Adams moved up the corporate ladder, earning an M.B.A. by taking night classes and eventually reaching a position with a $70,000 annual salary, he was not content. "I hated my work . . .," he told Andy Meisler in the *New York Times*. "It never seemed to me to be what I should be doing." Actually, before attempting to become a professional cartoonist, he tried his hand at invention. He worked on creating computer games and even a perpetual motion machine, but he also kept drawing. Adams doodled a lot at work, and gradually the character of Dilbert began to emerge in those drawings. Adams used Dilbert to illustrate points during meeting presentations, gaining his first fans among the coworkers that were his inspiration. "Dilbert is a composite of my co-workers over the years," Adams explained in an online biography. "He emerged over time as the main character of my doodles. . . . A co-worker suggested the name. Dogbert was created later just so Dilbert would have someone to talk to." Dogbert is Dilbert's diminutive but cynical pet dog who likes to plot corporate buy-outs and other money-making schemes. The "-bert" suffix later attached itself to other character names, including Ratbert and Catbert.

Adams cleverly mocks the corporate world in this bestselling collection of cartoons and essays based on his highly popular "Dilbert" comic strip.

By the time Adams was pushing thirty, he was itching for cartoon success. Never much of an artist, rejection letters from the *New Yorker* and other periodicals began rolling in. Adams, however, got encouragement from Jack Cassady, who was the host of a television show about cartooning. Adams had written to him asking for help. Cassady sent him letters urging him to keep trying and suggested he use a book on artists' markets. This Adams did, and he was able to catch the eye of an editor at United Feature Syndicate. Adams signed a contract with the syndicate in 1988, and "Dilbert" began to make its way into newspapers around the country in 1989. At first, the strip was about the middle-class life of the unmarried, unremarkable engineer who keeps pens in his short-sleeved shirt pocket and wears a tie that is always pointing upwards like a fish hook. While Dilbert's office life was often strange, there was also more about his home life, where the reader met odd characters like Bob the Dinosaur, who likes to give people wedgies. It was not long, however, before Adams realized that the strips poking fun at the ridiculousness of the modern corporate environment were the most popular with his readers.

Becoming a Success

In 1994, reported Tia O'Brien in the *San Jose Mercury News*, "Dilbert's fate was uncertain. Only about 100 newspapers had picked up the strip. . . . About 80 percent of the cartoon was generic humor, only about 20 percent about the idiosyncrasies—or idiocies—of corporate life. All that changed when Adams implanted his e-mail address in the strip, a first for a cartoonist." Adams got so many responses to his strips about the workplace that he refocused the strip. "I heard from all these people who thought that they were the only ones, that they were in this unique, absurd situation," Adams told Meisler. "That they couldn't talk about their situation because no one would believe it. Basically, there are 25 million people out there, living in cardboard boxes indoors, and there was no voice for them. So there was this pent-up demand."

Quickly earning a loyal following, Adams's strip appeared in more and more newspapers until "Dilbert" began to earn him more money than his desk job. (The comic strip now appears in over 1,900 newspapers and more than fifty countries.)

But Adams kept working at Pacific Bell for several years before finally quitting in 1995. One of the main reasons for this was that it was a terrific place to get new material for his cartoons. Now that Adams no longer works in an office, he still gets his ideas from the workplace—primarily from people who write to him via the cartoonist's e-mail address. Some of the messages he has received are published in his 1996 book, *The Dilbert Principal,* in which he mocks the idiocy of the modern business mentality. One section of the book, with the help of fan mail, pokes fun at actual memos distributed by various bosses. Phrases such as "utilize issue clarification processes" and "validate the supporting activities and remaining gaps" are such excellent examples of muddy thinking that they parody themselves.

The title of the book refers to Adams's theory that in the business world "the most ineffective workers are systematically moved to the place where they can do the least damage: management." But the book not only casts aspersions at corporate management, it also offers tips to average employees so that they can survive an environment where nothing really makes sense. Adams writes entire chapters on "Employee Strategies," "Pretending to Work," and "How to Get Your Way." Adams suggests that, since today's businesses prevent employees from working productively by bogging them down in bureaucracy, the best strategy for workers to survive is to simply play along. For example, in offering the useful formula "Real Work + Appearance of Work = Total Work," Adams says, "You can be a participant in nature's grand plan by actively pursuing the activities that create equilibrium. Try to keep your *Total Work* at a constant level without increasing your *Real Work.* Do that by beefing up your *Appearance of Work* using any of the following activities: Internet surfing; personal e-mail; attending meetings; talking to your boss; conventions; upgrading your computer; testing new software; waiting for answers from co-workers; project consulting; hiding behind voice mail."

The Dilbert Principle sold extremely well, appearing on the *New York Times* bestseller list, and received many positive reviews. "This cynical, satirical, all-too-familiar glimpse of corporate life is unabashed management bashing and is very funny," wrote Alan Farber in *Library Journal.* And a *Booklist* reviewer asserted that Adams's book "is on target and deliciously sardonic!" But while

---

If you enjoy the works of Scott Adams, you may also want to check out the following:

The writings of humorist Dave Barry.
Cathy, a syndicated cartoon strip by Cathy Guisewite.
Roger and Me, a documentary film by Michael Moore, 1989.

---

most satirical books do no more than criticize their subjects, Adams goes one step further by actually offering some solutions to business ills. His solution to cutting through all the corporate strategies du jour is summarized in a single sentence: "Companies with effective employees and good products usually do well." Anything that interferes or delays the ability of the employees to do their job—such as attending endless meetings and writing status reports—is counterproductive and should be avoided as much as possible. Some of the specific tasks that Adams labels "not fundamental" include process improvement teams, reorganizations, writing vision and mission statements, and forming recognition committees.

Fighting the "Induhviduals"

Adams has, however, devoted most of his efforts to pointing out stupidity. He runs his own Web site, "The Dilbert Zone," which logs over one million page views a day, and puts out a newsletter to anyone who joins "Dogbert's New Ruling Class." To join the DNRC, one simply has to send an e-mail request to Adams. This is the wise course of action to select, since anyone who isn't a DNRC member will become one of Dogbert's slaves when the scheming little puppy takes over the world. Everyone else is labeled an "induhvidual," with emphasis on the "duh." These are the dull-witted people in the world that go through life without a clue. Adams's newsletter publishes examples of induhvidual activity, such as the induhvidual who was convinced by a friend that he had to get up at two o'clock in the morning to change his clocks for daylight savings time because "it was the law," or the tire dealer who created the slogan "if it's in stock, we've got it!"

So, actually, Adams isn't so much against the modern business culture as he is against the stupidity that thrives within it. In Meisler's article, in fact, he commented that "stuff like 'total quality' and 'worker empowerment' are things that make a lot of sense. . . . But then the theory becomes a religion. People try to implement it everywhere because, well, you gotta get on board. So it gets misapplied. Secondly, there aren't that many smart people . . . [and] there's no idea that's so good you can't ruin it with a few well-placed idiots."

A few critics have not caught on to Adams's true theme, though. One writer, Norman Solomon, interprets "Dilbert" as a scheme by the cartoonist to appear sympathetic to the plight of office workers while actually playing them for fools and taking their money. In his *The Trouble with Dilbert: How Corporate Culture Gets the Last Laugh* Solomon accuses the cartoonist of being a "fraud," because Adams has profited so much from his cartoon and the merchandise that goes along with it, thus making him a corporate co-conspirator. Adams is the "loyal subject" who serves "the royal highness in a land where cash is king."

Adams has never denied that he enjoys making money, but he shows what he's really about in his 1997 book, *The Dilbert Future: Thriving on Stupidity in the 21st Century*. While there is the usual business humor in this work, Adams makes numerous tongue-in-cheek predictions based on his premise that there are too many idiots in the world (and he modestly includes himself among the ranks) for us to have a very bright future. In fact, Adams defines the three "Immutable Laws of Human Nature" as "Stupidity, Selfishness, Horniness." The other half of the problem, though, is that our world is becoming too complicated for ordinary people. This, according to Adams, causes "the incompetence line" to rise. "Every year," the cartoonist declares in his book, "it takes more brains to navigate this complicated world." Adams goes on to say that he recently fell below this line when he could no longer keep track of all the deals that airline companies were sending him. "I believe I have millions of dollars worth of unclaimed prizes now, if only I could figure out where they are and how to claim them." The book is also interspersed with a wide variety of predictions, such as "Democracy and capitalism will continue to give the shaft to lazy and stupid people. Neither group will complain," and "In the future, more people will actively ignore the news because it is irrelevant."

Another prediction, which has been made by other pundits, is that as more people get "downsized" there will be more people working out of their homes. This is actually not such a bad thing, as Adams himself can testify. Working from six in the morning until midnight, Adams admits he has had to "build fun" into the job, but he told an interviewer in *Business Ethics*, "There's nothing I do that is terribly unpleasant." He later added, "Based on my interviews with people who had been downsized, most are much happier afterward. Because if you were at a company that was downsizing, you probably weren't a happy camper for a long time before it happened. . . . And even people making less money seem happier."

Adams, of course, is not suffering from any economic hardships. "I am as surprised as anybody that ["Dilbert"] succeeded in the exact way that it has succeeded," he said in a *Time* article. "But still, the irrationally optimistic answer is that I always expect everything I do to change the world, not just because there's something special about me but because everything in the world was changed by one person." Whether this prediction will come true or not remains to be seen. What is certain is that the world will be seeing a lot more of Dilbert in the future, especially with an upcoming television series in the works. "Is this nebbishy comic-strip hero worth all the adulation: Frankly, yes," says *Entertainment Weekly* writer Lisa Schwarzbaum. "In nailing the Kafka-esque world of office existence . . . Adams captures the lunacy of our little lives just as surely as Pogo or Peanuts or Doonesbury did in their primes." As long as there are throngs of suffering cubicle dwellers in the world, the continued success of Adams's strip is assured.

■ Works Cited

Adams, Scott, *The Dilbert Principle: A Cubicle Eye's View of Bosses, Meetings, Management Fads & Other Workplace Afflictions*, HarperBusiness, 1996.

Adams, Scott, *The Dilbert Future: Thriving on Stupidity in the 21st Century*, HarperBusiness, 1998.

"Biography of Scott Adams," http://www.dilbert.com/comics/dilbert/scott/html/bio.html.

Review of *The Dilbert Principle, Booklist,* May 15, 1996, p. 1553.

"Dilbert: Working-Class Hero," *Time,* April 21, 1997, p. 59.

Business Ethics, July/August, 1996.

Farber, Alan, review of *The Dilbert Principle, Library Journal,* June 1, 1996, p. 120.

Meisler, Andy, "Yes, Dilbert's Dad Has a Cubicle of His Own," *New York Times,* January, 1995, pp. 120-22.

O'Brien, Tia, "From Obscurity in Cubicleland to a One-Man Media Empire," *San Jose Mercury News,* http://spyglass1.sjmercury.com/archives/dilbert/mission_scott.html.

Schwarzbaum, Lisa, review of *The Dilbert Principle, Entertainment Weekly,* January 31, 1997, p. 51.

Solomon, Norman, *The Trouble with Dilbert: How Corporate Culture Gets the Last Laugh,* Common Courage Press, 1997.

■ **For More Information See**

PERIODICALS

Chicago Tribune, June 22, 1997, Section 14, pp. 1-2.
Computer Life, August, 1997.
Entertainment Weekly, May 31, 1996, p. 54.
HR Magazine, February, 1997.
Publishers Weekly, May 26, 1997, p. 78; April 6, 1998, p. 19; August 24, 1998, p. 40; September 14, 1998, p. 20.

INTERNET SITES

"The Dilbert Zone" at http://www.dilbert.com.
United Media at http://www.comiczone.com.

—Sketch by Kevin S. Hile

Lloyd Alexander

■ Personal

Born January 30, 1924, in Philadelphia, PA; son of Alan Audley (a stockbroker and importer) and Edna (Chudley) Alexander; married Janine Denni, January 8, 1946; children: Madeleine (Mrs. Zohair Khalil). *Education:* Attended West Chester State Teachers College, Lafayette College, and Sorbonne, University of Paris. *Hobbies and other interests:* Music (particularly violin, piano, and guitar), animals (especially cats), drawing and printmaking.

■ Addresses

Home—1005 Drexel Ave., Drexel Hill, PA 19026. *Agent*—Brandt & Brandt, 1501 Broadway, New York, NY 10036.

■ Career

Writer and translator, 1946—. Author in residence, Temple University, 1970-74. Has also worked as a cartoonist, layout artist, advertising copywriter, and editor of an industrial magazine. *Military ser-*

vice: U.S. Army, Intelligence, 1943-46; became staff sergeant. *Member:* Authors Guild, Authors League of America, PEN, Amnesty International, Carpenter Lane Chamber Music Society (member of board of directors).

■ Awards, Honors

Isaac Siegel Memorial Juvenile Award, 1959, for *Border Hawk: August Bondi;* Newbery Honor Book, American Library Association (ALA), 1965, for *The Black Cauldron;* citation from American Institute of Graphic Arts Children's Books, 1967-68, for *The Truthful Harp;* Newbery Medal, ALA, and National Book Award nomination, both 1969, both for *The High King;* National Book Award, 1971, for *The Marvelous Misadventures of Sebastian;* Drexel Award, 1972 and 1976, for outstanding contributions to literature for children; *Boston Globe-Horn Book* Honor Book in fiction, 1973, for *The Cat Who Wished to Be a Man;* Laura Ingalls Wilder Award nomination, 1975; National Book Award nomination, 1979, Silver Pencil Award, 1981, and Austrian Children's Book Award, 1984, all for *The First Two Lives of Lukas-Kasha;* American Book Award nomination, 1980, for *The High King,* and 1982, for *The Wizard in the Tree;* American Book Award, 1982, for *Westmark;* Parents' Choice Awards, 1982, for *The Kestrel,* 1984, for *The Beggar Queen,* 1986, for *The Illyrian Adventure,* and 1992, for *The Fortunetellers;* Golden Cat Award, Sjoestrands Foerlag (Sweden), 1984, for excellence in children's literature; Regina Medal, Catholic Library Association,

1986; Church and Synagogue Library Association Award, 1987; Lifetime Achievement Award, Pennsylvania Center for The Book in Philadelphia, 1991; *Boston Globe-Horn Book* Award, and Otter Award, 1993, both for *The Fortune-tellers*.

Also recipient of various best book and notable book citations from ALA, *School Library Journal*, Child Study Association of America, the Library of Congress, and the *New York Times*; recipient of state reading awards from library organizations in Maryland and Pennsyl-vania.

■ Writings

And Let the Credit Go (novel), Crowell, 1955.
My Five Tigers, Crowell, 1956.
Janine Is French, Crowell, 1959.
My Love Affair with Music, Crowell, 1960.
(With Dr. Louis Camuti) *Park Avenue Vet*, Holt, 1962.
Fifty Years in the Doghouse, Putnam, 1963 (published in England as *Send for Ryan!*, W. H. Allen, 1965).
My Cats and Me: The Story of an Understanding, Running Press, 1989.

JUVENILES

Border Hawk: August Bondi (biography), illustrated by Bernard Krigstein, Farrar, Straus, 1958.
The Flagship Hope: Aaron Lopez (biography), illustrated by Bernard Krigstein, Farrar, Straus, 1960.
Time Cat: The Remarkable Journeys of Jason and Gareth, illustrated by Bill Sokol, Holt, 1963 (published in England as *Nine Lives*, Cas-sell, 1963).
Coll and His White Pig, illustrated by Evaline Ness, Holt, 1965.
The Truthful Harp, illustrated by Evaline Ness, Holt, 1967.
The Marvelous Misadventures of Sebastian, Dutton, 1970.
The King's Fountain, illustrated by Ezra Jack Keats, Dutton, 1971.
The Four Donkeys, illustrated by Lester Abrams, Holt, 1972.
The Foundling and Other Tales of Prydain, illustrated by Margot Zemach, Holt, 1973.
The Cat Who Wished to Be a Man, Dutton, 1973.
The Wizard in the Tree, illustrated by Laszlo Kubinyi, Dutton, 1975.
The Town Cats and Other Tales, illustrated by Laszlo Kubinyi, Dutton, 1977.

The First Two Lives of Lukas-Kasha, Dutton, 1978.
The Remarkable Journey of Prince Jen, Dutton, 1991.
The Fortune-tellers, illustrated by Trina Schart Hyman, Dutton, 1992.
The House Gobbaleen, illustrated by Diane Goode, Dutton, 1995.
The Arkadians, Dutton, 1995.
The Iron Ring, Dutton, 1997.

"PRYDAIN CHRONICLES" SERIES

The Book of Three, Holt, 1964.
The Black Cauldron, Holt, 1965.
The Castle of Llyr, Holt, 1966.
Taran Wanderer, Holt, 1967.
The High King, Holt, 1968.

"WESTMARK" TRILOGY

Westmark, Dutton, 1981.
The Kestrel, Dutton, 1982.
The Beggar Queen, Dutton, 1984.

"VESPER HOLLY ADVENTURES" SERIES

The Illyrian Adventure, Dutton, 1986.
The El Dorado Adventure, Dutton, 1987.
The Drackenberg Adventure, Dutton, 1988.
The Jedera Adventure, Dutton, 1989.
The Philadelphia Adventure, Dutton, 1990.

TRANSLATOR FROM THE FRENCH

Jean-Paul Sartre, *The Wall and Other Stories*, New Directions, 1948, published in England as *Intimacy and Other Stories*, Peter Nevill, 1949, New Directions, 1952.
Jean-Paul Sartre, *Nausea*, New Directions, 1949 (published in England as *The Diary of Antoine Roquentin*, Lehmann, 1949).
Paul Eluard, *Selected Writings*, New Directions, 1951, published as *Uninterrupted Poetry: Selected Writings*, 1975.
Paul Vialar, *The Sea Rose*, Neville Spearman, 1951.
Paul Eluard, *Ombres et Soleil—Sun and Shadows: Writings of Paul Eluard, 1913-1953*, Oyster River Press, 1992.

OTHER

Contributor to *Cricket's Choice*, Court, 1974. Also author of afterword to E. Nesbit's *Five Children and It*. Work included in New Directions anthologies. Contributor to *Contemporary Poetry*; contributor of articles to periodicals, including *School Library Journal, Harper's Bazaar,* and *Horn Book.* Member of editorial board, *Cricket.*

■ Adaptations

Stage versions of *The Cat Who Wished to Be a Man* and *The Wizard in the Tree* were produced in Japan; a television serial version of *The Marvelous Misadventures of Sebastian* was produced in Japan; *The Black Cauldron,* a film based on the Pry-dain novels, was made by Walt Disney Productions in 1985.

■ Work in Progress

Gypsy Rizka, for Dutton, expected 1999.

■ Sidelights

Lloyd Alexander is widely regarded as a master of twentieth-century children's literature. He is best-known for his fantasy fiction and modern fables: imaginative and adventurous stories, often rooted in historical fact and legend, which explore universal themes such as good versus evil and the quest of individuals for self-identity. Among Alexander's best-known works are the five novels which comprise his "Prydain Chronicles"—culminating with *The High King,* which in 1969 received the prestigious Newbery Medal for children's literature. "At heart, the issues raised in a work of fantasy are those we face in real life," Alexander stated in his Newbery Award acceptance speech printed in *Horn Book.* "In whatever guise—our own daily nightmares of war, intolerance, inhumanity; or the struggles of an Assistant Pig-Keeper against the Lord of Death—the problems are agonizingly familiar. And an openness to compassion, love, and mercy is as essential to us here and now as it is to any inhabi-tant of an imaginary kingdom."

Alexander was born in 1924 in Philadelphia, Pennsylvania, and was also raised there. His father, a former stockbroker who was bankrupted by the Stock Market Crash of 1929, struggled to support the Alexander family through a number of largely unsuccess-ful business ventures. Money was scarce, and little was available for lessons in the piano, an early love of Alexander's. Eventually he be-

came impassioned with books, scouring the odd assortment that lay about his household. "I learned to read quite young and have been an avid reader ever since, even though my parents and relatives were not great readers," he was quoted by Lee Bennett Hopkins in *More Books by More People.* "I was more or less left to my own devices and interests, which, after all, may not be such a bad idea." Alexander became very fond of Greek and Celtic mythologies, in addition to the Welsh tales and legends contained in the *Mabinogion.* He also discovered the novels of Charles Dickens, and was particularly impressed with *David Copperfield.* "Dickens was one of many authors who helped me grow up (and are still helping)," Alexander wrote in *Top of the News.* "For a long while he was both refuge and encouragement. If he helped me escape from my daily life, . . . he also sent me back somehow better able to face up to it."

At the age of fifteen, Alexander announced to his parents that he wished to become a poet—a decision which greatly concerned his father. As Alexander recalled in *More Books by More People,* "poetry, my father warned, was no practical career; I would do well to forget it." His mother interceded, however, and it was agreed upon that Alexander could pursue poetry—granted he also find practical work. "For my part, I had no idea how to find any sort of work—or, in fact, how to go about being a poet. For more than a year I had been writing long into the night and studying verse forms to the scandalous neglect of my homework." Upon graduation, his family's limited finances ruled out the possibility of college, and his prospects of becoming a successful writer looked equally dim. "In addition to poor marks, I collected rejection slips," Alexander recollected in *My Love Affair with Music.* "My goal was to become an author and it appeared that I would reach it only if I inserted the qualifying word 'unpublished'." Alexander was able to find work as a messenger boy in a bank, a job which, although low-paying and one he found miserable, allowed him to continue writing.

Alexander eventually saved enough money to enroll in a local college to formally study writing, yet he found the coursework inadequate. Instead, as he wrote in *My Love Affair with Music,* he decided that "adventure . . . was the best way to learn about writing," and he enlisted in the army. The year was 1943 and the United States was al-

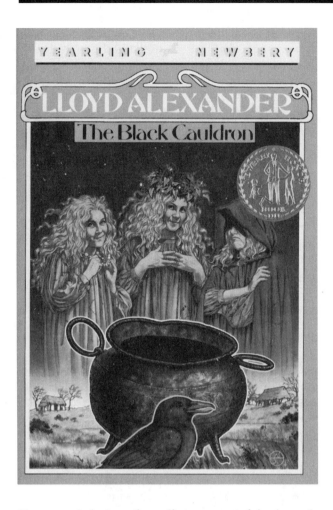

Taran must destroy the evil army created in Arawn's cauldron in this 1965 Newbery Honor book, the second in the "Prydain Chronicles" series.

ready fighting in World War II. Alexander was eventually assigned to military intelligence, and his unit was sent off to the country of Wales for combat training. "Wales was an enchanted world," Alexander continued. "The Welsh language fascinated me, as did English spoken with a Welsh lilt, more song than speech. . . . It seemed I recognized faces from all the hero tales of my childhood. . . . The Companions of Arthur might have galloped from the mountains with no surprise to me. Wales, to my eyes, appeared still a realm of bards and heroes; even the coal-tips towered like dark fortresses. Not until years afterwards did I realize I had been given, without my knowing, a glimpse of another enchanted kingdom."

Alexander was assigned to the Seventh Army in the Alsace-Lorraine region of France, and worked

as an interpreter-translator. When the war ended in 1945, he was sent to work with a counter-intelligence unit in Paris, and, as he wrote in *My Love Affair with Music*, "fell in love with the city at first sight and sound." Alexander requested a discharge from the army to resume his education, and received a scholarship from the French Foreign Ministry, with which he attended the Sorbonne, University of Paris. The same year he met his future wife, a young Parisian named Janine Denni, and the two were married three months later in January of 1946. Feeling, however, that he needed to be closer to his roots if he were to succeed as a writer, Alexander returned to the United States with his wife and her small daughter Madeleine, whom he had adopted. The three initially lived with Alexander's parents, until they moved into their own home, an old farmhouse in Drexel Hill, just outside of Philadelphia.

Alexander began writing novels, the first three of which were promptly rejected by publishers. Between 1948 and 1955, he worked at a variety of jobs to support his family, including being a cartoonist, advertising writer, layout artist, and an associate editor for an industrial magazine; he also translated several works from French, including Jean-Paul Sartre's *The Wall* and *Nausea*. Alexander was on the verge of giving up on writing when his fourth novel, *And Let the Credit Go*, was published. Based on his own experiences as a struggling writer, the book launched a number of biographically-based adult books by Alexander. "One thing I had learned during those seven years was to write about things I knew and loved," he explained in *Horn Book*. "Our cats delighted me. So did music; I had . . . tried to learn the violin, piano, and guitar. I relished Janine's war with the English language and her bafflement at the peculiar customs of Americans. All this found its way into books and was published. I was writing out of my own life and experience. But nearly ten years passed before I learned a writer could know and love a fantasy world as much as his real one."

Alexander made his first venture into children's fantasy with *Time Cat: The Remarkable Journeys of Jason and Gareth*. The story of a magical black cat who is able to transport a young boy into different historical periods, *Time Cat* brought Alexander into contact with ancient Wales once again. "Surely everyone cherishes a secret, private world from the days of childhood. Mine was Camelot, and

Arthur's Round Table, Malory, and the *Mabinogion*," Alexander wrote in *Horn Book*. "The Welsh research brought it all back to me. Feeling like a man who has by accident stumbled into an enchanted cavern lost since boyhood, both terrified and awestruck, I realized I would have to explore further." Originally intending to include a Welsh episode in *Time Cat*, Alexander decided to replace it with an Irish one, and began plans to devote a future book to his beloved Wales. "Not to the beautiful land of Wales I knew in reality," he told *Horn Book*, "but an older, darker one."

The Prydain Chronicles

Alexander didn't expect that his exploration would result in the five-novel Prydain Chronicles. In the

Among Alexander's best known novels, this work received the Newbery Medal in 1969 and was nominated for the American Book Award in 1980.

first novel, *The Book of Three*, Alexander's intent was to retell the convoluted tales of the *Mabinogion*. "I tried this at first, but strange things happened to me," he stated in an interview for *The Pied Pipers*. "I found I had been kidding myself: I didn't want simply to retell anybody's mythology. What I really wanted to do was invent my own, or at least use my own in some way. . . . The more I worked on *The Book of Three* the more I realized the personal importance it was taking on. . . . It was a tremendously liberating decision. I found myself, to my amazement, tapping into various areas of my personality that I never even knew existed."

The subsequent books of the series, *The Black Cauldron, The Castle of Llyr, Taran Wanderer,* and *The High King,* relate the adventures of a young hero, Taran, on several quests which lead him to understand the true meaning of heroism, goodness, and also evil. "Prydain grew into something much more than a thinly disguised ancient Wales," Laura Ingram comments in *Dictionary of Literary Biography*. "Undeniably, it was similar to that land, but reshaped by the addi-tion of contemporary realism, modern values, and a generous dose of humor, as well as the special depth and insight provided by characters who not only act, but think, feel, and struggle with the same kinds of problems that confuse and trouble people in the twentieth century." *The Black Cauldron* was a runner-up for the Newbery Medal in 1966, while *The High King* received the prestigious honor in 1969. Alexander's "total creation is a remarkable achievement," writes *Washington Post Book World* contributor Houston L. Maples, "a rich and varied tapestry of brooding evil, heroic action and great natural beauty, vividly conceived, romantic in mood yet curiously contemporary in its immediacy and fast action."

Alexander followed the Prydain Chronicles with several simpler tales geared more towards younger children. Some of these books, including *Coll and His White Pig, The Truthful Harp,* and *The Foundling and Other Tales of Prydain,* are special introductions for young readers into the world of Prydain. In 1970, Alexander went in a different direction with another children's book, *The Marvelous Misadventures of Sebastian,* which was honored with the National Book Award. The story, set in a country reminiscent of eighteenth-century Europe, charts the adventures of a young fiddler as he assists an orphaned princess who is trying to escape marriage to the repressive ruler of the land. As Alexander described in *The Pied Pipers*, the boy "comes into the possession of a fiddle that allows him to play and hear music as he has never done before. It changes his life." Alexander added that the story has parallels to his own discovery of the joys of writing for children. "The fiddle . . . is a mixed blessing because it also drains his life away the more he understands his magnificent discovery. Without being pretentious about it, I suppose *Sebastian* attempts to say something about what it feels like to be an artist."

The Westmark Trilogy

In 1981, Alexander published a new novel, *Westmark*, the first of a trilogy which would include *The Kestrel* (1982) and *The Beggar Queen* (1984). These novels became known as "The Westmark Trilogy," through which Alexander explores the political development of an imaginary land called Westmark, "a cross between colonial America and feudal Europe," as Ingram describes it. "Quite different in tone and setting from the *Prydain* series," according to critic Jill P. May in *Twentieth-Century Children's Writers*, Alexander's Westmark trilogy depicts "the horrors of revolution and unrest, and the conflicts caused by corrupt leadership."

In the first volume, Theo, a young printer's apprentice, escapes prosecution for the accidental killing of a royal officer by joining a theatrical troupe. There he falls in with a street girl, Mickle, and eventually joins a revolutionary group who is attempting to break the power of the evil minister Cabbarus. "A superb craftsman, Alexander has concocted a marvelous tale of high adventure," writes Zena Sutherland in the *Bulletin of the Center for Children's Books*, one which demonstrates the author's mastery of dialogue, plot, and character. In Theo's examination of the crime that led to his adventure, Alexander once again explores the meaning of good and evil. "The wisdom of the book lies in its difficult solution: good does not triumph over evil simply because it *is* good," observes Jean Fritz in the *New York Times Book Review*.

The next volumes of the Westmark trilogy turn from comic adventure to serious political struggle as Mickle, revealed as Westmark's missing princess, tries to retain her lawful position as queen

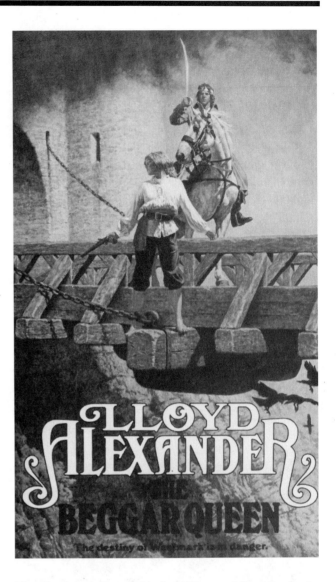

The final installment in the "Westmark" series finds Westmark engaged in an unforeseen war with a nearby country.

with the aid of her loyal friends. Theo, who loves his "beggar queen," is enlisted in an unexpected war against a neighboring country and faces questions about loyalty, duty, and the nature of combat. "The fast-paced plot, subtleties of character, ironic wit, quiet understatement and pervasive animal imagery—all work with superb concentration to undercut the heroics of war," *School Library Journal* contributor Hazel Rochman notes. "Alexander moves, as he did in the Prydain cycle, to deeper issues and subtler levels," Sutherland similarly comments. While the Westmark books examine ethical issues, the critic continues, they are "no less appealing as an adventure tale with a strong story line and rounded, consistent characterizations."

Adventures in Exotic Lands

A subsequent series of five books by Alexander recounts the adventures of a spirited young character named Vesper Holly. Set in the 1870s, the Vesper Holly books recount the exploits of a young Philadelphia girl as she travels to exotic locales with her guardians, becoming embroiled in intrigue and mystery. The first novel in the series, *The Illyrian Adventure,* was "in every way different from anything I'd written before," Alexander was once quoted as saying. "It was intended as an entertainment—for its author as much as anyone—with a gloriously fearless heroine, legendary heroes, inscrutable mysteries, and fiendish villains. What surprised me shouldn't have surprised me at all. In what was meant as sheer amusement, below the surface I realized that my own concerns and questions were still there, even though set in different terms." *Horn Book* writer Mary M. Burns concurs, observing about *The Illyrian Adventure* that "what makes [Alexander's] work truly excellent, rather than simply very good, is his strong sense of story, controlled but not dominated by a substantial theme, and his ability to meld the actual and the imagined into a plausible reality."

Other volumes in the series also combine excellence with entertainment. *The El Dorado Adventure,* in which Vesper travels to Central America, is "entertaining" and yet "offers some low-key history lessons," *Voice of Youth Advocates* contributor Brooke Dillon notes. Sutherland similarly remarks that the wild adventures and comic characters "will appeal to readers" while the writing quality "and pointed digs at the foibles of humankind will give them substance." Ethel L. Heins, writing in *Horn Book,* likewise finds the books filled with "elegant, witty, beautifully paced writing," while *Bulletin of the Center for Children's Books* critic Betsy Hearne concludes that "the whole series is valuable in that it bestows elegant writing on unsuspecting young readers looking to gallop through books."

Exotic locales characterize Alexander's next two works, the novel *The Remarkable Journey of Prince Jen* and the picture book *The Fortune-tellers.* The former, the story of a Chinese prince's voyage to

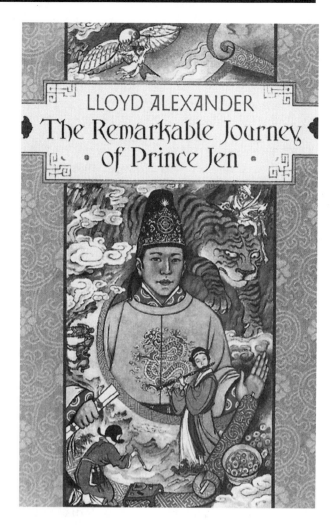

Bearing six gifts, a young Chinese prince embarks on a voyage to learn about true happiness in Alexander's 1991 novel.

study the way to govern a happy kingdom, "is a classic quest novel and classic Alexander," notes Kathleen Beck in *Voice of Youth Advocates.* "The adventures are exciting, the message subtly conveyed, and the characters as quirky and engaging as ever." *Horn Book* reviewer Ann A. Flowers concurs, writing that "Alexander's forte is the coming-of-age novel, and he skillfully uses symbolism and humor to reinforce his theme." *The Fortune-tellers* is set in the West African country of Cameroon, and tells of a young carpenter's visit to find out his future, a visit that turns into an interesting adventure. "The trickster's hand is hidden here," remarks Hearne; "it is the author's, and a clever tale he has turned, proving as adept at a picture book text as he is at complex fantasy series."

If you enjoy the works of Lloyd Alexander, you may also want to check out the following books and films:

Allen Appel, *Time After Time,* 1985.
Katherine Paterson, *Rebels of the Heavenly Kingdom,* 1991.
Philip Pullman, *The Ruby in the Smoke,* 1987.
Willow, a film by Ron Howard, 1988.

In a later novel, *The Arkadians,* Alexander borrows from the ancient Greek myths to tell the story of Lucian, a young man working in the palace who must flee for his life when he uncovers an embezzlement scandal involving the king's wise men. Lucian is joined by Fronto, a poet who has been transformed into a jackass, Joy-in-the-Dance, a mystical young woman, Catch-a-Tick, a goatboy, and others. Together they journey through Arkadia to see the legendary Lady of the Wild Things, finding danger and adventure along the way. Ilene Cooper, writing in *Booklist,* stated that "one of the most interesting things" about the work is the author's "focus on the goddess culture and its role in both history and myth."

The Iron Ring concerns young Tamar, ruler of Sundari, a mythical kingdom in India. When Tamar loses a dice game to King Jaya, a mysterious visitor from the north, an iron ring appears on his finger, signifying that he has become Jaya's slave. Bound by honor to accept his fate, Tamar travels to the king's land. Along the way, he is accompanied by a host of enchanted creatures, as well as a beautiful and sensible milkmaid. His journey becomes one of self-discovery as he learns about friendship, loss, and love. "The question of what constitutes being true to one's *dharma,* or code of ethics, is the solid, though occasionally slippery cord that ties the whole story together," according to Cooper in *Booklist.* A *Kirkus Reviews* critic stated that "Tamar comes to question everything he was brought up to believe in, especially the rigid caste system."

In her book *The Green and Burning Tree: On the Writing and Enjoyment of Children's Books,* Eleanor Cameron describes Alexander as "a perfect example of one who, before he could come into his own as a writer, had to discover that place which was, for him, the spiritual symbol or expression of something hidden." Alexander's varied contributions to children's literature have earned him not only many awards and critical accolades, but also a devoted and diverse readership. "I am amazed and delighted by how many adults read the 'Prydain Chronicles,'" Alexander was quoted in *The Pied Pipers.* "I don't think adults stop growing, or at least they shouldn't. If you stop growing you're dead. At any rate, I've never tried to pull any punches with the kids." For Alexander, the world of the imagination and fantasy has been a way to explore that which is most real. "Using the device of an imaginary world allowed me in some strange way to go to the central issues," he added in *The Pied Pipers.* "In other words I used the imaginary kingdom not as a sentimentalized fairyland, but as an opening wedge to express what I hoped would be some very hard truths. I never saw fairy tales as an escape or a cop out. . . . On the contrary, speaking for myself, it is the way to understand reality."

■ Works Cited

Alexander, Lloyd, *My Love Affair with Music,* Crowell, 1960.

Alexander, Lloyd, "The Flat-Heeled Muse," *Horn Book,* April, 1965, pp. 141-46.

Alexander, Lloyd, "A Personal Note by Lloyd Alexander on Charles Dickens," *Top of the News,* November, 1968.

Alexander, Lloyd, "Newbery Award Acceptance Speech," *Horn Book,* August, 1969.

Beck, Kathleen, review of *The Remarkable Journey of Prince Jen, Voice of Youth Advocates,* February, 1992, p. 378.

Burns, Mary M., review of *The Illyrian Adventure, Horn Book,* July/August, 1986, pp. 447-48.

Cameron, Eleanor, *The Green and Burning Tree: On the Writing and Enjoyment of Children's Books,* Little, Brown, 1969, p. 185.

Cooper, Ilene, review of *The Arkadians, Booklist,* May 1, 1995.

Cooper, Ilene, review of *The Iron Ring, Booklist,* May 15, 1997.

Dillon, Brooke, review of *The El Dorado Adventure, Voice of Youth Advocates,* February, 1988, p. 285.

Flowers, Ann A., review of *The Remarkable Journey of Prince Jen, Horn Book,* March, 1992, pp. 200-201.

Fritz, Jean, review of *Westmark, New York Times Book Review,* May 10, 1981, p. 38.

Hearne, Betsy, review of *The Jedera Adventure, Bulletin of the Center for Children's Books,* June, 1989, p. 242.

Hearne, Betsy, review of *The Fortune-tellers, Bulletin of the Center for Children's Books,* September, 1992, pp. 4-5.

Heins, Ethel L., review of *The Jedera Adventure, Horn Book,* September, 1989, pp. 624-25.

Hopkins, Lee Bennett, *More Books by More People,* Citation, 1974.

Ingram, Laura, "Lloyd Alexander," *Dictionary of Literary Biography,* Volume 52: *American Writers for Children since 1960: Fiction,* edited by Glenn Estes, Gale, 1986, pp. 3-21.

Review of *The Iron Ring, Kirkus Reviews,* May 1, 1997.

Maples, Houston L., review of *The High King, Washington Post Book World,* May 5, 1968, Part 2, p. 22.

May, Jill P., *Twentieth-Century Children's Writers,* 3rd edition, St. James Press, 1989, pp. 16-18.

Rochman, Hazel, review of *The Kestrel, School Library Journal,* April, 1982, pp. 64-65.

Sutherland, Zena, review of *Westmark, Bulletin of the Center for Children's Books,* June, 1981, pp. 185-86.

Sutherland, Zena, review of *The Kestrel, Bulletin of the Center for Children's Books,* June, 1982, pp. 181-82.

Sutherland, Zena, review of *The El Dorado Adventure, Bulletin of the Center for Children's Books,* April, 1987, p. 141.

Wintle, Justin and Emma Fisher, "Lloyd Alexander," *The Pied Pipers: Interviews with the Influential Creators of Children's Literature,* Paddington Press, 1974.

■ For More Information See

BOOKS

Children's Literature Review, Gale, Volume 1, 1976, Volume 5, 1983.

Contemporary Literary Criticism, Volume 35, Gale, 1985.

Jacobs, James S., and Michael O. Tunnell, *Lloyd Alexander: A Bio-Bibliography,* Greenwood Press, 1991.

Livingston, Myra Cohn, *A Tribute to Lloyd Alexander,* Drexel Institute, 1976.

May, Jill P., *Lloyd Alexander,* Twayne, 1991.

Something about the Author Autobiography Series, Volume 19, Gale, 1995.

Tunnell, Michael O., *The Prydain Companion,* Greenwood Press, 1989.

Tymm, Marshall B., Kenneth J. Zahorski, and Robert H. Boyer, *Fantasy Literature: A Core Collection and Reference Guide,* Bowker, 1979, pp. 39-44.

Wheeler, Jill C., *Lloyd Alexander (Tribute to the Young at Heart),* Abdo & Daughters, 1997.

PERIODICALS

Book Links, March, 1994, pp. 30-39.

Bulletin of the Center for Children's Books, November, 1991, p. 55.

Chicago Tribune Book World, November 26, 1967, p. 16.

Christian Science Monitor, May 2, 1968, p. B8; November 7, 1973, p. B5.

Cricket, December, 1976.

Elementary English, December, 1971, pp. 937-45.

Horn Book, June, 1967, p. 341; October, 1971, p. 508, 511-12; May/June, 1987, pp. 344-45; July/August, 1988, p. 499.

Language Arts, April, 1984.

The Lion and the Unicorn, Volume 9, 1985.

Los Angeles Times, July 24, 1985; July 27, 1985.

New York Times Book Review, December 3, 1964; June 19, 1966, p. 36; April 9, 1967, p. 26; March 28, 1968, p. 38; November 15, 1970, p. 42; November 13, 1977, p. 37; April 25, 1982, p. 47; June 7, 1987.

School Library Journal, May, 1967, p. 61; February, 1968, p. 86; September, 1992, p. 196.

Times Literary Supplement, November 24, 1966, p. 1089; May 25, 1967, p. 451; October 3, 1968, p. 1113; April 6, 1973, p. 379.

Washington Post Book World, August 21, 1966; November 8, 1970, p. 10; November 12, 1978, p. E4; May 10, 1981; January 9, 1983.

Writer's Digest, April, 1973.

OTHER

Meet the Newbery Author: Lloyd Alexander (filmstrip/cassette), Miller-Brody, 1975.

James Cameron

mid-1970s; New World Pictures, served various functions, including production assistant, second unit director, production designer, and miniature set builder. *Member:* Directors Guild of America, Screenwriters Guild of America.

■ Personal

Born August 16, 1954, in Kapuskasing, Ontario, Canada; immigrated to United States, 1971 (one source lists 1972); eldest of five children born to Philip (an electrical engineer) and Shirley Cameron (a nurse); married first wife (a waitress), circa 1973 (divorced); married second wife, Gale Anne Hurd (a motion picture producer), April, 1985 (divorced, 1988); married Kathryn Bigelow (a motion picture director), 1989 (divorced); married Linda Hamilton (an actress), 1997. *Education:* Studied physics at California State University at Fullerton in the early 1970s.

■ Addresses

Office—Alexandra Drobac, Lightstorm Entertainment, 3100 Damon Way, Burbank, CA 91505. *Agent*—International Creative Management, 8899 Beverly Blvd., Los Angeles, CA 90048.

■ Career

Director, screenwriter, and producer, since 1981. Truck driver for two to three years during the

■ Awards, Honors

The Terminator was named one of the ten best films of 1984 by *Time;* Best Director, Golden Globe Award, 1997, Best Director, Broadcast Film Critics Association Award, Best Screenplay, Writers Guild of America, Outstanding Directorial Achievement in Motion Pictures, Directors Guild of America Award, Academy Award for Best Director, Best Film Editing (with Conrad Buff IV and Richard A. Harris), and Best Picture (with Jon Landau), all 1998, all for *Titanic; Titanic* won a total of eleven Academy Awards. Honorary doctorate degree from Ryerson Polytechnic University, 1998.

■ Credits

FILM WORK

Art director, *Battle beyond the Stars*, New World, 1980.
Unit director and production designer, *Galaxy of Terror*, New World, 1981.
Director of special effects photography, *Escape from New York*, Avco-Embassy, 1981.
Director, *Piranha II: The Spawning*, New World, 1981.
Design consultant, *Android*, New World, 1982.

Director and co-screenwriter (with Gale Anne Hurd and William Wisher, Jr.), *The Terminator*, Orion, 1984.

Co-screenwriter (with Sylvester Stallone), *Rambo: First Blood, Part II*, Tri-Star, 1985.

Director and screenwriter, *Aliens* (based on story by Cameron, David Giler and Walter Hill; based on characters created by Dan O'Bannon and Ronald Shusett), Twentieth Century-Fox, 1986.

Director and screenwriter, *The Abyss*, Twentieth Century-Fox, 1989.

Director, producer, and co-screenwriter (with William Wisher, Jr.), *Terminator 2: Judgment Day*, Tristar, 1991.

Executive producer, *Point Break*, Twentieth Century-Fox, 1991.

Director, producer, and screenwriter, *True Lies*, Twentieth Century-Fox, 1994.

Producer and screenwriter, *Strange Days*, Twentieth Century-Fox, 1995.

Director, co-producer, co-editor, and screenwriter, *Titanic*, Twentieth Century-Fox and Paramount, 1997.

Also writer and director of *T2 3-D*, 1996.

■ Writings

(With William Wisher) *Terminator 2: Judgement Day: The Book of the Film: An Illustrated Screenplay*, Applause Theatre, 1991.

Strange Days: A "Script-Ment," Plume, 1995.

(With Ed W. Marsh) *James Cameron's Titanic*, photographs by Douglas Kirkland, HarperCollins, 1997.

Titanic: James Cameron's Illustrated Screenplay, HarperPerennial, 1998.

■ Adaptations

Characters from the "Terminator" movies and *Aliens* have been adapted to comic book and graphic novel form by Dark Horse Publications.

■ Overview

The phenomenal success of his Academy Award-winning historical epic *Titanic* has fundamentally changed the way the world views filmmaker James Cameron. Prior to the December 1997 release of *Titanic*, one of the most expensive Holly-

wood films and the biggest moneymaker of all time, most people would have agreed with Peter Waal of *Saturday Night* magazine when he described the Canadian-born movie screenwriter, director, and producer as "an action flick virtuoso." Cameron had earned considerable respect and media attention for an impressive, but relatively small body of work. But it was the commercial appeal of Cameron's films that most endeared him to major studios. At a time when movie formulas were no longer "sure-fire," he continued to enjoy consistent box-office success. Cameron insisted that his secrets were simple: common sense and good storytelling. "When I hear people shooting different endings for a movie I say 'God, how can you *do* that?'," he related to Michael Singer in *Film Directors: A Complete Guide.* "For me, the ending comes first and then you write backwards, and all the threads converge on that. And when it happens, there's a rightness about it that resonates through the rest of the film."

That "rightness" seems to strike a chord with critics, who had heaped an unusual amount of praise on his early films, which included such big-budget sci-fi blockbusters as *The Terminator, Aliens,* and *The Abyss.* "No one in the movies today can match Cameron's talent for . . . hyperbolic, big-screen action," declared Hal Hinson in the *Washington Post. Los Angeles Times* contributor Kirk Honeycutt simply proclaimed: "[He] is Hollywood's preeminent science fiction director." At the same time, Cameron was generally regarded as a difficult, egocentric perfectionist, who had little regard for production budgets or the feelings of people with whom he worked. "Obsessive and hot-tempered, [Cameron has] developed a reputation as a throwback to commandant-style Hollywood directors such as Michael Curtiz and Erich von Stroheim," Nancy Griffin reported in *Esquire.*

Titanic Success

However, in the wake of *Titanic*'s unprecedented success—eleven Oscars, a host of other major awards, almost universal critical praise, and (most important of all) a staggering $1 billion in gross revenues worldwide, Cameron is viewed much more sympathetically. After having created the biggest moneymaker and one of the great screen romances ever, he is no longer pigeonholed as a director of action films. In fact, Cameron now has creative license to make just about any film he

Cameron combined action and adventure with futuristic elements in his popular *The Terminator,* starring Arnold Schwarzenegger.

chooses. The great irony is that many people are now praising Cameron as a sensitive, albeit volatile, filmmaker who refuses to compromise his ideals or his creative vision in the bottom-line driven, dog-eat-dog world of the Hollywood studios. Peter Waal has gone so far as to describe *Titanic* as Cameron's "indictment of mainstream commercial film making." It is "a reaction against the fact that it's unsatisfying," Cameron told Waal. "It's satisfying on one level, but it's pizza, you know? Sometimes you want pizza, and sometimes you want something a little more epicurean. Not that I've never tried to make pizza, but at least I've tried to put a whole lot of different toppings on it."

Born and raised in the small northern Ontario mining town of Kapuskasing, Ontario, Canada, Cameron grew up in the community of Chippawa, not far from Niagara Falls. The Camerons immigrated to California in 1971, and there young James dreamed of becoming a marine biologist. "I thought I wanted to be the next Jacques Cousteau," he told *Film Directors.* However, foreseeing a career "counting fish eggs," Cameron instead turned his attention to astronomy and physics at California State University. By the end of four semesters he had lost interest in academics and decided to learn about the world firsthand. He quit school, became a truck driver, married a Big Boy waitress, and spent his spare time drinking beer, smoking dope, and trying to write. At the same time, Cameron dreamed of being a filmmaker—ever since he had seen Stanley Kubrick's wondrous 1968 film *2001: A Space Odyssey.*

Apart from some youthful experiments with his father's home movie camera, Cameron had little experience in film, so he sought training with Roger Corman, the celebrated king of B-Grade movies. Corman's New World Pictures had a reputation as a kind of prep school for influential directors—Francis Ford Coppola (the "Godfather" trilogy, *Apocalypse Now*), Peter Bogdonavich (*The Last Picture Show, Star 80*), and Martin Scorcese (*Taxi Driver, Raging Bull*) all started out working there. New World was also notorious for producing a large number of films on low budgets and short shooting schedules. Corman's staff was perpetually overworked and pushed to perform at a breakneck pace, but the ones who survived the pressure often emerged as skilled professionals. Cameron began his New World career as a member of the special effects team for a 1980 science fiction film called *Battle beyond the Stars.* When the art director was fired, Cameron was promoted to fill the vacancy—the first of several positions he held at New World. Working at Corman's frenetic pace, Cameron became a "jack-of-all-trades," receiving a crash course in virtually all aspects of filmmaking. He served as a production assistant and built miniature models for many of New World's science fiction films. The experience made Cameron realize that he wanted a larger role in the movie making process. "I had a dawning awareness that directing was the only place where you got perfect confluence of the storytelling, visual and technical sides," Cameron told Michael Singer. After working as a second unit director for the film *Galaxy of Terror,* Cameron was offered a job as the director of *Piranha II: The Spawning.* The experience proved to be less than satisfying.

Pitfalls for Piranha Producer

Cameron was working with an unscrupulous producer and a unilingual Italian crew. The producer proclaimed himself a second unit director and set about filming topless women frolicking aboard yachts—footage that contributed nothing to the storyline of carnivorous fish terrorizing humans. The producer proved to be a thorn in Cameron's side in other ways, too. When production was completed, he quickly took the print back to Italy to edit—without Cameron even seeing the final footage that he had shot. Cameron followed him to Rome in hopes of retaining some control over the final release.

When *Piranha II* was in preproduction, Cameron had wanted a character to break into a morgue using a credit card to unlock the door, but the producer did not believe this was possible. While the scene did not make it into the movie, Cameron did utilize the technique to enter the producer's locked office late one night. Once inside, Cameron taught himself to run the editing machine, and he viewed the uncompleted film. He later met with the producer to suggest changes to *Piranha II*—which the producer assumed the director had not seen. When Cameron's suggestions were refused, Cameron crept into the producer's office at night and made the changes himself. As a result, the confused producer had to scramble to correct these mysterious edits before the film's release date. Some of Cameron's

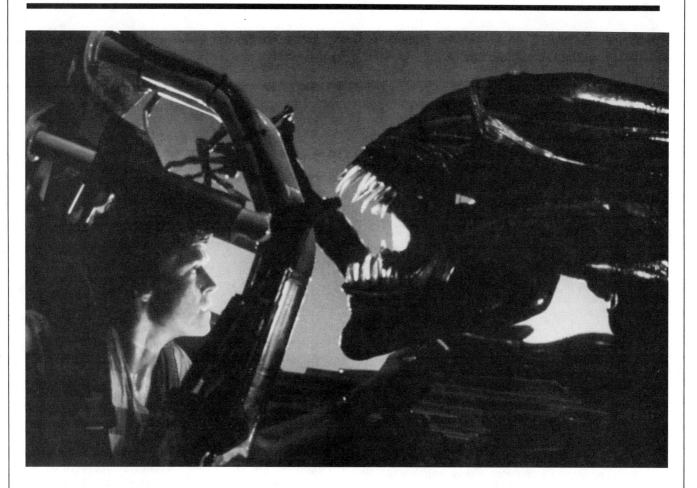

Sigourney Weaver starred in the highly successful film *Aliens*, written and directed by Cameron.

alterations ended up in the final print, though not enough to make a difference. *Piranha II* was a critical and financial failure.

While still in Rome, Cameron attempted to put his bad experiences behind him. He began to devise a film story involving cyborgs and time travel. Upon his return to Los Angeles, he contacted Gale Anne Hurd, a fellow alumnus of New World and his romantic interest. With a third writer, William Wisher, Jr., Cameron and Hurd set about writing the script for the 1984 film that would come to be known as *The Terminator*. Cameron and Hurd struck a deal with Hemdale, a production company, so that Hurd would produce and Cameron direct the film.

Terminator Terror

The Terminator opens with dark shots of a ragged future world. A narrator's voice explains that this

is the twenty-first century and that in the year 1997 a global nuclear holocaust will occur, an armageddon triggered by an automated defense system known as Skynet. In the wake of the war, the sentient Skynet computer controls the world. The surviving humans must now fight a second, more desperate war: the war with the machines. The film then cuts to the Los Angeles of 1984 and the arrival, on the city's outskirts, of a naked man amidst flashing light and electrical surges. The man, as played by Arnold Schwarzenegger, is large, muscular, and menacing. He dispassionately kills a gang of punks to get their clothes and makes his way into the city. He looks up in a phone book the name Sarah Connor, finding three people with that name. In a brutal and efficient manner, he tracks down the first two women and kills them. He arrives at the home of the third but mistakenly kills her roommate. Assuming his task is completed, he turns to leave when the voice of the real Sarah comes on the answering machine, unwittingly disclosing her whereabouts.

Meanwhile, another naked man has materialized in L.A. in the same fashion as the first. He is also seeking Sarah Connor. The second man locates the surviving Sarah and follows her into a nightclub. She notices him trailing her. By this time, news of a "phonebook killer" has spread throughout the city. Sarah mistakes this second man for the murderer, and in her terror she fails to notice the real killer's approach. As the large man aims his gun's laser sight at Sarah, the second man opens fire on him, knocking him to the ground. Almost instantly—and seemingly uninjured—the large man is back on his feet and continues his attack on Sarah. The second man pulls her out of the bar and into a car, the attacker following close behind. As they escape, Sarah's rescuer introduces himself as Kyle Reese, a traveller from the future sent to protect her from the Terminator now pursuing them. Reese explains to her that within the year, she will give birth to a son, John, who will survive the coming war and grow to be the leader of the human resistance against the machines. Skynet has sent the Terminator, a ruthless cyborg, back in time to perform a "retro-active abortion" on Sarah and eliminate the threat of John Connor. The John Connor of the future has sent Reese back in time to protect Sarah and his unborn self. While fleeing the Terminator, Reese and Sarah fall in love. They manage to find some quiet moments, but soon they must resume their flight. The film climaxes with Reese and Sarah squaring off against the Terminator to decide the fate of mankind.

By combining elements of traditional action/adventure films with the punk aesthetic of science fiction literature by authors such as William Gibson and Bruce Sterling (purveyors of a science fiction sub-genre often referred to as "Cyperpunk"), Cameron created a film that is credited with reviving a flagging genre. Science fiction devotees and film studio executives alike praised Cameron's unique cinematic style. Singer asked Cameron in *Film Directors* if he had consciously attempted to forge a new vision of science fiction cinema with the film. "I just came up with a way of juxtaposing futuristic elements with a kind of everyday reality," replied the director. This work ethic made *The Terminator* one of the most successful and popular films of the 1980s. The film became ensconced in the popular culture, especially Schwarzenegger's memorable "I'll be back" line. *The Terminator*'s themes of paradoxical time travel and its relentless energy popularized it with

a mass audience worldwide. Film critics seemed to agree with the ticket-buying public on the film's entertainment value. "This picture barrels with swank relentlessness through a giddily complicated premise and into an Armageddon face-off," declared Richard Corliss in *Time*. Reviewing *The Terminator* in the *Nation*, Andrew Kopkind proclaimed: "They hardly make good 'B' movies like this anymore, but they should."

Cameron was lauded as a forerunner in the new science fiction vanguard. He was also credited with creating, in the Terminator character, one of the truly terrifying prospects of the high-tech age; a lethal machine with a singular intent. "It can't be bargained with, it can't be reasoned with. It doesn't feel remorse or pity or fear. And it absolutely will not stop until you are dead," Reese tells Sarah in the film. In Cameron's view, the Terminator is an extreme end product of the worldwide voracity for technological gadgetry.

New Venues

While waiting for Schwarzenegger to complete his role in *Conan the Destroyer* so that filming could begin on *The Terminator*, Cameron worked as a screenwriter-for-hire. He was offered work on two major films, both sequels to popular movies. The first project was *First Blood II: The Mission*, which would continue the story of Vietnam veteran John Rambo, a character who first appeared in the Sylvester Stallone picture *First Blood*. Cameron wrote two drafts of a script dealing with Rambo's haunted return to Vietnam and the psychological effects of facing his darkest fears. He submitted his screenplay to the producers, who in turn gave it to Stallone, the film's star, to further revise. The motion picture that was released, under the title *Rambo: First Blood, Part II*, was vastly different from the screenplay that Cameron wrote. According to Cameron in *Film Directors*, Stallone rewrote large portions of Cameron's script to fit his own politics and ideals, omitting much of the psychological drama and character development along the way. However, the next script that Cameron would work on would incorporate many of the themes of self-doubt, psychological damage, and the confrontation of fears that *Rambo*—or Stallone—neglected.

Alien II was Cameron's second sequel, building on characters and events from director Ridley Scott's

1979 film, *Alien*. In addition to writing the script, Cameron also convinced the production company that he and Hurd, now husband and wife, were the best choices to respectively direct and produce the film, which was now titled *Aliens*. "I had a lot of emotional investment in [the script]," he told Fred Schruers in *Rolling Stone*, "I didn't want to see it botched up by somebody else."

Aliens opens with an intergalactic exploration team's discovery of warrant officer Ripley, *Alien's* sole human survivor, in deep space hibernation. Fifty-seven years have passed since she escaped on a small shuttle, and the reawakened Ripley learns that much has changed in her absence. Back on Earth, she is brought to an inquest regarding the fate of her old ship, the *Nostromo*, destroyed in the final battle with the alien in the first film. During the proceedings it is revealed that the planet where the *Nostromo* last landed—where the ship's crew discovered the murderous alien's breeding ground—has been colonized by the quasi-bureaucratic business entity known only as the Company. Ripley is incredulous that the Company has put so many lives, including families, in dangerous proximity to scores of vicious aliens. The Company officials coolly reply that the colony has existed for several years and that Ripley really isn't qualified to judge the safety of its inhabitants.

Ripley returns to a vague semblance of ordinary life, scarred and frail. She is tormented by nightmares of her experience with the alien. When a panicked Company employee calls and informs her that contact with the colonized planet has been lost and her help is requested to assist a squad of marines in the sweep and rescue, Ripley sees it as a means to exorcise her personal demons. She volunteers for the mission.

Ripley and the marine team arrive at the colony to find it deserted, save for one small girl who is found living in the heating ducts like a scavenger. When the marines ask the little girl where her family and the rest of the colony are, the child replies, "They're dead, okay? Can I go now?" Ripley is drawn to the girl, who, like herself, is the sole survivor of an alien attack. Ripley and the child, named Newt, quickly form a surrogate mother/daughter relationship. Meanwhile, the team has set off to survey the area. While exploring the dank subterranean levels of the colony, the marines come upon its missing inhabitants, encased in sticky, partial cocoons. As one of the colonists awakens, an alien creature bursts forth from her chest. The soldiers act quickly, using flamethrowers to destroy both the woman and the alien hatchling. The marines realize that the aliens have used the entire colony as incubators for their young creatures. Attempting to withdraw, the marines are beset by swarms of aliens in a bloody battle. Retreating to the upper levels, Ripley, Newt, and the surviving marines secure themselves in the infirmary against hordes of advancing aliens. The aliens break into the infirmary, sending the room's human occupants scrambling in different directions. Ripley loses Newt in the confusion that ensues. In her desperate search for the little girl, Ripley discovers the egg chamber of the alien queen on the bottom level of the colony. There she finds Newt, encased as the other colonists were, about to be impregnated with an alien fetus. The two "mothers," Ripley and the queen, now face each other, each determined to protect her children.

"For sheer intensity, the final forty-five minutes of *Aliens* is not likely to be matched," proclaimed *Newsweek* critic David Ansen. "Cameron is a master at choreographing ever-more astonishing catastrophes." Audiences impressed with *The Terminator* seemed even more excited by Cameron's efforts in *Aliens*. His ability to utilize themes from Scott's original film while forging a vision of his own impressed critics as well as the filmgoers, who pushed *Aliens* far beyond its predecessor in ticket sales. Cameron told Singer in *Film Directors*: "For me, the opportunity to do *Aliens* was to take a lot of what I liked from the first film and weld it together with my own imagery. I was in equal parts intimidated and seduced by it." Cameron's reputation as a master of kinetic, thrill-a-minute filmmaking was intensifying. "*Aliens* is a mother of a thriller," declared David Edelstein in *Rolling Stone*, "a royal chamber of horrors. And, as he proved in *The Terminator,* Cameron knows How Things Work in a fun house: each plunge down a chute and pop-out demon moves you faster along to the next frightful spill, choking you somewhere between a giggle and a scream."

Reputation Soars

Aliens's success having further solidified his reputation, Cameron spent the next three years making his most ambitious film to date, *The Abyss*.

Cameron's "Terminator" films feature bold, compelling storylines and innovative special effects.

Working with a budget that doubled the combined costs of *The Terminator* and *Aliens*, Cameron shot his underwater epic in abandoned nuclear cooling tanks. Rather than rely on miniatures, he built full-scale underwater sets within the massive tanks. As the film begins, an American nuclear submarine encounters an unidentified—and impossibly fleet—underwater object. The crew panics and crashes the sub onto a precipice, teetering on the brink of a deep abyss. A nearby underwater oil drilling colony, Deepcore, is enlisted to help a team of Navy SEALS (Sea-Air-Land specialists) ostensibly perform a rescue. The SEALs's real mission is to retrieve the sub's nuclear warheads before an enemy does. The undertaking becomes more intricate when the workers on Deepcore discover underwater aliens who appear to live down in the abyss. It was a craft belonging to these aliens that unintentionally caused the sub wreck. Most of the crew recognize that the aliens are intelligent and are in fact trying to make friendly contact. Trouble arises when the leader of the

SEALs succumbs to pressure sickness from the water depth. He becomes paranoid and unpredictable—psychotic—viewing the aliens as a threat to national security. He sends an armed nuclear warhead down into the abyss to take care of the "enemy." Seeking to avert the possible destruction of an intelligent, undiscovered race, the oil rig's foreman suits up to follow the bomb down into the abyss and diffuse it. Using a special liquid form of oxygen that enables humans to withstand extreme depth pressure, the foreman plummets into the five-mile abyss.

The Abyss met with mixed reviews. Some critics found it ambitious and thrilling, a competent reworking of several genre themes. As Ansen wrote in *Newsweek:* "There are variations on scenes you've seen a hundred times . . . yet Cameron renders them with such white-knuckle conviction they regain their primal force." Other critics complained that the film tried to be too many things at once—an action/adventure tale, an account of bonding between humans and aliens, and a love story—and as a result did not address any of those subjects well.

Many fans of Cameron's action pictures were disappointed that his new film displayed a markedly different tone from his previous efforts. Rather than offer nonstop, breathtaking action, *The Abyss* spends more time on atmosphere and suspense, carefully charting out the story. Cameron wanted to produce a film that elicited a degree of thought from the audience, rather than one that incited the audience to shout during a screening. "*The Abyss* does not strike me as an audience participation picture like *The Terminator* and *Aliens*. In a way that is good, really," Cameron explained to Ian Spelling in *Starlog*.

In terms of production scale and budgetary expenditure, *The Abyss* ranked as one of the biggest and most expensive motion pictures ever made to that point. In the light of *The Abyss*'s lukewarm showing at the box office (the film turned a respectable profit, but the studio, expecting a blockbuster, was disappointed), many industry observers felt that a film that matched or surpassed the cost and production scale of *The Abyss* would never be made. They were mistaken. Working with a budget that reportedly vacillated between $80 and $100 million dollars, Cameron next made *Terminator 2: Judgement Day*.

T-2

As *Terminator 2* begins, the audience learns that Sarah Connor has given birth to her savior son, John, who is now a young pre-teenager. The setting is ten years after the first movie and the nuclear war, judgement day, is approaching. Sarah has become near-crazy, obsessed with her knowledge of the impending war and the massive loss of human life it will entail. She has spent years training John in guerilla warfare, survival tactics, anything that will aid him in his future fight against the mechanized forces of the tyrannical Skynet computer. Unfortunately, Sarah's fanatical behavior has been detected by the authorities. As a result, she has lost custody of John. She is now locked away in a mental hospital, raving about the approaching apocalypse and the Terminator she encountered ten years before. Into these events come two separate men from the future. The first man resembles the Terminator in the

original film, played by Schwarzenegger in both pictures. The second is a much smaller man, though no less imposing. Both are Terminators searching for John Connor. The smaller man, a new state-of-the-art Terminator model called the T-1000, has come to kill John. The Schwarzenegger character is an older Terminator, the same production model that caused all of the havoc in the original film. The Schwarzenegger Terminator has been sent by the adult John Connor, living in the future, to protect the present-day John Connor. The two Terminators find young John at the same time and attack each other in a vicious battle for John's life. John escapes on his motorcycle amid the chaos. Schwarzenegger manages to catch John after the T-1000 has pursued the boy in a perilous truck and motorcycle chase. He informs John that he has been sent to protect him. When John finds out that the Terminator is programmed to obey all of his commands, he orders the machine to help him break Sarah out of the mental hospital. With the T-1000 still pursuing John, and the freed Sarah now a fugitive, the trio escapes into the desert.

Sarah realizes that even if they survive this encounter with the T-1000, Skynet will continue its assaults from the future until John is killed. She contends that the only solution to save John and the human race is to prevent judgement day from occurring. To do this they must reach the man responsible for developing Skynet, Miles Dyson. Dyson works for Cyberdyne Systems, the company that will create and then sell the Skynet system to the Defense Department in the near future. Cyberdyne is also the company that will one day manufacture the Terminator line (Cameron also used "Cyberdyne" in *Aliens* as the manufacturer of an android character in that film). Dyson has been studying the secret remains of the Terminator that terrorized Sarah ten years ago. Examining the technology in the fragments of the machine has enabled him to make incredible advances on a computer chip that will eventually lead to the invention of the Skynet computer. Sarah, John, and the Terminator find Dyson and inform him of the results of his research. As Sarah explains in the voice-over narration: "It's not everyday that you find out you're responsible for three billion deaths." Dyson agrees to help them destroy his Skynet research and the remains of the first Terminator. The T-1000 pursues them to the Cyberdyne complex and another monstrous battle, also involving an army of police, ensues. Escaping the site of the battle, the three protagonists are again pursued by the relentless T-1000 to a steel forgery. At this site they must destroy the T-1000 or surrender their hope of averting the nuclear disaster of judgement day.

With its elephantine price tag and its groundbreaking special effects, *Terminator 2* gained a considerable amount of attention during its production and upon its release. Speculation was that most of the money was spent on the elaborate effects for the T-1000. Using computer animation and prosthetic applications, the special effects team was able to take the human form of T-1000 actor Robert Patrick and melt it into any variety of liquid metal shapes. Attention to the film was divided between the storyline and the special effects. *Washington Post* contributor Hal Hinson assessed: "Cameron manages to create a neat balance between the technical and the human." *New York*

Times critic Janet Maslin enthused: "Mr. Cameron presents the T-1000 as a show-stopping molten metal creature capable of assuming or abandoning human form at will. Some of his tricks are cause for applause in their own right." Many critics lamented a lack of emotion in the film, though few doubted its ability to thrill an audience. "Cameron never relinquishes his grip on the audience, smoothly segueing from action sequence to action sequence and topping himself each time," praised Dave Kehr in *Chicago Tribune*.

Terminator 2 seems to have something for everyone willing to suspend disbelief for two hours of entertainment. Action fans enjoyed the fight and chase scenes, computer buffs took note of the technological aspect of the story, and Schwarzenegger fans liked the movie because it had Schwarzenegger. Filmgoers found Cameron's challenging time travel paradoxes particularly intriguing, es-

Arnold Schwarzenegger, Art Malik, and Jamie Lee Curtis starred in 1994's *True Lies*, with Schwarzenegger playing an international spy masquerading as a computer salesman.

pecially when Miles Dyson discovers the technology for creating Skynet and the Terminator line in the remains of a Terminator from the future—implying that the future is inventing itself. Despite its brain teasing plot and thrilling effects, the film drew criticism from some reviewers who felt it was nothing more than a heartless, calculated entertainment vehicle. As Kehr concluded in his review of the film: "The pathos of the film is the pathos of its leading character—it is a magnificent machine, but a machine it remains." The massive price tag that *Terminator 2* boasted also invited conjecture among critics as to the validity of making such a film. Cameron defended making the picture—and spending the large sum of money—as meeting supply and demand, delivering what audiences want. He told Kirk Honeycutt in *Los Angeles Times:* "State-of-the-art, mind-blower type of things aren't cheap. It's an epic film. That's what we planned to give people."

Mario Kassar, the chairman of Carolco, the company that financed *Terminator 2*, has called Cameron a "genius" at crafting high-tech entertainment. As Kassar explained to Honeycutt in the *Los Angeles Times*, the secret to Cameron's success is the fact he is a writer. "Everything has to make sense to him. He's a very logical person," said Kassar. However, by the standards of major motion picture studios, Cameron has gone against the grain, against the industry's logic. Before *Aliens*, the idea of building a major action/adventure film around a female hero was, to say the least, uncommon. Yet by successfully casting Sigourney Weaver's character of Ripley as the centerpiece of that film, Cameron dispelled the misconception that a woman could not carry a major action/adventure release. To some extent, each of Cameron's films has featured strong female characters that are in direct contrast to the stereotyped female roles so prevalent in popular entertainment. "I like the Forties thing," Cameron told Schruers in *Rolling Stone*, "a strong, Howard Hawks-type woman. . . . Strong male characters have been done so many times. With strong females, there's still a lot of room for exploration." Attention to detail in character is as much a focus in Cameron's filmmaking as creating riveting action sequences or suspenseful moods. "Audiences have to relate to people that they're seeing within a film, or they have no emotional attachment," Cameron told Singer. "I think you get more out of a movie when the characters are accessible and you can feel for their problems."

■ Update

In 1994 Cameron wrote and directed *True Lies*, an action/adventure tale starring Schwarzenegger as Harry Tasker, a top U.S. spy married to Helen, played by Jamie Lee Curtis, who believes her husband to be a computer salesman. Harry and his partner, Gib, are hot on the trail of Arab terrorists who are smuggling nuclear weapons into the United States. The film earned generally good reviews for its elaborate stunts and action-packed sequences. Cameron's fascination with strong characters and with the perils of modern technology continued in another film in which he got involved. He and Jay Cocks co-wrote the screenplay for *Strange Days,* a dark sci-fi tale directed by Kathryn Bigelow, Cameron's wife at the time. The film, which stars Ralph Fiennes (who would soon win fame for his role in the Academy Award-winning film *The English Patient*) is set in Los Angeles in the last two days of 1999; the city is a dark, forbidding, and dangerous place that is wracked by violent crime. Armed gangs rule the streets, and when the wealthy venture out, they do so in armored limousines. The city's jaded inhabitants have found escape in a virtual reality technology in which the ultimate high is to "jack-in" by attaching a "SQUID" to your head—SQUID being an acronym for Superconducting Quantum Interference Device. In essence, it is a high-tech electronic brainwave transmitter that allows the wearer to relive another person's memories. Cameron and Cocks provide viewers with a disturbing demonstration of this cybertechnology in the film's opening scenes; a "tapehead" goes on an armed robbery with a criminal, vicariously sharing the felon's experiences until he inadvertently plunges to his death from a rooftop. A tape of this horrible event is for sale, and it is offered to Lenny Nero, the character played by Ralph Fiennes. Nero is a grubby ex-cop turned tapehead, who supports his addiction by selling bootleg tapes. *Strange Days* recounts Lenny's adventures as he struggles to pull his life together again and to win back the love of a woman, who has dumped him for a high-powered rock star manager.

Strange Days was an unsettling film *noir* that evoked strong emotions in audiences; predictably, most reviewers were appalled by the film's apparent eagerness to delve into the excessive violence that it purports to condemn. Syndicated *Chicago Sun-Times* critic Roger Ebert hailed *Strange*

Days as a "technical *tour de force*" that challenges its viewers by examining the moral implications of virtual reality technology. However, he also noted: "Some of its scenes are deeply disturbing, involving the audience as voyeurs during scenes of death." David Denby of *New York* magazine shared Ebert's concerns, asking "How can Cameron, Cocks, and Bigelow preach against snuff films and jaded sicko thrillers after they've excited the audience with exactly those things?" Anthony Lane of the *New Yorker* termed the film "an unwatchable frenzy." Reviewer Peter Travers of *Rolling Stone* was in the minority when he praised *Strange Days*. While conceding that some scenes of "rape, mutilation, and murder . . . will leave you cringing," Travers argued that director Bigelow was not "getting off on what the film is criticizing."

The Epic

Reviewers and audiences alike were much more favorably disposed towards Cameron's next project, which also deals with the pitfalls and perils of mankind's reliance on technology. Paula Parisi of *Entertainment Weekly* aptly described the film as "the most technologically ambitious and most expensive" in Hollywood history. Given the story's grand historical sweep, it almost had to be. *Titanic* is a lavish historical epic about the sinking of the luxury liner *R.M.S. Titanic*, which hit an iceberg on its maiden voyage and went to the bottom of the North Atlantic on the night of April 14, 1912, with a loss of 1,500 lives. Not only did Cameron write the script for the film, he also directed and edited it. Like the great ship herself, the film *Titanic* and the story of its making have taken on a larger-than-life aura and become the stuff of Hollywood legend; the sheer amount of money involved in its creation—an estimated $200 million—and Cameron's at times outlandish behavior during the three years it took to make the film were enough to ensure that. However, the fact that the world fell in love with *Titanic* has only served to heighten the interest. Widely hailed as a cinematic masterpiece, it has become the top grossing film of all time.

Cameron's interest in the *Titanic* legend began in 1987, when he viewed a *National Geographic* documentary about the discovery of the shipwreck. Paula Parisi reported that Cameron scribbled these words on a piece of paper: "Do story with book-

ends of present-day [wreckage] scene . . . intercut with memory of a survivor . . . needs a mystery or driving plot element." It was eight years and a lot of musing before Cameron was able to flesh out that initial sketchy plot outline. What he finally devised was a plot about a modern-day salvage team that goes looking for a valuable jewel assumed to have gone down with the ship; the team's search provides the occasion for flashbacks that tell the story of a couple of young passengers who meet and fall in love aboard the *Titanic*. She is Rose, a wealthy seventeen-year-old Englishwoman from first class—the owner of the lost jewel. He is Jack, a handsome twenty-year-old starving artist from third class. When Cameron had written a draft script, he pitched his proposed film to then-Twentieth Century-Fox studio head Peter Chernin and a group of company executives. "It's 'Romeo and Juliet' on a sinking ship (that's how Cameron pitched it to Fox)," wrote Corie Brown and David Ansen of *Newsweek*. Cameron insisted that he could make the film he had in mind for "under $100 million," Parisi reported. Despite the success of Cameron's "Terminator" movies, Chernin was reluctant to commit so much money to the project until he had a firm idea of the costs; like everyone in Hollywood, he knew Cameron's reputation for going over budget. What the Fox head initially agreed to do was to provide the director with "a couple million dollars" to organize a research expedition to visit and film the *Titanic*'s wreckage, nearly two miles beneath the surface of the North Atlantic, southeast of Newfoundland.

Cameron spent the money to hire two Russian miniature deep-sea submersibles, one of which was equipped with a special remote-controlled movie camera that had been designed by Cameron's younger brother Mike, a former aerospace engineer; this ingenious unit was capable of withstanding the enormous water pressure at the wreck site, an estimated 10,000 pounds per square inch. Cameron made a dozen dives to the *Titanic* during a twenty-eight day period in the summer of 1995. Using the remote-controlled camera, Cameron was able to probe the wreckage and film the most stunning underwater footage ever taken of the great ship. The experience convinced him that the only way to tell the *Titanic*'s story was to build a ninety per cent scale model of the 820-foot vessel, rather than to go the conventional route: using tiny models or even a real ship on the open sea. To house such a large prop,

Kate Winslet and Leonardo DiCaprio find romance in *Titanic*, Cameron's 1997 film that garnered eleven Academy Awards, including best director and best picture.

Cameron planned a 360-thousand-square-foot water tank to be built at a new state-of-the-art film studio in the town of Rosarito, Mexico, where real estate and labor were inexpensive.

Twentieth Century-Fox, seeing other potential uses for the facility as well as the opportunities for tax write-offs, was interested in financing the film; when Paramount also agreed to come aboard as a partner and to contribute $65 million, Cameron had his money. This left him to find two charismatic young actors to play the star-crossed lovers, Rose and Jack. After much effort and considerable soul-searching, Cameron opted to take a chance on two relative unknowns who had caught his eye: English actress Kate Winslet and American actor Leonardo DiCaprio. Filming got underway in July 1996, and almost immediately there were problems. Costs quickly spiraled to worrisome levels. Tempers were frayed on the set. Fifty members of the cast and crew on location in Nova

Scotia, Canada, fell ill after someone poisoned their lobster chowder dinner with a hallucinogenic drug. Some stunt men were injured on the set; and, there were disquieting media reports about director Cameron being belligerent and "out of control," abusing his cast and crew unmercifully in his quest for perfection and absolute historical accuracy. As production costs rose, Bill Mechanic, the new head of Twentieth Century-Fox, nervously threatened to "pull the plug" on *Titanic*. "Film-making is war," a frustrated Cameron told Parisi. "There's no other way to look at it. It's a great battle. A battle between Business and Aesthetics."

However, money was not the *only* issue. Cameron's bosses were pressing him to give them a firm opening date. Although the director himself had assumed responsibility for the film's final editing, laboring night and day for several months, *Titanic*'s launch in theaters was twice delayed. First, it was from the summer of 1997 to Thanks-

If you enjoy the works of James Cameron, you may also want to check out the following:

Blade Runner, starring Harrison Ford, 1982.
A Night to Remember, an acclaimed film version of the Titanic disaster, 1958.
The Road Warrior, starring Mel Gibson, 1982.

giving, and then it was to December 19. The reason: Cameron was meticulously editing frame-by-frame the final version of the long film—which runs for more than three-hours. "[His] attention to detail now is astonishing," wrote Nancy Griffin in *Esquire.* "Current Hollywood dish says that Cameron has been holed up for so long in his cave that he's 'gone Kurtz' "—a disparaging allusion to the psychotic hermit character played by Marlon Brando in Francis Ford Coppola's now-legendary 1979 Vietnam war-era film *Apocalypse Now.*

In the end, all of this extra time and effort paid off in spades. Test audiences were wildly enthusiastic at sneak previews of *Titanic;* the all-important "buzz" was highly favorable. Almost immediately, some influential critics began comparing the film with such screen classics as *Gone with the Wind* and *Doctor Zhivago.* Richard Corliss of *Time* was not among them; in fact, he announced that he was less than impressed. "The film doesn't play to Cameron's strength as a ringmaster of burly metaphorical fantasy," Corliss wrote. "Ultimately, *Titanic* will sink or swim not on its budget but on its merits as drama and spectacle." Fortunately for Cameron, most other critics were much more enthusiastic in their opinions.

Moneymaking Phenomenon

Reviewer Mike Clark of *USA Today* gave *Titanic* a four-star rating, explaining that the film "can be picked at but, unlike its subject, not broken apart. To those seeking the full movie experience and the return of showmanship, welcome to one-stop Christmas shopping." Leah Rosen of *People* agreed, applauding *Titanic* for being "as big a blockbuster as its name implies." Owen Gleiberman of *Entertainment Weekly* hailed the film as a "lush and terrifying spectacle of romantic doom." James Cameron, he added, had recreated "the defining catastrophe of the early 20th century on a scale of such purified yearning and dread that he touches the deepest levels of popular moviemaking." Maslin, in the *New York Times,* described *Titanic* as "a huge, thrilling three-and-a-quarter hour experience that unerringly lures viewers into the beauty and heartbreak of its lost world."

As the favorable reviews and "word-of-mouth" recommendations from viewers continued to pile up, a series of major critics' awards followed. As they did, the *Titanic* marketing juggernaut rose to unprecedented heights. In the early weeks of 1998, the media was full of news stories about all aspects of the film, and about the historical details of the great ship's 1912 sinking. *Titanic* souvenirs, memorabilia, posters, and books were in huge demand; a paperback version of Cameron's screenplay for the film was reprinted ten times, selling more than 250,000 copies. And *Titanic's* young stars, DiCaprio and Winslet, and director-writer Cameron, became international celebrities. In late February 1998, just sixty-seven days after being released, *USA Today* reported that *Titanic* had surpassed *Jurassic Park* to become the "all-time box office champ," with a total gross of almost $920 million and counting—the film was still in theaters and the lucrative home video release was still to come.

So delighted by all of this was Twentieth Century-Fox head Bill Mechanic that he told reporter Andy Seiler of *USA Today* that he intended to work out a new compensation deal for Cameron, who had deferred his director's salary in order to help convince the film's financial backers not to pull the plug when production costs were rising. "We're in business long-term with Jim, and when all the dust settled down, we're likely to find a fair and equitable solution," Mechanic told Seiler. Almost as gratifying, from Cameron's perspective, was the fact that when the 1998 Academy Award ceremonies were held in March, *Titanic* sailed off with eleven Oscars, including the Best Picture and the Best Director awards. Cameron's faith in his vision of this epic film had won the ultimate accolade, and his place in the cinematic history was secured.

In the wake of *Titanic's* amazing success, Cameron seemed assured that Hollywood studios would now let him make whatever films he chooses. Industry speculation was that might be anything from a small, low-budget effort to a big screen version of the adventures of the comic book hero Spiderman, or perhaps an elaborate historical drama set in ancient Egypt. Asked what he planned to do next, Cameron told Peter Waal of *Saturday Night* that he did not know. "I just really want to keep doing new things," he said. "*Titanic* is a new thing. It proves that genre limitations need not apply if the filmmaker doesn't believe they apply. But you always have to make one film to prove that."

■ Works Cited

Ansen, David, *Newsweek*, July 21, 1986, p. 64.

Ansen, David, *Newsweek*, August 14, 1989, p. 56.

Brown, Corie, and David Ansen, "Rough Waters," *Newsweek*, December 15, 1997, pp. 64-68.

Cameron, James, Gale Anne Hurd, and William Wisher, Jr., *The Terminator*, Orion, 1984.

Clark, Mike, "Tale strikes unsinkable balance," *USA Today*, December 18, 1997.

Corliss, Richard, *Time*, November 26, 1984, p. 105.

Corliss, Richard, "Down, Down to a Watery Grave," *Time*, December 7, 1997, p. 91.

Denby, David, "People Are Strange," *New York*, October 16, 1995, pp. 60-61.

Ebert, Roger, review of *Strange Days*, *Sun-Times* (Chicago), October 13, 1995.

Gleiberman, Owen, review of *Titanic*, *Entertainment Weekly*, January 30, 1998, p. 47.

Griffin, Nancy, "James Cameron is the scariest man in Hollywood," *Esquire*, December, 1997.

Hinson, Hal, *Washington Post*, July 3, 1991, pp. B1-B2.

Kehr, Dave, *Chicago Tribune*, July 3, 1991, pp. 1, 4.

Kopkind, Andrew, *Nation*, January 26, 1985, p. 88.

Lane, Anthony, "Starkness Visible," *New Yorker*, October 9, 1995, pp. 95-97.

Los Angeles Times, July 2, 1991, pp. F1, F4.

Los Angeles Times, July 3, 1991, pp. F1, F6.

Maslin, Janet, *New York Times*, July 3, 1991.

Maslin, Janet, "A Spectacle as Sweeping as the Sea," *New York Times*, December 19, 1997, pp. E-1, 18.

Parisi, Paula, "Titanic: Man Overboard," *Entertainment Weekly*, November 7, 1997, pp. 26-28.

Rolling Stone, May 22, 1986, pp. 49-50.

Rolling Stone, August 28, 1986, pp. 41-42.

Rosen, Leah, review of *Titanic*, *People*, December 22, 1997, p. 18.

Seiler, Andy, *USA Today*, "Unsinkable 'Titanic' now all-time box-office champ," February 25, 1998, p. D-1.

Singer, Michael, *Film Directors: A Complete Guide*, Lone Eagle Press, 1987, pp. 3-5, 8-9.

Spelling, Ian, *Starlog*, January, 1990, pp. 29-32, 62.

Travers, Peter, review of *Strange Days*, *Rolling Stone*, October 19, 1995, pp. 156, 158.

Waal, Peter, "The Making of James Cameron," *Saturday Night*, March, 1998, pp. 26-34.

■ For More Information See

BOOKS

Heard, Christopher, and Kathryn A. Exner, *The Life and Films of James Cameron*, Bantam, 1998.

Parisi, Paula, *Titanic and The Making of James Cameron: The Inside Story of the Three-Year Adventure That Rewrote Motion Picture History*, Newmarket Press, 1998.

St. James Film Directors Encyclopedia, edited by Andrew Sarris, St. James Press, 1997.

PERIODICALS

Entertainment Weekly, January 13, 1995; January 10, 1997; May 2, 1997; August 8, 1997; December 26, 1997.

Los Angeles Times, May 19, 1991, pp. 22, 42.

Maclean's, December 8, 1997.

New York, June 3, 1985, p. 72.

New York Times, July 3, 1991.

People, August 11, 1986, pp. 93-95; February 9, 1998, p. 39.

Premiere, August, 1997, p. 63.

Time, December 8, 1997, p. 86.

Washington Post, July 5, 1991, p. 31.*

—Sketch by David Galens, updated by Ken Cuthbertson

Aidan Chambers

■ Personal

Born December 27, 1934, in Chester-le-Street, County Durham, England; son of George Kenneth Blacklin (a funeral director) and Margaret (Hancock) Chambers; married Nancy Harris Lockwood (a former editor of *Children's Book News*), March 30, 1968. *Education:* Attended Borough Road College, London, 1955-57.

■ Addresses

Home and office—Lockwood, Station Rd., South Woodchester, Stroud, Gloucestershire GL5 5EQ, England.

■ Career

English and drama teacher at various schools in England, 1957-68; full-time writer and editor, 1968—. Macmillan, London, general editor, "Topliners," "Club 75," and "Rockets" series, 1967-81; *Signal: Approaches to Children's Books*, South Woodchester, Gloucestershire, publisher, 1969—;

Thimble Press, proprietor and publisher, 1969—; Turton & Chambers, co-founder and editorial publisher, 1989—. Further Professional Studies Department, University of Bristol, tutor, 1970-82; Westminster College, Oxford, visiting lecturer, 1982—; May Hill Arbuthnot Lecturer, University of Kansas at Little Rock, 1986. Writer and presenter of radio programs, including (with wife, Nancy Chambers) *Bookbox,* Radio Bristol, 1973-75; *Children and Books,* BBC Radio, 1976; *Ghosts,* Thames-TV, 1980; and *Long, Short, and Tall Stories,* BBC-TV, 1980-84. Has produced children's plays for stage. *Military service:* Royal Navy, 1953-55. *Member:* Society of Authors.

■ Awards, Honors

Children's Literature Association Award, 1978, for article "The Reader in the Book"; *School Library Journal* Best Book designation, 1979, for *Breaktime;* (with Nancy Chambers) Eleanor Farjeon Award, 1982; American Library Association (ALA) Best Book for Young Adults designation, 1983, for *Dance on My Grave;* Silver Pencil Award (Netherlands), 1985 and 1986.

■ Writings

YOUNG ADULT NOVELS

Breaktime, Bodley Head, 1978, Harper, 1979.
Seal Secret, Bodley Head, 1980, Harper, 1981.

Dance on My Grave, Bodley Head, 1982, Harper, 1983.

The Present Takers, Bodley Head, 1983, Harper, 1984.

Now I Know, Bodley Head, 1987, published as *NIK: Now I Know,* Harper, 1987.

The Toll Bridge, Bodley Head, 1992, Harper, 1995.

CHILDREN'S FICTION

Cycle Smash, Heinemann, 1967.

Marle, Heinemann, 1968.

Don't Forget Charlie and the Vase, illustrated by Clyde Pearson, Macmillan, 1971.

Mac and Lugs, illustrated by Barbara Swiderska, Macmillan, 1971.

Ghosts Two (short stories), Macmillan, 1972.

Snake River, illustrated by Peter Morgan, Almqvist och Wiksell, 1975, Macmillan, 1977.

Fox Tricks (short stories), illustrated by Robin and Jocelyn Wild, Heinemann, 1980.

Also author of *Ghost Carnival,* 1977. Contributor to *Winter Tales for Children 4,* Macmillan.

PLAYS

Everyman's Everybody, produced in London, 1957.

Johnny Salter (produced in Stroud, Gloucestershire, 1965), Heinemann, 1966.

The Car (produced in Stroud, 1966), Heinemann, 1967.

The Chicken Run (produced in Stroud, 1967), Heinemann, 1968.

The Dream Cage: A Comic Drama in Nine Dreams (produced in Stroud, 1981), Heinemann, 1982.

EDITOR

(With wife, Nancy Chambers) *Ghosts,* Macmillan, 1969.

I Want to Get Out: Stories and Poems by Young Writers, Macmillan, 1971.

(With Nancy Chambers) *Hi-Ran-Ho: A Picture Book of Verse,* illustrated by Barbara Swiderska, Longman, 1971.

(With Nancy Chambers) *World Minus Zero: An SF Anthology,* Macmillan, 1971.

(With Nancy Chambers) *In Time to Come: An SF Anthology,* Macmillan, 1973.

The Tenth [Eleventh] Ghost Book, Barrie & Jenkins, 2 volumes, 1975-76; published in one volume as *The Bumper Book of Ghost Stories,* Pan, 1976.

Fighters in the Sky, Macmillan, 1976.

Funny Folk: A Body of Comic Tales, illustrated by Trevor Stubley, Heinemann, 1976.

Men at War, Macmillan, 1977.

Escapers, Macmillan, 1978.

War at Sea, Macmillan, 1978.

(Under pseudonym Malcolm Blacklin) *Ghosts Four,* Macmillan, 1978.

Animal Fair, illustrated by Anthony Colbert, Heinemann, 1979.

Aidan Chambers' Book of Ghosts and Hauntings, illustrated by Antony Maitland, Viking, 1980.

Ghosts That Haunt You, illustrated by Gareth Floyd, Viking, 1980.

Loving You, Loving Me, Viking, 1980.

Ghost after Ghost, illustrated by Bert Kitchen, Viking, 1982.

Plays for Young People to Read and Perform, Thimble Press, 1982.

(With Jill Bennett) *Poetry for Children: A Signal Bookguide,* Thimble Press, 1984.

Out of Time: Stories of the Future, Bodley Head, 1984, Harper, 1985.

Shades of Dark: Ghost Stories, P. Hardy, 1984, Harper, 1986.

A Sporting Chance: Stories of Winning and Losing, Bodley Head, 1985.

(And contributor) *A Haunt of Ghosts,* Harper, 1987.

A Quiver of Ghosts, Bodley Head, 1987.

Love All, Bodley Head, 1988.

On the Edge, Macmillan, 1990.

FOR ADULTS

The Reluctant Reader, Pergamon Press, 1969.

Introducing Books to Children, Heinemann, 1973, revised edition, Horn Book, 1983.

Axes for Frozen Seas (lecture), Woodfield and Stanley, 1981.

Booktalk: Occasional Writing on Literature and Children, Harper, 1985.

The Reading Environment: How Adults Help Children Enjoy Books, Thimble Press, 1990, Stenhouse, 1996.

Tell Me: Children, Reading and Talk, Thimble Press, 1993, Stenhouse, 1996.

Contributor to periodicals, including *Books and Bookmen, Books for Your Children, Children's Book News, Teachers' World,* and *Times Educational Supplement.* Author of columns "Young Reading," *Times Educational Supplement,* 1970-72, and "Letter from England," *Horn Book,* 1972-84.

OTHER

Haunted Houses, illustrated by John Cameron Jarvies, Pan, 1971.

More Haunted Houses, illustrated by Chris Bradbury, Pan, 1973.

Book of Ghosts and Hauntings, Viking, 1973.

Great British Ghosts, illustrated by Barry Wilkinson, Pan, 1974.

Great Ghosts of the World, illustrated by Peter Edwards, Pan, 1974.

Book of Flyers and Flying, illustrated by Trevor Stubley, Viking, 1976.

Ghost Carnival: Stories of Ghosts in Their Haunts, illustrated by Peter Wingham, Heinemann, 1977.

Book of Cops and Robbers, illustrated by Allan Manham, Viking, 1977.

■ Sidelights

"I can remember the day—evening rather—when I first learned to read," Aidan Chambers wrote in an essay for the *Sixth Book of Junior Authors and Illustrators*. "That evening in winter I sat staring at a page of print, and suddenly I started to hear the words in my head, making sense. And the sense they were making was a story, with people talking in it, about an adventure on an island. Hearing those printed words suddenly making sense in my head is one of the most vivid and valued moments in my life." From this moment, Chambers was inspired to begin a career in writing and editing young adult books, in addition to theorizing, criticizing, and advocating the same genre. "Whether editing anthologies or writing or reviewing children's books, Aidan Chambers takes his work seriously," asserts Anita Silvey in *Children's Books and Their Creators*. "He believes children, like adults, deserve good books written just for them."

Born in 1934 in Chester-le-Street, a small town in the northeast part of England, Chambers came from a working class family; his father was a skilled worker with wood and his mother stayed at home. His childhood home was dominated by the large, black iron fireplace where all the food was cooked and the water heated; only a few books could be found, including a dictionary, a volume of *Aesop's Fables*, and a do-it-yourself medical book. Chambers did not read for pleasure, nor did he excel in primary school. "Throughout my ninth year I was beaten twice

every Friday for not being able to do well enough in mental arithmetic tests," he recalled in the *Sixth Book of Junior Authors and Illustrators*. "School in Chester-le-Street was not a place you learned anything except how to avoid bullies."

Finds Literature a Few Miles South

Fortunately for Chambers, he and his family moved twenty-five miles south to Darlington when he was ten years old. Although he didn't like the town, the education system was a vast improvement over what he had left behind in Chester-le-Street; he was actually encouraged to read, and a new friend even took him to the local library. However, as Chambers later recalled, it was a teacher who inspired him with his eventual love of reading.

Transferred to the local grammar school at the age of thirteen, Chambers met P. J. Osborne, "a man who truly believed that the reading and writing of literature were the most important educational, cultural, and intellectual activities anyone could be concerned with," according to Chambers. And so he was introduced to several major American writers, including D. H. Lawrence, whose novel *Sons and Lovers* first led him to think that he, too, could write. Chambers saw himself in this book, for Lawrence came from a very similar cultural environment. After finishing *Sons and Lovers* in the middle of the night, Chambers started penning his first novel the very next day, setting it in the town in which he was born. Acknowledging that it was never finished, he admitted in his autobiographical essay that "It never will be. Everything I've written about since has been a failed attempt to write the book I started then."

Chooses Children's Literature Career

Osborne had an even greater effect on his student than making him a real reader—he inspired Chambers to become an English teacher. During the same time he was teaching, Chambers found the second phase of his career when he joined a new monastic order of the Anglican Church, an order founded for the purpose of working with young people. This led him to a position at a local secondary school where the boys and girls were far from great readers. Responsible for their library and drama work, Chambers spent several

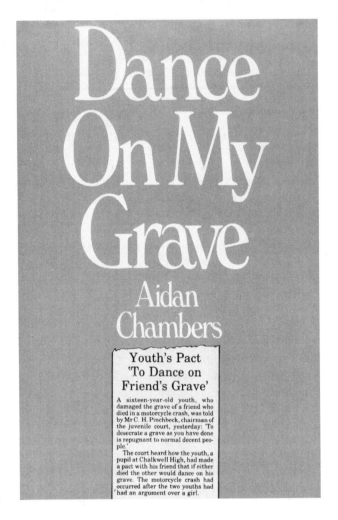

Chambers' 1982 novel recounts a passionate yet tragic affair between two young men.

he finished that D. H. Lawrence novel in the middle of the night. "Not without bother, I settled down to the unpredictable, anxiety-ridden and wholly satisfying life of the freelance writer," he revealed in his autobiographical essay.

Chambers' freelance career has since gone on to encompass many genres—criticism, novels, plays, anthologies, and more—but has always remained centered on children and young adults. "Chambers's work has forwarded children's literature in many respects," states Silvey. Focusing on Chambers' young adult novels in particular, Silvey adds that these "works of fiction . . . reflect his commitment to writing about situations and emotions familiar to his audience while simultaneously challenging and expanding their horizons with the unfamiliar." In order to convey these situations and emotions, Chambers employs a range of narrative techniques that many consider difficult for young readers. "His novels provide a challenge," continues Silvey, "as he often experiments with narrative technique, attempting to convey ideas or sensations as authentically as possible." S. David Gill similarly points out in *ALAN Review:* "Admittedly, the stylized writing found in these novels may intimidate readers who like their novels 'once and fast,' but Chambers is worth the work: his writing rewards rereading." Gill goes on to contend that "rarely does a writer possess the skill to integrate so many elements into a cohesive narrative. Underlying this skill, however, are universal stories about adolescents struggling to deal with their worlds."

The Search for Self

The first Chambers' "struggling adolescents" to be introduced to readers is seventeen-year-old Ditto, an English boy whose experiences during a spring holiday make up the 1978 novel *Breaktime*. After Ditto's classmate Morgan tells him that literature is "crap," Ditto sets out to prove him wrong by recording the events of his holiday. He does this through narration, letters, stream-of-consciousness, and a diary, all of which work together to reveal that he is in search of two things during his trip: an understanding of his failure to get along with his invalid father, and the loss of his virginity to a girl who has shown an interest in him. "Both themes are convincingly developed and resolved: The father-son material is unforced and poignant, and the love story is a sweet one," asserts Rich-

years in search of novels and plays appropriate for these students before finally deciding to write some of his own. Both the novels and plays were so successful that they were soon published.

From his first published works of fiction, Chambers moved on to write *The Reluctant Reader*, the first of several books he would author about children and reading. Quickly becoming a respected authority on children's literature, Chambers also started a paperback fiction list called "Topliners" and began to speak at conferences and meetings throughout his native England. By the time he reached his thirties, Chambers found himself immersed in three full-time careers—monk, teacher, and writer—and facing the very difficult decision of which one to pursue full-time. He chose the career he had discovered several years back, as

If you enjoy the works of Aidan Chambers, you may also want to check out the following books and films:

J. D. Salinger, *The Catcher in the Rye*, 1951.
Chaim Potok, *My Name Is Asher Lev*, 1972.
Nancy Garden, *Annie on My Mind*, 1982.
Jesus of Montreal, an award-winning Canadian film, 1989.

ard Yates in the *New York Times Book Review*. At the same time, Morgan is forced to realize that both he and Ditto have become characters in the story and he is unable to tell truth from fiction. "Like Morgan at the end," observes Robert Protherough in *Twentieth-Century Young Adult Writers*, "readers have to make their own sense of the narrative, to decide how much of it is true."

Similar to *Breaktime* in style, Chambers' 1982 novel *Dance on My Grave* opens with a newspaper story describing the arrest of Hal Robinson for dancing on the fresh grave of his lover, Barry. Hal's account of the events leading up to this crime is revealed through notes taken during sessions with his social worker as well as through letters, footnotes, and lists. After flipping over a boat on the Thames River in London, Hal is rescued by the older Barry, and the pair are brought together as both friends and eventually as lovers. Consumed by his first, passionate love, Hal is both angry and jealous when he discovers that Barry has casually been with a girl. A fight ensues and Barry leaves on his motorbike; he is killed in an accident a short time later. A fast and hard-living young man, Barry had made Hal promise to dance on his grave after his death, and Hal does so, revealing to the world his long-hidden sexual orientation.

"*Dance on My Grave* is inventive, witty, stimulating," in the opinion of Neil Philip in the *Times Educational Supplement*, who adds that Barry and Hal's relationship "is related with a cool matter-of-fact humour which is most refreshing." Mary K. Chelton similarly asserts in *Voice of Youth Advocates*: "To have male feelings so well depicted is a rare treat, and to have the protagonist be a young gay male who survives a lost love with insight and joy, is rarer still. . . . Everything about this book is superb."

Using similar framing devices to his previous young adult novels, Chambers begins his 1987 novel *NIK: Now I Know* with three separate narratives, taking place at three different times. As the three strands mesh together they form the story of Nik, a seventeen-year-old agnostic who is persuaded by a history teacher to do the background research for a youth group that is creating an amateur film about the Second Coming of Christ. During the course of this work, Nik meets and falls in love with Julie, a Christian feminist who eventually loses her sight when she is injured by a terrorist bomb. After witnessing this attack, Nik decides to conclude his research through an experiment in the local junkyard; he engineers a "practice version" of the crucifixion.

"With its time shifts, word play, and discussions on such vexing theological problems as free will, suffering and affliction, doubt and belief, the novel is compelling but demanding. Yet if offers enormous rewards to thinking, mature young adults," asserts *Horn Book* reviewer Ethel L. Heins. Patty Campbell concludes in her *Wilson Library Bulletin* review of *NIK: Now I Know*: "Chambers in this many-layered novel has given us a work of stunning impact, a book in the tradition of C. S. Lewis and George MacDonald that lights the search but begs no easy answers."

The theme of self-discovery through conflict is continued in Chambers' 1992 novel, *The Toll Bridge*. Borrowing from the Greek myth of Janus, the two-faced keeper of the gate to Hades, Chambers introduces Piers, who symbolically has two faces as well. To escape the pressures of his parents, girlfriend, and school, Piers takes a job as the gatekeeper of a private toll bridge, living in isolation in the gate house. The one friend Piers does make is Tess, the landowner's daughter, and the triangle is complete when a handsome, mysterious young man named Adam shows up one night. Unable to rid himself of his guest, Piers (renamed Jan when the three friends give each other new names) finds himself oddly drawn to Adam, as does Tess, though they know nothing of his past.

The Toll Bridge "is a rites of passage novel about identity and growth through friendship but it's also much more than that," maintains Melanie Guile in *Magpies*. "Moreover," continues Guile, "*The Toll Bridge*'s multifaceted form, together with its patterns of imagery (bridge, water, fire), enact crucial concerns in the novel: the fragmentation of personality that is an inevitable part of adolescence, and the struggle towards integration." A *Publishers Weekly* reviewer concludes: "Provocative in the best sense, this novel suggests even more than its intricate plot spells out, leaving readers with much for pleasurable contemplation."

Looking at Chambers' young adult novels as a whole, Protherough observes that their "originality and driving power . . . is undeniable. . . . Everything that Chambers has written can be seen as demonstrating the power of language and of active reading where 'the reader plays the text.'" And Gill concludes: "Chambers himself put it best when he wrote '. . . you discover yourself . . . and therefore learn to understand more about yourself.'"

■ Works Cited

Campbell, Patty, "The Young Adult Perplex," *Wilson Library Bulletin*, May, 1988, pp. 78-79.

Chambers, Aidan, autobiographical essay, *Sixth Book of Junior Authors and Illustrators*, edited by Sally Holmes Holtze, Wilson, 1989, pp. 53-54.

Chelton, Mary K., review of *Dance on My Grave*, *Voice of Youth Advocates*, October, 1983, p. 198.

Gill, S. David, "Aidan Chambers: Monk, Writer, Critic," *ALAN Review*, fall, 1997, pp. 11-12.

Guile, Melanie, review of *The Toll Bridge*, *Magpies*, May, 1993.

Heins, Ethel L., review of *NIK: Now I Know*, *Horn Book*, January/February, 1989, pp. 76-77.

Philip, Neil, "Adolescent Friction," *Times Educational Supplement*, September 10, 1982, p. 33.

Protherough, Robert, essay in *Twentieth-Century Young Adult Writers*, St. James Press, 1994, pp. 111-13.

Silvey, Anita, editor, *Children's Books and Their Creators*, Houghton, 1995, pp. 127-28.

Review of *The Toll Bridge*, *Publishers Weekly*, June 19, 1995, p. 62.

Yates, Richard, "You Can and Can't Go Home Again," *New York Times Book Review*, April 29, 1979, p. 30.

■ For More Information See

BOOKS

Townsend, John Rowe, *Written for Children: An Outline of English-Language Children's Literature*, 6th American edition, Scarecrow Press, 1996.

PERIODICALS

Books for Keeps, November, 1992, p. 27.
Bulletin of the Center for Children's Books, June, 1979, p. 171; June, 1981, p. 188; January, 1987, pp. 83-84.
Growing Point, November, 1984, pp. 4430-31.
Horn Book, June, 1984, pp. 326-27.
Kirkus Reviews, October 1, 1986, pp. 1514-15.
Publishers Weekly, April 15, 1983, p. 50.
School Library Journal, September, 1981, pp. 121-22; April, 1984, p. 112; November, 1987, p. 113; July, 1995, p. 92.
Times Literary Supplement, December 1, 1978, p. 1395; July 18, 1980, p. 812; November 30, 1984, p. 1381.
Voice of Youth Advocates, June, 1981, p. 28.

—Sketch by Susan Reicha

Daniel Defoe

■ Personal

Born Daniel Foe c. 1660, in St. Giles, London, England; name changed in 1703; died April 26, 1731, in Moorfields, London, England; buried in Bunhill Fields; son of James (a butcher, candlemaker, and merchant) and Alice Foe; married Mary Tuffley, January 1, 1684; children: Daniel, Benjamin Norton, Maria, Hannah, Henrietta, Martha, Sophia. *Education:* Studied at the Reverend James Fisher's school, Dorking, Surrey; studied for the Presbyterian ministry at Charles Morton's Academy, Newington Green, Middlesex.

■ Career

Journalist, pamphleteer, social and political commentator, and novelist, some religious and political writings resulting in arrests for libel and treason, fines, imprisonments, and a July 29-31, 1703 pillorying. Merchant in Cornhill, London, 1683; businessman in England in the hosiery and brick- and tile-making trades; investor in English land, ships, voyages, a diving bell, and a perfume concern; and a trader in tobacco and wines, 1685-92;

proprietor of brick and tile works, Tilbury, Essex, England, 1703; failed business dealings resulted in several lawsuits, two imprisonments, and two bankruptcies. Editor of periodicals, including *Review,* 1704-13, *Mercator,* 1713-14, *Manufacturer,* 1719-20, *Daily Post,* 1719-25, *Commentator,* 1720, *Mercurius Britannicus,* and *Flying Post.* Joined unsuccessful rebellion led by the Duke of Monmouth against King James II to establish a Protestant monarchy, Lyme Regis, England, 1685; participated in Glorious Revolution in which William of Orange deposed James II and, with wife, Mary II, was crowned William III, 1688-89; served William III in various capacities in England and Scotland, 1689-1702; secretary in the Glass Duty Office, 1695; agent for Robert Harley (a member of parliament and secretary of state), working as a propagandist, opinion pollster, and spy in England and Scotland, 1703-14.

■ Writings

NOVELS

The Memoirs of Majr. Alexander Ramkins, a High-Land-Officer, Now in Prison at Avignon: Being an Account of Several Remarkable Adventures during about Twenty-Eight Years' Service in Scotland, Germany, Italy, Flanders, and Ireland, R. King & W. Boreham, 1718.
The Life and Strange Surprising Adventures of Robinson Crusoe, of York, Mariner, W. Taylor, 1719, published as *The Life and Most Surprising*

Adventures of Robinson Crusoe, of York, Mariner, Robert Bell, 1776, published as *Robinson Crusoe,* illustrated by N. C. Wyeth, Running Press, 1991.

The Farther Adventures of Robinson Crusoe: Being the Second and Last Part of His Life, W. Taylor, 1719.

Memoirs of a Cavalier; or, A Military Journal of the Wars in Germany, and the Wars in England, from 1632-1648, A. Bell, 1720.

The Life, Adventures, and Pyracies of the Famous Captain Singleton, J. Brotherton, 1720.

Serious Reflections during the Life and Surprising Adventures of Robinson Crusoe, with His Vision of the Angelick World, W. Taylor, 1720.

The Fortunes and Misfortunes of the Famous Moll Flanders, W. Chetwood & T. Edling, 1722, published as *Moll Flanders,* Knopf, 1991.

A Journal of the Plague Year: Being Observations or Memorials, of the Most Remarkable Occurrences, as Well Publick as Private, Which Happened in London during the Last Great Visitation in 1665, Written by a Citizen Who Continued All the While in London, E. Nutt, 1722.

The History and Remarkable Life of the Truly Honourable Colonel Jacque, Commonly Call'd Colonel Jack, J. Brotherton, 1723.

The Fortunate Mistress; or, A History of the Life and Vast Variety of Fortunes of Mademoiselle de Beleau, Afterwards Call'd the Countess de Wintelsheim, in Germany, Being the Person Known by the Name of the Lady Roxana, in the Time of King Charles II, T. Warner, 1724, published as *Roxana,* Viking, 1982.

A New Voyage round the World, by a Course Never Sailed Before, A. Bettesworth & W. Mears, 1724, with illustrations by J. B. Yeats, AMS Press, 1974.

The Memoirs of an English Officer, E. Symon, 1728, published as *Memoirs of Captain George Carleton.*

POEMS

The Meditations of Daniel Defoe, 1681, edited by George H. Healey, Commington Press, 1946.

A New Discovery of an Old Intreague, [London], 1691.

The True-Born Englishman, [London], 1700.

The Pacificator, J. Nutt, 1700.

Reformation of Manners, [London], 1702.

The Mock Mourners, [London], 1702.

A Hymn to the Pillory, [London], 1703.

More Reformation: A Satyr upon Himself, [London], 1703.

A Hymn to Victory, J. Nutt, 1704.

The Dyet of Poland: A Satyr, [London], 1705.

The Vision, B. Bragg, 1706.

Caledonia: A Poem in Honour of Scotland, and the Scots Nation, Heirs and Successors of Andrew Anderson, 1706.

Jure Divino: A Satyr, [London], 1708.

HISTORIES

The History of the Kentish Petition, [London], 1701.

The Storm; or, A Collection of the Most Remarkable Casualties and Disasters Which Happen'd in the Late Dreadful Tempest, both by Sea and Land, G. Sawbridge, 1704.

The History of the Union of Great Britain, Heirs and Successors of Andrew Anderson, 1709.

A History of the Wars, of His Present Majesty Charles XII, King of Sweden . . . by a Scots Gentleman in the Swedish Service, A. Bell, 1715, expanded edition, 1720.

An Historical Account of the Voyages and Adventures of Sir Walter Raleigh, with the Discoveries and Conquests He Made for the Crown of England, W. Boreham, 1720.

A General History of the Robberies and Murders of the Most Notorious Pyrates, C. Rivington, Volume 1, 1724, Volume 2: *The History of the Pyrates,* 1728.

A General History of Discoveries and Improvements, four parts, J. Roberts, 1725-26.

The Political History of the Devil, as Well Ancient as Modern, two parts, T. Warner, 1726.

A System of Magick; or, A History of Black Art, J. Roberts, 1726.

An Essay on the History and Reality of Apparitions, A. Millar, 1727, AMS Press, 1973.

ECONOMIC TREATISES

A Tour thro' the Whole Island of Great Britain, three volumes, G. Strahan, 1724-27, abridged edition, Yale University Press, 1991.

The Royal Progress, J. Darby, 1724.

The Complete English Tradesman, two volumes, C. Rivington, 1725-27.

A Plan of the English Commerce, C. Rivington, 1728.

Atlas Maritimus and Commercialis; or, A General View of the World, So Far As It Relates to Trade and Navigation, James & John Knapton, 1728.

CONDUCT BOOKS

The Family Instructor, two volumes, E. Matthews, 1715-18, with an introduction by Paula R. Backscheider, Scholars' Facsimiles & Reprints, 1989.

Religious Courtship: Being Historical Discourses, on the Necessity of Marrying Religious Husbands and Wives Only, E. Matthews, 1722.

Conjugal Lewdness; or, Matrimonial Whoredom, T. Warner, 1727, published as *A Treatise concerning the Use and Abuse of the Marriage Bed*, T. Warner, 1727.

A New Family Instructor, T. Warner, 1727.

The Compleat English Gentleman, edited by Karl Buelbring, D. Nutt, 1890.

SELECTIONS

The Earlier Life and Chief Earlier Works of Daniel Defoe, edited by Henry Morley, Routledge, 1889.

Defoe, edited by John Masefield, G. Bell, 1909.

The Best of Defoe's Review, edited by William L. Payne, Columbia University Press, 1951.

Selections from the Prose of Daniel Defoe, edited by Roger Manvell, Falcon Press, 1953.

Daniel Defoe: Selections from His Writings, edited by James T. Boulton, Schocken, 1965.

Selections from Defoe, edited by Roger Manvell, Blackie, 1966.

Selected Poetry and Prose of Daniel Defoe, edited by Michael F. Shurgrue, Holt, 1968.

Robinson Crusoe, and Other Writings, edited by James Sutherland, Houghton, 1968.

Daniel Defoe: His Life and Recently Discovered Writing Extending from 1726-1729, Burt Franklin, 1969.

A Defoe Anthology: Writings on Politics, Economics, and History, edited by Laura Ann Goldsmith Curtis, Rutgers University Press, 1974.

Pirates, illustrated by Greg Irons, edited by Harry Knill, Bellerophon, 1975.

The Versatile Defoe: An Anthology of Uncollected Writings by Daniel Defoe, edited by Laura A. Curtis, Rowman & Littlefield, 1979.

COLLECTIONS

A True Collection of the Writings of the Author of The True-Born English-Man, [London], 1703.

A Second Volume of the Writings of the Author of "The True-Born Englishman," The Booksellers, 1705.

The Novels and Miscellaneous Works of Daniel Defoe, with prefaces attributed to Sir Walter Scott, twenty volumes, D. A. Talboys, 1840-41.

The Works of Daniel Defoe (includes a memoir of his life), edited by William W. Hazlitt, J. Clements, 1840-43.

The Novels and Miscellaneous Works of Daniel Defoe, seven volumes, Bell, 1856-84.

The Works of Daniel Defoe, edited by John S. Leltie, W. P. Nimmo, 1872.

Romances and Narratives, edited by George A. Aitken, sixteen volumes, Dent, 1895.

The Works of Daniel Defoe, edited by G. H. Maynadier, sixteen volumes, G. D. Sproul, 1903-04.

The Shakespeare Head Edition of the Novels and Selected Writings of Daniel Defoe, fourteen volumes, B. Blackwell, 1927-28.

Defoe's Review (facsimile edition of *The Review*, 1704-13), Columbia University Press, 1938.

Letters of Daniel Defoe, edited by George Harris Healey, Oxford University Press, 1955.

OTHER

A Letter to a Dissenter from His Friend at the Hague, concerning the Papal Laws and the Test; Showing That the Popular Plea for Liberty of Conscience Is Not Concerned in That Question, Hans Verdraeght, 1688.

The Character of the Late Dr. Samuel Annesley, by Way of Elegy, E. Whitlock, 1697.

An Essay upon Projects, R. R. for Tho. Cockerill, 1697.

A Poor Man's Plea, in Relation to All the Proclamations, Declarations, Acts of Parliament, etc., Which Have Been, or Shall Be Made, or Published, for a Reformation of Manners, and Suppressing Immorality in the Nation, [London], 1698.

The Villainy of Stock-Jobbers Detected, and the Causes of the Late Run upon the Bank and Bankers Discovered and Considered, [London], 1701.

The Apparent Danger of an Invasion, Briefly Represented in a Letter to a Minister of State, by a Kentish Gentleman, A. Baldwin, 1701.

Reasons against a War with France; or, An Argument Shewing That the French King's Owning the Prince of Wales as King of England, Scotland, and Ireland Is Not Sufficient Ground for a War, [London], 1701.

The Original Power of the Collective Body of the People of England, Examined and Asserted, [London], 1701.

The Shortest-Way with Dissenters; or, Proposals for the Establishment of the Church, [London], 1702.

More Short-Ways with the Dissenters, [London], 1704.

An Essay on the Regulation of the Press, [London], 1704.

Giving Alms, No Charity, and Employing the Poor, [London], 1704.

The Consolidator; or, Memoirs of Sundry Transactions from the World in the Moon, B. Bragg, 1705, Garland, 1972.

A True Relation of the Apparition of One Mrs. Veal, the Next Day after Her Death (short story), B. Bragg, 1706.

Atalantis Major (political satire), [Edinburgh], 1711, University of Illinois Press, 1973.

A Short Narrative of the Live and Actions of His Grace John D. of Marlborough, J. Baker, 1711, University of California Press, 1974.

Memoirs of John Duke of Melfort: Being an Account of the Secret Intrigues of the Chevalier de S. George, Particularly Relating to the Present Times, J. Moor, 1714.

The Secret History of the White Staff: Being an Account of Affairs under the Conduct of Some Late Ministers, and of What Might Probably Have Happened If Her Majesty Had Not Died, three parts, J. Baker, 1714-15.

An Appeal to Honour and Justice tho' It Be of His Worst Enemies: Being a True Account of His Conduct in Publick Affairs (autobiography), J. Baker, 1715.

A Vindication of the Press; or, An Essay on the Usefulness of Writing, of Criticism, and the Qualifications of Authors, [London], 1718, Garland, 1972.

The Dumb Philosopher; or, Great Britain's Wonder, T. Bickerton, 1719.

The History of the Life and Adventures of Mr. Duncan Campbell, [London], 1720, with illustrations by J. B. Yeats, AMS Press, 1974.

The King of Pirates: Being an Account of the Famous Enterprises of Captain Avery, the Mock King of Madagascar, A. Bettesworth, 1720, with illustrations by Yeats, AMS Press, 1974.

Due Preparations for the Plague, as Well as for Soul as Body, E. Matthews, 1722, with illustrations by Yeats, AMS Press, 1974.

An Impartial History of the Life and Actions of Peter Alexowitz, the Present Czar of Muscovy, from His Birth down to the Present Times . . . Written by a British Officer in the Service of the Czar, W. Chetwood, 1722.

The Great Law of Subordination Consider'd; or, The Insolence and Insufferable Behaviour of Servants in England Duly Enquir'd Into, S. Harding, 1724.

A Narrative of All the Robberies, Escapes, &c., of John Sheppard, J. Applebee, 1724.

(Under pseudonym Andrew Moreton, Esq.) *Every-Body's Business Is No-Body's Business,* T. Warner, 1725.

A True and Genuine Account of the Life and Actions of the Late Jonathan Wild, J. Applebee, 1725.

An Account of the Conduct and Proceedings of the Late John Gow, Alias Smith, J. Applebee, 1725, published as *Account of the Conduct and Proceedings of the Pirate Gow: The Original of Sir Walter Scott's Captain Cleveland,* Burt Franklin, 1970.

The Four Voyages of Captain George Roberts, A. Bettesworth, 1726, Garland, 1972.

Augusta Triumphans; or, The Way to Make London the Most Flourishing City in the Universe, J. Roberts, 1728, revised as *The Generous Protector; or, A Friendly Proposal to Prevent Murder and Other Enormous Abuses,* A. Dodd & E. Nutt, 1730.

Street-Robberies Consider'd: The Reason of Their Being so Frequent, with Probable Means to Prevent 'Em, J. Roberts, 1728.

An Effectual Scheme for the Immediate Preventing of Street Robberies, and Suppressing All Other Disorders of the Night, J. Wilford, 1730.

Of Royall Education: A Fragmentary Treatise, edited by Buelbring, D. Nutt, 1895.

Author of numerous essays of social and political commentary. Contributor to periodicals, including *Nathaniel Mist's Weekly Journal, Whitehall Evening Post, Original Weekly Journal, Director, Universal Spectator,* and *Applebee's Journal.*

■ Adaptations

PLAYS

Robinson Crusoe was adapted for the stage by R. B. B. Sheridan as *Robinson Crusoe; or Harlequin Friday,* T. Becket, 1781; by Issac Pocock as *Robinson Crusoe; or, The Bold Buccaniers* (two-act), Hodgson, 1822; by F. Fortescue as *Robinson Crusoe; or, The Island of Juan Fernandez* (operatic drama), [Boston], 1822; by J. F. Macardle and F. W. Green as *Robinson Crusoe,* Daily Post & Journal Offices, 1878; by Francis C. Burnand as *The Real Adventures of Robinson Crusoe* (burlesque), Bradbury, Agnew, 1893; and by Margaret Carter as *Robinson Crusoe* (two-act pantomime), S. French, 1949.

FILMS

Robinson Crusoe was adapted as a film of the same title by Henry W. Savage, 1916; Universal Film, 1917; Gaumont, 1927; and Guaranteed Pictures, 1936; adapted as *Adventures of Robinson Crusoe,* Universal (series of 18), 1922, and United Artists (UA), 1954; as *Mr. Robinson Crusoe,* starring Douglas Fairbanks, UA, 1932; as *Robinson Crusoe on Mars,* starring Paul Mantee and Adam West, Paramount, 1964; and as *Crusoe,* Island Pictures/Virgin Vision, 1988.

The Fortunes and Misfortunes of the Famous Moll Flanders was adapted for film as *The Amorous Adventures of Moll Flanders*, starring Kim Novak and Angela Lansbury, 1965; and as *Moll Flanders*, starring Morgan Freeman and Robin Wright, MGM, 1996; and adapted for British television, Granada, 1996.

■ Sidelights

The sheer weight of numbers is astounding. Daniel Defoe wrote over five hundred and sixty works of fiction, nonfiction prose, and poetry. His best-known novels were composed within five years of each other, three of them in 1722 alone. He penned millions of words in the last fifteen years of his life, after he left fiction behind, words scribbled in quill and ink and laboriously translated into hand-set type. Defoe's subjects were myriad: histories, travel books, guides to moral and societal conduct, proposals for improving society and industry, and biographies enough to fill a small library.

Defoe's span of influence is equally astounding. He has been dubbed variously the father of the novel and of modern journalism. Today he is largely known for several novels, the most famous being *The Life and Strange Surprising Adventures of Robinson Crusoe*. Next in line to these are *The Fortunes and Misfortunes of the Famous Moll Flanders, A Journal of the Plague Year,* and *A Fortunate Mistress* (later published as *Roxana*). In these works, to which he turned his hand between 1719 and 1724, Defoe combined elements of spiritual autobiography, allegory, and so-called rogue biography with stylistic techniques including dialogue, setting, symbolism, characterization, and, most importantly, irony to fashion some of the first realistic narratives in English fiction. With this winning combination, Defoe popularized the novel among a growing middle class readership.

But fiction was, in many ways, only a sideshow for this wordsmith; most of Defoe's professional life was spent writing prose nonfiction and in journalism, in both of which he made lasting contributions. A prolific pamphleteer and propagandist, Defoe wrote on topics ranging from religious tolerance to foreign trade to conjugal relations. "Perhaps no writer in human history has written so knowledgeably and sympathetically on so many subjects," noted Paula R. Backscheider in

Dictionary of Literary Biography. "Whatever kind of writing he took up, he transformed." Backscheider also observed the power Defoe wielded in his pamphleteering: "We may have forgotten pamphlets like *The Original Power of the Collective Body of the People of England* (1702), but they were enthusiastically and frequently quoted for two centuries and echoes of them exist in, for instance, the United States Constitution."

Journalism was equally transformed by Defoe, and in the *Review,* a periodical that he wrote singlehanded for nine years, he created the forerunner of such later papers as *Tatler* and *Spectator*. As Richard West noted in his *The Life and Strange Surprising Adventures of Daniel Defoe,* "Defoe was the principal pathfinder and pace-setter in what came to be seen as the golden age of journalism." According to West, Defoe was "the first master, if not the inventor, of almost every feature of modern newspapers." These included the lead article, investigative reporting, advice and gossip columns, letters to the editor, human interest features, background articles, and foreign news analysis. If Defoe pioneered the best of what would become modern journalism, he also opened the Pandora's box to what might be the worst, for tabloid journalism also took its inspiration from Defoe's *Review,* with its fake letters to the editor and hyperbolic lampoons.

Defoe did not accomplish all this from an ivory tower, but was most definitely a man *of* and *in* the world. It was his own religious convictions as a Dissenter to the Anglican Church of England that brought him to writing in the first place, and throughout his career he remained a spokesman for that conviction. He was a husband and a father, as well as a businessman and investor—though bankrupt twice over, hounded until his death by creditors. He also was a political prisoner who on one occasion spent three days in the pillory for his writing, an experience which would change his life. And there was also Defoe the spy, the double agent, who worked at times for the Tories, at other times for the Whigs. As a young man, Defoe had learned how to write persuasively from many points of view; it was as if this early training allowed him to slip in and out of allegiances at will as an adult. A complex man, Defoe escapes the psychological scalpel of modern biographers because so little is known or recorded about his private life. What we do know comes largely from what he wrote, where he lived, what debtors' prison he may have frequented. For Defoe, the writings are all that is known of the man.

The Foe Family of Cripplegate

"Daniel Defoe began his life as he was to spend it, and as he eventually ended it, in the utmost secrecy," West noted in his biography. Defoe was born sometime in 1660—the fall, it is supposed—to James and Alice Foe in the parish of St. Giles Cripplegate, just north of the old center of London. There were also two older sisters in the family: Mary, born in 1657, and Elizabeth, born in 1659. The year 1660 has another significance, for it marked the restoration of the monarchy in England. The Foes were followers of Oliver Cromwell during the Commonwealth (the period, beginning in 1649 following the execution of King Charles I, when a wholly representative government ruled England) and also Presbyterians. Thus the return of the Royalists (supporters of Charles II) was something of a tragedy for them and others of their faith, for they were Nonconformists or Dissenters to the established Church of England. The Royalists set a series of punitive laws against Dissenters, much as the Puritans had done to Anglicans during Cromwellian times. Thus young Daniel Defoe was plagued from his earliest years by a sense of ostracism and discrimination on account of his beliefs.

James Foe was a butcher and a candle merchant whose fortunes improved over the years despite his religious beliefs. Little is known of Defoe's youth, but it is highly likely that he was on some level influenced by two significant historical events: the Plague of 1665 and the Great Fire of London in 1666. He would later write of the plague, though West, among other biographers, is doubtful whether he actually experienced it on a personal level. The Great Fire, however, certainly touched Defoe more closely, for it inaugurated the transformation of London from a city of wood to a modern metropolis rebuilt in brick and stone, stretching out into the countryside. The London that Defoe loved was built during his own lifetime.

Defoe's mother died when he was about ten and he attended a school in Dorking, Surrey, run by the Reverend James Fisher. When he was sixteen, Defoe was sent to an academy in Newington Green, north of London, operated by the Reverend Charles Morton. As Dissenters, members of the Foe family were barred from attending elite universities at Oxford or Cambridge, but at Morton's academy Defoe gained an enduring love of science and also developed an ability to write with not only clarity but "Energy", as he termed it. Typical exercises at the academy involved writing letters from various points of view: for example from that of a merchant or an ambassador abroad. The writing in such letters was to reflect both the character of the would-be writer as well as to hint at the personality of the letter's intended recipient. Such practice developed in the young Defoe an acute sense of character and point of view, both of which skills he would later employ in his fiction.

Instead of an emphasis on Latin and Greek as found at most universities, Morton's small academy stressed philosophy and the sciences, and generally trained its scholars for the ministry. But such was not the case for Defoe: after three years at the academy, he set out into the world of business. In 1680 he became a factor, or middleman, between manufacturers and sellers of hosiery, setting up as a partner with two brothers. Defoe, however, never seemed content with only one iron in the fire; he branched out into wine and tobacco and traveled widely on the Continent in the course of his business duties. In 1684 he married Mary Tuffley, the daughter of a successful merchant who brought him the substantial dowry of thirty-seven hundred pounds. They would have seven children together (though by some accounts Mary is believed to have given birth to at least eight), yet little is known about Mary and the relationship the couple shared. What is known is that their marriage had its financial ups and downs caused both by Defoe's commercial as well as political convictions.

From Merchant to Writer to Spy

In 1685, just one year after his marriage, Defoe took part in a short-lived rebellion against the recently crowned Catholic King James II that was led by the Duke of Monmouth. It is not known to what extent Defoe participated, but the rebellion was quickly put down and several of its leaders were executed. Defoe won a pardon in 1687, and when William III drove James out, Defoe was once again able to return to London. Where he

Marooned on a Caribbean island, Robinson Crusoe uses all available resources to create a permanent home, as seen in an illustrated edition of Defoe's classic 1719 novel.

stayed until that time remains a matter for speculation, but he, like many other followers of Monmouth, most likely sought refuge in Scotland and Holland. Defoe's earliest writing, a pamphlet inspired by the need for religious toleration, appeared in 1688.

During the 1680s and 1690s, Defoe's activities centered on two fronts: commerce and political involvement. His far-flung business and investment ventures culminated in bankruptcy in 1692, and he was left owing his creditors the monumental sum of seventeen thousand pounds. Before this point he had already spent two terms in debtors' prison; with bankruptcy he sought refuge in Whitefriars where warrants could not be served. There he came into contact with thieves and pros-

titutes, characters who would later fill the pages of his fiction. Similar to the experience of the young Charles Dickens over a century later, debtors' prison provided a writer's education for Defoe.

Defoe quickly sought patrons among the powerful and found a position as a secretary to a brick works near Tilbury, England. Eventually he became chief owner of the works, and was able to pay off all but five thousand pounds of his debt. In 1697 he published his first important work, *Essay upon Projects,* and four years later made his name known with his long poem, *The True-Born Englishman,* his effort to counter a growing xenophobia in England. This poem, which satirized the prejudices of his fellow countrymen and called the English a race of mongrels, sold more copies in a single day than any other poem in English history. It was about this time, also, that Daniel Foe began styling himself Defoe, upgrading the family name in the process.

Fame of a very different sort came Defoe's way with publication of his next major work, 1702's *The Shortest Way with Dissenters.* He wrote anonymously in the voice of Tories who would further constrict the rights of Dissenters, exaggerating their positions in an attempt to make them appear absurd. Unfortunately, this time Defoe's satire was grossly misunderstood. He won scorn from both sides of the issue and was accused of seditious libel. Resorting to a response that was, by now, becoming habit, Defoe ran, and remained in hiding until he received some assurances that he would serve only a short prison term. However, once arrested, he was forced to spend three consecutive days in the stocks, each day in a different part of London. The authorities thought that such a punishment might lead to death for the headstrong writer, as did Defoe, who attempted to mellow public sentiment against him by writing another poem, *A Hymn to the Pillory.* It was published on the very day he was put into the stocks; instead of stones those who came to see his punishment threw flowers.

Defoe's time in hiding and his prison term in Newgate sent his brick business into chaos, forcing him to declare bankruptcy for a second time. Thus when a proposal to work for the Tories was put to him, Defoe readily agreed. His prison term was cut short on condition that he become an instrument for the Catholic monarchy, turning his considerable propaganda powers to the service of the state rather than the criticism of it. Working for Secretary of State Robert Harley for a fee of two hundred pounds a year, Defoe founded the *Review* in 1704 and continued writing it for over nine years. That the paper promoted Harley's views—pro-Anglican, anti-Dissenter, against foreign entanglements—did not seem to bother Defoe, who had the ability to write from different perspectives. In 1706 Defoe was a silent partner in negotiations for the union of Scotland and England and thereafter wrote *The History of the Union of Great Britain*, still a respected resource for historians of the period. During his tenure as a government agent, he also set up an information network all over England to report to the Tories on political unrest.

The death of Queen Anne in 1714 and the fall of the Tory government put Defoe out of a job for a time. But soon enough he was hired by the new power elite, the Whigs, and sent as a secret agent to work for a Tory publication, the *Weekly Journal*, published by one Nathaniel Mist. Defoe's job here was to sabotage the newspaper, yet all the while he was able to continue his growth as a writer and propagandist. Never fully comfortable with the Whig position, he found that he could honestly write from the Tory point of view at times. However, throughout these years, he was still periodically arrested for his writings and continually dogged by creditors.

One port for Defoe amid the hectic storms of his life seems to have been his family. In 1709 he moved to Stoke Newington, a suburb of London heavily populated with Dissenters, and it was there, with a pleasant garden and an ample library, that Defoe could escape some of the cares of the political world. Another escape was afforded him by turning his hand to fiction.

Robinson Crusoe

As early as 1717 Defoe wrote a fictionalized memoir by one of the participants in the peace treaty negotiations with France. With another work, *The Memoirs of Major Alexander Ramkins* in 1718, "Defoe finally depicts a fully developed fictional character," according to Maximillian E. Novak in an overview of Defoe's novels in *Dictionary of Literary Biography*. But Defoe's lasting fame for most readers lies with the book that he published in

1719, *The Life and Strange Surprising Adventures of Robinson Crusoe of York, Mariner,* better known to modern readers simply as *Robinson Crusoe.*

Defoe had long been developing the tools of his trade: point of view, dialogue, characterization, and a sense of scene. With *Robinson Crusoe* he put these together for the first time in a continuous creative product. Employing the form of travel biography, the work tells the story of a man marooned on a Caribbean island. Seemingly fanciful, such a story did not simply appear to its author from nowhere, but was the result of several worldly inspirations. First was the real-life story of the querulous Alexander Selkirk, master of a ship exploring the South Seas in the early 1700s. A difficult man by all accounts, Selkirk voluntarily agreed to be put ashore on an island hundreds of miles off the coast of Chile after arguing with another commander in the expedition. There Selkirk remained, on his own, for over four years until an expedition in 1709 stopped on the island. Accounts of Selkirk's solitary life were still popular in London when Defoe set to write his tale.

Also important in the development of his novel was the proposal, in early 1719, by England's South Sea Company to establish a colony near the mouth of the Orinoco River in Guiana—very close to the fictional location of Crusoe's island, in fact. Added to this topical inspiration was Defoe's perennial interest in utopian colonies, as well as his search for a literary mouthpiece to give voice to his Christian doctrines. These varied impulses resulted in the creation of *Robinson Crusoe* as well as its sequels, *The Farther Adventures of Robinson Crusoe* (1719) and *Serious Reflections during the Life and Surprising Adventures of Robinson Crusoe* (1720).

Brought up in the comfortable middle classes, Robinson Crusoe is destined for a life in business until he opts for a more adventurous career at sea, rejecting both his father's mercantile as well as his spiritual beliefs. Crusoe's first voyage is almost his last, however, as his ship is caught in a violent storm at sea. Once he returns to England, Crusoe vows never again to leave land. However, his vow does not last long; Crusoe's longing for adventure soon overwhelms him. He takes to sea again, this time on a trading ship bound for Africa. When his ship is captured by Turkish pirates he is made a slave and forced to endure terrible treatment. Finally he manages to escape in a small boat. Rescued by a Portuguese cargo ship, he is taken to Brazil where he begins a new life as a planter.

The need for adventure takes Crusoe to sea again, however, when he joins another English planter on a voyage to Africa to secure slaves. Off the coast of South America, however, the ship breaks apart on a reef and Crusoe is the only one to survive. Washed ashore on a remote island, he sets about to create a life for himself. Building a raft, he manages many trips back to the wrecked ship to salvage food, water, weapons, tools, lumber, sail cloth, clothing, and various other articles he will need to survive on the island. His first home is a tent on the side of a hill that he encircles with stakes to create a crude fort or stockade. Discovering a quill pen and ink among the salvaged material, Crusoe begins to keep a journal of his experiences. He also begins to make his dwelling more permanent and also to find local food and water sources, thus become self-sufficient.

For twenty-four years Crusoe lives something of a utopian existence on the island, kept company only by the animals he domesticates and entertained by reading a Bible salvaged from the wrecked ship. After surviving a serious illness, Crusoe eventually undergoes something of a re-conversion back to the faith of his father. His long-absent contact with humans resumes when cannibals from a nearby island come ashore on Crusoe's beach to feast on an unhappy victim. Chasing them off, Crusoe saves the life of their intended meal, and dubs the man Friday, after the day he is saved. Friday becomes Crusoe's faithful friend and servant, and Crusoe teaches Friday enough English to learn that some seventeen white men are being held captive on Friday's home island. Crusoe builds a canoe, planning to sail to the island and rescue the men, but before he can leave his island is once again visited by savages. Among their prisoners this time is a European, and once again Crusoe saves the intended victims, a Spaniard and an islander who turns out to be Friday's father.

Subsequently, the Spaniard and Friday's father are sent back to the neighboring island to try and save the seventeen white captives. But before they return an English ship anchors in the bay off Crusoe's island. Crusoe makes contact with the captain of the ship and two crew members after the three are set ashore by a mutinous crew. With Crusoe's help, the men recapture their ship. Five of the mutinous crew choose to stay on the island rather than face hanging in England, and Crusoe, along with Friday, sets sail for England.

In a sequel to this story that Defoe quickly cobbled together after finding his novel to be immensely popular, Crusoe has more adventures. Finding that most of his family in England has died after his long absence, Crusoe and Friday travel to his holdings in Lisbon, where Crusoe discovers he has become wealthy from his Brazilian estates. Returning to England, he marries and has three children. But with the death of his wife, he and Friday set out for more adventures on a trading ship bound for China. En route, his ship puts in at his former island, where the mutineers who stayed behind have taken native wives and established a community. At sea again, Crusoe's ship is attacked by pirates and Friday is killed. Crusoe is set ashore in China by the pirate crew, which has grown tired of his preaching at them. There he joins an overland caravan to Siberia, and eventually, an old man near death, Robinson Crusoe returns home to England, where he awaits the greatest voyage of all.

Like all great creative works, *Robinson Crusoe* lends itself to myriad interpretations: as an allegorical representation of the British Empire, an attack on economic individualism and capitalism, a further installment in the author's spiritual biography, and as a lightly veiled allegory of Defoe's own life. Most importantly, however, is the fact that the novel was read widely by Defoe's contemporaries in England. It was indeed the first work to become popular among the middle and even lower classes, who could identify with Crusoe's adventures. As John Robert Moore noted in an essay in *Twentieth-Century Interpretations of Robinson Crusoe*, before Defoe's book "there was no English novel worth the name, and no book (except the Bible) widely accepted among all classes of English and Scottish readers."

Despite its popular acceptance, *Robinson Crusoe* received a mixed reception from scholars of Defoe's time, who found the novel to be un-Christian in tone. Academics also attacked it for being wildly improbable. As with all his novels, though Defoe attaches moral overtones of sin and redemption, the realistic action supplies an ironic counter-balance to such high moral aims. For example, in Defoe's work Crusoe has a spiritual conversion and returns to the religion of his father as a result of his experiences. Yet his further adventures and self-reliance seem to ironically belie this message. Crusoe seeks the extremes of existence, not the boring middle path of mercantilism and piety.

Enlightenment philosopher Jean-Jacques Rousseau was one of the first to applaud *Robinson Crusoe* as a highly instructive book when, in 1762, Rousseau noted that "The surest way of rising above prejudice and ordering one's opinions according to the real relations of things is to put oneself in the place of a solitary man, and to judge everything as he would, having regard to its particular utility."

A distinct shift in tone among Defoe's critics came about with the writings of novelist Sir Walter Scott who, in 1827, praised *Robinson Crusoe* for its realism. Defoe's stature continued to grow during the nineteenth century. His eighteenth-century reputation as a literary hack who was willing to write

for any cause was replaced by a close study of his work that showed he was the equal of Jonathan Swift and one of the fathers of the English novel. A temporary late-nineteenth century reversal in this judgment was again displaced by twentieth-century critics, who have pointed to Defoe's use of irony and his economic theories. Virginia Woolf, in her *Collected Essays,* called *Robinson Crusoe* "a masterpiece," and went on to note that "it is a masterpiece because Defoe has throughout kept consistently to his own sense of perspective." Defoe's Crusoe has long been regarded as the symbol of economic man. As John J. Richetti observed in his *Daniel Defoe,* "what Crusoe attempts on his island is much more than survival; he tries to duplicate the civilization from which he has been separated and in his dogged way he recapitulates European society's technological transformation of nature." This "economic man" critique has been broadened into what some scholars see as Defoe's criticism of capitalism itself.

Aidan Quinn starred in *Crusoe*, a 1989 film adaptation of Defoe's work.

Ian Watt, in his influential *The Rise of the Novel*, pointed out the importance of both economics and Puritanism in Defoe's work: "Economic individualism explains much of Crusoe's character; economic specialisation and its associated ideology help to account for the appeal of his adventures; but it is Puritan individualism which controls his spiritual being." Other critics have also noted a pattern of Puritan regeneration in the novel and have speculated on the extent to which the novel is actually a spiritual autobiography of Defoe himself. Yet in the end, it is the continuing popularity of the book and not the opinion of the critics that has made it a classic. As Novak pointed out in *Dictionary of Literary Biography*, "in *Robinson Crusoe* [Defoe] created a work which was to be read throughout the world. It was quickly translated and started a rage for the island tale—the 'Robinsonade'—which has yet to show signs of fading away."

The Miraculous Five Years

Novak noted in *Dictionary of Literary Biography* that between 1719, with publication of *Robinson Crusoe,* and 1724 and the publication of *Roxana,* "Defoe singlehandedly gave to prose fiction a power and imagination which it had never attained in England before." Other books written during this period of intense creative work include Defoe's best known works after Crusoe: *Moll Flanders* and *Journal of the Plague Year*. With the success of *Robinson Crusoe,* Defoe saw that he might turn even a better profit than he had with his poetry and pamphlets. Thus this five-year period represents the enterprise of the hunger artist.

Moll Flanders has maintained the same reader interest as *Robinson Crusoe* over the years. It is the product of one incredible year of work on Defoe's part. In 1722 he published *Moll* as well as *Journal of the Plague Year* and *Colonel Jack*. Defoe was not content, however, with this achievement, but interspersed the fiction with several nonfiction books of history and social and religious manners. One wonders where he found the time to even breathe with such a prodigious output. *Moll* fits in well with such a flurry, for its title character's own life is filled with action. Yet another of Defoe's fictional biographies, *Moll Flanders* is told by Moll herself to a rather abashed editor who cleans up her language. In the pages of *Moll Flanders*, Defoe was able to use the criminals and prostitutes he

If you enjoy the works of Daniel Defoe, you may also want to check out the following books and films:

Theodore Taylor, *Timothy of the Cay,* 1993.
Gary Paulsen, *The Voyage of the Frog,* 1989.
Robert Louis Stevenson, *Kidnapped,* 1886.
Lord of the Flies, based on the novel by William Golding, 1963.

had rubbed shoulders with during his spells in prison for either sedition or debt. As with Dickens in his novel *Oliver Twist,* Defoe brings the criminal element vibrantly to life within the pages of his fiction.

Moll, who has been left an orphan when her mother is transported to the colonies, is befriended for a time by a band of gypsies. When they abandon her, she becomes a charge of the parish of Colchester and soon is a favorite of the mayor and his wife. Left on her own again at age fourteen, she is taken in by a kindly woman of means and treated like a third daughter. Subsequently she is taken advantage of by one of the sons and discovers the power she has over others because of her beauty and cleverness.

There follows a series of adventures and misadventures, marriages and affairs on both sides of the Atlantic. Moll spends some eight years in Virginia, married to a sea captain who turns out to be her half brother, and then returns to England to live in Bath, leaving both her husband and a son behind. As mistress to a gentleman in Bath, she gives birth to three children; this relationship is followed by a banker, who in turn is followed by an Irishman who is as much a confidence trickster as Moll is. She returns to the banker, whom she marries and lives with for five years until he dies. Left with two children, middle-aged Moll now suffers from reduced means and takes to stealing for the next dozen years.

Moll is finally caught and sent to Newgate Prison—the very place Defoe spent some time for his sedition conviction—but is saved from hanging when she repents her sinful ways. Transported to America, she discovers her former Irish husband has been given the same sentence and they reunite aboard ship bound for Virginia. The couple prosper beyond their wildest dreams and at age seventy, Moll returns to England, resolved to live a penitent life for her former sins.

As Novak noted in *Dictionary of Literary Biography*, "*Moll Flanders* is a lesson in survival." Much like Crusoe, Moll must live by her wits, and Defoe supplies ample detail to make the story seem as if it is in fact the actual biography of such a woman. Not considered quite decent in its day, the book was nonetheless popular with the reading public. Its form is an extension of what was known as rogue biography. As Richetti observed in *Daniel Defoe*, "most critics would agree that Moll is Defoe's most memorable character," and the critic went on to note that the book is less a novel than a series of episodes.

Most modern criticism of *Moll Flanders* focuses on the sense of sin and repentance in the novel. On the surface, Moll repents the sinful ways of her past, yet Defoe's realistic tone in describing these past events somewhat debunks this high moral purpose. After all, Moll flourishes despite her sinful ways. Some critics attribute conscious irony to Defoe and maintain that Defoe was satirizing the Puritanical rules of his day. On the other side of the argument are critics such as Ian Watt, who believes that if there is irony in Defoe, it is unintended. But as Richetti noted, "The moral ambiguity in Moll's thanksgiving, with its irrepressible self-promotion, is a link with the unrepentant Moll of earlier times. For some readers, this particular inconsistency and adamant inability to become simply moral types are what make Defoe's characters a uniquely living collection."

Other notable Defoe novels are *A Journal of the Plague Year*, a historical novel set during the London Plague of 1665 and 1666. Called, by Novak, "Defoe's masterpiece of descriptive realism," the novel is narrated by one "H. F.", a man likely modeled on Defoe's own uncle, Henry Foe. The book developed new fictional ground that would later be taken over by the gothic novel. *Colonel Jack*, another biographical novel, is once again set in the underworld of thieves and pickpockets, and traces the fortunes of Jack as he tries to succeed through honest work. Once again, the New World provides the opportunity for success; Jack's return to England is thence "a downward path to gentility," according to Novak. *Roxana*, the last of Defoe's novels, introduces Defoe's first introspec-

tive narrator, foreshadowing the psychological novels that would some day follow. Many critics claim *Roxana* to be Defoe's most complex and artistic work, though it has not retained the same popularity as has *Robinson Crusoe* or *Moll Flanders*.

Return to Nonfiction

After *Roxana*, Defoe concentrated almost exclusively on longer nonfiction works, including the justly famous *A Tour thro' the Whole Island of Great Britain*, *The Political History of the Devil*, *The Complete English Tradesman*, and *Conjugal Lewdness; or, Matrimonial Whoredom*. By the mid-1720s, his journalistic career came to an end when Nathaniel Mist finally discovered that Defoe had been working as a Whig agent all the while. Over the years, he founded several journals, but these also had ceased publication by 1925, leaving Defoe free for longer prose fiction works. In 1729 legal proceedings were initiated against Defoe; with creditors on his track again, the writer once more went into hiding to avoid the questionable pleasures of Newgate Prison.

Leaving his family behind in the suburbs, Defoe took lodgings in a section of London near where he was born, but he was no longer youthful and suffered from gout and kidney stones. His last letters—addressed to his daughter and son-in-law—are among the few personal inscriptions that survive to give the modern reader any indication of the passions boiling beneath the surface of this multi-talented word-smith. As Novak noted, "Only in these letters does one have a glimpse of the emotional force that could create Crusoe's solitude and Moll's horror at finding herself in Newgate." Defoe died in hiding on April 26, 1731.

As Backscheider noted in *Dictionary of Literary Biography*, obituaries of the day spoke of Defoe's varied writing abilities and his promotion of civic and religious freedom, but none mentioned that he was the author of either *Robinson Crusoe* or *Moll Flanders*. Modern readers, of course, know him by little else. "Defoe's literary reputation is probably higher today than it has ever been," concluded Novak in *Dictionary of Literary Biography*. "Many modern critics look to *Robinson Crusoe*, along with Cervantes's *Don Quixote*, as a key work in the formation of the novel; and *Moll Flanders*, *A Journal of the Plague Year*, and *Roxana* have been praised as masterpieces."

■ Works Cited

Backscheider, Paula R., "Daniel Defoe," in *Dictionary of Literary Biography*, Volume 101: *British Prose Writers, 1660-1800*, Gale, 1991, pp. 103-26.

Moore, John Robert, "Robinson Crusoe," in *Twentieth-Century Interpretations of Robinson Crusoe*, edited by Frank H. Ellis, Prentice-Hall, 1969, p. 55.

Novak, Maximillian E., "Daniel Defoe," in *Dictionary of Literary Biography*, Volume 39: *British Novelists, 1660-1800*, Gale, 1985, pp. 143-66.

Richetti, John J. *Daniel Defoe*, Twayne, 1987, pp. 59, 87, 103-04.

Rousseau, Jean-Jacques, "Rousseau on 'Robinson Crusoe,'" translated by Pat Rogers, in *Defoe: The Critical Heritage*, edited by Pat Rogers, Routledge, 1972, pp. 52-54.

Watt, Ian, *The Rise of the Novel: Studies in Defoe, Richardson, and Fielding*, University of California Press, 1957.

West, Richard, *The Life and Strange Surprising Adventures of Daniel Defoe*, HarperCollins, 1997, pp. xiii, 1.

Woolf, Virginia, "Robinson Crusoe," in *Daniel Defoe's 'Robinson Crusoe,'* edited by Harold Bloom, Chelsea, 1988, p. 7.

■ For More Information See

BOOKS

Backscheider, Paula R. *Daniel Defoe: Ambition and Innovation*, University Press of Kentucky, 1986.

Defoe, Daniel, *Robinson Crusoe*, edited by Michael Shinagel, Norton, 1975.

Dictionary of Literary Biography, Volume 95: *Eighteenth-Century British Poets*, Gale, 1990.

Meigs, Cornelia, Anne Thaxter Eaton, Elizabeth Nesbitt, and Ruth Hill Viguers, *A Critical History of Children's Literature*, revised edition, Macmillan, 1969.

Montgomery, Elizabeth Rider, *The Story behind Great Books*, McBride, 1946.

Moore, J. R., *Daniel Defoe: Citizen of the Modern World*, University of Chicago Press, 1958.

Moore, J. R., *A Checklist of the Writings of Daniel Defoe*, second edition, Shoe String Press, 1971.

Stirland, Dorothy J., *First Book of Great Writers*, Cassell, 1959.

Sutherland, James, *Defoe*, Lippincott, 1938, revised as *Defoe: A Critical Study*, Methuen, 1950.

Wilson, Walter, *The Life and Times of Daniel Defoe*, Volume 2, Hurst, Chance, 1830.

—Sketch by J. Sydney Jones

Loren D. Estleman

■ Personal

Born September 15, 1952, in Ann Arbor, MI; son of Leauvett Charles (a truck driver) and Louise (a postal clerk; maiden name, Milankovich) Estleman; married Carole Ann Ashley (a marketing and public relations specialist), September 5, 1987; married Deborah Morgan (a writer). *Education:* Eastern Michigan University, B.A., 1974.

■ Addresses

Home—Whitmore Lake, MI. *Agent*—Barbara Puechner, Ray Peekner Literary Agency, 3418 Shelton Ave., Bethlehem, PA 18017.

■ Career

Writer, 1980—. *Michigan Fed*, Ann Arbor, MI, cartoonist, 1967-70; *Ypsilanti Press*, Ypsilanti, MI, reporter, 1973; *Community Foto-News*, Pinckney, MI, editor in chief, 1975-76; *Ann Arbor News*, Ann Arbor, special writer, 1976-77; *Dexter Leader*, Dexter, MI, staff writer, 1977-80. Has been an instruc-

tor for Friends of the Dexter Library, and a guest lecturer at colleges. *Member:* Western Writers of America (vice president/president-elect, 1998), Private Eye Writers of America.

■ Awards, Honors

American Book Award nomination, 1980, for *The High Rocks; New York Times Book Review* notable book citations, 1980, for *Motor City Blue,* and 1982, for *The Midnight Man;* Spur Award for best western historical novel, Western Writers of America, 1982, for *Aces and Eights;* Shamus Award nomination for best private eye novel, Private Eye Writers of America, 1984, for *The Glass Highway;* Pulitzer Prize in Letters nomination, 1984, for *This Old Bill;* Shamus Award, both 1985, for novel *Sugartown* and short story "Eight Mile and Dequindre"; Spur Award for best western short story, 1986, for "The Bandit"; Michigan Arts Foundation Award for Literature, 1986; American Mystery Award for best private eye novel, 1988, for *Downriver;* Shamus Award for best private eye short story, 1988, for "The Crooked Way"; American Mystery Award, for *Whiskey River;* Spur Award for best western short fiction, 1996, for "The Alchemist"; Michigan Author's Award, Michigan Library Association, 1997; Estleman has also received two Stirrup Awards for outstanding articles in the *Western Writers of America* magazine, and two Outstanding Mystery Writer of the Year awards from *Popular Fiction Monthly.*

■ Writings

The Oklahoma Punk, Major Books, 1976.

Sherlock Holmes vs. Dracula; or, The Adventure of the Sanguinary Count (mystery-horror novel), Doubleday, 1978.

Dr. Jekyll and Mr. Holmes (mystery-horror novel), Doubleday, 1979.

The Wister Trace: Classic Novels of the American Frontier (criticism), Jameson Books, 1987.

Red Highway, PaperJacks, 1988.

Peeper, Bantam, 1989.

The Best Western Stories of Loren D. Estleman, edited by Bill Pronzini and Martin H. Greenberg, Ohio University Press, 1989.

Crooked Way, Eclipse Books, 1993.

The Judge, Forge, 1994.

The Rocky Mountain Moving Picture Association, Forge, 1999.

"AMOS WALKER" MYSTERY SERIES

Motor City Blue, Houghton, 1980.

Angel Eyes, Houghton, 1981.

The Midnight Man, Houghton, 1982.

The Glass Highway, Houghton, 1983.

Sugartown, Houghton, 1984.

Every Brilliant Eye, Houghton, 1986.

Lady Yesterday, Houghton, 1987.

Downriver, Houghton, 1988.

General Murders (short stories), Houghton, 1988.

Silent Thunder, Houghton, 1989.

Sweet Women Lie, Houghton, 1990.

Never Street, Mysterious Press, 1997.

Witchfinder, Mysterious Press, 1998.

"DETROIT" SERIES

Whiskey River, Bantam, 1990.

Motown, Bantam, 1992.

King of the Corner, Bantam, 1993.

Edsel, Mysterious Press, 1995.

Stress, Mysterious Press, 1996.

Jitterbug: A Novel of Detroit, Forge, 1998.

"PETER MACKLIN" MYSTERY SERIES

Kill Zone, Mysterious Press, 1984.

Roses Are Dead, Mysterious Press, 1985.

Any Man's Death, Mysterious Press, 1986.

WESTERN NOVELS

The Hider, Doubleday, 1978.

Aces and Eights, Doubleday, 1981.

The Wolfer, Pocket Books, 1981.

Mister St. John, Doubleday, 1983.

This Old Bill, Doubleday, 1984.

Gun Man, Doubleday, 1985.

Bloody Season, Bantam, 1988.

Western Story, Doubleday, 1989.

Sudden Country, Bantam, 1992.

Billy Gashade, Forge, 1997.

Journey of the Dead, Forge, 1998.

"PAGE MURDOCK" WESTERN SERIES

The High Rocks, Doubleday, 1979.

Stamping Ground, Doubleday, 1980.

Murdock's Law, Doubleday, 1982.

The Stranglers, Doubleday, 1984.

City of Widows, Tor Books, 1994.

OTHER

Contributor to anthologies, including *The Eyes Have It: The First Private Eye Writers of America Anthology*, edited by Robert J. Randisi, Mysterious Press, 1984; *The Year's Best Mystery and Suspense Stories*, edited by Edward D. Hoch, Walker & Co., 1986; *P. I. Files*, edited by Estleman with Martin H. Greenberg, Ivy Books, 1990; and *The Fatal Frontier*, edited by Edward Gorman and Martin H. Greenberg, Carroll & Graf, 1997.

Contributor to periodicals, including *Alfred Hitchcock's Mystery Magazine, Baker Street Journal, Fiction Writers Magazine, A Matter of Crime, Mystery, New Black Mask, Pulpsmith, Roundup, Saint Magazine, TV Guide, Writer,* and *Writer's Digest.* Estleman's work has been published in twenty-three languages.

■ Adaptations

Several of Estleman's books, including the Amos Walker mysteries *Motor City Blue, Angel Eyes, The Midnight Man, Sugartown, The Glass Highway,* and *Every Brilliant Eye,* have been recorded on audio cassette. *Sherlock Holmes vs. Dracula* was broadcast by the British Broadcasting Corporation. One of Estleman's western novels has been optioned by a California film company.

■ Work in Progress

A short story series titled "Valentino!", to appear in *Ellery Queen's Mystery Magazine;* an Amos

Walker mystery; a seventh installment of the "Detroit" series.

■ Sidelights

Loren D. Estleman, the prolific author of what James Kindall describes in *Detroit* as "hard-bitten mysteries, a herd of reality-edged westerns and an occasional fantasy or two," is perhaps best known for his series of hard-boiled mysteries that unravel in an authentically evoked Detroit. "A country boy who has always lived outside of Detroit, he writes with convincing realism about inner city environments," states Kindall, adding that "probably no other area pensmith can lay as convincing a claim to the title of Detroit's private eye writer as Estleman." Had it not been for the success of fellow Detroiter and mystery writer Elmore Leonard, pronounces William A. Henry in *Time*, "Estleman would doubtless be known as the poet of Motor City."

Trained as a journalist, Estleman researches his work thoroughly and draws deeply from his experience as a reporter who covered the police beat of a small-town newspaper: He "killed a lot of time . . . just listening to cops," notes Beauford Cranford in a *Detroit News* interview with the author; and according to Kindall, he "sometimes rode with police and held shotgun during arrests." Kindall proposes that Estleman's "affection for the street life which permeates his detective books" can be attributed partially to the stories he heard as a child from his family: "His mother nearly married a member of Detroit's Purple Gang and his father told tales of his rowdy but harmless past. Only in later years after talking to his Austrian-born grandmother, a professional cook who took hotel jobs across the country, did he find out her roving was because of an insatiable thirst for gambling, he says. And one of her casino acquaintances was Al Capone."

For Estleman, writing is an avowed compulsion: "Can't not write," he admits to Kindall. Devoting six hours a day, seven days a week to his craft, he tries to produce five pages of manuscript daily. "Clarity distinguishes Estleman's writing," declares Bob McKelvey in the *Detroit Free Press*. "Just what you'd expect from a guy who sneers at murky, avant-garde authors who go in for what Estleman calls 'ropy subjunctives and diarrhetic stream-of-consciousness.'" Estleman concurs with *Contempo-*

rary Authors interviewer Jean W. Ross that his style, which he characterizes in *Twentieth-Century Western Writers* as "highly visual," has been influenced by television and motion pictures. Critics commend the clarity, good dialogue, and cinematic framing that hallmark Estleman's writing and frequently compare him to his predecessors in the genre, Dashiell Hammett and Raymond Chandler. However, Estleman is "a genre writer with ambitious intent," discerns Cranford, to whom Estleman explains: "I'm trying to delve into crime as a metaphor for society. One of the reasons crime novels are so popular now is that crime isn't something that always happens to the other guy any more. Everybody has been touched by crime, and you can't turn on the television without hearing about it. So more and more, crime and law and cops and robbers tend to become a metaphor for the way we live. Crime is probably our basic conflict."

Estleman has crafted an increasingly popular series of mysteries around the character of Amos Walker, a witty and rugged Detroit private investigator who recalls Chandler's Philip Marlowe and Hammett's Sam Spade. Considered "one of the best the hard-boiled field has to offer" by Kathleen Maio in *Wilson Library Bulletin*, "Walker is the very model of a Hammett-Chandler descendant," observes the *New York Times Book Review*'s Newgate Callendar. "He is a big man, very macho, who talks tough and is tough. He hates hypocrisy, phonies and crooks. He pretends to cynicism but is a teddy bear underneath it all. He is lonely, though women swarm all over him." Conceding to Ross that the character represents his "alter ego," Estleman once refused a six-figure offer from a major film company for exclusive rights to Walker, explaining to Kindall: "Twenty years from now, the money would be spent and I'd be watching the umpteenth movie with Chevy Chase or Kurt Russell playing Amos with the setting in Vegas or L.A. and blow my brains out."

Amos Walker "deals with sleaze from top to bottom—Motor City dregs, cop killers and drug dealers," remarks Andrew Postman in *Publishers Weekly*, and reviewers admire the storytelling skills of his creator. Walker made his debut searching the pornographic underworld of Detroit for the female ward of an aging ex-gangster in *Motor City Blue*, a novel that Kristiana Gregory appraises in the *Los Angeles Times Book Review* as "a dark gem of a mystery." About *Angel Eyes*, in which a dancer who anticipates her own disappearance hires Walker to search for her, the *New Republic's* Robin W. Winks believes that "Estleman handles the English language with real imagination . . . so that one keeps reading for the sheer joy of seeing the phrases fall into place." In *The Midnight Man,* which Callendar describes as"tough, side-of-the-mouth stuff, well written, positively guaranteed to keep you awake," Walker encounters a contemporary bounty hunter in his pursuit of three cop killers; and writing about *The Glass Highway,* in which Walker is hired to locate the missing son of a television anchor and must contend with a rampaging professional killer, Callendar believes that Estleman "remains among the top echelon of American private-eye specialists."

Although critics generally enjoy Estleman's narrative skill, plots, dialogue, and well-drawn characters, they are especially fond of his realistic portraits of the Motor City. Estleman and his private-eye character "share a unique view" of the city of Detroit, observes Kindall: "The things I like about Detroit are everything the mayor hates," states Estleman. "I love the warehouse district, for instance; that's Detroit to me . . . I like the character of a city that grew up without anybody's help." According to Jean M. White in a *Washington Post Book World* review of *Angel Eyes:* "Estleman knows the seamy underworld of Detroit's mean streets. He has a nice touch for its characters and language. His knife-sharp prose matches the hurtling pace of the action." Bill Ott suggests in *Booklist* that "Detroit becomes more than merely a setting" in Estleman's Shamus Award-winning *Sugartown,* in which an elderly Polish immigrant hires Walker to find her grandson who has been missing for nineteen years: "As the city's neighborhoods fall prey to the wrecker's ball, the dreams and even the very histories of its residents become part of the rubble." Maio believes that "Estleman writes so well of the threadworn respectability of working people stranded on the edge of an urban wasteland. His vivid and merciless descriptions of the revitalized Detroit root his complex story in reality."

As "one of the major current practitioners of the tough-guy private-eye novel," proclaims Callendar, Estleman is "at his best" in *Downriver,* a novel in which Walker investigates the claim of an intimidating black ex-convict that he was framed for the murder that sent him to prison for twenty years. "The dialogue is crackling, the writing is unpad-

ded," Callendar continues, "and one can smell and even taste the city of Detroit." In a Chicago *Tribune Books* review of the novel, Kevin Moore considers Estleman a "polished craftsman," commending especially his "sharp, cleanly defined writing." Reviewing *Every Brilliant Eye,* in which Walker searches for a vanished friend, Callendar thinks that there exists "a kind of poetry in his snapshots of the underside of a city with which he so clearly has a love-hate relationship." Resolved, according to Kindall, to continue the series until "it begins to be [like] pulling boxcars to write another one," Estleman intends to keep Walker in Detroit, remarking to Cranford: "If L.A. was where the American dream went wrong, then Detroit is where it bellied up dead. But there's still a nobility to Detroit, a certain kind of grittiness among

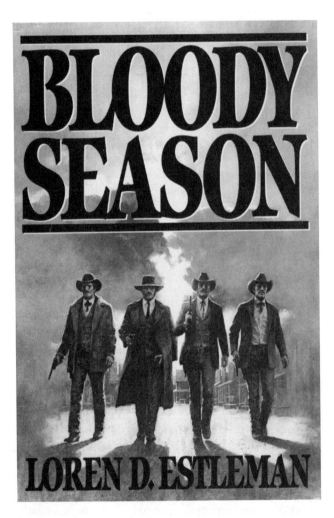

In this 1988 work, Estleman explains the events that led up to the legendary 1881 shoot-out at the O.K. Corral in Tombstone, Arizona.

people who can live here from day to day that may not be so true for L.A."

Although some reviewers fault Estleman's tough-guy fiction for occasional cliched conventionality, most find his Walker novels especially well-written and riveting. Henry, for instance, faults Estleman for generally resolving his plots "unsatisfyingly" through withheld information, but nevertheless believes that Estleman's "ear for diverse patois seems impeccable, and so does the inner mechanism that tells him when an unlikely escape can be plausible." Estleman's vibrant renderings of Detroit's jazz world also elicit a favorable critical response. For example, in a *Washington Post Book World* review of *Lady Yesterday*, in which Walker helps an ex-prostitute hunt for her missing father, Alan Ryan praises the novel's "great narrative and dialogue," adding: "All of this is good. I'm caught up in the story, but best of all is the way Estleman writes about jazz, the sound of it, the smoky clubs it lives in and the musicians who play it. . . . Well done. I like Estleman." And although Kindall regards Estleman as "one of those rare people who can write about deadly things in poetic terms," he perceives that a few critics have difficulty determining "who's zoomin' who," especially since Walker himself seems to border on parody rather than a realistic portrayal. "There are some critics out there who don't know what I'm doing," Estleman responds. "Some don't know if I'm parodying the form, if I'm being serious or what. The only answer to that is I'm doing both."

In another series of mysteries, Estleman slants the perspective to that of a criminal, Peter Macklin, who also freelances out of Detroit. "Macklin is the result of my wanting to do an in-depth study of a professional killer," Estleman tells McKelvey. "It presents a challenge to keep a character sympathetic who never has anything we would call morals." Kindall suggests that "although a killer, he always seems to end up facing opponents even lower on the evolutionary scale, which shades him into the quasi-hero side." However, in a review of *Kill Zone*, the first novel in the Macklin series, Callendar feels that "not even Mr. Estleman's considerable skill can hide the falsity of his thesis" that even hired killers can be admirable characters. The plot of the novel concerns the seizure of a Detroit riverboat by terrorists who hold hundreds of passengers hostage, attracting other professional killers from organized crime and a gov-

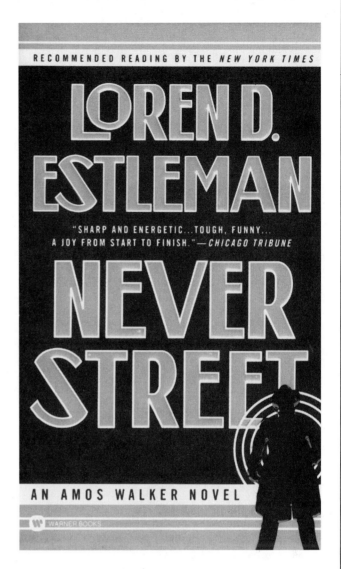

Walker is hired to find a missing *film noir* enthusiast in this 1997 installment of the "Amos Walker" mystery series.

ernmental agency as well—a plot that a *Publishers Weekly* contributor finds "confusing and glutted with a plethora of minor characters who detract from the story's credibility." And although Peter L. Robertson detects an implausibility of plot in the second of the series' novels, *Roses Are Dead*, in which Macklin tries to determine who and why someone has contracted to kill him, he says in *Booklist* that the novel is "a guaranteed page-turner that features an intoxicating rush of brutal events and a fascinating anti-hero in Macklin." Describing the action of *Any Man's Death*, in which Macklin is hired to guard the life of a television evangelist and is caught in the struggle between rival mob families for control of a proposed casino gambling industry in Detroit, Wes Lukowsky suggests in *Booklist* that Estleman "has created a surprisingly credible and evolving protagonist." And as a *Time* contributor remarks: "For urban edge and macho color . . . nobody tops Loren D. Estleman."

Estleman explains to Kindall that the hard-boiled mystery genre is particularly popular in this country because "America has always tended to revere the revolutionary types . . . who are not allied with any official organization . . . someone who lives pretty much according to his own rules." Estleman's work enjoys popularity in several other countries as well, though, including West Germany, Holland, Great Britain, Spain, and Japan, where his Detroit-based mysteries are enthusiastically received, notes Kindall. "Genre fiction is just American literature," Estleman tells Cranford, adding that "mysteries and westerns are our contribution to world literature." He further suggests to Ross that "private-eye fiction is the modern counterpart of the western story" because its solitary hero, when confronted with dreadful odds, must depend solely on his own "wits and personal sense of integrity." Estleman alternates between writing mysteries and westerns to keep the ideas fresh, he tells Ross, dubbing it "literary crop rotation."

The Hider, a novel about the last buffalo hunt in America, was Estleman's first western novel and was purchased immediately—a rarity in the genre. He has since written several other successful western novels plus a critical analysis of western fiction itself, *The Wister Trace: Classic Novels of the American Frontier;* and several of his books about the American West have earned critical distinction. *The High Rocks,* for instance, which is set in the mountains of Montana and relates the story of a man's battle with the Indians who murdered his parents, was nominated for an American Book Award. And the first two books of his proposed historical western trilogy have also earned honors: *Aces and Eights,* about the murder of Wild Bill Hickok, was awarded the Spur; and *This Old Bill,* a fable based on the life of William Frederick "Buffalo Bill" Cody, was nominated for a Pulitzer Prize.

In the *Los Angeles Times Book Review,* David Dary discusses Estleman's *Bloody Season,* an extensively researched historical novel about the gunfight at

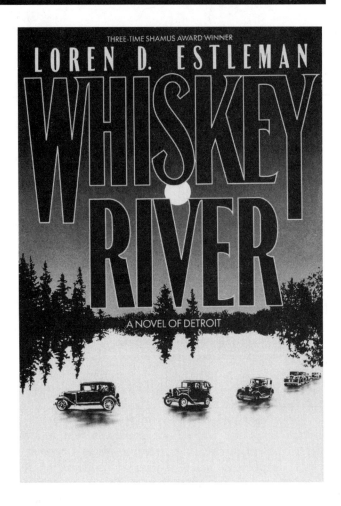

Narrated by a female journalist, this work about gang wars during the Prohibition years is the first in a series of crime novels set in Detroit.

the O. K. Corral: "The author's search for objectivity and truth, combined with his skill as a fine writer, have created a new vision of what happened in Tombstone . . . , and he avoids the hackneyed style that clutters the pages of too many Westerns." Dary concludes that although it is a fictional account, the novel "probably comes closer to the truth" than anything else published on the subject. In *Twentieth-Century Western Writers,* Bill Crider observes: "All of Estleman's books appear solidly researched, and each ends in a way which ties all the story threads together in an effective pseudo-historical manner, giving each an air of reality and credibility."

The city of Detroit is the central character of Estleman's crime series originally projected to be a trilogy but now encompassing additional volumes. The first installment, *Whiskey River*, covers the wars between rival gangs during the Prohibition years and is narrated by newspaper columnist Connie Minor. "Estleman's novel is a wizard piece of historical reconstruction, exciting as a gangster film but with a texturing of the characters and the times that rises well above genre," hails Charles Champlin in the *Los Angeles Times Book Review.* "Occasionally the details fail," remarks Walter Walker in the *New York Times Book Review.* "But [Estleman] does a marvelous job of setting clues, bringing seemingly loose ends together and surprising his readers, leaving them nearly incapable of stopping at the end of any given chapter." *Motown* is set in the turbulent year of 1966, when big cars, mobs, labor unions, racial tension, and power politicians dominated Detroit. Intertwining real and fictional events, Estleman weaves plots concerning race wars between the black and Italian mobs, racketeering, and the safety records of the cars produced by the Big Three automakers. Connie Minor appears again, this time as an investigative reporter who finds an incriminating photograph of a labor leader. Thomas Morawetz declares in the *Washington Post Book World* that "this wonderful cornucopia of a novel [has] quicksilver dialogue, incisive characterizations and canny interweaving of observations and events." The series' third novel is *King of the Corner*, which continues the themes of racial tension, dirty politics, and organized crime. The central character is "Doc" Miller, an overweight ex-Tigers baseball pitcher just out of prison for the death of a girl in his hotel room. Though he intends to do honest work, Miller soon finds himself involved with Detroit's black drug dealers and political corruption. "Neither as colorful nor as vigorous as the earlier volumes-but, still, a pleasing if rather rambling mystery-thriller," states a *Kirkus Reviews* contributor.

The additional novels in the series focus on other decades in the Motor City. In *Edsel* Connie Minor has become a copywriter for the Ford Motor Company touting its new dream car of the 1950s, the Edsel. But because of his questioning of guys on the line, Minor comes under suspicion of spying on the rank-and-file and gets caught up in intrigue by the unions. "The conspiracy he ultimately discovers and untangles may be fairly anticlimactic, but Minor's observation and irreverence combine to keep the reader comfortably-even avidly-in the passenger's seat," declares Jean Hanff Korelitz in the *Washington Post Book World.* Notes

Marilyn Stasio in the *New York Times Book Review,* "Mr. Estleman is a pithy, punchy writer who can also deliver the action by spitting images out of the side of his mouth." *Stress* takes place in the 1970s as Detroit is recovering from the sixties riots. Charlie Battle is a young black cop confronting a racist department and violent black militant groups. Wes Lukowsky of *Booklist* calls the novel "a fine installment in an innovative series," while a *Publishers Weekly* reviewer states: "It's difficult to believe that Detroit will ever find a more eloquent poet than Estleman, who here . . . celebrates the gristle and sinew of the city as well as its aching heart." *Jitterbug* takes place during

A black police officer struggles with the aftermath of the 1968 Detroit race riots in this 1996 novel.

If you enjoy the works of Loren D. Estleman, you may also want to check out the following books and films:

Louis L'Amour, *The Lonesome Gods,* 1983.
Larry McMurtry, *Lonesome Dove,* 1985.
Elmore Leonard, *LaBrava,* 1983.
The Maltese Falcon, a classic private eye film starring Humphrey Bogart, 1941.

World War II and focuses on Lieutenant Zagreb, who heads a group of detectives investigating a series of murders. Tensions mount over the killings until the city explodes into a race riot. "Terrific, tough characters, snappy dialogue, crackling action . . . make this a triumph for Estleman," praises a critic in *Publishers Weekly.*

In 1997, after an absence of seven years, hardboiled private eye Amos Walker returned in *Never Street.* Walker is hired to locate a businessman A *Publishers Weekly* contributor writes, "Estleman expertly manipulates a complex plot, boobytrapping his tale with movie lore and arty imagery." Writing in the Chicago *Tribune Books,* Gary Dretzka declares, "What's wonderful here is Estleman's ability to construct a convincingly Chandler-esque scenario . . . while also maintaining his contemporary voice." In *The Witchfinder,* an architect's deathbed wish propels Walker into a case of fraud and murder. "With his classical job skills and austere code of ethics, this no-nonsense shamus is one of the most efficient guys in the profession," maintains Marilyn Stasio in the *New York Times Book Review.*

Estleman once stated: "The three writers whose works have had the most profound influence on my writing are all dead, which should prove some indication of my opinion of most writers who have since arisen. Edgar Allan Poe, Jack London, and Raymond Chandler have impressed me since childhood with their lyrical, poetical approach to action and adventure. The literature of violence is purely an American development and only the English language, that most elusive, infinitely fascinating of tongues, fulfills all the requirements for its proper expression. The icy deliberation of the murderer in Poe's 'A Cask of Amontillado,' the tortured psyche of the brutal Wolf Larsen in

London's *The Sea Wolf,* and the parade of grotesques that march through all of Chandler's best works are products of the American experience beside which the elements of the great fiction of Europe seem tame as a houseplant. That there is a prejudice in literary circles against these three masters is evidence of how far we still have to go to cast off the shackles forged by those potentially great writers who accepted the restrictions of Victorian society during literature's so-called Golden Age. Shakespeare was aware of the importance of violence in human nature, as were Homer and Dostoevski, but today's civilization prefers to forget that it even exists.

"All of this may sound strange coming from the author of *Sherlock Holmes vs. Dracula.* Indeed, one or two reviewers commented upon a rather bloody scene in that book and said that Conan Doyle would have been repelled by it. If they'd taken the trouble to read one or two of the original Holmes adventures, they'd have recognized his debt to Poe and his own 'morbid' fascination with brutality and the grotesque.

"I've never killed anyone off the written page. I am, however, a hunter, and I doubt that I'm being original in saying that people and animals die similarly. I'm a good boxer, a fair wrestler, and with a name like Loren I saw my share of schoolyard fights. Although I hardly appreciated it then, those tussles have come in handy every time I've sat down to write a fight scene. Since we have no memory of pain, though, I've occasionally had to remind myself of certain sensations, which has entailed slugging myself in the jaw while seated at the typewriter. Writing was never more painful than this."

■ **Works Cited**

Review of *Any Man's Death, Time,* December 22, 1986.

Callendar, Newgate, review of *The Midnight Man, New York Times Book Review,* August 22, 1982, p. 26.

Callendar, Newgate, review of *The Glass Highway, New York Times Book Review,* October 23, 1983, p. 38.

Callendar, Newgate, review of *Kill Zone, New York Times Book Review,* December 2, 1984, p. 62.

Callendar, Newgate, review of *Sugartown, New York Times Book Review,* March 24, 1985, p. 29.

Callendar, Newgate, review of *Every Brilliant Eye, New York Times Book Review,* April 20, 1986, p. 32.

Callendar, Newgate, review of *Downriver, New York Times Book Review,* March 6, 1988, p. 22.

Champlin, Charles, review of *Whiskey River, Los Angeles Times Book Review,* September 9, 1990, p. 10.

Dary, David, review of *Bloody Season, Los Angeles Times Book Review,* January 24, 1988, p. 12.

Dretzka, Gary, "A hard-boiled but thoroughly modern tale," *Tribune Books* (Chicago), April 13, 1997.

Estleman, Loren D., interview with Beauford Cranford in *Detroit News,* August 21, 1983.

Estleman, Loren D., interview with Jean W. Ross in *Contemporary Authors, New Revision Series,* Volume 27, Gale, 1989.

Gregory, Kristiana, review of *Motor City Blue, Los Angeles Times Book Review,* August 21, 1983, p. 7.

Henry, William A., "To Be or Not to Be Continued," *Time,* August 17, 1987, pp. 63-64.

Henry, William A., review of *Downriver, Time,* February 1, 1988, p. 66.

Review of *Jitterbug, Publishers Weekly,* July 20, 1998, p. 205.

Review of *Kill Zone, Publishers Weekly,* July 13, 1984.

Kindall, James, *Detroit,* March 8, 1987.

Review of *King of the Corner, Kirkus Reviews,* April 1, 1992, p. 412.

Korelitz, Jean Hanff, review of *Edsel, Washington Post Book World,* March 26, 1995, p. 2.

Lukowsky, Wes, review of *Any Man's Death, Booklist,* October 15, 1986.

Lukowsky, Wes, review of *Stress, Booklist,* March 15, 1996, p. 1242.

Maio, Kathleen, review of *Sugartown, Wilson Library Bulletin,* March, 1985, p. 487.

McKelvey, Bob, *Detroit Free Press,* September 26, 1984.

Moore, Kevin, review of *Downriver, Tribune Books* (Chicago), January 31, 1988, p. 6.

Morawetz, Thomas, review of *Motown, Washington Post Book World,* July 26, 1992, p. 1.

Review of *Never Street, Publishers Weekly,* February 10, 1997, p. 70.

Ott, Bill, review of *Sugartown, Booklist,* November 15, 1984.

Robertson, Peter L., review of *Roses Are Dead, Booklist,* September 1, 1985, p. 4.

Ryan, Alan, review of *Lady Yesterday, Washington Post Book World,* May 17, 1987, p. 6.

Stasio, Marilyn, review of *Edsel, New York Times Book Review,* March 19, 1995, p. 29.

Stasio, Marilyn, review of *The Witchfinder, New York Times Book Review,* May 17, 1998, p. 17.

Review of *Stress, Publishers Weekly,* January 29, 1996, p. 84.

Twentieth-Century Western Writers, Gale, 1982.

Walker, Walter, review of *Whiskey River, New York Times Book Review,* October 14, 1990, p. 50.

White, Jean M., review of *Angel Eyes, Washington Post Book World,* October 18, 1981, p. 6.

Winks, Robin W., review of *Angel Eyes, New Republic,* November 21, 1985.

■ For More Information See

BOOKS

Contemporary Literary Criticism, Volume 48, Gale, 1988, pp. 102-7.

Contemporary Popular Writers, St. James Press, 1997.

Twentieth-Century Crime and Mystery Writers, 2nd edition, St. Martin's, 1985.

PERIODICALS

Ann Arbor News, September 24, 1978.

Ann Arbor Observer, July, 1978.

Armchair Detective, summer, 1987, p. 311; spring, 1988, p. 218; summer, 1989, p. 329; fall, 1989, p. 434; summer, 1990, p. 250; spring, 1991, p. 250; winter, 1991, pp. 5-11, p. 28; summer, 1995, p. 285.

Booklist, September 15, 1988, p. 123; April 1, 1990, p. 1530; June 15, 1991, pp. 1932, 1948; March 15, 1994, p. 1327.

Chicago Tribune Book World, January 18, 1981; August 10, 1986.

Detroit News, May 18, 1979.

Eastern Echo, September 8, 1978.

Kirkus Reviews, August 1, 1988, p. 1100; August 1, 1989, p. 1116; June 15, 1991, p. 746; February 15, 1994, p. 160; February 1, 1995, p. 90; September 15, 1998, p. 1334.

Library Journal, September 1, 1989, p. 219; March 15, 1994, p. 100; March 1, 1996, p. 109.

Los Angeles Times Book Review, January 19, 1986, p. 9; April 11, 1991, p. 5; August 11, 1991, p. 5; May 10, 1992, p. 17.

New Black Mask, Number 4, 1986.

New York Times Book Review, November 11, 1979, p. 24; October 26, 1980, p. 20; November 1, 1981, p. 41; August 14, 1983, p. 27; December 23, 1984,

p. 24; November 24, 1985, p. 43; October 26, 1986, p. 47; January 29, 1989, p. 34; April 9, 1989, p. 42; April 16, 1989, p. 31; October 15, 1989, p. 45, p. 56; May 20, 1990, p. 53; July 8, 1990, p. 28; September 15, 1991, p. 34; February 9, 1992, p. 28; July 5, 1992, p. 17; May 8, 1994, p. 18.

Observer, September 16, 1990, p. 55.

Publishers Weekly, August 23, 1985; August 12, 1988, p. 442; January 22, 1988; May 3, 1991, p. 64; March 14, 1994, p. 64.

School Library Journal, October, 1998, p. 161.

Time, July 31, 1978, p. 83.

Times (London), November 20, 1986; November 29, 1986; December 31, 1987.

Times Literary Supplement, March 14, 1986; April 10, 1987; August 12, 1988, p. 893; September 8, 1989, p. 969; August 10, 1990, p. 855; September 13, 1991, p. 22.

Tribune Books (Chicago), February 24, 1987, p. 41; March 1, 1987, p. 8; March 26, 1989, p. 6; November 5, 1989, p. 6; July 21, 1991, p. 3; May 3, 1992, p. 6.

Village Voice, February 24, 1987.

Washington Post Book World, September 21, 1980, p. 14; October 21, 1990, p. 10; August 18, 1991, p. 10; August 16, 1992, p. 6.

Web site

Estleman's author profile can be found at www.cyberzone-inc.net/ws/morgan/.*

—Sketch by Sharon Malinowski

Terry Goodkind

■ Personal

Born in 1948, in Omaha, NE. *Education:* Studied drawing at the Omaha School of Fine Arts.

■ Addresses

Home—Maine. *Office*—c/o Tor Books, 175 Fifth Ave., New York, NY 10010.

■ Career

Author. First worked in his father's mail-order business before moving on to careers as an artist, hypnotherapist, violin maker, carpenter, restorer of rare artifacts, and wildlife artist.

■ Writings

"SWORD OF TRUTH" FANTASY SERIES

Wizard's First Rule, Tor, 1994.
Stone of Tears, Tor, 1995.

Blood of the Fold, Tor, 1996.
Temple of the Winds, Tor, 1997.

■ Adaptations

Some of Goodkind's books have been released on audio cassette, Brilliance, 1997.

■ Sidelights

Fantasy author Terry Goodkind is living evidence that good teachers really do make a difference. As a boy, he had been made to hate reading because most adults chastised him for being so slow at it. It wasn't that the young Goodkind didn't like the stories that were in books, but he had a great deal of difficulty sorting out the words. He had dyslexia, though he didn't learn this until later. His teachers—most of them, anyway—taught him that what was important in reading and writing was getting the grammar and spelling correct. What's more, students were judged on how many books they could read, whether they were literary works or not. Goodkind liked to read adventure stories, such as the Edgar Rice Burroughs books, which he found in his local library.

But then in his senior year of high school Goodkind met Ann Hansen, his English composition teacher. "This teacher read the stories I wrote for her class and saw something more than a collection of misspelled words," the author recalled in an online interview with James Frenkel. "Although she admonished me over my poor spelling and grammatical errors, she also told me that there was something beyond the mechanics of writing that was profoundly important. She saw the story. She encouraged me to write stories. She let me touch something noble. This changed my world."

It did, indeed. For now, Goodkind is the author of a bestselling fantasy series that has earned him a six-figure income. It has also gained him more satisfaction than he has had in any other profession, and Goodkind has worked in a lot of pro-

The wizard's first rule—that people are stupid—is central to this initial work in the "Sword of Truth" fantasy series.

fessions. Although he was constantly dreaming up stories and writing them in his head all the time he was growing up, Goodkind didn't write down many of his tales. Writing wasn't a practical pursuit, and so he searched for another career.

An Author in Waiting

Always a good artist, Goodkind had been drawing ever since he could remember, and he started selling his work when he was in high school. He later worked as a wildlife artist, as well as becoming involved in other artistic professions, including making violins and restoring rare artifacts. In addition, he had stints as a hypnotherapist and cabinet maker. But he told Stacy Trevenon in *Half Moon Bay Review,* "All these things were in search of writing. . . . The thing you desire most is the last thing you get to because you're afraid to fail at it."

Goodkind didn't feel that he was ready to write until he was about forty-five years old. By that time, he had already moved from his home in Omaha to his favorite state, Maine, a place he had fallen in love with just after finishing high school. There, using his skills as a carpenter, he built his own home. It is just the sort of house one would expect from a creative mind. Along with the expected wood-paneled library, he has an office with panels hand painted to look like granite, and a kitchen with cabinets made out of a heavy, stonelike material. His home is decorated with objects showing his interest in antiquities, including masks from Indonesia, medieval weaponry, and a variety of antiques.

It was while building his private sanctuary in the Maine woods that Goodkind finally decided to write his first novel. "I don't think I could have written what I did any earlier," the author told Lynn Flewelling in a *Bangor Daily News* article. "I had to live this long, had the experiences I've had, to create what I do. I knew I wanted to write for years, but I had to be ready so I wouldn't blow it. The move to Maine was the final step." In an online Barnes & Noble author chat, Goodkind related how the character of Mother Confessor Kahlan Amnell came to him: "I was building my house at the time Kahlan first came to me, and I let the story grow in my mind for a year when I finished the house. Then I started writing, and it took 13 months to write *Wizard's First Rule.* Ten

Richard, Kahlan, and the wizard Zedd contend with a host of powerful dark forces in this sequel to *The Wizard's First Rule.*

weeks after I wrote the end, I had an agent and the book was sold and auctioned for the highest price ever paid for a first fantasy novel." Goodkind received a $275,000 two-book deal from Tor for *Wizard's First Rule* and his then-unfinished *Stone of Tears.* "I hate telling that story to people who've been struggling for years . . . ," the author told Flewelling. "They look at me and I kind of back up in case they go for my throat."

Goodkind's Debut

But Goodkind's success wasn't a fluke. The publishing house knew what it was doing, for the first book in what was to become the "Sword of Truth" series became a best seller, and the author quickly drew a loyal following. Sometimes compared to authors such as Robert Jordan, Tad Williams, Terry Brooks, and J. R. R. Tolkien—but not always in a favorable light—Goodkind's books are traditional fantasy quest tales in which the forces of Good are pitted against the Dark. There is mystery, magic, and romance aplenty, plus what some say is the author's strength: strong characters. The hero of *Wizard's First Rule* is Richard Cypher, a simple woodsman who loves living in the forest. His life quickly becomes complicated when he meets Kahlan Amnell, who has fled her kingdom from the evil wizard Darken Rahl. Richard, whose father has just been slain for refusing to reveal the location of the Book of Counted Shadows, learns that he has inherited magical abilities, and that he must become a Seeker and wield the Sword of Truth in a fight against Rahl. Together with Kahlan and the kindly wizard Zedd, Richard sets out for the Midlands to defeat Rahl. He does so by using the "Wizard's First Rule"—the knowledge that people are stupid. Richard tricks Rahl into thinking he is opening the magical Box of Orden which will give Rahl dominion over all the world. The mistake proves fatal to Rahl, who turns out to be Richard's real father, therefore revealing Richard Cypher to be Richard Rahl and explaining the source of Richard's magical abilities.

Wizard's First Rule is a rather dark story, full of bloodshed, torture, and other violent scenes. Some have commented on this grim aspect of Goodkind's work, to which he has responded that, though he is writing fantasy, when it comes to the realities of the ugliness of war he wishes to remain realistic. In response to a Barnes & Noble online chat question, Goodkind said, "I write to be true to the characters and also to be true to the way things really are. . . . I know a lot about how war is fought, and I don't clean it up to make it look grand and glorious. War is a dirty, messy business, and I try to tell it as true as possible."

Despite the stupendous advance Goodkind received for *Wizard's First Rule*, critics had mixed feelings about the book. Carolyn Cushman, writing in *Locus*, commented that the story was "involving, even compelling," but she also judged Goodkind's style to be "simplistic, overexplained, and occasionally sanctimonious." However, a *Pub-*

lishers Weekly reviewer observed that the author's writing "improves as the book winds on . . . but, for the most part, his prose is flat." Chris Gilmore, on the other hand, felt that Goodkind's writing abilities are his saving grace. Writing in the *St. James Guide to Fantasy Writers* about the novel's lengthy passage in which Richard is tortured for over fifty pages by a sadistic sorceress, Gilmore averred that "the quality of writing sustains the interest of what in other hands would be monotonous, distasteful and incredible."

Themes and Characters

Despite its mixed reception by critics, Goodkind's epic fantasy debut was popular with many readers. As *Voice of Youth Advocates* contributor Elaine M. McGuire stated, "those who aren't intimidated by the book's size will be sucked into the adventure." And thousands of fans have been sucked in. Not only does Goodkind's debut novel have a lot of action and an intricate plot, but there are some weighty themes as well. "The themes of sacrifice and teamwork recur constantly," remarked Gilmore. The main characters who fight on the side of good are always fighting the odds, and dire prophecies predicting their failure constantly dog them. Good characters die or suffer other grievous consequences as the author constantly works to stack the odds against them, making their final victory all the more satisfying and triumphant. And another theme, as Gilmore also pointed out, is that only those who "recognize themselves for what they are" can be victorious and triumph over fate. Darken Rahl fails to do this and therefore is defeated by Richard.

Goodkind's novel has yet another theme: the use of magic as a metaphor for technology. Some of the characters in his books have an irrational fear of magic, a fear that has the same psychology behind it as the fear many people in the real world have for modern advances. "There is absolutely no difference," the author told Frenkel, "between the forensic psychology of 'My joints be aching because there's a witch down the road who be casting evil spells on me,' and 'My joints are aching because the power lines down the road are emitting low frequency electromagnetic radiation.' None." Goodkind is condemning a similar ignorance in his novel when Kahlan is chased out of her kingdom and persecuted by people who fear her magic.

Even more important than themes to Goodkind, however, are his characters. To him, they are not heroes and heroines living in a fantasy but more like real people, with real strengths and weaknesses, who just happen to be living in a world where magic is possible. As when Goodkind was building his house and first envisioned the character of Kahlan, the author's characters come to him, bringing their stories with them. "The point of my writing," Goodkind explained in the Barnes & Noble online chat, "is how these characters relate to us in terms of their desires, ambitions, and what really matters in their lives. . . . Magic is a

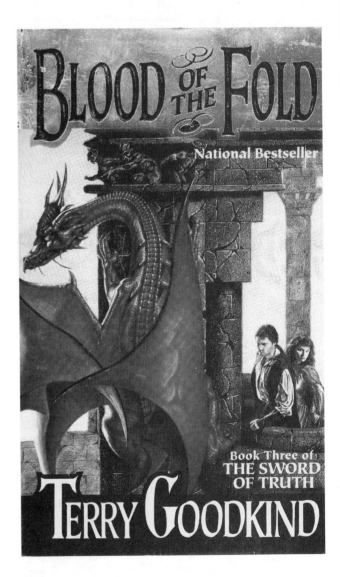

Richard must use all his magical powers to seal off the Old World and protect the New World from its evil forces.

new way of looking at emotions that are common to all of us."

Once Kahlan and Richard started telling their stories, their world just grew and grew. Goodkind came out with his second novel, *Stone of Tears,* a year after the first. When Richard destroyed his father in the first book, he accidentally opened a gateway between his world and the Underworld, allowing Emperor Jagang, the Keeper of the Underworld, a portal through which to enter the world of the living. To beat the Keeper, Richard must train with the Sisters of Light to become a real wizard while Kahlan leads a ragtag army against Darken Rahl's surviving army. As with the first book, the heroes of *Stone of Tears* face impossible odds against demons from Hell, the Sisters of the Dark, and loathsome monsters. Richard, Kahlan, and the wizard Zedd—who turns out to be Richard's grandfather—suffer and sacrifice much. Zedd, for example, gives up his vast magical powers.

The "Sword of Truth"—Will It Last?

Roland Green, writing in *Booklist,* noted that Goodkind, in keeping with a number of modern fantasies, reverses the traditional roles of hero and heroine. Roland goes on a magical quest of self-discovery while Kahlan fights bloody battles. Green stated that the author handles this "particularly well," and observed, as others have, that the series resembles Robert Jordan's "Wheel of Time" saga. While not equal to Jordan's, Goodkind's work, according to Green, is full of "engaging characters," a well-realized imaginary world, and lots of action. In addition to comparing Goodkind to Jordan, several critics have compared the "Sword of Truth" books to the "Star Wars" movies "for its epic proportions," as *Voice of Youth Advocates* McGuire noted, concluding that "as a high fantasy/quest/action novel, it's nearly perfect."

Another comparison that critics and readers alike have made is between Goodkind's stories and British author J. R. R. Tolkien's "Lord of the Rings" trilogy, the whetstone against which so many fantasy writers hone their stylistic edge. Goodkind, however, denies having ever read a word of the late master's works about Middle Earth. But Goodkind reads omnivorously—everything from technical nonfiction books to adven-

If you enjoy the works of Terry Goodkind, you may also want to check out the following books and films:

Terry Brooks' "Shannara" trilogy, 1977-85.
Robert Jordan's "Wheel of Time" series, 1990—.
Joan D. Vinge, *The Snow Queen,* 1980.
The Dark Crystal, Universal, 1982.

ture novels. What he doesn't like to read is a dull book, whatever the genre, such as the ones he was constantly made to read in school. The trick for an author is to grab the reader's interest immediately and keep it, Goodkind has averred.

In *Blood of the Fold* the gate between the Underworld and the world of the living is still open and still a threat, for Emperor Jagang has yet to be destroyed. Richard's task is to use all his magical capabilities to destroy the Keeper and close the gateway once and for all. Again there is treachery, violence, self-sacrifice, and action in another thick tome. The novel, as several critics remarked, does not disappoint. Readers—especially newcomers, as a *Publishers Weekly* reviewer wrote—"will delight in a complex epic fantasy that crackles with vigor and magical derringdo." Goodkind writes his novels with the intention that they be understandable independently of the other books in the series, though some reviewers felt that readers starting with *Blood of the Fold* "may find the references to previous events confusing," as one *Kirkus Reviews* contributor wrote. By this third book, Goodkind was really beginning to establish his reputation, especially for his skills with character development. Green, writing again in *Booklist,* praised the author's development of Kahlan Amnell, who "emerges here as one of the outstanding female principals in current fantasy."

The formula of intricate plotting, gruesomeness, and personal sacrifice hold true again in the series' fourth installment, *Temple of the Winds,* in which Jagang once more wages war. But the Emperor uses a different tactic this time, sending a magically spread plague that causes a horrible death to the afflicted, especially children. To find a cure Richard must locate the lost Temple of the Winds. Worst of all, both Richard and Kahlan must forsake their love by marrying other people—what is for them the ultimate sacrifice. Of course, Goodkind resolves all the issues happily by the book's conclusion. Reviewers of the novel found it met their expectations. Although "Goodkind's prose sometimes lags," in the opinion of a contributor to *Publishers Weekly*, " . . . his ingenuity rarely does." And Green concluded that "Goodkind's fantasy epic will still have its readers turning pages."

It looks as if Goodkind found his niche late in life. Although he still dabbles in art—he illustrated the endpapers for *Wizard's First Rule* and created all the maps—the author has never found art quite as satisfying as writing. As he wrote to an online fan, "[W]hile I enjoy doing artwork, once I started writing I discovered that writing is my true passion, and now I paint with words." The novelist also seems content to keep on writing new installments in the "Sword of Truth" series with no end in sight. When asked by Frenkel whether he had a fixed set of stories in mind for Richard and the others, Goodkind replied, "I hope to keep [readers] interested in the adventures of Richard and Kahlan . . . for a long time to come. I know what the last book in the series will be about, but there are a myriad of exploits yet to unfold along the way." Fans of the series have much more to look forward to.

■ Works Cited

"Author Chat Transcripts," http://www.barnesandnoble.com, October 24, 1997.

Review of *Blood of the Fold*, *Kirkus Reviews*, October 1, 1996, p. 1434.

Review of *Blood of the Fold*, *Publishers Weekly*, October 7, 1996, p. 66.

Cushman, Carolyn, review of *Wizard's First Rule*, *Locus*, June, 1994, p. 35.

Flewelling, Lynn, interview with Terry Goodkind, *Bangor Daily News*, November, 1995.

Frenkel, James, "An Interview with Terry Goodkind," www.tor.com/interviews.html.

Gilmore, Chris, "Terry Goodkind," *St. James Guide to Fantasy Writers*, St. James Press, 1996, pp. 237-38.

Green, Roland, review of *Stone of Tears*, *Booklist*, October 1, 1995, p. 254.

Green, Roland, review of *Blood of the Fold*, *Booklist*, November 15, 1996, p. 576.

Green, Roland, review of *Temple of the Winds*, *Booklist*, November 1, 1997, p. 457.

McGuire, Elaine M., review of *Wizard's First Rule*, *Voice of Youth Advocates*, February, 1995, p. 347.

McGuire, Elaine M., review of *Stone of Tears*, *Voice of Youth Advocates*, June, 1996, p. 107.

Review of *Temple of the Winds*, *Publishers Weekly*, October 13, 1997, p. 60.

Trevenon, Stacy, "Top Fantasy Author Terry Goodkind Visits," *Half Moon Bay Review*, October 23, 1996.

Review of *Wizard's First Rule*, *Publishers Weekly*, August 29, 1994, p. 65.

■ For More Information See

PERIODICALS

Booklist, September 1, 1994, pp. 28, 31.

Kirkus Reviews, July 1, 1994, p. 892; August 15, 1995, p. 1147.

Kliatt, July, 1998, p. 52.

Library Journal, September 15, 1994, p. 94; October 15, 1995, p. 91.

Locus, October, 1994, p. 53; February, 1995, p. 76.

Publishers Weekly, September 25, 1995, p. 48.

Voice of Youth Advocates, April, 1995, p. 347; April, 1997, p. 12.*

—Sketch by Kevin S. Hile

Karen Hesse

■ Personal

Born August 29, 1952, in Baltimore, MD; married Randy Hesse, November 27, 1971; children: Kate, Rachel. *Education:* University of Maryland, B.A., 1975.

■ Addresses

Office—c/o Scholastic, Inc., 555 Broadway, New York, NY 10012.

■ Career

Writer, 1969—. Leave benefit coordinator for the University of Maryland, 1975-76; worked variously as a teacher, a librarian, an advertising secretary, a typesetter, and a proofreader. Affiliated with Mental Health Care and Hospice, 1988—; Newfane Elementary School board chair, 1989; board member of Moore Free Library, 1989-91.

Member: Society of Children's Book Writers and Illustrators (leader of South Vermont chapter, 1985-92).

■ Awards, Honors

Hesse's work has won many awards, including Children's Book of Distinction, *Hungry Mind Review*, 1992, for *Wish on a Unicorn*; poetry awards from *Writer's Digest* and Poetry Society of Vermont; *School Library Journal* Best Book selection, New York Public Library Book for Sharing selection, Best Book for Young Adults and Notable Book selections, American Library Association, all 1992, Christopher Award, International Reading Association, 1993, all for *Letters from Rifka*; Heartland Award for Excellence in Young Adult Literature, 1998, for *Phoenix Rising*; Newbery Medal for distinguished writing for children, American Library Association, and Scott O'Dell Award for Historical Fiction, both 1998, both for *Out of the Dust*.

■ Writings

Wish on a Unicorn, Holt, 1991.
Letters from Rifka, Holt, 1992.
Poppy's Chair (picture book), illustrated by Kay Life, Macmillan, 1993.
Lester's Dog (picture book), illustrated by Nancy Carpenter, Crown, 1993.
Lavender (early chapter book), illustrated by Andrew Glass, Holt, 1993.
Sable (early chapter book), illustrated by Marcia Sewall, Holt, 1994.
Phoenix Rising, Holt, 1994.

A Time of Angels, Hyperion, 1995.
The Music of Dolphins, Scholastic, 1996.
Out of the Dust, Scholastic, 1997.
Just Juice (early chapter book), illustrated by Robert Andrew Parker, Scholastic, 1998.
Come On, Rain! (picture book), illustrated by Jon J. Muth, Scholastic, 1999.

Contributor of short story to *When I Was Your Age, II,* Candlewick, 1999.

■ Sidelights

"A profound and visceral sense of place is one of the qualities that is most memorable about Karen Hesse's writing." This evaluation, written for *Horn Book* by Brenda Bowen, Hesse's long-time editor, on the occasion of Hesse's winning the 1998 Newbery Medal, cuts to the heart of Hesse's work. This "sense of place" encompasses not only landscape—physical locations from Russia to Vermont to Oklahoma—but also spaces in the heart and mind. Whether taking on questions of death and hope in *Phoenix Rising,* of the meaning of being human and its relationship to language in *The Music of Dolphins,* of the plight of refugees in *Letters from Rifka,* or of the tenacity of the human spirit as in her Newbery Medal-winning *Out of the Dust,* Hesse explores her chosen emotional terrain with a deft hand and a poet's eye for telling detail.

History is also part of Hesse's sense of place. Her three historical novels, *Letters from Rifka, A Time of Angels,* and *Out of the Dust,* have transported readers from Russia, Belgium, and the United States in the early 1900s, to Boston and Vermont just following World War One, and to the American Dust Bowl in the 1930s. "I was once told that writing historical fiction was a bad idea," Hesse commented in her Newbery acceptance speech, reprinted in *Horn Book.* "No market for it. I didn't listen. I love research, love dipping into another time and place, and asking questions in a way that helps me see both the question and answer with a clearer perspective. . . . Often, our lives are so crowded, we need to hold to what is essential and weed out what is not." Reading historical fiction, she continued, "gives us perspective, respite from the bustle of everyday life, and helps us come to grips with the notion that there are not always answers to life's questions. It gives us a safe place in which we can grow, transform,

transcend. It helps us understand that sometimes the questions are too hard, that sometimes there are no answers, that sometimes there is only forgiveness."

Karen Hesse was born in Baltimore, Maryland, in 1952, long after the events of which she so lovingly writes. She grew up in a row house, and later in an apartment in the Baltimore suburbs. Hesse once described her childhood persona in *Something about the Author:* "Thin and pasty, I looked like I'd drifted in from another world and never quite belonged in this one." A sickly child, she could only be soothed by a ride in the family car. Her older brother, Mark, was a close ally, and books became another. Hesse recalled in an

When the Coast Guard discovers Mila, a teenage girl who was rescued and raised by dolphins from the age of four, she begins to grapple with what it means to be human and whether she belongs in the world of humans.

essay for *Something about the Author Autobiography Series* (*SAAS*) that her "childhood home provided few places for private retreat." To find privacy, she would go out the back door and climb into an apple tree. "There, cradled in the boughs of the tree, I spent hours reading. Often my bony bottom would go numb, but I loved it up there so much, I ignored the discomfort."

Another sanctuary for the young Hesse was the Enoch Pratt Free Library near her house. "Beginning with Dr. Seuss, I read my way through the picture books, the shorter chapter books, and finally the novels," she wrote in *SAAS*. As she neared the teenage years, she began to read adult novels, and one of these was John Hersey's *Hiroshima*, a book "that changed my life," Hesse recalled. "The courage, the profound compassion, dignity, and humanity of the Japanese people in the face of such unfathomable destruction helped me see the world in a way I never had before. When I closed the covers of *Hiroshima*, I closed the door on my childhood." The impact of this book would later be felt in her own novel about nuclear disaster, *Phoenix Rising*.

Reading provided one alternate world for the shy Hesse; an active imagination provided yet another. As a young girl she believed she could fly and once had to be restrained by her mother from jumping out of an upstairs window in an attempt to take wing. She also had a favorite cat whose ghost she saw after its death. There were angels, too, in her childhood cosmology. "I saw the sky open late one night when I was no older than ten or twelve," she noted in *SAAS*. "As I watched, angels descended earthward." These, and other events of her childhood were filed away, to be used decades later in the pages of her fiction.

Hesse's father was a collection man, and sometimes father and daughter would drive around together on his rounds, an experience that taught her a degree of sympathy for people who were less well off than she was. When her mother remarried, the new domestic package included not only a stepfather, with whom she became very close, but also a stepsister who was exotic looking, beautiful, and a professional dancer. Hesse jealously began to compete for attention—a new impulse for her. In high school she joined in amateur dramatics. "I loved being on stage," she wrote in *SAAS*, "being someone else. And I definitely got noticed. . . . I lost myself in my char-

acter to the point that I'd forget I was on stage. Suddenly I sort of 'woke up' and noticed people were crying."

Hesse's grades were poor in her freshman and sophomore years, but they improved in her last two years of high school. With the help of an enthusiastic drama teacher, she was admitted to Towson State College. However, her studies were cut short after just two years, when she met her future husband. "I fell in love . . . my very first year at college and figured out pretty quickly that I couldn't be in love and in the theater at the same time," she noted in *SAAS*. "Both commitments required 100 per cent of my heart and soul. I gave up theater. I've never regretted my decision." In 1971, the young couple eloped, and soon after that Hesse's husband was shipped out with the navy for Vietnam.

Literary Beginnings

Hesse lived in Norfolk, Virginia, while she waited for her husband's return. She also finished her undergraduate work, transferring to the University of Maryland, where she helped to pay her way by working in the university library. During this time she began writing and giving readings, gaining a reputation for herself as a poet. Upon graduation, Hesse worked for a time as a leave-benefit coordinator for her alma mater, but mostly she took work that was close to books and words: as an advertising secretary, a typesetter, and a proofreader. Upon settling in Vermont, Hesse and her husband had two children, in 1979 and 1982; both were born at home. Hesse's poetry was put on hold by motherhood, but soon she was experimenting with writing books. "It was typesetting that led me to believe I could succeed as a children's book writer," she noted in *SAAS*. "Some of the work I set struck me as very unsatisfying. I thought I could write at least as well if not better." But it was from 1980, when that thought first struck, to 1991 before her first book was published.

Hesse's editor, Bowen, recalled in *Horn Book* receiving an early attempt by the Newbery winner: the story of a family's encounter with Bigfoot. "The story was not credible, but the time and place were palpable," Bowen commented. "The voice was something to remember. I thought: This is a writer." Bowen also recalled the fledgling writer's intriguing address: Star Route in Vermont. When several years later Bowen received another submission from Star Route, she was eager to see the new work. Enclosed were story ideas for picture books, one of them titled "Wish on a Unicorn." While Bowen liked the story, she felt it needed to be fleshed out. The result was Hesse's first novel, *Wish on a Unicorn*. According to Bowen, it "held in it so many seeds of [Hesse's] later work: an underprivileged family; a child who has had to shoulder more responsibility than she should; a longing to fix things for people who can't fix them for themselves. And that strong sense of place."

Sixth-grade Maggie, the protagonist of *Wish on a Unicorn*, loves her younger brother, Mooch, and her slightly brain-damaged sister, Hannie, but sometimes feels overwhelmed with the responsibility of looking after them while their single-parent mom works nights. At school, the kids give the whole family a hard time, especially when Hannie wets herself. As a result, Maggie's afraid that she'll never have friends. When Hannie finds a dirty stuffed unicorn, she begins to believe that the toy animal has magical powers to grant wishes. In spite of herself, Maggie also begins to believe in the powers of the unicorn, and some wishes even come true—though not necessarily in the way she hoped. Eventually a family crisis—the disappearance of Hannie and her unicorn—crystallizes the importance of family for Maggie.

Reviewing this debut novel in *Horn Book,* Nancy Vasilakis noted that "Hesse has written a compassionate story of a family who have little in the way of worldly goods but who are rich in solidarity and spirit." Vasilakis also observed that the "use of the unicorn as a symbol of this family's essential strength is understated and effective." *Booklist*'s Hazel Rochman commented that "the poverty is palpable," and that kids "will be moved by the burdens on the oldest girl, who resents adult responsibility and yet finds the loving strength to reach beyond her years."

Delves Into Family History

Hesse's next book drew its inspiration from her own family's history. Based on the experiences of her great-aunt, *Letters from Rifka* tells of the adventures of a young Jewish girl and her family. The letters of the title, written in the margins and blank pages of a treasured book of Alexander Pushkin's poetry, are penned by the young girl, Rifka, to her cousin Tovah. Fleeing the harsh conditions for Jews in Russia in the wake of the Bolshevik Revolution, Rifka's family first crosses into Poland in 1919. There they are humiliatingly examined by a doctor and are stricken by typhus. They survive, make their way to Belgium and then sail for America. However, Rifka catches ringworm trying to help a fellow passenger on the way to Warsaw, and she is denied passage on the ship. Rifka lives with a Belgian family while she recovers. When she finally leaves to join her family in America, Rifka survives a storm at sea and then is detained by immigration officials at Ellis Island because of the baldness caused by ringworm. During the weeks of detainment, she befriends a young Russian boy who is in a similar predicament. At her hearing, Rifka makes an eloquent plea on behalf of both herself and her new friend. Thus reunited with her family, she begins a new life.

Hesse's second book was enthusiastically received by reviewers. Writing in *Horn Book*, Hanna B. Zeiger commented that this "moving account of a brave young girl's story brings to life the day-to-day trials and horrors experienced by many immigrants as well as the resourcefulness and strength they found within themselves." Rochman, writing in *Booklist*, noted that "the narrative flashes occasionally with lively Yiddish idiom" and that "the emerging sense of Rifka's personality" is what "especially raises it above docu-novel." Writing in *Bulletin of the Center for Children's Books*, Betsy Hearne observed that while many novels have focused on the immigration experiences of the Jews of Russia, *Letters from Rifka* "is vivid in detailing the physical and emotional toll exacted for passage." A reviewer for *Publishers Weekly* concurred: "Hesse's vivacious tale colorfully and convincingly refreshes the immigrant experience."

Tragedy in Fiction

A pair of picture books and two chapter books followed for Hesse: warm family and pet stories. Hesse returned to books for older readers with *Phoenix Rising*, a futuristic tale of nuclear disaster and its aftereffects. A nuclear power plant spreads radiation throughout New England, but thirteen-year-old Nyle and her grandmother continue tending their sheep on a Vermont farm, wearing pro-

Hesse earned the 1997 Newbery Award for her series of free-verse poems portraying life in the 1930s Oklahoma dust bowl from the point of view of a young girl.

tective masks and praying that the winds keep the contamination away. Then two evacuees arrive from Boston, fifteen-year-old Ezra and his mother, who stay in the back bedroom on the farm—the same room where Nyle's mother and grandfather died. Nyle is afraid of intimacy and keeps her distance at first from the deathly ill Ezra. However, she slowly goes beyond her own fear and self-protectiveness, and comes to love the youth stricken with radiation poisoning. She takes care of him until his death, learning at this moment how to let go of a loved one. "Nyle's emotional growth allows her to face his death with newfound strength," explained Vasilakis in *Horn Book.* "The story is told in measured, laconic

tones," Vasilakis continued, and "by focusing on the love story between the two main characters, Hesse has made this story essentially one of hope and determination." Hearne also noted Hesse's focus on the human element in such a tragedy in *Bulletin of the Center for Children's Books.* "It's a credit to Hesse that she concentrates on character dynamics instead of exploiting situational dynamics," Hearne wrote, concluding that the "friends, family, and loyal dogs that personalize this tragedy will move kids to their own thoughts about social action." A critic in *Kirkus Reviews* stated that "Hesse portrays her characters' anguish and their growing tenderness with such unwavering clarity and grace that she sustains the tension of her lyrical, understated narrative right to her stunning, beautifully wrought conclusion."

Catastrophic events are also at the heart of Hesse's fourth novel for older readers, *A Time of Angels.* However, instead of the future, the reader is transported to the past to the influenza epidemic which spread throughout the world following World War I. Hannah and her sisters are living in Boston with Tanta Rose, waiting for their parents to return from Europe. Rose is killed by the flu and her sisters are also infected. Evacuated from the city, Hannah, too, comes down with the flu, and ends up in Brattleboro, Vermont, guided by an angel who has saved her life before. She is brought back to health by an old German farmer, a local outcast because of his former nationality. A *Publishers Weekly* reviewer noted that "Hesse intensifies the apocalyptic mood of *Phoenix Rising,* palpably recreating the terror in the streets as the influenza spreads," while Hearne commented in *Bulletin of the Center for Children's Books,* "Hesse has taken on a lot here and managed to do justice to it all."

Doing justice to the characters in her fiction is what most concerns Hesse. "Let me tell you," she said in her Newbery acceptance speech. "I never make up any of the bad things that happen to my characters. I love my characters too much to hurt them deliberately, even the prickly ones. It just so happens that in life, there's pain; sorrow lives in the shadow of joy, joy in the shadow of sorrow. The question is, do we let the pain reign triumphant, or do we find a way to grow, to transform, and ultimately transcend our pain?" These are questions Hesse asks herself every day as she sits down to her work. A methodical writer, she sticks to a routine as much as possible. Up at 5:00 A.M., she begins work. Even on weekends she maintains the early hours, though on those days she busies herself answering mail from readers around the world.

Hesse's fifth novel for older readers, *The Music of Dolphins,* was described by a *Publishers Weekly* reviewer as being as "moving as a sonnet, as eloquently structured as a bell Curve" and that "poignantly explores the most profound of themes—what it means to be human." The narrator of the tale, Mila, is a so-called feral child, raised by dolphins. As a four-year-old, she survived a plane crash off the coast of Cuba and has been nurtured by dolphins for ten years, until her discovery by the Coast Guard. Dubbed Mila, "miracle" in Spanish, the girl becomes the subject of a government study. She is taught language and music by a team of scientists, and learns with amazing speed, attempting in turn to teach the scientists dolphin language. But all the while, the call of the wild continues to echo in Mila's head, and she longs to return to her island. "Mila's rich inner voice makes her a lovely, lyrical character," noted Mary Arnold in *Voice of Youth Advocates.* Arnold went on to observe that the book was a "profound study of being human and the ways in which communication unites and separates human beings." A critic in *Kirkus Reviews* lauded the book, calling it a "probing look at what makes us human, with an unforgettable protagonist." A *Publishers Weekly* contributor further commented that "Hesse succeeds" in pulling off the tricky plot in a "frequently dazzling novel," while Kate McClelland, in a *School Library Journal* review, concluded that this "powerful exploration of how we become human and how the soul endures is a song of beauty and sorrow, haunting and unforgettable."

Out of the Dust

The same adjectives have been used to describe Billie Jo and the events of Hesse's next novel, *Out of the Dust.* Hesse worked on the novel for several years, drawing inspiration from a car trip to Colorado in 1993. She was awestruck by the country she saw, amazed by the subtle varieties of color and by the wind that never ceased. It took her years to internalize these feelings, to assimilate them into a creative direction, and meld them with a historical look at the Dust Bowl years of the 1930s. Next she saturated herself in research,

---

If you enjoy the works of Karen Hesse, you may also want to check out the following books and films:

Thomas Baird, *Where Time Ends*, 1988.
Hila Colman, *Rachel's Legacy*, 1979.
Erika Tamar, *Good-Bye, Glamour Girl*, 1984.
The Grapes of Wrath, a classic film starring Henry Fonda, 1940.

---

reading her way through newspapers of the time, getting the feel of the life of those days in details of how people actually lived. Then came characters, Billie Jo and her family, and the format, free verse. Hesse's roots in writing were with poetry; now she returned to those roots. "I never attempted to write this book any other way than in free verse," she noted in her Newbery acceptance speech. "The frugality of the life, the hypnotically hard work of farming, the grimness of conditions during the dust bowl demanded an economy of words."

Hesse's intent was a spare understatement, and that is what the book provides in its glimpse of a bygone way of life. The family barely scrape together a living, with the father refusing to plant anything but wheat. Yet this crop is destroyed by the winds and dust time after time. Dust is everywhere, in the sills, on the piano keys, in the body: "Daddy came in, / he sat across from Ma and blew his nose. / Mud streamed out. / He coughed and spit out / mud. / If he had cried, / his tears would have been mud too, / but he didn't cry. / And neither did Ma." Billie Jo takes solace in her piano playing, until her mother and infant brother are killed in a kitchen fire. Billie Jo is scarred on her hands and soul, and both her father and Billie Jo bottle up their grief for a time. The young girl becomes an outcast until finally both she and her father build hope out of utter desolation, and redefine what it means to be a family.

Reviewers enthusiastically praised *Out of the Dust.* *Booklist*'s Susan Dove Lempke commented that although the story was bleak, "Hesse's writing transcends the gloom and transforms it into a powerfully compelling tale of a girl with enormous strength, courage, and love." Sarah K. Hetz noted in *Voice of Youth Advocates* that this "novel celebrates the tenacity of the human spirit." Peter D. Sieruta observed in *Horn Book* that Billie Jo's voice, "nearly every word informed by longing, provides an immediacy that expressively depicts both a grim historical era and one family's healing." Thomas S. Owens, writing in the *Five Owls*, felt that Hesse's novel was more than "vivid storytelling," and that it "gives a face to history." Owens went on to conclude that *"Out of the Dust* seems destined to become [Hesse's] signature work, a literary groundbreaker as stunning as Oklahoma's dust bowl recovery." The 1998 Newbery Medal was presented to Hesse for this vivid historical recreation.

"Occasionally, adult readers grimace at the events documented in *Out of the Dust,*" the author noted in her Newbery acceptance speech. "They ask, how can this book be for young readers? I ask, how can it not? The children I have met during my travels around the country have astounded me with their perception, their intelligence, their capacity to take in information and apply it to a greater picture, or take in the greater picture and distill it down to what they need from it." Hesse also commented that young readers ask for substance in the books they read, for books that challenge. That is something that she hopes to keep providing.

"I love writing," Hesse explained in *SAAS.* "I can't wait to get to my desk every morning. I wish everyone felt that way about their chosen profession. Writing is not easy. I work for long hours and sometimes all that work disappoints me and I throw it out and begin again. . . . The thing about writing . . . until your words become a book you can change them, mold them, shape and reshape them until they look and sound and feel precisely the way you want."

■ Works Cited

Arnold, Mary, review of *The Music of Dolphins, Voice of Youth Advocates,* February, 1997, p. 328.

Bowen, Brenda, "Karen Hesse," *Horn Book,* July-August, 1998, pp. 428-32.

Hearne, Betsy, review of *Letters from Rifka, Bulletin of the Center for Children's Books,* October, 1992, p. 44.

Hearne, Betsy, review of *Phoenix Rising, Bulletin of the Center for Children's Books,* June, 1994, pp. 321-22.

Hearne, Betsy, review of *A Time of Angels, Bulletin of the Center for Children's Books,* January, 1996, p. 161.

Hesse, Karen, comments in *Something about the Author,* Volume 74, Gale, 1993, pp. 120-21.

Hesse, Karen, *Out of the Dust,* Scholastic, 1997.

Hesse, Karen, entry in *Something about the Author Autobiography Series,* Volume 25, Gale, 1998.

Hesse, Karen, "Newbery Medal Acceptance," *Horn Book,* July-August, 1998, pp. 422-27.

Hetz, Sarah K., review of *Out of the Dust, Voice of Youth Advocates,* April, 1998, p. 46.

Lempke, Susan Dove, review of *Out of the Dust, Booklist,* October 1, 1997, p. 330.

Review of *Letters from Rifka, Publishers Weekly,* June 29, 1992, p. 64.

McClelland, Kate, review of *The Music of Dolphins, School Library Journal,* November, 1996, pp. 120, 123.

Review of *The Music of Dolphins, Kirkus Reviews,* August 15, 1996, p. 1235.

Review of *The Music of Dolphins, Publishers Weekly,* September 2, 1996, p. 131.

Owens, Thomas S., review of *Out of the Dust, Five Owls,* January-February, 1998, pp. 60-61.

Review of *Phoenix Rising, Kirkus Reviews,* April 1, 1994, p. 480.

Rochman, Hazel, review of *Wish on a Unicorn, Booklist,* March 15, 1991, p. 1493.

Rochman, Hazel, review of *Letters from Rifka, Booklist,* July, 1992, p. 1931.

Sieruta, Peter D., review of *Out of the Dust, Horn Book,* January-February, 1998, p. 73.

Review of *A Time of Angels, Publishers Weekly,* October 23, 1995, p. 70.

Vasilakis, Nancy, review of *Wish on a Unicorn, Horn Book,* July-August, 1991, pp. 457-58.

Vasilakis, Nancy, review of *Phoenix Rising, Horn Book,* September-October, 1994, p. 599.

Zeiger, Hanna B., review of *Letters from Rifka, Horn Book,* September-October, 1992, p. 585.

■ For More Information See

PERIODICALS

ALAN Review, Spring, 1998, p. 50.

Booklist, July, 1992, p. 1931; March 15, 1993, p. 1359; October 1, 1993, p. 344; May 15, 1994, p. 1674; June 1 & 15, 1994, p. 1820; December 1, 1995, pp. 618, 620; October 1, 1997, p. 330.

Bulletin of the Center for Children's Books, November, 1993, p. 84; May, 1994, p. 289.

Five Owls, May-June, 1996, pp. 116-17.

Horn Book, March-April, 1994, pp. 190-91; July-August, 1994, p. 452; September-October, 1994, p. 599; September-October, 1995, p. 634.

Kirkus Reviews, March 1, 1991, p. 318; February 15, 1993, p. 227.

New York Times, January 13, 1998, p. B 3.

New York Times Book Review, June 19, 1994, p. 28.

Publishers Weekly, August 30, 1993, p. 95; October 25, 1993, p. 59; August 25, 1997, pp. 72-73; November 3, 1997, p. 50; September 21, 1998, p. 85.

School Library Journal, August, 1992, pp. 154-55; July, 1993, p. 61; October, 1993, p. 100; December, 1993, p. 89; May, 1994, p. 114; June, 1994, p. 148; December, 1995, p. 131; September, 1997, pp. 131, 217; February, 1998, p. 13; May, 1998, p. 26; October, 1998, pp. 100, 102.

Voice of Youth Advocates, August, 1994, p. 146; February, 1997, p. 328; April, 1998, p. 46.*

—Sketch by J. Sydney Jones

Julie Johnston

■ Personal

Born January 21, 1941, in Smiths Falls, Ontario, Canada; daughter of J. A. B. (a lawyer) and Sarah Mae (a homemaker; maiden name, Patterson) Dulmage; married Basil W. Johnston (an orthopedic surgeon), 1963; children: Leslie, Lauren, Andrea, Melissa. *Education:* University of Toronto, received degree, 1963; Trent University, B.A., 1984. *Hobbies and other interests:* Old wooden boats, vegetable gardening, cycling, hiking, traveling, reading, stone masonry.

■ Addresses

Home and office—463 Hunter St. W., Peterborough, Ontario, Canada K9H 2M7.

■ Career

Smiths Falls, Ontario, occupational therapist at a school for mentally handicapped children, 1963-65; occupational therapist at a rehabilitation centre, Kingston, Ontario, 1965-69. Peterborough Board of Education, Continuing Education Department, creative writing instructor, 1988-89. *Member:* Canadian Society of Children's Authors, Illustrators, and Performers (CANSCAIP), Canadian Children's Book Centre, The Writer's Union of Canada, Ottawa Independent Writers.

■ Awards, Honors

Runner-up, *Chatelaine* Fiction Contest, 1979, for short story "Canadian Content"; first prize, Solange Karsh Award, Birks Gold Medal, and cash prize, Canadian Playwriting Competition, Ottawa Little Theatre, 1979, for *There's Going to Be a Frost;* Kawartha Region Best Play award, 1980, for *There's Going to Be a Frost,* and co-winner for best play, 1984, for *Lucid Intervals;* Canadian Library Association Young Adult Honour Book, 1993, shortlist for Mister Christie's Book Award, 1993, National Chapter of Canada Independent Order Daughters of the Empire (IODE) Violet Downey Book Award, 1993, Governor General's Literary Award for children's literature, 1993, School Library Journal Best Book, 1994, New York Public Library's 1994 Books for the Teen Age list selection, Ontario Library Association 1994 Silver Birch Award nomination, and American Library Association notable book selection, all for *Hero of Lesser Causes;* American Library Association notable book selection, Governor General's Literary Award for children's literature, 1994, both for *Adam and Eve and Pinch-Me;* honorary D.L., Trent University, 1996.

■ Writings

YOUNG ADULT NOVELS

Hero of Lesser Causes, Lester Publishing, 1992, Joy Street Books, 1993.
Adam and Eve and Pinch-Me, Lester Publishing, 1994, Little, Brown, 1994.
The Only Outcast, Tundra, 1998.

OTHER

There's Going to Be a Frost (one-act play), first produced at the Sears Drama Festival, 1980.
Lucid Intervals (one-act play), first produced at the Sears Drama Festival, 1984.

Also author of screenplay based on *Hero of Lesser Causes*, Roy Krost Productions, 1994. Contributor of the novella *The Window Seat* to *Women's Weekly Omnibus*, 1984, and the story "Mirrors" to the anthology *The Blue Jean Collection*, Thistledown Press, 1992. Contributor of fiction to periodicals, including *Buzz*, *Chatelaine*, *Matrix*, *Woman and Home*, and *Women's Weekly*; contributor of nonfiction to periodicals, including *Wine Tidings*, *Homemakers*, *Doctor's Review*, and *Canadian Author and Bookman*. Johnston's work has been translated into French, and it has been published in Canada, Denmark, France, Great Britain, and the United States.

■ Sidelights

Imagine that you are twelve years old, living in Canada in the years just after World War II. Your thirteen-year-old brother, who is also your best friend, has been paralyzed after a bout with polio. Now he is bedridden, and he has lost the will to live. Or, imagine that you are a teenage girl in the 1990s who has been passed from foster home to foster home for the first fifteen years of your life. You feel that you have never been loved, and you do not want to love anyone. Just when you determine to leave your foster family in rural Canada to strike out on your own, you begin to grow close to this family. To make matters even more confusing, a woman shows up who thinks that she is your birth mother. Author Julie Johnston has put herself and her readers into the shoes of both of these characters, Keely in *Hero of Lesser Causes* and Sara in *Adam and Eve and Pinch-Me*.

Johnston's first two books have been lauded by critics; both received the prestigious Governor General's Literary Award. Before reading *Hero of Lesser Causes* and *Adam and Eve and Pinch-Me*, Jean Little, a contributor in *Canadian Children's Literature*, wondered if a new author "deserved so great an honor *twice*." The critic found that they "are both beautifully written books;" in fact, Little stated that she wished that she had written *Adam and Eve and Pinch-Me* herself. What makes Johnston's novels so good, as several reviewers have noted, is the people portrayed in them. According to Deborah Steven-son in *Bulletin of the Center for Children's Books*, "Johnston's particular gift is in the authenticity of her characters and relationships."

Johnston did not grow up intending to become a writer. She wrote her first young adult novels only after her children were grown, and these books were published after a number of years. Yet Johnston's life, from her own early childhood to her education and career, provided her with some of the substance of her stories. She was born in Smiths Falls, Ontario, during World War II. Her father, a lawyer, served at the National Defence Headquarters in nearby Ottawa. At home, where Johnston lived with her mother, grandmother, and older sister, the war affected her life and imagination in various ways. "My first memories . . . are of uniforms," she wrote in the *Something about the Author Autobiography Series* (SAAS). "I remember hearing my mother once describe the telegram her family received saying that one of my uncles was missing during the war and presumed dead. After the war I used to imagine going to Europe and searching for my uncle and finding him and bringing him home safe and sound." As Johnston noted, her character Keely ponders a similar feat in *Hero of Lesser Causes*.

A nurse named Margaret came to live with the family after Johnston's grandmother suffered a stroke. Johnston was just three years old at the time, but Margaret's arrival provided her with another enduring memory. Margaret, "strong," "superstitious," and blessed with talents that left Johnston "believing in her superhuman power," became a part of the family. Margaret departed at the death of Johnston's grandmother, when Johnston was nine years old, but aspects of her personality, as Johnston revealed in her autobiographical essay, reappear in the character of Peggy, the nurse in *Hero of Lesser Causes*.

Hero of Lesser Causes Julie Johnston

When her beloved brother is paralyzed by polio, Keely must find a way to improve his emotional state in this award-winning 1992 novel set during World War II.

Julie, along with her sisters Diane and Kathie (Kathie was born when Johnston was five), spent their childhood playing together in the family's home. In *SAAS* Johnston recalled telling her sisters stories that she made up. These stories featured the girls' neighbors and often ended with Johnston herself rescuing them from imaginary dangers. "I think Keely in *Hero of Lesser Causes* owes something to these early days," she stated. After the war, the family also spent time at a cottage built on an island in a lake, where Johnston swam, played games, read, and enjoyed the outdoors. When Johnston was older, a friend at the lake taught her to ride a horse. She wrote plays in school, and in high school she worked on the yearbook and student newspaper. She also

wrote a novel that was serialized in the town newspaper.

Johnston was still a teenager when she met her future husband, Basil Johnston, at the lake. Johnston enrolled at the University of Toronto, where Basil was a medical student. She began studying physical and occupational therapy, which involved everything from dissecting cadavers to learning arts and crafts and working in hospitals. There Johnston "met so many people whose lives were so different from my own that I began to feel that at last I was beginning to get an education." In *SAAS*, she commented that she "probably would not have written about such a severe disability" as the one Patrick has in *Hero of Lesser Causes* if it were not for her "background in rehabilitation."

Julie and Basil Johnston married in 1963. That same year, Johnston graduated from university and began her career as an occupational therapist. Initially, she worked at a school for mentally handicapped children in her hometown of Smiths Falls. She wrote in her *SAAS* essay that she "was very idealistic in those days. I really thought I could make a big difference in the lives of some of those kids by practicing what I'd been taught, but it was extremely frustrating. . . . Nothing I could do would help relieve their severe and multiple handicaps. The saddest thing I learned was how quickly one can become inured to tragic circumstances." Johnston and her husband, who also worked at the school, eventually went to work in England. After touring Europe on a camping holiday, they returned to Canada. Johnston began work at a rehabilitation centre in Kingston, Ontario, as an occupational therapist. Johnston left this job after some years to take care of her four daughters.

Long Years of Waiting

When her girls were older, Johnston began taking courses at Trent University in Peterborough, Ontario. Although she felt insecure and self-conscious about her age, she continued to take courses for nine years, until finally she earned a degree in English literature. Johnston practiced the writing craft in a variety of ways. She had been recording her dreams since the late 1970s, and when her daughters were in school she wrote a play which they performed at home and at the lake. Next, she entered a one-act play in a national competition. As she recalled in *SAAS*, she was astonished to win first prize. "Three weeks later I had a letter from *Chatelaine* magazine saying that they wanted to publish a story I had sent them, and a few weeks after that a British magazine accepted another story. It was a banner year," she wrote. Yet it was another seven long years and countless rejection letters before Johnston's career as a writer took off. "The only thing that made me keep on trying was that initial good luck," she explained.

Johnston originally sent the manuscript for *Hero of Lesser Causes* to publishers in 1986. At first, the book met with rejection. "I stuck the manuscript in the back of a cupboard and started another novel, the one that was to become *Adam and Eve and Pinch-Me*," Johnston recalled in *SAAS*. She also began teaching creative writing and sent *Hero of Lesser Causes* out again to publishers in the late 1980s. After some difficulties, it was eventually published in 1992.

"A Fine First Novel"

Hero of Lesser Causes, set in Ottawa in 1946, tells the story of twelve-year-old Keely and her brother Patrick. Keely adores her older brother, and joins him in outdoor play and contests. She is determined to become a warrior of sorts, fighting for great causes. However, not even Keely seems able to help Patrick when he contracts polio after a swim in a public pool. When he returns home from the hospital, Keely finds that her brother has been paralyzed both in body and spirit. Unable to move, Patrick is depressed and even suicidal. The children's mother is physically exhausted and emotionally devastated.

Keely refuses to let her brother fade away. Full of youthful enthusiasm, she insists that he show courage and do what he can to recover. She attempts to engage him in a plan to find nurse Peggy's fiance, who is listed as killed during the war. Keely's efforts, as well as those of nurse Peggy, are at first met with bitterness. It takes time—and an unsuccessful suicide attempt—before Patrick regains his will to live. As Donna Houser of *Voice of Youth Advocates* pointed out, Keely learns that "she can't be the big hero." Instead, "she'll have to settle for being one of the lesser causes."

If you enjoy the works of Julie Johnston, you may also want to check out the following books and films:

Alden R. Carter, *Up Country*, 1989.
Sharon Creech, *Walk Two Moons*, 1994.
Cynthia Voight, *Izzy, Willy-Nilly*, 1986.
Gas Food Lodging, a film based on a novel by Richard Peck, 1992.

Johnston's first novel won praise. "The unique period details create a strong sense of the place and the time without slowing down the action," Nancy Vasilakis commented in *Horn Book*. According to Stephanie Zvirin in *Booklist*, Johnston includes the "practical adjustments of being dependent on a wheelchair and on other people." Floyd Spracklin of *Canadian Materials* described *Hero of Lesser Causes* as "very funny and insightful," and a *Kirkus Reviews* critic called it a "fine first novel with an intense, beautifully developed sibling relationship." "With its charismatic people and engaging plot, this book is just terrific!" concluded Cindy Darling Codell in *School Library Journal*. *Hero of Lesser Causes* also won several notable literary awards.

Life on a Computer

The title of Johnston's second novel, *Adam and Eve and Pinch-Me*, comes from a children's rhyme. Published in 1994, *Adam and Eve and Pinch-Me* features Sara, a fifteen-year-old who narrates the story as she records her life story on a computer. Sara has had a traumatic childhood. She was given up for adoption as a baby, and her adoptive parents were killed in a fire. Since then, Sara has lived with many foster families. One of the latest gave her the computer, but now she lives with the Huddlestons on their farm. Foster-father Hud does not speak, while foster-mother Ma talks too much. Sara is not pleased with the placement; she dislikes farm life and the two foster boys who also live with the Huddlestons. Sara cannot wait to turn sixteen, so she can legally live on her own.

Yet Sara's wish to remain isolated begins to dwindle. She takes a job working in a cafe, and then another typing for a writer. She learns to speak up for herself, to deal with the attentions of a boy, and to sort out her feelings when a woman who thinks she may be Sara's birth mother comes to town. Sara, who has always felt free to write on the computer because she knows she can erase what she has written, accidentally prints out her diary near the end of the novel. She decides not to destroy the hard copy. According to Sarah Ellis of *Horn Book*, this means that the computer, "which began as an escape for Sara and then became an instrument for self-discovery, has now become . . . a route to communication." Sara seems to be on her way to emotional recovery, and now has the potential to develop relationships with others.

Critics praised *Adam and Eve and Pinch-Me.* As Barbara Greenwood of *Quill and Quire* noted, "Johnston captures flawlessly a sarcastic, self-deprecating teen-aged voice while revealing with great sensitivity the gradual, painful thawing of Sara Moone." Carolyn Noah of *School Library Journal* stated that each of the supporting characters "emerges distinctly." According to a *Kirkus Reviews* critic, *Adam and Eve and Pinch-Me* has "keen pacing and a wonderfully nimble narrative." Sarah Ellis of *Horn Book* appreciated the "device of the electronic diary," which "lends a plausible immediacy to the story as Sara retreats to her computer at times of stress." *Horn Book*'s Nancy Vasilakis, noting Johnston's "robust and original" heroine in *Hero of Lesser Causes*, stated that Johnston "succeeds to an even greater extent" with *Adam and Eve and Pinch-Me.*

In 1998, Johnston published *The Only Outcast,* a coming-of-age novel set in the early twentieth century and featuring a male protagonist. Sixteen-year-old Fred Dickinson travels with his three younger siblings for a vacation at their grandparents' cottage. Still troubled by the death of his mother three years earlier and burdened by a harsh, demanding father, Fred gains wisdom and maturity through a series of sometimes dangerous and mysterious incidents. A reviewer in *Publishers Weekly* called *The Only Outcast* a "subtle, beautifully polished work."

Johnston's life has changed since she became a successful writer. "My time is almost completely taken up with writing, traveling to do readings, to give speeches, and to take part in workshops," she explained in *SAAS.* While Johnston enjoys traveling and spending time with her family at the lake she loves, she is happiest when she is

writing. She added that her lakeside cottage "is the place above all others that provides me with continuity, with a sense of well-being and with a sense of identity, things I find important to my ability to write and to live, which for me, now, are one and the same."

■ Works Cited

Review of *Adam and Eve and Pinch-Me, Kirkus Reviews,* May 15, 1994, p. 700.

Codell, Cindy Darling, review of *Hero of Lesser Causes, School Library Journal,* June, 1993, p. 107.

Ellis, Sarah, "News from the North," *Horn Book,* September-October, 1994, pp. 626-28.

Greenwood, Barbara, review of *Adam and Eve and Pinch-Me, Quill and Quire,* May, 1994, p. 37.

Review of *Hero of Lesser Causes, Kirkus Reviews,* May 15, 1993, p. 663.

Houser, Donna, review of *Hero of Lesser Causes, Voice of Youth Advocates,* August, 1993, pp. 152-53.

Johnston, Julie, *Something about the Author Autobiography Series,* Volume 24, Gale, 1997, pp. 163-80.

Little, Jean, "Julie Johnston: An Exciting New Voice," *Canadian Children's Literature,* Number 77, 1995, pp. 33-38.

Noah, Carolyn, review of *Adam and Eve and Pinch-Me, School Library Journal,* July, 1994, p. 119.

Review of *The Only Outcast, Publishers Weekly,* August 24, 1998, p. 58.

Spracklin, Floyd, review of *Hero of Lesser Causes, Canadian Materials,* October, 1992, p. 272.

Stevenson, Deborah, review of *Hero of Lesser Causes, Bulletin of the Center for Children's Books,* April, 1993, p. 254.

Vasilakis, Nancy, review of *Hero of Lesser Causes, Horn Book,* July-August, 1993, p. 457.

Vasilakis, Nancy, review of *Adam and Eve and Pinch-Me, Horn Book,* September-October, 1994, pp. 599-600.

Zvirin, Stephanie, review of *Hero of Lesser Causes, Booklist,* July, 1993, p. 1966.

■ For More Information See

PERIODICALS

Booklist, May 15, 1994, p. 1678.
Bulletin of the Center for Children's Books, May, 1994, p. 290.

Children's Book News, Spring, 1992, p. 17.
Emergency Librarian, March, 1993, p. 14.
Kliatt, March, 1996, pp. 8, 10.
Publishers Weekly, April 18, 1994, p. 64.
Quill and Quire, April, 1992, p. 31.
Toronto Star, December 22, 1992.
Voice Of Youth Advocates, August, 1994, pp. 146-
47.

—Sketch by R. Garcia-Johnson

Annette Curtis Klause

■ Personal

Born June 20, 1953, in Bristol, England; came to the United States, June, 1968; daughter of Graham Trevor (a radiologist) and Mary Frances (a homemaker; maiden name, Kempe) Curtis; married Mark Jeffrey Klause (a library assistant), August 11, 1979. *Education:* University of Maryland, B.A., 1976, M.L.S., 1978. *Politics:* "Sometimes." *Religion:* "Never." *Hobbies and other interests:* "Reading science fiction, fantasy, and horror; messing around with my computer; and listening to rock music."

■ Addresses

Home—Hyattsville, MD. *Office*—c/o Bantam Doubleday Dell, Books for Young Readers, 1540 Broadway, New York, NY 10036.

■ Career

Various positions for library contracting companies, 1979-81; various positions in the Montgomery County, MD, Department of Public Libraries, in-cluding Silver Spring Community Library, Silver Spring, MD, children's librarian I, 1981; substitute librarian, 1981-82; Kensington Park Community Library, Kensington Park, MD, part-time children's librarian I, 1982-84; Bethesda Regional Library, Bethesda, MD, full-time children's librarian I, 1984-89; Olney Community Library, Olney, MD, head of children's services, 1989-91; Kensington Park Community Library, head of children's services, 1991-92; Aspen Hill Community Library, Rockville, MD, head of children's services, 1992—. *Member:* American Library Association (ALA), Association of Library Services to Children, Young Adult Library Services Association, Society of Children's Book Writers and Illustrators, Children's Book Guild.

■ Awards, Honors

American Library Association (ALA) Best Book for Young Adults and Best Book for Reluctant Readers, 1990, *School Library Journal* Best Book, 1990, *Booklist* Best Book and Editor's Choice, 1990, Best Book of the Year Honor Book, Michigan Library Association Young Adult Division, 1990, California Young Reader Medal, young adult category, 1993, Sequoyah Young Adult Book Award, Oklahoma Library Association, 1993, Maryland Library Association Black-eyed Susan award for grades six through nine, 1992-93, and South Carolina Library Association Young Adult Award, all for *The Silver Kiss*; ALA Notable Book for Children, *Booklist*

Editor's Choice, *School Library Journal* Best Books designation, and New York Public Library One Hundred Best Children's Books designation, all 1993, all for *Alien Secrets*; Top Ten Best Books for Young Adults and Quick Picks for Reluctant Readers designations, ALA, both 1998, both for *Blood and Chocolate.*

■ Writings

The Silver Kiss, Delacorte, 1990.
Alien Secrets, Delacorte, 1993.
Blood and Chocolate, Delacorte, 1997.

Also author of short stories "Librarians from Space," published in *The U*n*a*b*a*s*h*e*d Librarian*, Number 51, 1984; "The Hoppins," published in *Short Circuits*, edited by Donald Gallo, Delacorte, 1992; and "The Bogey Man," published in *Night Terrors: Stories of Shadows and Substance.* Contributor of poetry to periodicals, including *Takoma Park Writers 1981*, Downcounty Press, 1981; *Cat's Magazine; Aurora; Visions;* and others. Contributor of articles to professional journals, including *School Library Journal* and *Voice of Youth Advocates;* contributor of book reviews to periodicals, *School Library Journal*, 1982-94.

■ Sidelights

Combining her early passion for fantasy and science-fiction literature with the insights into human behavior that developed due to her own introspective nature, Annette Curtis Klause has written several acclaimed novels for teen readers. Interweaving a seductive vampire and a strong dose of grisly goings-on into the plot of her 1990 debut novel, *The Silver Kiss*, broke many of the rules of writing for young adults, and Klause's more recent books have continued in that same vein, combining romance, horror, science-fiction, and even mystery genres in unique ways. Her readable, flowing style and ability to draw readers into complex philosophical issues in a non-confrontational way have also contributed to Klause's growing reputation as a writer of unique, quality YA fiction. "I find I often deal with the positive aspects of difference," she once told *Something about the Author* interviewer J. Sydney Jones. "Difference is good. People contribute to life and society in different ways, but everybody has something to contribute."

As a child, Klause was weaned on offbeat stories, many told to her by her father, a science-fiction buff who was also a fan of American monster and gangster films. Born in Bristol, England, Klause played in the ruins of homes destroyed during the Blitz, the bombing raids flown over England by the Nazis during World War II. At age seven, she and her family moved north to Newcastle-upon-Tyne, where Klause embarked upon a lifelong love affair with books and reading during one of her first visits to the local library. The stories of such authors as C. S. Lewis, with his "Chronicles of Narnia" series, fascinated her, and she also began to do some writing of her own: self-illustrated stories about cats and kittens, poems, and even plays that she performed with her schoolmates.

From Pulp Fiction to Poetry

Klause's early exposure to fantastic literature—via the pulp novels and science fiction magazines collected by her father and scattered in piles around the house—gave her imagination a rather horrific bent. One of her first longer written works, which actually reached several chapters in length, was *The Blood Ridden Pool of Solen Goom*, a story that involved gallons of blood. Her first exposure to vampire stories came when Klause read Jane Gaskell's *The Shiny Narrow Grin*, at age fourteen. *The Shiny Narrow Grin* would serve as a major influence when Klause plotted her own debut novel, *The Silver Kiss*, many years later.

Klause spent her high school years in the United States, where her family moved due to her father's career. Now living in Washington, D.C., she had left prose and now concentrated on writing poetry about the things most teen girls ponder: namely, boys, love, and how to acquire both. A naturally shy person, Klause had been an outsider in England; in the United States she was sought after as a friend due to her fellow students' fascination with her British background. "It's the British accent," Klause once explained. "It made people want to find out about me."

Poetry can be one of the most accessible mediums for adolescent writers, and Klause certainly found it so. "I wrote poetry because it could be short and I wanted instant gratification," she explained to *Authors and Artists for Young Adults* (*AAYA*). "It was especially important to an emo-

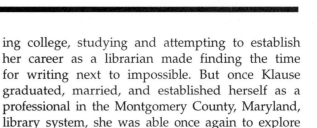

A girl whose mother is dying of cancer befriends a troubled vampire in Klause's award-winning debut novel.

tional teen because poetry cuts right to the emotional nub. You don't have to waste time with the frills, you can get right to the agonized point." Looking back at her early writing, she also reflected that poetry can be good training for most writers, "since it teaches you to hone down to the exact words you want, and to use startling new images that make your reader see commonplace things with new eyes."

Klause attended the University of Maryland, earning her bachelor's degree in 1976 and an advanced degree in library science two years later. Despite attending several poetry workshops dur-

ing college, studying and attempting to establish her career as a librarian made finding the time for writing next to impossible. But once Klause graduated, married, and established herself as a professional in the Montgomery County, Maryland, library system, she was able once again to explore her gift with words. Becoming frustrated with the quality of her poetry, she gradually switched to writing prose; "I realized I could apply all I loved about poetry to prose and not worry about iambic pentameter," she recalled. It was while attending a writer's workshop led by children's author Larry Callen that Klause decided to challenge herself: she would write a full-length novel.

Deciding to write her novel for a young adult readership rather than for adults was one of the easiest aspects of her future book for Klause to plan; as she told Jones, like many adults, she's "still working through my own adolescence, so [writing for teens] seems appropriate." Thinking back to some of her favorite books during her teen years, she remembered her fascination with *The Shiny Narrow Grin*, and the seeds of her first novel took root. Klause reread the poems she had written while under the influence of Gaskell's vampire story, and was happy to discover more than a few good ideas and well-turned phrases within those notebook pages. In a way, Klause would later admit, it was kind of like plagiarizing herself.

The Silver Kiss Wins Kudos

In *The Silver Kiss*, seventeen-year-old Zoe finds her whole world in chaos as she watches her mother slowly die of cancer and her father withdraws into both his job and his sorrow. To make matters worse, her best friend and confidante is moving away. Even with her personal turmoil, Zoe remains aware of the things going on in her community—including a series of unsolved murders involving young women whose throats have been savagely cut and their bodies drained of all blood. Unafraid, she continues her evening walks in a nearby park, where she first catches sight of Simon, a handsome young man with silver hair, who turns out to be a three-hundred-year-old vampire.

Simon is not the vampire responsible for the evil that has befallen Zoe's community, however; that is the work of his younger brother, Christopher, who Simon is attempting to stop. Simon feels drawn to the attractive, melancholy young woman he sees walking alone in the dark, and he and Zoe ultimately become friends, their relationship based on both a strong physical and emotional attraction. Through their friendship, Simon and Zoe help each other come to terms with their inner turmoils and fears.

Highly praised by critics almost before it was released to bookstores, *The Silver Kiss* was based more on Klause's imagination than on her personal experiences. "My mother is still very much alive," she told *AAYA*, "and no one I know has gone through the experience of losing their mother to cancer while I've known them. The situation

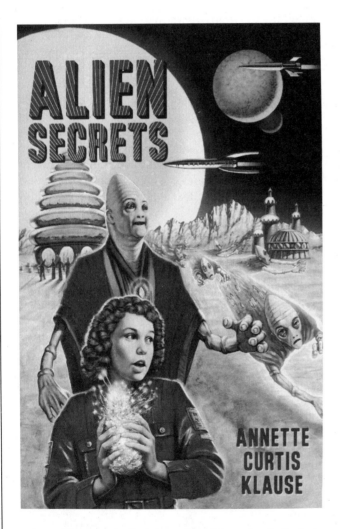

Having been expelled from boarding school, Puck is on her way back to the planet Shoon when she meets Hush, who is searching for a valuable treasure that has been stolen from him.

of Zoe's mother dying was suggested by a question my writing workshop teacher asked me. (The same person who talked me into writing a novel in the first place.) I told him my idea of a romance between a girl and a vampire, and he asked me, 'What would make a teenage girl so lonely and isolated that she would be susceptible to the charms of a vampire?' Once I decided that a dying mother and a friend moving away were both perfect answers, I discovered that the subplot leant all sorts of shadings to Zoe's relationship with Simon."

Calling Klause's debut novel "a unique contribution to the [vampire fiction] genre and to YA fiction," *Voice of Youth Advocates* contributor Samantha Hunt enthused that *The Silver Kiss* "raises larger issues such as the nature of good and evil, and the acceptance (or denial) of mortality" within its entertaining, horror-novel format. Commenting on the sexual aspects of the novel, Roger Sutton stated in a review for *Bulletin of the Center for Children's Books* that Klause's take on the "darkly erotic" traditional vampire story is "evoke[d] without over-the-top exploitation." And *Wilson Library Bulletin* reviewer Cathi MacRae contended that *The Silver Kiss* "marries every surefire ingredient of YA appeal with literary vision and graceful style. Gutwrenching horror, spine-tingling suspense, a romance of impossible longing, and realistic challenges all probe a sympathetic teen heroine into new growth and insight."

Takes Aim at the Stars with *Alien Secrets*

While Klause had a solid grounding in vampire lore before she began *The Silver Kiss*, her second novel would take her into the unknown—the world of science fiction. In *Alien Secrets*, readers are introduced to thirteen-year-old Puck, a girl from Earth going to join her parents on the planet Shoon in disgrace, having just been kicked out of school due to her bad grades. During her space voyage, Puck meets Hush, a Shoon native who is attempting to discover who robbed him of a valuable statue that has great spiritual value for his people. Puck and Hush soon become fellow sleuths, helping each other work through their personal issues while they jointly uncover the perpetrator of the robbery.

Because its mystery unfolds on a spaceship, *Alien Secrets* required more than the usual mystery novel's amount of preliminary research of its author. To construct her fictional world, Klause explained: "I did a certain amount of astronomy research. Which stars did scientists think might have planets around them? How far away were they and in which direction? If you were going on a trip, in which order would you go to them?" While the novel is less "hard" science-fiction—or SF—than an entertaining mystery story with some truly unique characters, Klause found that the answers to such technical questions were necessary before she could get the story off the ground.

Unlike the scientific aspects of the story, the futuristic elements of *Alien Secrets* were brainstormed rather than researched; Klause took the facts she had gathered, peppered them with the SF conven-

A beautiful teenage werewolf is caught between two worlds when she falls in love with two boys, one a human and the other a wolf.

tions she has been picking up since the fifth grade through her science-fiction reading, and then "tried to give things my own twist." In fact, she found that constructing the mystery was far more challenging than constructing the future world that frames it. "There were plenty of times I became stuck or wrote myself into a corner," Klause admitted to *AAYA.* "I had to make sure I planted enough clues and red herrings so the conclusion would never be obvious but would be perfectly logical and believable when it arrived. The technology and plot may not be fact, but the behavior of individuals must ring true no matter what the circumstances, else the reader won't believe the story. A writer must always be consistent and remain true to the rules of the universe she creates."

Alien Secrets "demonstrates Klause's versatility and affirms her talent," declared *Voice of Youth Advocates* contributor Donna L. Scanlon. Praising the novel's well-constructed plot and engaging characters, as well as its author's "mastery of the English language," Scanlon went on to note that Klause "maintains the suspense throughout and keeps the reader guessing until the very end." While Roger Sutton's enthusiasm was more restrained for Klause's second effort, he characterized Puck as a "plucky heroine" and praised the novel's non-stop action. Also praising Puck for a resilience and determination comparable to teen sleuth Nancy Drew, *School Library Journal* reviewer Susan L. Rogers added that Puck's "experiences with alien friends and enemies provide lessons applicable to the changing relationships between races and ethnic groups here on Earth."

"Sci-fi is a term usually used by people who don't read science fiction," Klause explained to *AAYA* regarding one of her favorite fiction genres and the type of person attracted to it. "It's often sarcastically applied by SF fans to bad science fiction movies. I have told the concerned parents of adolescent SF readers that they should celebrate. The young person who reads SF is often smarter than his or her schoolmates, has made the leap to abstract thought earlier than his or her colleagues, and is now engaged in exercising newfound powers of imagination and reasoning. Young SF readers have a greater ability to make leaps in perception, and the twists and turns of good science fiction are like brain candy to them. This doesn't mean they are always socially well-adapted if they spend too much time inside their heads, but many people strike a good balance. I'm sure there must be a research paper in what personality traits keep a person reading SF, but part of it is the need for adventure and a sense of wonder at the universe. While many people who read SF also read horror, I think different psychological needs are involved, and a person who loves one genre doesn't necessarily love the other. I think one of the unconscious reasons to read horror is to develop coping skills, to put a face on the fears we all have inside and fight them in the open."

Blood and Chocolate

Like *The Silver Kiss*, which contained "gruesome bits" that *Bulletin of the Center for Children's Books* contributor Roger Sutton deemed "viscerally effective, . . . with their well-spaced restraint and . . . controlled discretion," *Blood and Chocolate* contains more than a dash of violence. In an update of the werewolf legends, Klause spins a story of a beautiful young woman named Vivian, who can turn from woman to wolf at will. Living among others of her kind in a suburb of Maryland, she finds her affections caught between the virile Gabriel—a werewolf like herself—and the sensitive human Aiden, a "meat-boy" to her carnivorous companions. Meanwhile, pressures within her wolf pack force Vivian to come to terms with her dual nature—part socially acceptable human and part uninhibited wild animal.

If Klause "cooled her vampire's *Silver Kiss* for the puberty set, . . . she allows her werewolves all the unbounded heat and urgency of prime adolescence," in the opinion of *Horn Book* reviewer Lauren Adams. Remarking on the intense sexuality of the novel's protagonist, *Bulletin of the Center for Children's Books* contributor Deborah Stevenson stated that Klause's story is both "powerful" and "sexy", its author "reveling in the ferality of her characters and the overtones of legend." In *Voice of Youth Advocates*, contributor Beverly Youree maintained that young women in particular would empathize with Vivian's "desire for popularity, her rebellion against . . . other adults, her feeling of invincibility, and her wish to be part of a group." *Booklist* contributor Stephanie Zvirin also had high praise for *Blood and Chocolate*, calling Klause's book a "totally convincing" story "that can be read as feminist fiction, as smoldering romance, as a rites of passage

If you enjoy the works of Karen Hesse, you may also want to check out the following books and films:

Thomas Baird, *Where Time Ends*, 1988.
Hila Colman, *Rachel's Legacy*, 1979.
Erika Tamar, *Good-Bye, Glamour Girl*, 1984.
The Grapes of Wrath, a classic film starring Henry Fonda, 1940.

novel, or as a piercing reflection on human nature."

Brings Feminist Sensibility to Writing

Like Zvirin, several other critics have commented on the strong female characters that appear in Klause's stories. "I've often been able to relate to the way that guys look at things," the novelist stated, responding to the label. "I've never been much of a 'girl' girl either—none of that stereotype frills and make-up stuff for me—so perhaps that accounts for the idea that my writing is feminist. I just write about the sort of strong girls I would like to be, and I think my female readers want to be." Klause's ultimate aim is to create characters that she wants to spend time developing; although the "feminist" label pleases her, it is not something she consciously set out to acquire. "It especially pleases me that young men like my books," she stated. "I love it that I am breaking that stereotype that boys won't read about girls. They will if the girls are those they can respect." Of her ability to convincingly express a male character's viewpoint, she noted that "people are people, they just have different personalities that come into play. I've always gotten on well with guys and have had many male friends. Maybe that helps."

Working in a library setting has allowed Klause to not only stay close to her potential audience—kids who read books—but also to the kind of books being published for the young adult market. While she noted that the majority of teens prefer a quick read, "there are those who will tackle books of enormous length if they discover an author they love. There is plenty of rubbish out there and kids gobble it down the same way adults consume their own fluff, which doesn't mean they won't read 'good' books, too. . . . Young people are assigned plenty of classics by their teachers so I have no fear of them missing those; I worry more that they will hurry on to the adult section too fast and miss some of the brilliant books being written for teens. There are some truly excellent writers of young adult books that are much better writers than those writing many of the best sellers."

If her career as a librarian has exposed Klause to the wide range of new writers publishing in the YA field, her continued participation in a local writer's group has helped her career as a writer immeasurably. "It helps to know that there is a group of people eagerly awaiting what you have written and will help you out of jams when you're stuck," she acknowledged. Being in such a group "means trusting the people you are working with and not taking critiques personally," explained Klause, characterizing her own group as "tough but caring." Klause advises those who wish to start a writers' group of their own to seek out a number of people "writing at about the same level that are willing to listen to each other and not hog the limelight. People must be honest but not cruel. Some people pass out copies of their work for people to look at as they read aloud, others just have the group listen. Members can take turns reading aloud their work then listening to comments. Comments can be given by anyone jumping in, or the group could go around the circle one at a time." She recommended soliciting members of a new writing group through a local school, library, or by enrolling in a creative writing class at a local adult education community recreation program.

Klause, who resides in Maryland, is currently at work on her fourth YA novel, which she would only describe as having "a weird setting, a strange love story, and bizarre characters." While her books have continued to appeal to primarily a young adult market, she looks ahead to someday writing a picture book or, at the other end of the spectrum, books for older adults—"when my inner voice grows up." "Some of my poetry has been published in the past," she also admitted, "but I don't mention Cat's Magazine to serious poets." The most gratifying aspect Klause finds about being a novelist? "When teenage girls write to me and tell me they read my books over and over. Wow!"

■ Works Cited

Adams, Lauren, review of *Blood and Chocolate, Horn Book,* July-August, 1997, pp. 459-60.

Hunt, Samantha, review of *The Silver Kiss, Voice of Youth Advocates,* December, 1990, p. 299.

Klause, Annette Curtis, interview with J. Sydney Jones for *Something about the Author,* March 11, 1994.

Klause, Annette Curtis, interview with Pamela Shelton for *Authors and Artists for Young Adults,* September 25, 1998.

MacRae, Cathi, "Young Adult Perplex," in *Wilson Library Bulletin,* December, 1990, p. 124.

Rogers, Susan L., review of *Alien Secrets, School Library Journal,* September, 1993, p. 233.

Scanlon, Donna L., review of *Alien Secrets, Voice of Youth Advocates,* August, 1993, pp. 165-66.

Stevenson, Deborah, review of *Blood and Chocolate, Bulletin of the Center for Children's Books,* July-August, 1997, p. 400.

Sutton, Roger, review of *The Silver Kiss, Bulletin of the Center for Children's Books,* September, 1990, p. 10.

Sutton, Roger, review of *Alien Secrets, Bulletin of the Center for Children's Books,* September, 1993, p. 15.

Youree, Beverly, review of *Blood and Chocolate, Voice of Youth Advocates,* August, 1997, p. 193.

Zvirin, Stephanie, review of *Blood and Chocolate, Booklist,* June 1-15, 1997, p. 1694.

■ For More Information See

BOOKS

Seventh Book of Junior Authors and Illustrators, edited by Sally Holmes Holtze, H. W. Wilson, 1996.

Speaking for Ourselves, Too, edited by Donald Gallo, National Council of Teachers of English, 1993.

PERIODICALS

ALAN Review, spring, 1997.

Booklist, October 15, 1990, p. 439.

Horn Book, September-October, 1993, pp. 599-600.

Locus, July, 1990, p. 56; November, 1993, pp. 31, 56.

New York Times Book Review, April 21, 1991.

Publishers Weekly, July 27, 1990, p. 236; July 5, 1993, p. 74.

School Library Journal, September, 1988, pp. 120-23;
  September, 1990, p. 255.
Voice of Youth Advocates, April, 1993, p. 20.
Wilson Library Bulletin, March, 1991, p. 4.

—Sketch by Pamela Shelton

Susan Kuklin

■ Personal

Born September 6, 1941, in Philadelphia, PA; daughter of Albert E. (a builder) and Bertha (maiden name, Gussman) Greenbaum; married Bailey H. Kuklin (a professor of law), July 7, 1974. *Education:* New York University, B.S., 1963, M.A. (Asian theater), 1966. *Hobbies and other interests:* Dance, traveling, gardening (in pots on her roof terrace), reading (especially Chinese and Japanese fiction and the classics), visiting museums, theater concerts, opera.

■ Addresses

Home—New York, NY. *Office*-c/o Hyperion Press for Children, 114 Fifth Ave., New York, NY 10011.

■ Career

Photographer and writer. New York City Public Schools, New York City, English teacher, 1965-74; New York City Board of Education, New York City, curriculum developer, 1970-74; University of Tennessee, Knoxville, teacher of film studies, 1974-76; photojournalist, 1974—. Member of executive committee, Works Ballet Company. *Exhibitions:* "Fifty Years at the New York City Ballet," Lincoln Center Library, 1973; "Camera Infinity—Fourteen Photographers," Lever House, New York City, 1986. Work also exhibited in group shows in and around New York City. *Member:* PEN America, Authors Guild, Society of Children's Book Writers and Illustrators.

■ Awards, Honors

Outstanding Science Trade Book for Children award, National Science Teachers Association, 1980, for *The Story of Nim: The Chimp Who Learned Language;* Notable Children's Trade Book in the Field of Social Studies, National Council for Social Studies/Children's Book Council (NCSS/CBC), 1984, for *Mine for a Year; Thinking Big* named a Best Book of the Year by *School Library Journal* and International Board on Books for Young People, both 1986, and one of Child Study Association's Children's Books of the Year, 1987; *Reaching for Dreams: A Ballet from Rehearsal to Opening Night* named a best book of 1987, American Library Association (ALA) and the New York Public Library; best children's book award, San Francisco *Chronicle*, Names Project Award, "Words Project for AIDS," and Association of Childrens' Librarians of Northern California Best Book, all 1989, Best Book of the Year and Best Book for Reluctant Readers, ALA, all for *Fighting Back: What Some People Are*

Doing about AIDS; Carter G. Woodson award, Outstanding Merit Book award, NCSS, and Pick of the List, American Book Sellers, all 1992, all for *How My Family Lives in America;* Best Book for Reluctant Young Adult Readers, Best of the Year, New York Public Library, both 1993, and *Hungry Mind* best nonfiction book of 1994, all for *Speaking Out: Teenagers Take on Race, Sex, and Identity;* ALA Best Books, Best Book for Reluctant Young Adult Readers, Best of the Year, New York Public Library, and Suicide Prevention Award, Robert Wood Johnson Medical School Annual Regional Survivors of Suicide Conference (Piscataway, NJ), all 1994, all for *After a Suicide: Young People Speak Up;* Christopher Award, 1997, Cooperative Children's Book Center Choice Book, and Voice of Youth Advocates Nonfiction honor list, 17 & 74 Books award, Amnesty International, all 1996, all for *Irrepressible Spirit: Conversations with Human Rights Activists.*

■ Writings

NONFICTION

Fighting Back: What Some People Are Doing about AIDS, Putnam, 1988.
What Do I Do Now: Talking about Teenage Pregnancy, Putnam, 1991.
Speaking Out: Teenagers Take on Race, Sex, and Identity, Putnam, 1993.
After a Suicide: Young People Speak Up, Putnam, 1994.
Irrepressible Spirit: Conversations with Human Rights Activists, Putnam, 1996.
Iqbal Masih and the Crusaders Against Child Slavery, Holt, 1998.

PHOTO-ESSAYS FOR YOUNG PEOPLE

Mine for a Year, Coward, 1984.
Thinking Big: The Story of a Young Dwarf, Lothrop, 1986.
Reaching for Dreams: A Ballet from Rehearsal to Opening Night, Lothrop, 1987.
When I See My Doctor, Bradbury Press, 1988.
When I See My Dentist, Bradbury Press, 1988.
Taking My Cat to the Vet, Bradbury Press, 1988.
Taking My Dog to the Vet, Bradbury Press, 1988.
Going to My Ballet Class, Bradbury Press, 1989.
Going to My Nursery School, Bradbury Press, 1990.
Going to My Gymnastics Class, Bradbury Press, 1991.

How My Family Lives in America, Bradbury Press, 1992.
Fighting Fires, Bradbury Press, 1993.
From Head to Toe: How a Doll Is Made, Hyperion, 1994.
Kodomo: Children of Japan, Putnam (New York City), 1995.
Fireworks: The Science, the Art, and the Magic, Hyperion, 1996.
(With Bill T. Jones) *Dance,* Hyperion, 1998.

PHOTOGRAPHER

Herbert Terrace, *Nim,* Knopf, 1979.
(With Herbert Terrace) Anna Michel, *The Story of Nim: The Chimp Who Learned Language,* Knopf, 1979.
Paul Thompson, *The Hitchhikers,* F. Watts, 1980.
Linda Atkinson, *Hit and Run,* F. Watts, 1981.
Gene DeWesse, *Nightmares in Space,* F. Watts, 1981.
(Contributor) *How Animals Behave,* National Geographic Society Books, 1984.
(Contributor) Terry Miller, *Greenwich Village and How It Got That Way,* Crown, 1990.
(Contributor) Robert Lacy, editor, *Balanchine's Ballerinas,* Simon & Schuster, 1984.

Contributor of photos and essays to periodicals, including *Time, Newsweek, Psychology Today, New York, New York Times, Pegasus, Us, Der Spiegel, Science, Dance, Discovery, Cricket, Woman, Junior Scholastic, Viva, Family Weekly,* and *Planned Parenthood Review.*

■ Work in Progress

An untitled book about a criminal trial for middle-graders, for Penguin.

■ Sidelights

Photojournalist Susan Kuklin follows her natural curiosity, her strong desire to promote social justice, and her fascination with people when embarking on each new project for children. She explains that her books take on a life of their own once the subjects get involved. "Sometimes the books seem to be writing themselves, taking me someplace extraordinary where I have never been before," the New York City-based former schoolteacher told *Authors and Artists for Young Adults (AAYA).* Working as an author and illustrator of photo-essays for young children since the early-1980s—among her many books are *Reaching for Dreams: A Ballet from Rehearsal to Opening Night, How My Family Lives in America*, and *Kodomo: Children of Japan*, Kuklin has also written several topical nonfiction books for older teens that grapple with controversial subjects. The straight-talking *Speaking Out: Teenagers Take on Race, Sex, and Identity*, published in 1993, would be among her most popular works for older teen readers.

Born in Philadelphia, Pennsylvania, in 1941, Kuklin developed an early interest in the arts. "Going to the opera, ballet, or theater with my family was my idea of a wonderful time," she once recalled. "At night my grandmother would read to me Russian fables and short stories, and I spent a great deal of time at the public library. I fondly remember looking at long wooden shelves filled with books thinking that I must read all of them before I grow up." Despite her love of reading, Kuklin's childhood career aspiration was to become a dancer; by the time she was in her teens, her dream of being a dancer had changed to being an actress, and after graduation she enrolled at New York University with a major in theatre arts, going on to further study in world theatre during graduate school. Living in Manhattan also provided Kuklin with the opportunity to work alongside some of the most notable stage actresses of the 1960s; while apprenticing with Joseph Papp's famous Shakespeare Festival along with summers at Philadelphia's Playhouse in the Park she got to know Jessica Tandy, Geraldine Page, and Hume Cronin.

Learning to "See" in a New Way

During graduate school at New York University, Kuklin's interest in acting began to lessen in relationship to her growing interest in directing stage productions. "While acting [had] taught me how to interpret a part, directing forced me to look at the big picture which included a visual application of the art," she once explained. "I learned about framing, position, lighting, movement, and so on." This new way of seeing would prove useful in Kuklin's ultimate career: as a photographer and an author and illustrator of nonfiction. She also balanced her interest in the stage with an interest in art, particularly the art and literature of Asia, the spareness of which would also later characterize her photography.

However, Kuklin didn't jump immediately from stage direction to photography. During the late 1960s she worked as an English teacher in New York City public schools, using drama to inspire her students—mostly from the inner city—with a love of words. In 1973 she and her husband, law professor Bailey Kuklin, moved to Knoxville, Tennessee, where she got a job teaching film studies at the University of Tennessee. It was during this point in her life that her talent for photography, which had mostly been confined to vacation and family snapshots, became apparent. The "rugged individualism" of the people living in the rural regions of the area fascinated her, and to meet and photograph them, she began to travel with a local Planned Parenthood branch that visited rural families, thus gaining the confidence of these wary people. Coupling her visual skills with her natural curiosity, Kuklin compiled her first photo-essay, a study of the hill people of the Smoky Mountain region titled "Appalachian Families." Her new career as a photojournalist was born.

As more and more publishers became interested in using works from her growing portfolio, Kuklin taught herself everything she could about photography—from shooting technique to darkroom chemistry and the works of major photographers. Her first book-length illustration assignment, Anna Michel and Herbert Terrace's *The Story of Nim: The Chimp Who Learned Language*, was published in 1979. This project opened the way for a wide variety of journalist assignments, from accompanying policemen in the South Bronx to photographing a New York City Ballet production choreographed by George Balanchine. Although working on such projects was interesting, Kuklin liked the feeling of really understanding a subject that she had acquired while working on *The Story of Nim*; she decided to tackle another children's book. In 1984 *Mine for a Year*, the story of an almost-blind boy who is given the opportunity to care for a puppy destined to be trained as a seeing-eye dog, was published. Created for young children, it would be the first of many photo-essays with first-person text that she has published.

People Can Make a Difference

Kuklin believes that if people—both kids and adults—are given clear information, they become empowered to go out into the world and do something with that knowledge. This belief is the motivation behind her books for teens. "There are many subjects that people are not really willing to touch on," she explained in her *AAYA* interview, "and some of those subjects are very, very close to my heart." She continued, "I want to bring information to teenagers and then let them make their own decisions about whether or not to deal with it. I try not to judge; its my readers' job to judge." Kuklin added that she thinks of her books as "the beginning of a conversation. They are simply the tools to start the conversation. Then I hope the teens will take it from there."

Kuklin's *What Do I Do Now: Talking about Teen Pregnancy* presents the many issues, questions, and ethical dilemmas that teenagers and their families confront when a young woman becomes pregnant. It took Kuklin more than two years to research and write the book. In order to interview the pregnant teenagers, she had to gain the confidence of the professionals—doctors, nurses, counselors—who worked at a Planned Parenthood clinic, an abortion clinic, an adoption center, and a hospital. She attended clinic meetings and retreats. After a while she was invited to meet the teenagers. "None of the pregnant teenagers took their situation lightly," Kuklin recalled. "They were frightened and vulnerable. Their decision about whether or not to continue their pregnancy was very carefully thought out." In time, some of these young women were comfortable enough to talk candidly about their choices, such as giving up their newborn to adoptive parents. Some of the young women allowed Kuklin to be present during the abortion procedure itself.

What Do I Do Now deals with a controversial topic, which Kuklin attempted to present in a balanced way, although making clear her own feelings about abortion. Her efforts have met with success, according to many reviewers. "The experiences these girls describe are more informative than a factual compendium. . . . Kuklin has . . . [created] a natural flow to ease young readers through a series of stories that may help prevent them from becoming a statistic," according to Betsy Hearne in *Bulletin of the Center for Children's Books*. Libby K. White commented in *School Library Journal* that "Kuklin is frank about her sympathies for the Planned Parenthood approach," in contrast to her more negative slant on experiences with pro-life groups. However, White continues, the book contains "Solid information, soberly presented, without moralization or strident activism."

Praising Kuklin's empathy for the young mothers portrayed in the book, Laura L. Lent stated in *Voice of Youth Advocates* that in *What Do I Do Now?* "Kuklin does not attempt to judge any of these young woman or to anger the reader. Her motivation is simple—to inform her audience, not to moralize." Reviewers also applauded Kuklin's addition of a glossary of medical terms included in the volume.

Confronts Prejudice with *Speaking Out*

The publication of *Speaking Out* was the culmination of a year spent at Manhattan's Bayard Rustin High School for the Humanities; it includes interviews with numerous students and faculty reflecting their feelings about the effects of racial, cultural, and gender-based prejudice on their lives. "Choosing the school was the easy part," Kuklin explained. "I called the Superintendent of Schools in Manhattan, who I knew. She said, 'I have just the school for you.' Bayard Rustin is the city's most ethnically diverse school—one quarter each Latino, Asian American, African American, and white. The student body includes children from homeless families to children of ambassadors. Also, it was a well-run, caring school with an excellent administration and faculty."

Kuklin spent the entire first semester "just hanging out with the kids" and sitting in on classes before beginning the interview process. She wanted time to get to know them, and soon felt confident in letting the teens take charge of the direction of the book. "*They* led *me*," the author explained. "The students told me, 'Go to this teacher; there's a really good lesson being taught tomorrow.' Or 'You should meet such and such a person.'" Kuklin was at the high school almost everyday, which after working as a teacher made her feel right at home. "I didn't have the responsibility of lesson plans and marking exams; I could just enjoy the kids," she laughed.

Taping interviews began during the second semester. Cooperation from the students was so extensive that, before she knew it, Kuklin had what amounted to a six hundred-page book on her hands. "I told everyone that I could not guarantee that they were going to get in," she remembered, "so if they were going to be hurt and feel left out, they should think about that before the interviews. But I kept sixty to seventy percent of the interviews." Finally, after over a year of taping and listening and interviewing, it was time for photographs. And, once again, Kuklin let the teens take charge. "They said they wanted their photographs to be a cross between the styles of Robert Mapplethorpe and Richard Avedon. I explained that would require special lighting. We converted a classroom into a studio, and I put one student in charge of setting up photography appointments and making sure that the posers—students and teachers—were there on time." Each person then worked with the author to select which photos they wanted included in the book. By the time *Speaking Out* reached bookstore shelves in 1993 it had truly become a collaborative effort.

Speaking Out received praise from both readers and reviewers. Noting that the author does not editorialize in any way, Stephanie Zvirin commented in *Booklist* that the volume "makes clear the insidious nature of prejudice, and it will inspire readers to think about the stereotypes they

REACHING
FOR DREAMS
A Ballet from Rehearsal to Opening Night

BY SUSAN KUKLIN

The result of in-depth interviews as well as observation, the author's 1987 photo essay chronicles the work of the Alvin Ailey American Dance Theater.

have acquired from their parents, from television, from their friends, and from what they read." "Many of these testimonies are heartbreaking, some are uplifting, some are terrifying; every single one is memorable," maintained Susan Dunn in *Voice of Youth Advocates*, while Roger Sutton noted in his appraisal for *Bulletin of the Center for Children's Book* that Kuklin's black-and-white photos "have a candor and immediacy missing in yearbook pictures, and many teens will see themselves within these pages."

Suicide: A Teen Tragedy

During the year she spent at Bayard Rustin High School, Kuklin learned that suicide was a topic that came up frequently; she was shocked to learn how many young people's lives it had touched. This insight sparked her 1994 book *After a Suicide: Young People Speak Up,* which is divided into sections dealing with survivors—school friends and family members left to deal with their grief after a teen takes his or her own life—and interviews with a teen who attempted suicide and another who thought seriously about it. "For *After a Suicide,* I purposefully did not pick anyone who was very close in time to the suicide," Kuklin noted of her interviewing technique, "because those families were going through such a difficult time. There were too many unanswered questions." She wanted to illustrate the mourning process; what happens after a teen commits suicide and what the people left behind can expect to experience in reaction. "Unfortunately," Kuklin explained in describing the audience for her book, "they'll be new families who have to deal with this issue. With *After a Suicide* the reader can see many differing aspects of the healing process and perhaps identify with the people in the book. Hopefully, the families will be able to talk about what they are experiencing. The pain never goes away, but they can learn they are not alone, and how others deal with it."

Kuklin has received many letters from readers in response to her books, letters that, she told *AAYA,* "mean a great deal to me." One in particular touched her deeply. "A young man from Texas told me that he bought my book *After a Suicide* for a friend who admitted to feeling suicidal. The friend read the book and was able to hear what the interviewees had to say. He then was able to talk to his family and get professional help." The

If you enjoy the works of Susan Kuklin, you may also want to check out the following books:

Russell Freedman, *Lincoln: A Photobiography*, 1987, and *Kids at Work: Lewis Hine and the Crusade against Child Labor*, 1994.
Brent Ashabranner, *Into a Strange Land: Unaccompanied Refugee Youth in America*, 1987.

letter-writer credited the book with saving the boy's life. "I was thrilled," Kuklin stated. "Helping that one unidentified young man made the year's work worthwhile." Reviewers have been equally moved; William R. Mollineaux declared in *Voice of Youth Advocates* that "The book merits its greatest praise for being a suicide deterrent, for I believe that any reader contemplating suicide will reconsider this final act." "Many books on teen suicide discuss aspects of the effects on survivors," added *School Library Journal* contributor Libby K. White, "but Kuklin's is the only one that considers their predicament so thoroughly, sympathetically, and intelligently."

Gives Voice to Human Rights Activists

Of all the books Kuklin has written, *Irrepressible Spirit* is closest to her heart. Containing interviews with eleven human rights activists from around the world, the book recounts both the history and motivation of each individual and the basic human rights—among them the right to live, to have free speech, to chose one's own religion, and to have equality before the law—they are attempting to restore. Abuses committed in China, Cuba, Haiti, Bosnia, and the United States are among those covered in a book that critics have noted addresses a difficult subject matter. As Susan Dove Lempke commented in *Booklist*, "Readers will find [*Irrepressible Spirit*] depressing, but with the personal messages . . . they may find it inspiring as well."

"I don't think that reliance on pat, sound-bite endings where everybody lives happily ever after does a service to a young person," Kuklin responds. "Also, I don't think one should leave young readers with a sense of total hopelessness. I want to try to empower them, not depress them. For all the atrocities that take place in *Irrepressible Spirit*, there's always a person there who stands up and confronts it or is able to deal with it in an unusual way." Noting that the work requires a mature readership, Tracey Kroll wrote in *School Library Journal* that *Irrepressible Spirit* "is a quality book that will stir strong emotions and raise awareness," and *Bulletin of the Center for Children's Books* reviewer Deborah Stevenson called it "far more energizing than series nonfiction about global strife," noting that Kuklin's book "will offer teens an idea of the varied forms 'good works' can take and how challenging and exciting they can be."

A Balance between Tragedy and Joy

Kuklin's books for teens have required her to spend a great deal of time with people who have experienced tragedy in their lives, so she also works on more lighthearted fare to maintain a balance. Her photo-essays for younger children have been a way to achieve this balance. While working on *After a Suicide*—which Kuklin admitted would sometimes "really get me down, because I felt so bad for the families"—she also photographed *From Head to Toe: How a Doll Is Made*, spending hours at the Madame Alexander doll factory. *Irrepressible Spirit* was balanced by work on *Fireworks: The Science, the Art, and the Magic*. Even though the subjects of some of the YA books were heart-wrenching to work on, the people she interviewed in all the books were always inspirational. In *After a Suicide*, she explained, "the families were so wonderful that they made me want to dig deeper and deeper, in order to do a good job for them." And about *Irrepressible Spirit*, she commented: "I thought the people in that book were so brave, so inspiring. They just blew me away."

One of the noteworthy aspects of Kuklin's books for young adult readers is her ability as a photographer. As she explained to *AAYA*, during the interview process the photography comes after she has established a bond with her subject. The photography is then "a way of graphically pinpointing who some of the people are in my books. A photographic portrait is different from a snapshot. There needs to be a strong connection between the photographer and the subject. I try to get everyone to be completely relaxed when they pose in front of my camera."

In contrast to her books for teen readers, Kuklin's books for younger children, full-color photo essays, are "photography-driven. For my pre-school books I start with the camera; the text comes much later," she explained to *AAYA*. "Actually I'm more comfortable working this way because I started as a photographer, not a writer."

The Creation of a Story

Kuklin explained the process of creating *How My Family Lives in America* as an example of the way her books evolve. The 1992 work, which focuses on the family traditions of three children—Sanu is part Senegalese, part American; Eric's parents are from Puerto Rico; and April's parents were born in Taiwan. Creating this book required the participation of not only the three children but also their families. "I met a number of families from each ethnic group to determine who would be articulate and who would be willing to participate in the project," Kuklin recalled of the first stages. Once the three families were chosen, "we start to get to know one another and spend time together—a couple of hours just chatting or having a meal." However, Kuklin believes the participation of the children are the key to her projects. In *How My Family Lives in America*, she asked Sanu, Eric, and April each to make a list of everything they thought other children should know about them. Afterward she reviewed the lists to be sure that each child contributed something slightly different. Then she began photographing.

Kuklin's equipment is bulky, particularly the heavy lighting necessary to take photographs indoors. She has to create a "set." "I use a medium format camera and heavy strobes. There are assistants running about taking light readings and moving cables. The children must be very careful or they could get hurt. Everyone pitches in and does his or her part." In one instance, Kuklin had to light the different areas of the house to photograph the family's activities during meal preparation. "Sanu's family and I were comfortable with each other. They were devoted to the book. They cooked in their kitchen while I photographed. As I moved the hot lights into the dining area, the family changed to their traditional clothing and began eating. It was a delicious production." The relaxed atmosphere Kuklin manages to create with her subjects has come across to reviewers as well; noting that the photographs "are clear, informal, affectionate, upbeat," *Booklist* contributor Hazel Rochman remarked that *How My Family Lives in America* allows "kids [to] see the richness in diversity and the connections among the human family."

Kuklin traveled to Asia for her 1995 photo-essay, *Kodomo: Children of Japan.* "My husband and I visited a friend who was the director of the Radiation Effects Research Foundation in Hiroshima. Some of the youngsters who appear in *Kodomo* are the children of the doctors and nurses who made up his staff." Kuklin spent six weeks with seven children, ranging in age from eight to fourteen, communicating with them through a translator. Despite the language barrier, the book was created using the same process as *How My Family Lives in America.* The Japanese children "told me what they wanted American kids to know about themselves. They were friendly and affectionate and fun and giggly. I had a great time getting to know them." While Kuklin was in Japan, she developed a close relationship with not only the children but their families as well. "The mothers and I did a lot of comparison shopping," she laughed. "I think that when you go into any culture you find that some of the trappings are different, but basically the wants and the needs are the same."

Kodomo—the word means "children" in Japanese—would prove to be popular with both young children and critics. Commenting on the background information on Japanese culture that Kuklin provides throughout the book, *Bulletin of the Center for Children's Books* reviewer Roger Sutton noted that *Kodomo* "is quite browsable and the excellent photos offer their own rewards." In *School Library Journal*, contributor John Philbrook observed that Kuklin's "full-color photographs are excellent, lively, and sometimes humorous, capturing the variety and individuality of these young people far better than the text."

Continues Broadening Young Readers' Minds

A story that captured Kuklin's imagination has been transformed by her into *Iqbal Masih and the Crusaders Against Child Slavery.* "This book is the true story about a little boy, Iqbal, who at age four was sold by his parents in Pakistan for $12.00 to pay for his older brother's wedding," she explained. "He was sold to a carpetmaker and worked chained to a loom until he was ten. He escaped, learned to read and write, and then went on to free three thousand other children. Iqbal visited Boston where he was eventually awarded the Reebok Human Rights award."

The book concerns child slavery, another complicated and difficult subject. The story was especially difficult because Iqbal was tragically murdered soon after he returned from Boston to Pakistan. To learn more about Iqbal Masih, Kuklin worked with a number of human rights organizations, such as UNICEF, Human Rights Watch, and the Human Rights Commission of Pakistan. She interviewed people who had met Iqbal, including a group of middle-school students in Quincy, Massachusetts, a small town near Boston. Iqbal's death shocked the young American students. They resolved to do something to help the bonded children in Pakistan. The children set up a Web site on the Internet where they described modern child slavery and the amazing odyssey of Iqbal Masih. They asked other children their age to send them a nominal donation of $12. The number "twelve" was chosen as a symbol because Iqbal had been sold into bondage for that sum and was killed when he was twelve. With the money they continue to raise, the students built a school in Pakistan in Iqbal's memory. *Iqbal Masih and the Crusaders Against Child Slavery* is also about these (and other) dedicated people who are working to end contemporary child slavery.

Kuklin has gained a great deal of personal satisfaction from devoting her career to creating books for young people. She has been impressed by the cooperation she has received from her youngest subjects. "When it's time to photograph or do an interview, they know this is 'business'; its time to be serious." She never has problems with tantrums or children acting out. Barring parents from the set is a help in keeping younger children focused on the job of being a photographers' model. "The kids are wonderful, and the teenagers are wonderful," she exclaimed. "I love that they are so open; much more open than adults. If you ask them a simple question—and if you listen—they'll give you a simple answer. It's that easy. Young people say 'This is who I am; this is what I think about; this is where I'm coming from.' And that's

it. It's marvelously rewarding for me to be able to work with them."

■ Works Cited

Dunn, Susan, review of *Speaking Out, Voice of Youth Advocates,* June, 1993, pp. 116-17.

Hearne, Betsy, review of *What Do I Do Now?, Bulletin of the Center of Children's Books,* November, 1991, pp. 66-67.

Kroll, Tracey, review of *Irrepressible Spirit: Conversations with Human Rights Activists, School Library Journal,* April, 1996, p. 162.

Kuklin, Susan, interview with Pamela Shelton for *Authors and Artists for Young Adults,* June, 1998.

Lempke, Susan Dove, review of *Irrepressible Spirit: Conversations with Human Rights Activists, Booklist,* May 1, 1996, p. 1503.

Lent, Laura L, review of *What Do I Do Now?, Voice of Youth Advocates,* August, 1991, p. 190.

Mollineaux, William R., review of *After a Suicide, Voice of Youth Advocates,* February, 1995, p. 360.

Philbrook, John, review of *Kodomo: Children of Japan, School Library Journal,* August, 1995, p. 148.

Rochman, Hazel, review of *How My Family Lives in America, Booklist,* March 1, 1992, pp. 1282-83.

Stevenson, Deborah, review of *Irrepressible Spirit: Conversations with Human Rights Activists, Bulletin of the Center for Children's Books,* September, 1996, p. 19.

Sutton, Roger, review of *Speaking Out, Bulletin of the Center for Children's Books,* October, 1993.

Sutton, Roger, review of *Kodomo: Children of Japan, Bulletin of the Center of Children's Books,* April, 1995, p. 279.

White, Libby K., review of *What Do I Do Now?, School Library Journal,* July, 1991.

White, Libby K., review of *After a Suicide, School Library Journal,* December, 1994, p. 135.

Zvirin, Stephanie, review of *Speaking Out, Booklist,* August, 1993, p. 2061.

■ For More Information See

PERIODICALS

Booklist, September 1, 1984, p. 67; March 1, 1987, p. 1005; May 1, 1988, p. 1525; September 15, 1989, p. 185; June 1-15, 1996, pp. 1710-11.

Bulletin of the Center for Children's Books, July-August, 1984, p. 207; May, 1986, p. 170; April, 1987, pp. 149-50; March, 1989, p. 174; October, 1989,

p. 36; November, 1991, p. 66; April, 1992, pp. 212-13; October, 1993, p. 49; January, 1995, p. 170; April, 1995, p. 279; September, 1996, p. 19; November, 1998, pp. 103-4.

Horn Book, September, 1984, p. 607; July-August, 1986, p. 466; May/June, 1987, p. 357; January, 1989, p. 91; September-October, 1989, p. 639.

Kirkus Reviews, March 1, 1987, p. 383; April 15, 1988, p. 620; December 15, 1988, p. 1813.

New York Times Book Review, July 1, 1984, p. 23; January 22, 1989, p. 29.

Publishers Weekly, March 18, 1988, p. 84.

School Library Journal, October, 1984, p. 158; August, 1986, pp. 83-84; May, 1987, p. 114; August, 1988, p. 89; October, 1988, p. 133; December, 1988, p. 99; February, 1989, p. 106; September, 1989, p. 241; November, 1990, p. 104; December, 1991, p. 111; March, 1992, p. 231; July, 1993, p. 108; September, 1993, p. 225; December, 1994, pp. 135-36; August, 1995, p. 148; April, 1996, pp. 146, 162.

Voice of Youth Advocates, December, 1987, p. 250; April, 1989, p. 59; August, 1991, p. 190; February, 1995, pp. 359-60.

—Sketch by Pamela Shelton

Marie G. Lee

Book Writers and Illustrators, Authors Guild, Authors League of America, Asian American Arts Alliance, Committee Against Anti-Asian Violence, National Coalition Against Censorship, Asian American Writer's Workshop (president and member of board of directors, 1992-97).

■ Personal

Born April 25, 1964, in Hibbing, MN; daughter of William Chae-Sik (a physician) and Grace Koom-Soon (a social worker) Lee; married Karl H. Jacoby (a history professor), June 28, 1997. *Education:* Brown University, A.B., 1986. *Politics:* Independent. *Religion:* Christian. *Hobbies and other interests:* Tae kwon do, skiing, rollerblading.

■ Addresses

Agent—Wendy Schmalz, Harold Ober Associates, 425 Madison Ave., New York, NY 10017.

■ Career

Data Resources/Standard and Poor's, New York City, consultant, 1986-88; Goldman Sachs and Co., New York City, editor, equity research, 1988-90; instructor of literature and creative writing, Yale University, 1996; freelance writer. Member, Read Aloud (New York City school volunteer program). *Member:* PEN, Society of Children's

■ Awards, Honors

Best Book Award, Friends of American Writers, Best Book for Reluctant Readers citation, American Library Association (ALA), and New York Public Library Books for the Teen Age citation, all 1992, and Children's Choice citation, International Reading Association, 1994, all for *Finding My Voice;* Books for the Teen Age citations, New York Public Library, for *If It Hadn't Been for Yoon Jun* and *Saying Goodbye;* honorable mention, O. Henry Awards, 1997, for a short story; Books for the Teen Age citation, New York Public Library, 1997, and Best Books for Young Adults citation, ALA, 1998, for *Necessary Roughness;* Fulbright Scholar in Korea, 1997-98; Lee's work has been cited by the National Conference of Christians and Jews in *The Human Family . . . Learning to Live Together.*

■ Writings

Finding My Voice, Houghton, 1992.
If It Hadn't Been for Yoon Jun, Houghton, 1993.
Saying Goodbye, Houghton, 1994.

Necessary Roughness, HarperCollins, 1996.
Night of the Chupacabras, Avon, 1998.
F is for Fabuloso, Avon, 1999.

Lee's works have been anthologized in *Matters of Fact,* Prentice-Hall, 1992, *New Worlds of Literature,* Norton, 1994, and *New Year, New Love,* Avon, 1996. Also author of an editorial opinion essay in the *New York Times,* "We Koreans Need an Al Sharpton," 1991. Lee's adult fiction has also appeared in the *Kenyon Review* and *American Voice.*

■ Work in Progress

A collection of short stories for adults.

■ Sidelights

In her young adult novels, *Finding My Voice, If It Hadn't Been for Yoon Jun, Saying Goodbye,* and *Necessary Roughness,* Marie G. Lee has created a blueprint for what it is like to grow up an outsider in America: the racial taunts, the feeling of otherness, the gestalt and internal disharmony that result from finally *discovering* that you are "different." Lee, an Asian American, has written out of her own deeply felt experiences growing up in America's heartland, the only Korean in her small hometown. "I write coming-of-age stories of people who, for some reason, feel different than those around them," Lee told *Authors and Artists for Young Adult (AAYA)* in an interview. For Lee, that "reason" is most often ethnic background. "I didn't have anything like [my books] when I was growing up and wish I did," Lee continued. "I really wish there was a book describing how it felt to be called a 'chink,' to have teachers making nasty jokes about how Koreans eat dog. Asian Americans inhabit a tricky place because while our looks will always deny us from looking totally 'American,' we do not have that 'angry minority' spot to identify with. Black Panthers, A.I.M., La Raza—but Angry Asians?"

Lee's characters must contend with many of the obstacles Lee herself did growing up. Ellen Sung in *Finding My Voice* is the only Asian in a small American high school, anxious to get on with all the normal adolescent desires—hanging out with her girl friends, finding a boy friend, and getting into a good college—but first she must learn to deal with racism. Ellen's story is also featured in the sequel, *Saying Goodbye,* in which she deals with another form of discrimination as a freshman at Harvard. Alice Larsen in *If It Hadn't Been for Yoon Jun* is another Korean American protagonist, but in this scenario, Alice, who was adopted at birth by American parents, must confront her own unconscious racism. The narrowness of small town America is also examined in *Necessary Roughness* when Chan Kim and his twin sister, Young, move to all-white Iron River, Minnesota, from multicultural Los Angeles.

"I have been asked more than once when I am going to be through with the 'race thing' and go onto more 'universal themes,'" Lee noted in an *ALAN Review* article. "I always answer that with a 'probably never.' Toni Morrison has gone so far as to say that she's never ever really felt she was an American. I don't take that extreme a view, but I do feel that growing up a person of color in this country, one that traces its history back to Anglo-European foundations, has had the effect that my perceptions of American life are inevitably filtered through a prism of race. . . . [A] writer has to know herself first, or her work won't be honest; and for me, being an American of Korean descent and being a writer are inextricably linked."

Through the Prism of Race

"I grew up in a very small town in Minnesota— Hibbing—which, perhaps not coincidentally, is where Bob Dylan also grew up," Lee told *AAYA.* "In a small town it's easy to know who's 'in' or 'out,' and not only was I a shy, bookish kid, but our family was the only family of color in town. So I spent a lot of time holed up in the library, not only because I liked to read (which is still true) but also because it was easier than dealing with the kids from school." Lee's parents immigrated from Korea in 1953; her father was a physician and her mother a social worker. Theirs was a comfortable upper-middle class life. "My parents were not the typical Korean American parents. They let me have a lot of privacy, and, besides bugging me to study, basically left me alone." It was this time on her own in her youth, "just dreaming," that Lee credits with making her a writer. She also spent much of her time with a best friend, "having those kinds of conversations you have when you're a kid."

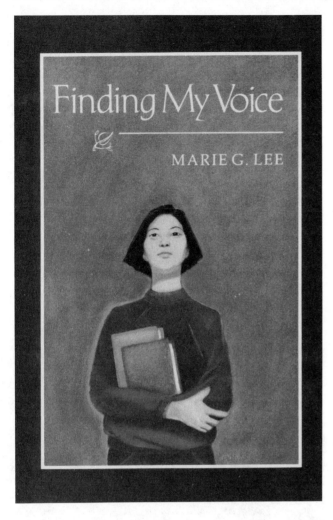

Finding My Voice

MARIE G. LEE

The only Asian person at her school, Ellen spends her senior year struggling with racism and her parents' expectations for her.

But there was always the background noise of race and difference for Lee. "Throughout my life—starting from age three or four—I heard a lot of racist insults. Mostly it was people calling me chink, yelling from cars. But it also included teachers saying things right to my face, and in high school, there were always these girls who were trying to beat me up." Lee did well at school, a motivated student whose father hoped that she and her three siblings would follow in his career. "I was basically a nerd but tried to hide it," she told *AAYA*. "It was definitely not cool to be smart at my school. I was writing a lot all through my childhood and teenage years but didn't share it with people, although my friends and I sometimes showed each other our poems." There were no books on growing up

Asian American in Lee's youth, so she "devoured" books about alienation, such as *The Catcher in the Rye* and *The Outsiders.*

Lee also recounted in *ALAN Review* her desire to fit in. She and her friends were avid readers of *Seventeen* magazine, where she first published an essay at age sixteen. She, like her friends, identified with the all-white models who posed for the magazine. Lee saw herself as one of the blond, Scandinavian types she was growing up with, though all the while she felt like someone trying to "force your feet into a pair of shoes that you love but that don't fit." At a state hockey tournament as captain of the cheerleaders, Lee was offered a *Seventeen*-style make over by a local department store. "At last, I thought. *Seventeen* was going to turn me into one of those All-American girls!" But when the hairdresser and beautician were finished, Lee looked in the mirror and saw that she had been given a "China chop" haircut and eyes teased into a Cleopatra look with eyeliner. "I was humiliated," Lee wrote in *ALAN Review.* "Looking back to that time, I can see that there was definitely a sort of two-way cognitive dissonance going on: I thought of myself as culturally white, or least All-American; other people—even my friends—saw me as a China doll. I was neither."

Finding Her Voice

Lee attended Brown University, and there she gave up the idea of someday becoming a doctor like her father. "I realized that would be impossible for me, someone as squeamish as I was," Lee told *AAYA*. "I was still a dutiful daughter and majored in economics so I could get a 'real' job, but all this time I was still planning to be a writer." She had come to that determination when she got her first typewriter. Publication of her essay in *Seventeen* was a confirmation of this early desire, and by the time she left for college, her drawers were crammed with finished stories.

Out of college, Lee worked in a research firm that used computer-generated models to predict what the economy would do. "Of course, as an aspiring writer, this wasn't a great job. Later I moved to Goldman Sachs, an investment bank. This made my parents really happy, but it only solidified my desire to get out of the corporate world." Meanwhile, Lee was learning how to write in her free time. She had several fine teachers, including Nancy Willard, who taught her a new way to look at her work. "Nancy basically confirmed for me that what I was writing was really valuable. It wasn't until then that I really started writing with confidence," Lee explained to *AAYA*.

What Lee was writing was her first novel, *Finding My Voice*. As Lee once described it in *Something about the Author*, the inspiration for that book resulted from a ski trip. "I was back home in Minnesota, and my dad and I were driving to go skiing. To get to the local ski hill, you have to pass through a few towns even smaller than the one we lived in. When we were going through Biwabik (the name even *sounds* small), I saw two guys in football letter jackets walking down the main street. I thought to myself, I want to write a story that will capture all this: what it's like to live in the snow and the cold, what it's like being in these small towns where everybody knows everybody, and having a letter jacket means you are really *something*." That was Lee's initial inspiration; as she was writing the book the themes of fitting in, racism, and peer and parental pressure came to her work almost of their own accord. The resulting novel was autobiographical in some respects. "My high school life wasn't exactly like Ellen's [the protagonist of *Finding My Voice*], but some of the things that happened to her were similar to things that happened to me. I had people call me names because I was Asian, and I also had very strong, close friends who helped me see that these names had little to do with me as a person."

Ellen Sung, in *Finding My Voice*, is caught between two worlds. A senior at a Minnesota high school, she is prodded to succeed and become more "American" by her immigrant parents; at the same time, she feels the effects of racism from some classmates and even teachers. A gymnast and straight A student, still Ellen is made to feel an outsider, different from the other kids. Her crush on one of the most popular boys in her class, Tomper, will probably come to nothing, she knows, as she is so shy and studious. Tormented with the epithet "chink," Ellen must learn to stand up for herself. Ellen is expected to enter Harvard as her older sister did and become a doctor, like her father, and these pressures are added to by the racist attitudes of her rival, Marsha, on the gymnastics team. Eventually

Tomper and Ellen become romantically involved, and this, coupled with Ellen's visits to prospective colleges, gives her a newfound sense of confidence. She begins to understand that she needs to see a bigger world beyond the confines of her small Minnesota town. A final confrontation with Marsha sends Ellen to the hospital, but she has taken a step toward individual freedom by standing up for herself.

Critical response to Lee's debut novel was very positive. Penny Blubaugh in *Voice of Youth Advocates* called the book "a sensitive coming-of-age story" and went on to note that it "should provoke anger and thought." Writing in *Bulletin of the Center for Children's Books*, Betsy Hearne ob-

Alice, a Korean child adopted by American parents as a baby, isn't interested in the new Korean immigrant girl at school, until Yoon Jun ignites Alice's curiosity about her own heritage.

served that although the plot is episodic, "the tension increases steadily with Ellen's emotional stress, and the characterization deepens credibly. . . ." Hearne concluded that "Readers will empathize with Ellen's pain and celebrate her emerging confidence." A critic in *Kirkus Reviews* praised this "portrait of a quietly sensitive teenager" which "is filled with searing truths about day-to-day racism," and went on to remark that the book was a "gently self-possessed work, told in economical language that veils its earnestness and depth." Concluding her review in *School Library Journal*, Libby K. White noted that Lee's first novel "gives voice to a point of view that has been wanting until recently in fiction about Asian-Americans. It is a welcome addition."

Further Explorations along the Color Line

Lee's next book, *If It Hadn't Been for Yoon Jun*, was inspired by a woman several years younger than the author who had come to her town as a Korean adoptee. "I felt like I'd had a hard time growing up being Korean with Korean parents," Lee told *AAYA*. "So I became interested in learning about her experiences of growing up in an all-white town with white parents." Alice Larsen, the central character in *If It Hadn't Been for Yoon Jun*, thinks of herself as white and has never considered her Korean heritage. Then a Korean boy, a recent immigrant, transfers to her junior high and suddenly Alice's world is turned upside down. Alice is assimilated: she is a cheerleader who is gaining the attention of one of the cutest boys in school. But when Yoon Jun arrives, Alice's pastor father asks her to meet the new boy and help bring him into American society.

But making Yoon Jun "American" will not be an easy task; his English is poor, and he is pudgy and foreign-looking to Alice. Alice wants no part of him, and no part of the epithets, such as "gook," which are thrown their way. But working together on a school project about Korea helps to bring her closer to Yoon Jun and to her own cultural heritage. Yoon Jun becomes Alice's friend, a friendship made tighter when the boy pushes her out of the way of a speeding car. A *Publishers Weekly* reviewer noted that "Alice's turnaround is well handled and instructive; she's a character readers will understand and recognize." Unlike her first novel, Lee's second is geared toward younger readers, and *Booklist*'s

In this sequel to *Finding My Voice*, Ellen, now a freshman at Harvard, is just beginning to discover her Asian roots when she faces discrimination and is forced to take a side.

Janice Del Negro remarked that the book "is one of the few elementary grade novels that deal with racial pride and prejudice in an accessible fashion." Writing in the *New York Times Book Review*, Karen Ray observed that Lee's second novel "will appeal to children who, for whatever reason, feel they don't quite fit in." Ray concluded that Lee "deals with the subject of racism in a way that is both explicit and sensitive. Alice's delicately developed friendship with Yoon Jun teaches her about Korea, but more important, it teaches her about doing the right thing."

Lee returned to the story of Ellen Sung in her third novel, *Saying Goodbye*. Ellen is now a college freshman at Harvard, in premed. Her new f you enjoy the works of Marie G. Lee, you may also want to check out the following books and films:

Jeanne Betancourt, *More Than Meets the Eye*, 1990.
Linda Crew, *Children of the River*, 1989.
Anna Myers, *Rosie's Tiger*, 1994.
Eat Drink Man Woman, a film directed by Ang Lee, 1994.

friend and roommate at college, Leecia, assumes that Ellen is as passionately involved in her cultural heritage as Leecia is in her own African American background. But Ellen is far more interested in studying creative writing than in multiculturalism. She begins to fall in love, however, with a Korean American named Jae whose family's shop was destroyed in the 1992 Los Angeles riots. This and a tae kwon do class she takes initiate an interest for Ellen in her Korean heritage. Meanwhile, a short story she has written—based on the life of her best friend from high school—is published, and this friend subsequently tells Ellen she never wants to speak to her again. When Leecia and her African American Alliance sponsor a black rap singer on campus, Ellen is forced once again to confront racism in society. The singer in question is infamous for one piece that threatens inner-city Korean shopkeepers. Jae is affronted, and Ellen sides with him, helping in a demonstration against the rap musician. Ellen's friendship with Leecia is destroyed over the matter, though there is a partial reconciliation at the end.

Once again, reviewers and critics found much to praise in *Saying Goodbye*. *Horn Book*'s Maeve Visser Knoth noted that this "topical novel addresses pressures faced by young adults to align themselves with one group, and see the world in terms of stark contrast. . . . Lee writes an intriguing story which addresses issues of growing independence and self-awareness faced by young people as they begin to cross the threshold into adulthood." Gail Richmond, writing in *School Library Journal*, observed that Lee's blend of questions about cultural as well as socio-economic identity would induce readers to "reflect on Ellen's experiences and learn from them," while Hearne concluded in *Bulletin of the Center for*

Children's Books that "Lee doesn't cop out on the ending: neither of her friendships will ever be quite the same, nor does her stabilized relationship with Jae alleviate the pain of alienation she feels from the women in her life. Readers will be curious to see if a third book continues the story of these honest and interesting personae."

Necessary Roughness was Lee's next novel for older readers, a story about finding and making a place for oneself in a new environment. The twins Chan and Young Kim are uprooted from their home in Los Angeles and move with their family to a small town in northern Minnesota. There Chan tries to fit in by turning his soccer skills to the use of high school football; his twin sister plays flute in the band. The two fight the cultural wars at home and at school. Chan's father, for example, derides his participation in athletics as childish. At school, he faces racist taunts and a locker-room attack. The death of his sister in a car crash only exacerbates things for Chan; the "necessary roughness" his football coach is always talking about has spread into unnecessary dimensions and Chan must learn to come to terms with all these conflicting forces in his life. A contributor in *Kirkus Reviews* observed that football "is the central metaphor for how a Korean family confronts life, death, and assimilation in this gritty and moving novel." *Booklist*'s Stephanie Zvirin noted that "Lee's at her strongest when writing about prejudice and describing Chan's classic confrontational relationship with his father," while Alan McLeod, writing in *ALAN Review,* called the book "moving, entertaining, and painful."

Lee has also written what she describes as a "multicultural R. L. Stine-ish" mystery set in Mexico, *Night of the Chupacabras*, as well as *F Is for Fabuloso*, a story about growing up as an immigrant. Both are middle-grade novels. In her books, Lee has created a new genre in multicultural literature for young readers—the Asian American novel, detailing more specifically the Korean American experience. Lee writes her novels not only for those, like herself, who have been the victim of racial prejudice and harassment, but also the potential harassers. Lee commented in *ALAN Review*, "I want readers to know . . . that behind every racial slur there's a person, and in this light, I believe books have the capacity to educate." As she stated in her *AAYA* interview, "There is an optimistic side to my rather pessimistic self, and it lies in my work. I believe literature can be transformative because it can help develop people's humanity by literally putting themselves in other people's shoes. I even had a fan letter from one of the name-callers, saying something like 'I didn't know that bugged you so much.' Even opening the eyes of one person is worth it."

■ Works Cited

Blubaugh, Penny, review of *Finding My Voice, Voice of Youth Advocates,* December, 1992, p. 282.

Del Negro, Janice, review of *If It Hadn't Been for Yoon Jun, Booklist,* July, 1993, p. 1966.

Review of *Finding My Voice, Kirkus Reviews,* September 15, 1992, p. 1190.

Hearne, Betsy, review of *Finding My Voice, Bulletin of the Center for Children's Books,* October, 1992, pp. 47-48.

Hearne, Betsy, review of *Saying Goodbye, Bulletin of the Center for Children's Books,* July-August, 1994, p. 364.

Review of *If It Hadn't Been for Yoon Jun, Publishers Weekly,* May 19, 1993, p. 72.

Knoth, Maeve Visser, review of *Saying Goodbye, Horn Book,* July-August, 1994, p. 458.

Lee, Marie G., *Something about the Author,* Volume 81, Gale, 1995, pp. 123-26.

Lee, Marie G., "How I Grew," *ALAN Review,* Winter, 1995.

Lee, Marie G., interview with J. Sydney Jones for *Authors and Artists for Young Adults,* conducted July, 1998.

McLeod, Alan, review of *Necessary Roughness, ALAN Review,* Spring, 1997.

Review of *Necessary Roughness, Kirkus Reviews,* November 1, 1996, p. 1602.

Ray, Karen, review of *If It Hadn't Been for Yoon Jun, New York Times Books Review,* June 27, 1993, p. 21.

Richmond, Gail, review of *Saying Goodbye, School Library Journal,* August, 1994, p. 168.

White, Libby K., review of *Finding My Voice, School Library Journal,* October, 1992, pp. 143-44.

Zvirin, Stephanie, review of *Necessary Roughness, Booklist,* January 1, 1997, p. 844.

■ For More Information See

BOOKS

The Asian American Almanac, Gale, 1995.

Lives of Famous Asian Americans: Literature, Chelsea House, 1995.

Rosey Grier's All-American Heroes: Multicultural Success Stories, MasterMedia, 1993.

Oxford Companion to Women's Writing in the United States, Oxford University Press, 1995.

PERIODICALS

Book Links, January, 1994, p. 28.

Booklist, September 1, 1992, p. 48.

Bulletin of the Center for Children's Books, April, 1993, p. 256; April, 1995, p. 256.

Emergency Librarian, November, 1995, p. 28.

Five Owls, January-February, 1994, pp. 69-70.

Horn Book, January-February, 1997, pp. 61-62.

Kirkus Reviews, October 15, 1998, p. 1533.

Kliatt, January, 1995, p. 9; September, 1995, p. 11; July, 1998, p. 14.

New York Times Book Review, November 6, 1994, p. 32.

Publishers Weekly, July 6, 1992, p. 57; November 25, 1996, p. 76.

Sassy, February, 1993, p. 36; July, 1994, p. 39.

School Library Journal, April, 1993, p. 121.

Stone Soup, November-December, 1993, pp. 40-41.

Voice of Youth Advocates, June, 1994, p. 86.

—Sketch by J. Sydney Jones

Ursula K. Le Guin

■ Personal

Surname pronounced "luh-gwin"; born October 21, 1929, in Berkeley, CA; daughter of Alfred L. (an anthropologist) and Theodora Covel Brown (a writer; maiden name, Kracaw) Kroeber; married Charles Alfred Le Guin (a historian), December 22, 1953; children: Elisabeth, Caroline, Theodore. *Education:* Radcliffe College, A.B., 1951; Columbia University, A.M., 1952.

■ Addresses

Home—Portland, OR. *Agent*—Virginia Kidd, 538 East Harford St., Milford, PA 18337. *Dramatic Agent*—Matthew Bialer, William Morris Agency, Inc., 1325 Avenue of the Americas, New York, NY 10019. *Speakers Bureau*—Quest, 9 Meriam St., Lexington, MA 02173.

■ Career

Writer and educator. Part-time instructor in French at Mercer University, 1954-55, and University of Idaho, 1956; Emory University, department secretary, 1955; visiting lecturer and writer in residence at various locations, including Clarion West, Pacific University, Portland State University, University of California, San Diego, University of Reading, Kenyon College, Tulane University, Indiana University Writers Conference, Bennington Writing Program, Beloit, Flight of the Mind, Stanford, and First Australian Workshop in Speculative Fiction; guest of honor at science fiction conventions, including World Science Fiction Convention, 1975. Creative consultant for Public Broadcasting Service for television production of *The Lathe of Heaven,* 1979. *Member:* Authors League of America, Writers Guild, PEN, Science Fiction Research Association, Science Fiction and Fantasy Writers of America, Science Fiction Poetry Association, Writers Guild West, Amnesty International of the USA, National Abortion Rights Action League, National Organization for Women, Nature Conservancy, Planned Parenthood Federation of America, Women's International League for Peace and Freedom, Phi Beta Kappa.

■ Awards, Honors

Fulbright fellowship, 1953; *Boston Globe-Horn Book Award,* 1968, Lewis Carroll Shelf Award, 1979, *Horn Book* honor list citation, and American Library Association Notable Book citation, all for *A Wizard of Earthsea;* Nebula Award nomination for best novelette, Science Fiction Writers of America (now Science Fiction and Fantasy Writers of America), 1969, for "Nine Lives."

Nebula Award and Hugo Award, International Science Fiction Association, both for best novel, 1970, for *The Left Hand of Darkness*; Nebula Award nomination, 1971, and Hugo Award nomination and *Locus* Award, both 1973, all for best novel, for *The Lathe of Heaven*; Newbery Silver Medal Award and finalist for National Book Award for Children's Literature, both 1972, and American Library Association Notable Book citation, all for *The Tombs of Atuan*; Child Study Association of America's Children's Books of the Year citation, Junior Library Guild selection, 1972, and National Book Award for Children's Books, 1973, all for *The Farthest Shore*; Nebula Award nomination, 1972, and Hugo Award, 1973, both for best novella, for *The Word for World Is Forest*; Hugo Award for best short story, 1974, for "The Ones Who Walk Away from Omelas"; American Library Association's Best Young Adult Books citation, 1974, Hugo Award, Nebula Award, and Jupiter Award, all for best novel, 1975, and Jules Verne Award, 1975, all for *The Dispossessed: An Ambiguous Utopia*; Nebula Award and Jupiter Award, both for best short story, 1975, for "The Day before the Revolution"; Nebula Award nomination for best novelette, 1975, for "The New Atlantis"; Nebula Award nomination for best novelette and Jupiter Award, both 1976, both for "The Diary of the Rose"; National Book Award finalist, American Library Association's Best Young Adult Books citation, Child Study Association of America's Children's Books of the Year citation, and *Horn Book* honor list citation, all 1976, and Prix Lectures-Jeunesse, 1987, all for *Very Far Away from Anywhere Else*; Gandalf Award (Grand Master of Fantasy) nomination, 1978; D.Litt., Bucknell University, 1978, and Lawrence University, 1979; Gandalf Award, 1979; Balrog Award nomination for best poet, 1979; Nebula Award nomination for best novelette, 1979, for "The Pathways of Desire."

D.H.L., Lewis and Clark College, 1983, and Occidental College, 1985; *Locus* Award, 1984, for *The Compass Rose*; American Book Award nomination, 1985, and Janet Heidinger Kafka Prize for Fiction, University of Rochester English Department and Writer's Workshop, 1986, both for *Always Coming Home*; Nebula Award nomination, 1987, and Hugo Award 1988, for *Buffalo Gals, Won't You Come Out Tonight*.

Nebula Award nomination, 1990, for "The Shobies' Story"; Nebula Award for best novel, 1991, for *Tehanu: The Last Book of Earthsea*; Pushcart Prize, 1991, for "Bill Weisler"; Harold Vursell Award, American Academy and Institute of Arts & Letters, 1991; H. L. Davis Award, Oregon Institute of Literary Arts, 1992, for *Searoad*; *Hubbab* Annual Poetry Award, 1995, for "Semen"; Nebula Award nomination for best novelette, 1994, and James Tiptree Award, 1995, for "The Matter of Seggri"; Nebula Award nomination for best novella, 1994, *Locus* Readers Award, Asimov Readers Award, and Sturgeon Award, 1995, all for "Forgiveness Day"; Nebula Award, 1996, for "Solitude"; Tiptree Retrospective Award, 1996, for *The Left Hand of Darkness*; Readers Award, *Locus* Magazine, 1996, for *Four Ways to Forgiveness*; Pulitzer Prize nomination, 1997, for *Unlocking the Air*; Tiptree Award, 1997, for "Mountain Ways."

■ Writings

"EARTHSEA" BOOKS

A Wizard of Earthsea, illustrated by Ruth Robbins, Parnassus Press (Berkeley, CA), 1968.
The Tombs of Atuan, illustrated by Gail Garraty, Atheneum (New York City), 1971.
The Farthest Shore, illustrated by Gail Garraty, Atheneum, 1972.
Earthsea (omnibus; contains *A Wizard of Earthsea*, *The Tombs of Atuan*, and *The Farthest Shore*), Gollancz, 1977, published as *The Earthsea Trilogy*, Penguin (London), 1979.
Tehanu: The Last Book of Earthsea, Atheneum, 1990, Bantam (New York), 1991.

REALISTIC FICTION AND FANTASY NOVELS

Very Far Away from Anywhere Else, Atheneum, 1976, published in England as *A Very Long Way from Anywhere Else*, Gollancz (London), 1976.
The Beginning Place, Harper, 1980, published in England as *Threshold*, Gollancz, 1980.

"CATWINGS" SERIES

Catwings, illustrated by S. D. Schindler, Orchard Books (New York City), 1988.
Catwings Return, illustrated by S. D. Schindler, Orchard Books, 1989.
Wonderful Alexander and the Catwings, illustrated by S. D. Schindler, Orchard Books, 1994.

STORIES AND PICTURE BOOKS

Solomon Leviathan's Nine Hundred and Thirty-First Trip around the World (picture book; originally published in collection *Puffin's Pleasures*), illustrated by Alicia Austin, Puffin, 1976, Cheap Street (New Castle, VA), 1983.

Leese Webster, illustrated by James Brunsman, Atheneum, 1979, Gollancz (London), 1981.

The Adventures of Cobbler's Rune, illustrated by Alicia Austin, Cheap Street, 1982.

Adventures in Kroy, Cheap Street, 1982.

A Visit from Dr. Katz (picture book), illustrated by Ann Barrow, Atheneum, 1988, published as *Dr. Katz,* Collins (London), 1988.

Fire and Stone (picture book), illustrated by Laura Marshall, Atheneum, 1989.

Fish Soup (picture book), illustrated by Patrick Wynne, Atheneum, 1992.

A Ride on the Red Mare's Back (picture book), illustrated with paintings by Julie Downing, Orchard Books, 1992.

NOVELS FOR ADULTS

Rocannon's World (bound with *The Kar-Chee Reign* by Avram Davidson; also see below), Ace Books (New York City), 1966.

Planet of Exile (bound with *Mankind under the Leash* by Thomas M. Disch; also see below), Ace Books, 1966.

City of Illusions (also see below), Ace Books, 1967.

Three Hainish Novels (contains *Rocannon's World, Planet of Exile,* and *City of Illusions*), Doubleday (New York City), 1967.

The Left Hand of Darkness, Walker (New York City), 1969, with new afterword and appendixes by author, 1994.

The Lathe of Heaven, Scribner (New York City), 1971.

The Dispossessed: An Ambiguous Utopia, Harper (New York City), 1974.

Malafrena, Putnam (New York City), 1979.

The Eye of the Heron, and Other Stories (includes a novella originally published in collection *Millennial Women;* also see below), Panther, 1980, Harper, 1983.

The Visionary: The Life Story of Flicker of the Serpentine (bound with *Wonders Hidden: Audubon's Early Years,* by Scott Russell Sanders), Capra (Santa Barbara, CA), 1984.

Always Coming Home (includes audiocassette of "Music and Poetry of the Kesh," with music by Todd Barton; also see below), illustrated by

Margaret Chodos, diagrams by George Hersh, Harper, 1985, published without audiocassette, Bantam (New York City), 1986, Gollancz (London), 1986.

World of Exile and Illusion, St. Martin's Press, 1996.

POETRY

Wild Angels (collection of early works), Capra, 1975.

(With mother, Theodora K. Quinn) *Tillai and Tylissos,* Red Bull, 1979.

Torrey Pines Reserve (broadsheet), Lord John (Northridge, CA), 1980.

Hard Words, and Other Poems, Harper, 1981.

Gwilan's Harp, Lord John, 1981.

(With artist Henk Pander) *In the Red Zone,* Lord John, 1983.

Wild Oats and Fireweed, Harper, 1988.

Buffalo Gals, Won't You Come Out Tonight, illustrated by Susan Seddon Boulet, Pomegranate Artbooks (San Francisco, CA), 1994.

Going Out with Peacocks and Other Poems, HarperPerennial (New York City), 1994.

(With Diana Bellessi) *The Twins, The Dream: Two Voices / Las Gemelas, El Sueno: Dos Voces,* Arte Publico (Houston, TX), 1996.

OTHER

The Word for World Is Forest (novella; originally published in collection *Again, Dangerous Visions;* also see below), Berkley (New York City), 1972.

From Elfland to Poughkeepsie (lecture), introduction by Vonda N. McIntyre, Pendragon Press (Portland, OR), 1973.

The Wind's Twelve Quarters: Short Stories, Harper, 1975.

Dreams Must Explain Themselves (critical essays), Algol Press (New York City), 1975.

(With Gene Wolfe and James Tiptree, Jr.) *The New Atlantis and Other Novellas of Science Fiction,* edited by Robert Silverberg, Hawthorn Books (New York City), 1975.

Orsinian Tales (short stories), Harper, 1976, Gollancz (London), 1977.

The Water Is Wide (short story), Pendragon Press, 1976.

(With others) *The Altered I: An Encounter with Science Fiction* (includes Le Guin's play *No Use to Talk to Me*), edited by Lee Harding, Norstrilia Press (Melbourne, Australia), 1976.

(Editor) *Nebula Award Stories 11,* Gollancz, 1976, Harper, 1977.

The Language of the Night: Essays on Fantasy and Science Fiction (critical essays), edited by Susan Wood, Putnam, 1979, revised edition, edited by Le Guin, Women's Press, 1989.

(Editor with Virginia Kidd) *Interfaces: An Anthology of Speculative Fiction*, Ace Books, 1980.

(Editor with Kidd) *Edges: Thirteen New Tales from the Borderlands of the Imagination*, Pocket Books (New York City), 1980.

The Compass Rose (short stories), Harper, 1982, Gollancz (London), 1983.

King Dog: A Screenplay (bound with *Dostoevsky: The Screenplay*, by Raymond Carver and Tess Gallagher), Capra, 1985.

(With Barton) *Music and Poetry of the Kesh* (audiocassette), Valley Productions, 1985.

(With David Bedford) *Rigel Nine: An Audio Opera* (recording), Charisma, 1985.

(With composer Elinor Armer) *Uses of Music in Uttermost Parts* (music and text), first performed in part in San Francisco, CA, and Seattle, WA, 1986, 1987, and 1988.

Buffalo Gals and Other Animal Presences (short stories and poems), Capra, 1987, published as *Buffalo Gals*, Gollancz, 1990.

Dancing at the Edge of the World: Thoughts on Words, Women, Places (essays), Grove (New York City), 1989, Gollancz (London), 1989.

The Way of the Waters Going: Images of the Northern California Coastal Range, photographs by Ernest Waugh and Alan Nicolson, Harper, 1989.

Searoad: Chronicles of Klatsand (short stories), HarperCollins (New York City), 1991, Gollancz (London), 1992.

Myth and Archetype in Science Fiction, Pulphouse, 1991.

Talk about Writing, Pulphouse, 1991.

Blue Moon over Thurman Street, photographs by Roger Dorband, NewSage Press (Portland, OR), 1993.

Earthsea Revisioned (lecture), Children's Literature New England (Cambridge, MA), 1993.

The Ones Who Walk Away from Omelas (short story), Creative Education (Mankato, MN), 1993.

(Editor with Brian Attebery) *The Norton Book of Science Fiction: North American Science Fiction, 1960-1990*, Norton (New York City), 1993.

A Fisherman of the Inland Sea: Science Fiction Stories, HarperPrism (New York City), 1994.

Four Ways to Forgiveness (contains "Betrayals," "Forgiveness Day," "A Man of the People," and "A Woman's Liberation"), HarperPrism, 1995.

Unlocking the Air: And Other Stories (includes "Standing Ground," "Poacher," "Half Past Four," and "Limberlost"), HarperCollins, 1996.

(With J. P. Seaton) *Lao Tzu: Tao Teh Ching: A Book about the Way and the Power of the Way*, Shambhala, 1997.

Author of postcard short story, *Post Card Partnership*, 1975, and *Sword & Sorcery Annual*, 1975. Contributor to anthologies, including *Orbit 5*, 1969, *World's Best Science Fiction*, 1970, *The Best Science Fiction of the Year #5*, 1976, and *The Norton Anthology of Short Fiction*, 1978. Contributor of introductions to *A Home-Concealed Woman: The Diaries of Magnolia Wynn Le Guin, 1901-1913*, edited by husband Charles A. Le Guin, 1990, and the Oxford University Press edition of Mark Twain's *The Diaries of Adam and Eve (1904, 1906)*, 1997.

Contributor of short stories, novellas, essays, and reviews to numerous science fiction, scholarly, and popular periodicals, including *Amazing Science Fiction*, *Science-Fiction Studies*, *New Yorker*, *Antaeus*, *Parabola*, *New Republic*, *Redbook*, *Playboy*, *Playgirl*, *New Yorker*, *Western Humanities Review*, *Yale Review*, and *Omni*.

Le Guin has made recordings of several of her works, including *The Ones Who Walk Away from Omelas* (includes excerpt from *The Left Hand of Darkness*), Alternate World, 1976, *Gwilan's Harp and Intracom*, Caedmon, 1977, and *The Left Hand of Darkness* (abridged recording), Warner Audio, 1985; an abridged version of *The Earthsea Trilogy* was made into a sound recording by Colophone, 1981; *The Word for World Is Forest* was made into a sound recording by Book of the Road, 1986. Le Guin has also provided the texts for "Lockerbones/Airbones," music by Elinor Armer, 1985, and "Wild Angels of the Open Hills," music by Joseph Schwantner, 1983. Le Guin's papers are housed in a permanent collection at the University of Oregon Library, Eugene.

■ Adaptations

The Lathe of Heaven was televised by the Public Broadcasting Service in 1979; *The Tombs of Atuan* was adapted as a filmstrip with record or audiocassette by Newbery Award Records, 1980; "The Ones Who Walk Away from Omelas" was performed as a drama with dance and music at the Portland Civic Theatre in 1981. *A Wizard of Earthsea*, *The Tombs of Atuan*, *The Farthest Shore*, and *The Beginning Place* were made into sound recordings in 1992.

■ Work In Progress

Two books of short stories, *Love Stories* and *Science Fiction Stories*, for HarperCollins.

■ Sidelights

Considered one of the most significant authors of science fiction and fantasy to have emerged in the twentieth century, Le Guin is recognized as a gifted and original writer whose works address essential themes about the human condition in prose noted for its beauty and clarity. A prolific author of great range and variety, she has written novels, novellas, short stories, poetry, plays, essays, reviews, and texts for musical compositions and has also edited collections of science fiction; she directs her books, which she categorizes as science fiction, fantasy, realism, and magical realism, to children and young adults as well as to adults. Le Guin is regarded as a groundbreaking writer who brought sophisticated themes and literary craftsmanship to the genre of science fiction; in addition, she is credited for being the first female writer to have made a major contribution to the genre. In her works, Le Guin characteristically explores issues important to humanity, such as relationships, communication, the uses of power, the search for identity, and the acceptance of death. Since the 1970s, her works have incorporated a marked feminist perspective—she has addressed topics with special relevance to women, such as abortion—and have also reflected a strong environmental consciousness.

Le Guin is often credited as an exceptional maker of worlds; her books, which take place on earth, on different planets, and in settings outside of our universe, are acknowledged for the author's invention and attention to detail in her depiction of landscapes and societies. Her works also reflect Le Guin's fascination with myths, archetypes, and dreams, especially in her use of language and symbols. Most critics regard Le Guin as the creator of provocative, profound books that insightfully articulate the concerns of humanity in the context of imaginative literature. In a jacket note to Le Guin's short story collection *Searoad: Chronicles of Klatsand,* Carolyn Kizer called Le Guin "our wise woman, our seeress, a writer of rage and power," while Frank Allen of *Library Journal* named her "our foremost woman of letters in fantasy and science fiction." Theodore Sturgeon, writing in the *Los Angeles Times,* noted that "above all, in almost unearthly terms, Ursula Le Guin examines, attacks, unbuttons, takes down and exposes our notion of reality." In her *Reading for the Love of It,* Michele Landsberg called Le Guin "the leading writer of fantasy in North America," while Derek de Solla Price of the *New Republic* wrote that no writer "inside the field of science fiction or outside of it [has] done more to create a modern conscience."

Prized Fantasy Quartet

Since the first publications of her adult science fiction and fantasy, young people have been drawn to Le Guin's writings. She has directed several of her works specifically to young people and younger children; in several of these books, Le Guin outlines some of the same themes she addresses in her novels and stories for adults. Le Guin is perhaps best known for a series of fantasy novels that were published and marketed for readers in the upper elementary grades through high school: the Earthsea Quartet, which is composed of *A Wizard of Earthsea, The Tombs of Atuan, The Farthest Shore,* and *Tehanu: The Last Book of Earthsea.* The novels, which delineate the life of their main protagonist, the wizard Ged, from youth to old age, are set on various locations in Earthsea, a rural archipelago complete with its own anthropology, geology, and language. A world that is both like and unlike our own, Earthsea is a land of forests, islands, and bodies of water that incorporates many nations and customs. Although Earthsea is governed by secular rulers, its real laws are made by a hierarchy of wizards, men whose inborn affinity for magic is augmented by disciplined study that teaches them to know, and, importantly, to be able to name, the essence of each person or thing in the world. The basis of the magic in Earthsea is, therefore, in language: in knowing the true name of someone or something, one has power and control. Due to this fact, true names are given only to the trusted. The magi of Earthsea are also responsible for keeping the balance or equilibrium of the world: since order is not imposed by a deity, the wizards and other powerful humans act or refrain from acting based on their insights into both the world and themselves. Thus, individual responsibility and the acceptance of oneself as both good and evil are pivotal qualities in maintaining the balance of Earthsea.

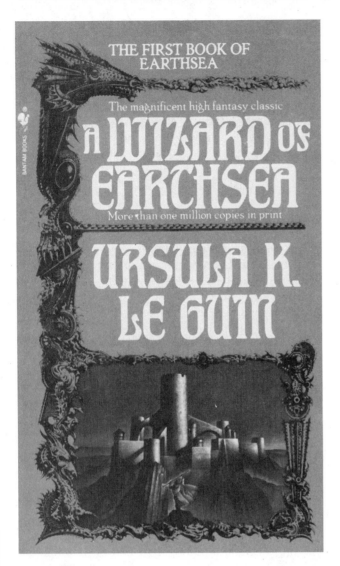

THE FIRST BOOK OF EARTHSEA

The magnificent high fantasy classic

A WIZARD OF EARTHSEA

More than one million copies in print

URSULA K. LE GUIN

The first in a series that is considered among the best fantasy ever written, this novel introduces the sorcerer Ged and the world of Earthsea, where the series takes place.

Le Guin depicts her wizards as artists, poets and shamans who devote themselves to retaining an integrated universe, a world in which light and darkness, life and death are equally acknowledged and revered. Throughout the quartet, Le Guin stresses the importance of self-knowledge through each stage of life, especially as it relates to the world. In the first three novels, Ged overcomes pride and fear and learns to accept himself and his own mortality as well as to love and trust others; as Archmage of Earthsea, he succeeds in laying the groundwork for a society based on justice and peace through his selfless and profoundly

dangerous acts of will. In the fourth novel, Le Guin suggests that the responsibility for maintaining the equilibrium of the world, instead of belonging exclusively to male wizards such as Ged, whose final act as Archmage causes his loss of power, will henceforth be shared by women.

The Earthsea quartet is considered a major achievement as both fantasy literature and children's literature; in addition, the novels are often regarded as the best of Le Guin's oeuvre. Compared in stature to J. R. R. Tolkien's *The Lord of the Rings* and *The Chronicles of Narnia* by C. S. Lewis, the Earthsea books are generally considered works of genuine epic vision and depth that are good stories as well as moving, incisive examinations of basic human concerns such as achieving maturity, acknowledging individual responsibility and responsibility to others, learning to trust and love, and accepting death. The quartet also reflects Le Guin's integration of Eastern philosophy, especially Taoism; her use of Jungian archetypes; and her interest in cultures as diverse as medieval European and Native American. As a prose stylist, Le Guin invests the Earthsea books with rich, taut language that ranges from action-filled in the earlier titles to more meditative in the final volume; Michele Landsberg called Le Guin's prose in the series "vigorous, precise, clear, and sturdy enough to sustain a whole archipelago." The novels are often noted for their appeal to young readers: Le Guin provides her audience with a series of suspenseful adventures and magical events in an otherworldly setting while developing themes regarding coming of age and good versus evil, topics with which young people can identify; in addition, young adults are drawn to the characters, especially Ged, who faces crises successfully and finds the resources within himself to successfully complete his rite of passage.

Reviewers are generally captivated by the Earthsea Quartet, praising the novels for their intelligence, consistency, and sensitivity as well as for their emotional and psychological resonance. Writing in *Book World* about the first three volumes, Michael Dirda said, "Perhaps no modern work of fantasy has been more honored and loved than Ursula Le Guin's Earthsea trilogy. Though marketed as young-adult novels, [they] are as deeply imagined, as finely wrought, as grown-up, as any fiction of our time. They deserve the highest of all accolades: Everyone should read them"; in a later review in the same periodical, Dirda noted that the four Earthsea novels "are the finest juvenile fantasies of our time." Meredith Tax of the *Village Voice* claimed, "The *Earthsea* books are children's literature like the *Odyssey* and *Beowulf* are children's literature. Composed sparely and shaped by narratives so basic they must be inscribed upon our cells, they read as if they were not written but found, dug out like jewels from rock." Calling Le Guin "a prophet unhonored in her own country," Tax concluded, "Kid stuff? Sure, . . . if children are the only ones who need stories that remind us of the firelight flickering on the walls of the cave." Writing in *English Journal* about the first three volumes, Richard Erlich commented that the highest art "is that which can entertain and instruct an entire culture. Le Guin's trilogy meets that criterion. . . . If it is 'kiddie lit,' well, 'The Tempest' is the world's greatest kid's show." In her essay on Le Guin in *Twentieth Century Children's Writers*, Jill Paton Walsh claimed, "No paraphrase of plot or setting can do justice to the profound originality of these books, which have been repeatedly imitated, and always far exceed the imitation. . . ."; the critic Fantastes of *Cambridge Review* noted, "Behind the brilliance of her books are some very subversive notions indeed." T. A. Shippey of the *Times Literary Supplement* concluded that the Earthsea books "challenge comparison with Virgil or Dante or James Frazer, exploring themes which can perhaps now only be treated outside realistic fiction, but doing so with the severity and power of modern rationalism. . . . [Le Guin] is an iconoclastic writer as much as a 'mythopoeic' one; but if ever myths were to come again, they would come from creations like her name-magery, her Shadowland."

"Mrs Le Guin," Shippey wrote, "is the daughter of famous anthropologists . . . and the achievements of that science are embodied in her work." Le Guin herself noted, "My father studied real cultures and I make them up—in a way, it's the same thing." Born in Berkeley, California, to the noted anthropologist and educator Alfred Louis Kroeber and the writer Theodora Kroeber, Le Guin noted of her early life, "My father was a professor at the University of California at Berkeley, and our summer house . . . was a gathering place for scientists, writers, students, and California Indians. Even though I didn't pay much attention, I heard a lot of interesting, grown-up conversation. What I did pay close attention to were tales. My father occasionally told us stories around a fire; stories he had heard from Indians in their

native language. He translated them into very impressive renditions of rolling skulls and other such horrifying things. My mother kept many collections of myths around the house. The ice and fire of Norse mythology were my special favorites and were much unlike the Greeks whose interests revolved around sex—so boring to me at the time. . . . The Norse, on the other hand, were always hitting each other with axes and so on— much more up a kid's alley, I would say." Le Guin began writing poetry at five and then graduated to stories, mostly fantasy and science fiction. "I wrote my first story at the age of nine," she noted, "about a man persecuted by invisible evil elves. Speculative fiction. My parents encouraged anything we did and took us seriously." She continued, "My closest brother and I used to save

George Orr's dreams become reality in this highly praised 1971 book.

our quarters to buy *Astounding Stories*. We'd laugh a lot over the stories, because most of them were junk. At twelve I submitted one of my science fiction pieces to them only to have it promptly rejected. It was all right with me. It was junk. At least I had a real rejection slip to show for it."

As a child, Le Guin said, "I read everything I could—no holds barred." She was especially drawn to Celtic and Teutonic lore as well as to such authors as Hans Christian Andersen, Padraic Colum, and her main inspiration J. R. R. Tolkien, a writer to whom she is often compared. Le Guin was also inspired by the anthropological views of Sir James Frazer, whose study of the development of religion and folklore, *The Golden Bough*, first thrilled her as a child when she discovered a juvenile adaptation written by Frazer's wife and Bronislaw Malinowski. Another major influence was the Irish writer Lord Dunsany: "I was very impressed by the age of twelve," she commented, "with the 'Inner Lands' of Toldees, Mondath, and Arizim, bounded to the east by desert, to the south by magic, to the west by a mountain, and to the north by the polar wind in Lord Dunsany's *A Dreamer's Tale*. In spite of my familiarity with legends and myths, Dunsany came to me as a revelation." She continued, "What I hadn't realized, I guess, is that people were still making up myths. One made up stories oneself, of course; but here was a grownup doing it, for grownups, without a single apology to common sense, without an explanation, just dropping us straight into the Inner Lands. Whatever the reason, the moment was decisive. I had discovered my native country."

While they express definite humanistic values, the Earthsea books and several of Le Guin's other works have often been acknowledged for their independence from traditional Christian beliefs. Le Guin, who has described herself as an "unconsistent Taoist and a consistent unChristian," has been accused by fundamentalist groups of advocating foreign religions. She once commented about the influence of her background: "My father was a cultural relativist. He had been brought up in the Ethical Culture movement in New York in the late nineteenth century, which was a nonreligious but, as the title implies, highly moral system of thought. I was brought up in an unreligious household; there was no religious practice of any kind. There was also no feeling that any religion was better than another, or worse; they just

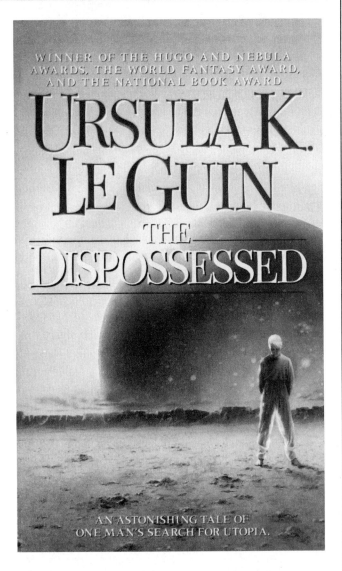

Le Guin's highly celebrated book concerns a scientist who journeys beyond his anarchist planet to discover the civilized universe.

weren't part of our life. . . . Not having been brought up with a religion gives me a slightly different viewpoint, I realize, from a great many people. I look at Christianity not in any way as belonging to it, not in any way against it." As a child, Le Guin discovered the *Tao te ching* by Lao Tse. She remembered, "It was one of the books in my house when I was a kid. And it answered my need. It's a very quiet way of looking at the world which was developed at a time of great trouble and stress in China, rather like the twentieth century here. . . . Without being a religion, it has a lot of feeling in it, and it allows for being very much in tune with nature, which is very important to me. It seemed to fit my bill, and I love the poetry in it, too; it's paradoxical and ironic."

An Educated Woman

After graduating from high school, Le Guin attended Radcliffe College in Massachusetts, where, she said, "I received an excellent education. . . . Though Harvard and Radcliffe were far from coed at the time, women students were essentially attending Harvard classes." Although she claimed that she is "grateful to Harvard/Radcliffe for a splendid education," Le Guin added that she has had "to *unlearn* a great deal of what I learned there. We were taught a sense of being *better* than other people. And yet, girls were taught to think that they were not as valuable as boys. I've had to fight against both these attitudes in myself—one is so easily influenced and malleable at eighteen." In 1951, Le Guin received her bachelor's degree in French from Radcliffe, graduating Phi Beta Kappa. "I never thought I wanted to be a writer," she noted, adding, "I always thought I was one. The big question was how could I earn a living at it? My father wisely suggested I get some training in a money-making skill so that I would not have to live off my writing. . . . With this in mind, I decided to work toward a higher degree in Romance languages and teach."

In 1953, Le Guin received her master's degree from Columbia University, again graduating Phi Beta Kappa. After starting on her Ph.D. in French and Italian Renaissance Literature, she received a Fulbright Fellowship to France. En route aboard the Queen Mary, she met Charles Le Guin and had a shipboard romance; the couple married six months later. After returning to the United States, Charles Le Guin finished his doctorate in history at Emory University in Atlanta while Ursula, deciding against getting her doctorate, taught French, worked at part-time jobs, and continued the serious writing she had begun two years earlier. Over the next eight years, she published poetry and wrote five unpublished novels, four of them about Orsinia, an imaginary country in central Europe. Then she discovered science fiction: "When I became aware of Philip K. Dick, Cordwainer Smith and other science fiction writers," she said, "I thought to myself, 'Hey, this stuff is just as crazy as what I'm doing.' I knew where my work might

fit in." After selling a short story to the pulp magazine *Fantastic,* she was on her way.

After the publication of her first science fiction novel, *Rocannon's World,* a work that blends elements from both science fiction and fantasy, Le Guin determined to, as she wrote, keep "pushing at my own limitations and at the limits of science fiction. That is what the practice of art is, you keep looking for the outside edge. When you find it you make it a whole, solid, real, and beautiful thing; anything less is incomplete." With the publication of *A Wizard of Earthsea* in 1968 and her adult novel *The Left Hand of Darkness*—a work that explores the differences between the sexes in the context of science fiction—in 1969, Le Guin claimed that she "finally got my pure fantasy vein separated from my science fiction vein . . . and the separation marked a large advance in both skill and content. Since then I have gone on writing, as it were, with both the left and right hands; and it has been a matter of keeping on pushing out towards the limits—my own and that of the medium."

In her book *Dreams Must Explain Themselves,* Le Guin explained, "I did not deliberately invent Earthsea. I am not an engineer, but an explorer. I discovered Earthsea." In 1964, Le Guin submitted a story to *Fantastic* magazine called "The Word of Unbinding," which had a wizard as its main character; soon after, *Fantastic* published "The Rule of Names," a story in which the author developed the island setting and the rules of magic that she introduced in her first story. A few years later, Le Guin wrote a longer unpublished story about a prince who travels through the archipelago of the earlier stories in search of the Ultimate. In 1967, the publisher of Parnassus Press, Herman Schein, asked Le Guin to write a book directed to the young adult audience, a request that led the author to reconsider her ideas about wizards. In her essay in *Dreams Must Explain Themselves,* Le Guin remembered that she asked herself, "What were they before they had white beards? How did they learn what is obviously an erudite and dangerous art? Are there colleges for young wizards. . . . And so on." After drawing a map of Earthsea, she named her characters and islands. "People often ask me," she wrote, "how I think of names in fantasies, and again I have to answer that I find them, that I hear them. This is an important subject in this context." She added, "For me, as for the wizards, to know the name of an island or a character is to know the island or the person. . . . This implies a good deal about the 'meaning' of the trilogy, and about me. The trilogy is, in one aspect, about the artist. The artist as magician. The Trickster. Prospero. That is the only truly allegorical aspect it has of which I am conscious. . . . Wizardry is artistry. The trilogy is then, in this sense, about art, the creative experience, the creative process. There is always this circularity in fantasy. The snake devours its tail. Dreams must explain themselves."

Earthsea

The first volume of the quartet, *A Wizard of Earthsea*, is considered a classic story of coming of age as well as the most popular book of the series. In it, Le Guin describes how Sparrowhawk, a richly gifted but impetuous student of magic, unleashes an evil shadow through hubris; when the boy confronts the shadow, they call each other by the same name—Ged, Sparrowhawk's true name—and he and the shadow become one. Through this act, Ged is made whole, thus beginning his preparation to become Archmage of Earthsea; in addition, he has restored balance to the world. In her essay in *Dreams Must Explain Themselves*, Le Guin wrote that the "most childish thing about *A Wizard of Earthsea*, I expect, is its subject: coming of age. Coming of age is a process that took me many years; I finished it, so far as I ever will, at about age 31; and so I feel rather deeply about it. So do most adolescents. It's their main occupation, in fact." Reviewers were almost uniformly enthusiastic about *A Wizard of Earthsea*. In her review in *Horn Book*, Ruth Hill Viguers said that it "is wholly original, but has the conviction of a tale told by a writer whose roots are deep in great literature of many kinds, including traditional lore and fantasy. . . . Unusual allegory or exciting quest, it is an unforgettable and a distinguished book." A critic in the *Times Literary Supplement* noted that a survey of the outstanding books for the young of the last forty years "will reveal that almost all have drawn on the extra dimension of magic or fantasy—Tolkien, White, Lewis, Pearce, Garner, Hoban and the rest. . . . To find one novel a year to join the first group noted above is as much or more than one may expect, but there seems little doubt that *A Wizard of Earthsea* is the likeliest candidate that we have had for some time; if a book as remarkable as this turns up in the next twelve months,

we shall be fortunate indeed." Writing in *Crosscurrents of Criticism: Horn Book Essays 1968-1977*, Eleanor Cameron concluded that *A Wizard of Earthsea* "is a work which, though it is fantasy, continually returns us to the world about us, its forces and powers; returns us to ourselves, to our own struggles and aspirations, to the very core of human responsibility."

The next Earthsea book, *The Tombs of Atuan*, examines feminine coming of age as it describes the rite of passage of fifteen-year-old Arha, who has been hailed as the reincarnation of the Priestess of the Tombs of Atuan. At the age of five, Arha was taken away from her parents and placed in a desert environment where death is worshipped and no men are allowed. Arha, who is in her apprenticeship as priestess, encounters Ged in a lightless underground labyrinth, where he is seeking the lost half of an ancient ring that contains a lost rune of wholeness; once the two halves of the ring are joined, order can be restored to Earthsea. Since Ged has defiled a holy place, it is Arha's duty to have him put to death. However, the girl—who holds the other half of the silver ring—pities the wizard and saves his life; in return, Ged convinces Arha to renounce the darkness and choose freedom and liberation. He tells the girl her real name, Tenar, and entrusts her with the restored ring. After Tenar and Ged escape, an earthquake swallows the tombs and the labyrinth, which ends the worship of death and allows the kingdoms of the world to reunite. *The Tombs of Atuan* is regarded as both an account of religious experience and an exploration of adolescent sexuality; in addition, reviewers have noted the lesson that Ged receives—"the necessity of mutuality," in the words of Francis J. Molson in *Twentieth Century Children's Writers*.

In her book *Dreams Must Explain Themselves*, Le Guin said, "The subject of *The Tombs of Atuan* is, if I had to put it in one word, sex. . . . [The] symbols can all be read as sexual. More exactly, you could call it a feminist coming of age. Birth, rebirth, destruction, freedom are the themes." Writing in *Horn Book*, Paul Heins noted that the storytelling in *The Tombs of Atuan* "is so good and the narrative pace so swift that a young reader may have to think twice before realizing that the adventures that befell Tenar were really the experiences that marked the growth of her personality. . . . Atuan, like Earthsea, is located in the mind of its maker, but was created out of the very stuff of mythology and reflects universal patterns that were once embodied in Stonehenge and in the Cretan labyrinth." Aidan Warlow of *School Librarian* called *The Tombs of Atuan* "a cold, colourless, humourless novel whose rather formal style and slowly unfolding plot make considerable demands on the young reader. But, for those who can manage it, this is very powerful stuff." Writing in *Book World*, Virginia Haviland concluded, "Children who love the strange will indeed revel in the drama of Ged's unlikely survival and the awesome aspects of the vast underworld—and will find them unforgettable."

Le Guin ends *The Tombs of Atuan* with the hope that Earthsea might be united under its true king; in the third volume of the quartet, *The Farthest*

Le Guin examines the notion of freedom through four interconnected novellas in this 1995 work.

Shore, Ged guides teenage Arren, the future king of Earthsea, on a quest to discover the source of the evil that is demoralizing the archipelago. The wizard and the prince journey to an island peopled by the walking, silent dead, where a former classmate of Ged's has achieved a macabre immortality. In order to restore death to its rightful place in the universe, Ged heals the crack in the fabric of the world that has been caused by the crazed wizard; however, the difficulty of the task causes Ged to lose all of his mage power. Through his apprenticeship with Ged, Arren comes to understand his role in keeping the balance of the universe and accepts his position as Earthsea's governor, thus fulfilling the prophecy of the coming of a great king who restores peace to Earthsea.

In her *Dreams Must Explain Themselves*, Le Guin wrote, "*The Farthest Shore* is about death. That's why it is a less well-built, less sound and complete book than the others. They were about things I had already lived through and survived. . . . It seemed an absolutely suitable subject to me for young readers, since in a way one can say that the hour when a child realizes, not that death exists—children are intensely aware of death—but that he/she, personally, is mortal, will die, is the hour when childhood ends, and new life begins. Coming of age again, but in a larger sense." The author concluded, "The book is still the most imperfect of the three, but it is the one I like best. It is the end of the trilogy, but it is the dream I have not stopped dreaming." A reviewer in the *Times Literary Supplement* noted, "Opinions may always differ on whether *A Wizard of Earthsea* or its current sequel, *The Farthest Shore*, is the greater book. . . . But few will dispute that both Le Guin books are cut from the same cloth, offer the same heady range of scene and plan, pose and meet no less audacious problems, in no less seductive style." Margery Fisher of *Growing Point* noted, "This book seems to me the most impressive of the three so far written. . . . In her imaginative embodying of the archipelago Ursula Le Guin has shown herself to be the only writer at present able to challenge Tolkien on his own ground."

Eighteen years after the publication of *The Farthest Shore*, Le Guin wrote *Tehanu: The Last Book of Earthsea*, a novel that begins twenty-five years after the end of its predecessor. In the process of raising her feminist consciousness, the author realized that she needed to tell another story about Earthsea, one about the power of womanhood; with this volume, then, Le Guin felt that she would provide a balance to the male-dominated trilogy. In an interview with Meredith Tax in the *Village Voice*, the author referred to the "long, purely male tradition of heroic adventure fantasy. My Earthsea trilogy is part of this male tradition—that is why I had to write this fourth volume. Because I changed, I had to show the other side." In *Tehanu*, Le Guin describes how Ged, who has entered a life of contemplation on his home island of Gont after the loss of his mage power, is joined once again with Tenar, the heroine of *The Tombs of Atuan*. Now a middle-aged widow, Tenar has chosen to forego her own powers and to live anonymously. Le Guin introduces a new and pivotal character, the abused child Therru, a six-year-old girl who is found by Tenar after she has been raped and beaten by her father and uncle and left to die in a fire. Therru begins to heal emotionally through her relationship with Tenar and Ged; when she discovers her power to call dragons, she saves her friends from the last of the wizards who have chosen to defy death. Receiving the name "Tehanu" from the eldest of the dragons, the child fulfills the prophecy that "a woman on Gont" will be Ged's successor. Thus, the power on Earthsea and the responsibility to keep its balance will be shared by men and women, and the patriarchal system is balanced by female power.

Writing in *Locus* about the origins of *Tehanu*, Le Guin said that her novel "starts at the end of *The Farthest Shore*. There's no gap in time between the books, although there was a huge gap in my life. That in itself was a bit of an enchantment for me—like I was being carried around on dragons. It's strange to go back that way and yet be a different person, carrying the story on. . . . I was able to write it because I had changed, but of course a book changes you as you write it. That's why I write books. I was tremendously free—the experience of writing it was really like flying." Writing in *Book World*, Michael Dirda said of *Tehanu*, "[Though] less sheerly exciting than the earlier books, it may be the most moving of them all." Robin McKinley of the *New York Times Book Review* called *Tehanu* "a major novel by a major novelist. . . . Ursula Le Guin shows courage in writing a sequel to an accomplished series that demonstrated the full but traditional intellectual and magical gifts of wizards who were always male. The astonishing clearsightedness of *Tehanu*

If you enjoy the works of Ursula K. Le Guin, you may also want to check out the following books:

Octavia E. Butler's "Patternist" series, including *Wild Seed*, 1980.
Nancy Kress, *Beggars in Spain*, 1993.
C. S. Lewis, the seven volumes of *The Chronicles of Narnia*, 1950-56.
J. R. R. Tolkien, *The Hobbit; or, There and Back Again*, 1937, and *The Lord of the Rings*, 1954-55.

---

is in its recognition of the necessary and life-giving contributions of female magic—sometimes designated as domesticity." Writing in the *Times Literary Supplement*, John Clute claimed that after the trilogy, *Tehanu* comes "as kind of a shock. This is clearly deliberate. The first half of *Tehanu* is a forcible—and at times decidedly bad-tempered—deconstruction of its predecessors. It is a statement that the wholeness of the trilogy is an artefact and an imposition, because the order which expresses that wholeness is inherently male." The reviewer concluded, "[In] the end one resents the corrosiveness of *Tehanu*, for in telling this particular tale, Le Guin has chosen to punish her own readers for having loved books she herself wrote." Ann Welton of *Voice of Youth Advocates* noted that the strength of *Tehanu* lies in "the fact of its being a woman's book—about women, their lives, their concerns." Noting that the novel presents a yin view of Earthsea in order to balance the male-empowered yang of the trilogy, the critic claimed that Le Guin's "attempt to balance something already in harmony results in a serious weakening of both works. . . . Let us hope that in her concern for the rights of women, Ursula Le Guin has not lost sight of that human face." In a counter-argument in a later issue of the same periodical, Margaret Miles explained that for her, *Tehanu* "brought completion instead of disappointment." Calling the novel "by far the best book of the year but . . . probably too good to win the Newbery," Miles concluded that with *Tehanu*, the shape of the series "is complete: what had been an uneasy, unbalanced triangle as a 'trilogy' now reveals itself as a completed cycle of interlinked smaller circles. The missing parts of the ring have been found and joined in *Tehanu*, and Tenar and

Ged both can now be at peace together. Equilibrium has been restored."

Novels for Teens

Although the Earthsea books are the best known examples of Le Guin's juvenile literature, she has written several additional stories and picture books for children and novels for young adults. Her first contribution to the latter category is *Very Far Away from Anywhere Else*, published in England as *A Very Long Way from Anywhere Else*. The author's first purely realistic novel for young people, *Very Far Away* is a contemporary story about Owen Griffin and Natalie Field, talented high school seniors—Owen in science, Natalie in music—who become close friends. When Owen feels pressured to introduce sex into their relationship, Natalie gently but firmly rejects his advances; distraught, Owen flips his car over while driving recklessly. After his recovery, Owen and Natalie are reunited and realize that each of them has grown from their relationship; as the characters leave for separate colleges, it appears that they will remain friends. Writing in *Horn Book*, Ethel L. Heins called *Very Far Away* a "small jewel of a book. . . . For some readers the book may come as a revelation; for others it may provide welcome reassurance." A reviewer in *Junior Bookshelf* commented, "This for me, was the most sensitive book I read in 1976, in fact I could almost say for a long time." Margery Fisher of *Growing Point* acknowledged, "In this quiet, ironic, compressed story readers in their 'teens should find much to concern them," while Andrew Gordon, writing in the *Dictionary of Literary Biography*, noted, "Like all of Le Guin's fiction, *Very Far Away from Anywhere Else* concerns the painful effort in becoming a whole human being."

The Beginning Place is a novel that, according to a reviewer in *Publishers Weekly*, brought Le Guin "back to the field in which she first gained fame (SF/fantasy) and simultaneously breaks new ground in her writing." Marketed as an adult book and reviewed as both an adult and young adult title, the novel, published in England as *Threshold*, features the adolescent characters Hugh Rogers and Irene Pannis. After running away from home to escape from his domineering mother and dead-end job, Hugh discovers a gateway to Tembreabrezi, a parallel world of eternal twilight. Irene, who has left home because of the sexual advances of her stepfather, had discovered Tembreabrezi years before and has made a home for herself there; in addition, she has become the lover of the master of the townspeople, who are reminiscent of figures from the Middle Ages. Hugh is hailed as a long-awaited savior of the town, which is under a dragon's curse. He agrees to slay the dragon, and he and Irene, who has left the town's master, go into the mountains. Although he kills the dragon, Hugh is wounded and has to be rescued by Irene. At the end of the novel, the protagonists go back to their suburban world; when Hugh's mother refuses to let him come home, Hugh and Irene rent an apartment and begin their life together. "Read as a creation of a secondary world. . . ." wrote Francis J. Molson in *Twentieth Century Children's Writers*, "the novel seems incomplete and, hence, teasing. Read as Hugh and Irene's struggle to trust in themselves and in each other, however, the novel satisfies and compares favorably with the best young adult fiction today." Writing in another edition of the same source, Jill Paton Walsh commented, "There are multiple resonances in this book, of Oedipus as well as of Sigurd among many others, and the position of the fantasy geography as a land of the inner world, of the mind, is clearer than in Earthsea, though less compellingly beautiful." Andrew Gordon noted, "The achievement of *The Beginning Place* is its vivid, detailed realism, which brings alive both the plastic suburb and the haunting twilight land and makes us believe in the possibility of crossing the threshold between the two." The critic also praised the author's "admirable new restraint in not spelling out her moral for the reader but allowing the story to speak for itself." In her review in *School Library Journal*, Amy Rolnick claimed that Le Guin's devoted fans "will recognize the artful melding of the real and the fantastic as the author at her best."

In assessing Le Guin's oeuvre since the completion of the Earthsea quartet, Michael Dirda commented that the author has "had trouble with some of her books for younger kids, which have seemed a little inconsequential compared to the moral seriousness of *A Wizard of Earthsea* or *Tehanu*." Andrew Gordon of the *Dictionary of Literary Biography* added another perspective, noting that the Earthsea books are "her finest work thus far, but as her later works indicate, she is continuing to experiment with different modes of writing and to grow in artistic range." In her entry in *Twentieth Century Children's Writers*, Jill Paton Walsh concluded, "It is hard to see how Le Guin could exceed the merit of her existing work; but also hard to put any limit on what might be expected from a writer of such variety, such force, and such psychological depth."

■ Works Cited

Allen, Frank, review of *Going Out with Peacocks and Other Poems*, *Library Journal*, June 1, 1994, pp. 110-12.

Review of *The Beginning Place*, *Publishers Weekly*, December 3, 1979, p. 47.

Cameron, Eleanor, "High Fantasy: 'A Wizard of Earthsea,'" *Crosscurrents of Criticism: Horn Book Essays 1968-77*, edited by Paul Heins, Horn Book, 1977, pp. 333-41.

Clute, John, "Deconstructing Paradise," *Times Literary Supplement*, December 28, 1990, p. 1409.

Dirda, Michael, "The Twilight of an Age of Magic," *Washington Post Book World*, February 25, 1990, pp. 1, 9.

Erlich, Richard, "Why I Like the Earthsea Trilogy," *English Journal*, October, 1977, pp. 90-93.

Fantastes, "Enchantress of Earthsea," *Cambridge Review: Fantasy in Literature*, November 23, 1973, pp. 43-45.

Review of *The Farthest Shore*, *Times Literary Supplement*, April 6, 1973, p. 379.

Fisher, Margery, review of *The Farthest Shore*, *Growing Point*, July, 1973, p. 2200.

Fisher, Margery, review of *A Very Long Way from Anywhere Else*, *Growing Point*, January, 1977, pp. 3041-42.

Gordon, Andrew, essay in *Dictionary of Literary Biography, Volume 52: American Writers for Children Since 1960—Fiction*, Gale, 1986, pp. 233-41.

Haviland, Virginia, "A Magical Tour," *Washington Post Book World*, November 7, 1971, p. 4.

Heins, Ethel L., review of *Very Far Away from Anywhere Else*, *Horn Book*, February, 1977, pp. 57-58.

Heins, Paul, review of *The Tombs of Atuan*, *Horn Book*, October, 1971, p. 490.

Kizer, Carolyn, jacket note for *Searoad: Chronicles of Klatsand*, HarperCollins, 1991.

Landsberg, Michele, "Fantasy," *Reading for the Love of It: Best Books for Young Readers*, Prentice Hall, 1987, pp. 157-82.

Le Guin, Ursula K., "Dreams Must Explain Themselves," *Dreams Must Explain Themselves*, Algol Press, 1975, pp. 4-13.

Le Guin, Ursula K., interview with Rachel Koenig in *Something about the Author*, Gale, Volume 52, 1988, pp. 103-04.

Le Guin, Ursula K., interview with Jean W. Ross in *Contemporary Authors New Revision Series*, Gale, Volume 32, 1977, p. 253-54.

Le Guin, Ursula K., *The Language of the Night: Essays on Fantasy and Science Fiction*, edited by Susan Wood, Putnam, 1979.

Le Guin, Ursula K., essay on *Tehanu*, *Locus: The Newspaper of the Science Fiction Field*, January, 1990.

McKinley, Robin, "The Woman Wizard's Triumph," *New York Times Book Review*, May 20, 1990, p. 38.

Miles, Margaret, "'Earthsea Revisited' Revisited," *Voice of Youth Advocates*, December, 1991, pp. 301-02.

Molson, Francis J., essay in *Twentieth Century Children's Writers*, 2nd edition, edited by D. L. Kirkpatrick, *St. Martin's Press*, 1983, pp. 466-67.

Price, Derek de Solla, commentary in *New Republic*, February 7, 1976.

Rolnick, Amy, review of *The Beginning Place*, *School Library Journal*, April, 1980, p. 132.

Shippey, T. A., "Archmage and Antimage," *Times Literary Supplement*, July 15, 1977, p. 863.

Sturgeon, Theodore, commentary in *Los Angeles Times*, September 5, 1982.

Tax, Meredith, "Fantasy Island," *Village Voice*, October 30, 1990, p. 75.

Review of *Very Far Away from Anywhere Else*, *Junior Bookshelf*, April, 1977, pp. 116-17.

Viguers, Ruth Hill, review of *A Wizard of Earthsea*, *Horn Book*, February, 1969, pp. 59-60.

Walsh, Jill Paton, essay in *Twentieth Century Children's Writers*, 3rd edition, edited by Tracy Chevalier, St. James Press, 1989, pp. 569-71.

Warlow, Aidan, review of *The Tombs of Atuan*, *School Librarian*, September, 1972, p. 258.

Welton, Ann, "Earthsea Revisited: 'Tehanu' and Feminism," *Voice of Youth Advocates*, April, 1991, pp. 14-16, 18.

Review of *A Wizard of Earthsea*, *Times Literary Supplement*, April 2, 1971, p. 383.

■ For More Information See

BOOKS

Bittner, James, *Approaches to the Fiction of Ursula K. Le Guin*, UMI Research Press, 1984.

Bucknall, Barbara, *Ursula K. Le Guin*, Ungar, 1981.

Children's Literature Review, Gale, Volume 3, 1978, Volume 28, 1992.

Cogell, Elizabeth Cummins, *Ursula K. Le Guin: A Primary and Secondary Bibliography,* G. K. Hall, 1983.

Contemporary Literary Criticism, Gale, Volume 8, 1978, Volume 13, 1980, Volume 22, 1982, Volume 45, 1987, Volume 71, 1992.

Cummins, Elizabeth, *Understanding Ursula K. Le Guin,* University of South Carolina Press, 1990.

De Bolt, Joe, editor, *Ursula K. Le Guin: Voyager to Inner Lands and to Outer Space,* Kennikat Press, 1979.

De Montreville, Doris, and Elizabeth D. Crawford, *Fourth Book of Junior Authors and Illustrators,* Wilson, 1978.

Dictionary of Literary Biography, Volume 8: Twentieth-Century American Science Fiction Writers, Gale, 1981.

Haviland, Virginia, *The Openhearted Audience: Ten Authors Talk about Writing for Children,* Library of Congress, 1980.

Olander, Joseph D., and Martin Harry Greenberg, editors, *Ursula K. Le Guin,* Taplinger, 1979.

Reginald, Robert, and George Edgar Slusser, editors, *Zephyr and Boreas: Winds of Change in the Fiction of Ursula K. Le Guin,* Borgo Press, 1996.

Reid, Suzanne Elizabeth, *Presenting Ursula K. Le Guin,* Twayne's United States Authors Series, Simon Schuster (New York), 1997.

Silvey, Anita, editor, *Children's Books and Their Creators,* Houghton Mifflin, 1995.

Slusser, George Edgar, *The Farthest Shores of Ursula K. Le Guin,* Borgo, 1976.

Slusser, George Edgar, *Between Two Worlds: The Literary Dilemma of Ursula K. Le Guin,* Borgo Press, 1995.

St. James Guide to Science Fiction Writers, St. James Press, 1996.

Twentieth-Century Young Adult Writers, St. James Press, 1994.

PERIODICALS

Belle Lettres, spring, 1992, pp. 53-54.

Booklist, June 15, 1992, p. 1847; November 15, 1993, p. 598; February 1, 1997, p. 921.

Boston Globe, July 13, 1994, p. 65.

Children's Literature in Education, July, 1972, pp. 21-29; March, 1995, p. 90.

Extrapolation (Ursula K. Le Guin issue), fall, 1980.

Foundation, January, 1974, pp. 71-80.

Kirkus Reviews, July 1, 1995, p. 905.

Locus, October, 1994, pp. 17, 19.

Publishers Weekly, January 29, 1996, p. 86.

School Library Journal, April, 1996, p. 168.

Science-Fiction Studies (Ursula K. Le Guin issue), March, 1976.

—Sketch by Gerard J. Senick

Sharyn McCrumb

Beautiful Daughter, and 1994, for *She Walks These Hills*; Macavity Award for best novel, for *If Ever I Return, Pretty Peggy-O*; *She Walks These Hills* received the Nero Award, Agatha Award, Anthony Award, and Macavity Award for best novel; Outstanding contribution to Appalachian Literature, 1997.

■ Personal

Born in North Carolina; married, husband's name, David (a corporate environmental director); children: Spencer, Laura. *Education:* Graduated from University of North Carolina; Virginia Tech, M.A. in English.

■ Career

Full-time novelist and lecturer, 1988—. Teacher of journalism and Appalachian Studies at Virginia Tech. Has worked as a reporter.

■ Awards, Honors

Best Appalachian Novel Award, 1985, for *Lovely in Her Bones*, and 1992, for *The Hangman's Beautiful Daughter*; Edgar Award, Mystery Writers of American, 1988, for *Bimbos of the Death Sun*; *New York Times* Notable Book citations, 1990, for *If Ever I Return, Pretty Peggy-O*, and 1992, for *The Hangman's Beautiful Daughter*; *Los Angeles Times* Notable Book citations, 1992, for *The Hangman's*

■ Writings

"BALLAD" SERIES

If Ever I Return, Pretty Peggy-O, Scribner, 1990.
The Hangman's Beautiful Daughter, Scribner, 1992.
She Walks These Hills, Scribner, 1994.
The Rosewood Casket, Dutton, 1996.
The Ballad of Frankie Silver, Dutton, 1998.

"ELIZABETH MACPHERSON" SERIES

The Windsor Knot, Ballantine, 1990.
Lovely in Her Bones, Ballantine, 1990.
Missing Susan, Ballantine, 1991.
MacPherson's Lament, Ballantine, 1992.
Sick of Shadows, Ballantine, 1992.
Highland Laddie Gone, Ballantine, 1992.
If I'd Killed Him When I Met Him . . ., Ballantine, 1995.
Paying the Piper, Ballantine, 1996.

"JAY OMEGA" SERIES

Bimbos of the Death Sun, TSR Books, 1987.
Zombies of the Gene Pool, Simon and Schuster, 1992.

SHORT STORIES

Foggy Mountain Breakdown and Other Stories, Ballantine, 1997.

■ Sidelights

Sharyn McCrumb, who has won several major literary awards for her southern crime fiction, likens her bestselling books to Appalachian quilts. "I take brightly colored scraps of legends, ballads, fragments of rural life, and local tragedy, and I piece them together into a complex whole that tells not only a story, but also a deeper truth about the culture of the mountain South," McCrumb said in an interview in Armchair Detective. Her signature style traces the connection between the culture of the British Isles and the Appalachian Mountains of east Tennessee, incorporating elements from such distinct genres as historical fiction, mystery, and fantasy.

A voracious reader even as a child, McCrumb was seven when she knew that she wanted to be a writer. Reading a book a day nurtured an early love for storytelling, a trait that ran in her family. McCrumb's great-grandfathers were circuit preachers in North Carolina's Smoky Mountains, riding horseback from community to community. She attributes her own talent to these ancestors. Her father's family lived in the Smoky Mountains that divide North Carolina and Tennessee in the late 1700s. McCrumb's books also delve into other branches of her family tracing back to her Scottish ancestor, Malcolm McCourry, who, as legend had it, was kidnapped when he was a boy living on Islay in the Hebrides in 1750 and was forced to work as a ship cabin boy. He grew up to become an attorney in New Jersey, fought in the American Revolution, and settled in Mitchell County, North Carolina, in 1794.

Followed Her Heart

McCrumb grew up in North Carolina close to Chapel Hill and graduated with a bachelor's degree from the University of North Carolina at Chapel Hill. "I wanted to be an English major, but my father said that there was no future in that," McCrumb said in the Armchair Detective interview. "So I majored in Communications and Spanish and therefore could have been a Cuban disk jockey, but as it was I did journalism for a while and all those sorts of things that liberal arts majors do while they're trying to figure out what they want to be. Finally, after about ten years of that sort of thing I went back and got my master's in English [from Virginia Tech], damn it. And then I became a writer."

During that discovery period, McCrumb taught journalism and Appalachian Studies at Virginia Tech. She also worked as a newspaper reporter at a small newspaper in Bryson City in the North Carolina mountains (and in fact her popular "Ballad" series features a small-town newspaper). Since 1988, she has worked full-time writing books and lecturing at halls around the world, including the University of Bonn, the American Library in Berlin, Oxford University, the Smithsonian Institution, and at literary festivals and universities throughout the United States.

MacPherson Charms Readers

McCrumb's first book, Sick of Shadows, introduces the southern-born heroine, Elizabeth MacPherson, a forensic anthropologist who "finds death all over the place but more often than not in Scotland," explained Peter Robertson in Booklist. MacPherson attends the wedding of her cousin, Eileen Chandler, to a man nobody much likes, because they suspect he's after her $200,000 inheritance. A murder occurs before the wedding, and everyone in the wedding party becomes a suspect.

Highland Laddie Gone, and Paying the Piper are also part of the "MacPherson" series. Highland Laddie Gone centers around Elizabeth's adventures at the Scottish-American Highland Games. There is no shortage of suspects when the head of the Campbell Clan is murdered; it seems everyone wanted him dead. Paying the Piper is about a crew of American and British archaeologists—amateurs and experts alike—who meet during an archaeological dig into prehistoric burial rites on a small Scottish island. Suspense builds when an American is found dead in his tent, and then another crew member dies mysteriously. MacPherson looks for the reason behind the deaths.

In The Windsor Knot, MacPherson rushes to marry her Scottish fiancee; he has been invited to the Queen's garden party and only immediate relatives of the guest share such an invitation. When

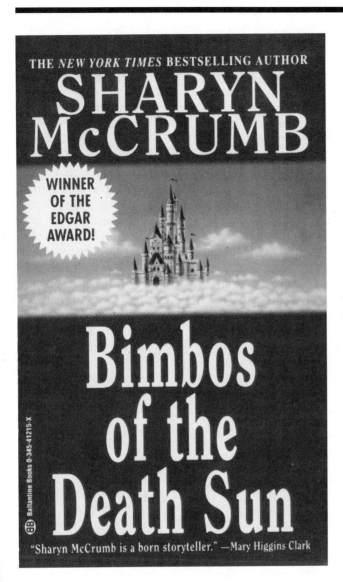

THE *NEW YORK TIMES* BESTSELLING AUTHOR

SHARYN McCRUMB

WINNER OF THE EDGAR AWARD!

Ballantine Books 0-345-41215-X

Bimbos of the Death Sun

"Sharyn McCrumb is a born storyteller." —Mary Higgins Clark

A science fiction and fantasy convention provides a colorful setting for the mystery of a murdered best-selling author.

Elizabeth arrives in Georgia for the wedding preparations, she encounters a mystery about a local woman's husband who has apparently died twice—several years apart. "McCrumb writes with a sharp-pointed pen," according to Charles Champlin in *Los Angeles Times Book Review*. In *Missing Susan* MacPherson takes a busman's holiday of England's most notorious murder sites. Unknown to her, the tour guide, catty Rowan Rover, plans to murder one of the other tourists. According to Ira Hale Blackman in *Armchair Detective*, *Missing Susan* is "a strong, but humorous, cozy-thriller." Marilyn Stasio of the *New York Times*

Book Review stated: "Whenever Sharyn McCrumb suits up her amateur detective, Elizabeth MacPherson, it's pretty certain that a trip is in the offing and that something deadly funny will happen on the road."

In another novel, *MacPherson's Lament*, Elizabeth travels to Virginia to save her brother, Bill, a lawyer, from a charge that could land him in prison. Bill also makes an appearance in *If I'd Killed Him When I Met Him. . . .* The book tells of a jilted wife who kills her former husband and his new bride; a middle-aged woman whose husband has brought home a sixteen-year-old girl to serve as his second wife; and a female sculptor who wants Bill to challenge laws that prohibit her from marrying a dolphin. McCrumb manages "not only to make a reader laugh out loud but also to shed a tear or two," according to Pat Dowell in the *Washington Post Book World*.

McCrumb won a 1988 Edgar Award for *Bimbos of the Death Sun*, a "send-up of science fiction fandom," according to Edward Bryant in *Locus*. That work introduced Dr. James Owen Mega, a university professor who, under the pseudonym "Jay Omega," has published some science fiction novels, and fellow professor Marion Farley. In the sequel, *Zombies of the Gene Pool*, James and Marion attend a reunion of science fiction writers and fans. The weekend includes the opening of a time capsule buried beneath a lake and, of course, a murder. A critic in *Kirkus Reviews* applauded the work, saying that McCrumb's "deadpan humor and bull's-eye accuracy skewers the science fiction genre, its eccentric authors, outlandish fans, and their nitpicking fanzines." A reviewer for *Analog: Science Fiction/Science Fact* wasn't impressed by *Zombies of the Gene Pool*, calling it "not terribly complex, subtle, or difficult," though Blackman, in *Armchair Detective*, found the work "sensitive, funny, and clever."

"Ballad" Series Takes New Slant

Some of McCrumb's most widely read and acclaimed books are part of the "Ballad" series that includes *If Ever I Return, Pretty Peggy-O* and *The Hangman's Beautiful Daughter*. McCrumb told Robertson in *Booklist* that while these stories are important to her because they are set in Appalachia, where her ancestors from Scotland first settled. *If Ever I Return, Pretty Peggy-O* takes place in Hamelin, Tennessee, where a series of gruesome crimes occur while preparations are underway for the twentieth reunion of Hamelin High's class of 1966. The classmate's internal struggles are also represented; this is the generation that lost its innocence to the Vietnam War . Kathleen Maio, writing in the *Wilson Library Bulletin*, thought McCrumb tried to include too many issues: "Because McCrumb is trying to say so much about an entire generation, her narrative remains frustratingly unfocused." However, Maio concluded that the book is a "worthwhile read by a talented writer." And *New York Times Book Review* critic

While at a Scottish festival, Elizabeth MacPherson investigates two murders, the first a man whom everyone disliked.

Marilyn Stasio remarked that "the author threads the theme of self-awareness thoughout her suspenseful narrative."

The Hangman's Beautiful Daughter concerns Nora Bonestell, an elderly Tennessee mountain woman who is said to have "the Sight," a gift of clairvoyance which allows her to foretell tragic events. The story focuses on the slaughter of a new family in the area during a teenager's murderous rampage; a fire that kills a mother leaving her young child orphaned; and incidents of cancer and stillbirths attributed to a polluted river. Marilyn Stasio of the *New York Times Book Review* stated that McCrumb "writes with quiet fire and maybe a little mountain magic about these events and the final, cleansing disaster that resolves them. . . . Like every true storyteller, she has the Sight." Champlin, in the *Los Angeles Times Book Review*, noted that McCrumb is one of "the funniest crime writers. . . . But she can also be movingly serious, a side of her versatility wonderfully displayed in *The Hangman's Beautiful Daughter*." He went on to say that McCrumb makes readers care about the characters and leaves them believing "that what has gone on has been not invention but experience recaptured."

A *Publishers Weekly* reviewer said that in *She Walks These Hills*, the third novel in the "Ballad" series, McCrumb "weaves . . . colorful elements into her satisfying conclusion as she continues to reward her readers' high expectations." The novel takes place in the hills and hollows of present day Appalachia, and McCrumb strings together an intriguing cast of characters: the ghost of Katie Wyler, a teenager kidnapped by Shawnees in 1779; Hiram Sorley, an elderly escaped convict who cannot recall recent events because of a rare mental illness; Sorley's former wife and daughter; a radio talk show host interested in Sorley's past; and a frightened girl with an abusive husband and a demanding baby. Mary Carroll in *Booklist* surmised that McCrumb revels in her homeland, "probes the multilayered puzzles of past and present, and meditates on human suffering and the survival instinct with sensitivity and compassion." Clyde Edgerton of the *New York Times* noted that in *She Walks These Hills* McCrumb "handles several scenes deftly by not overexplaining. In these, the economy allows the reader to visualize action that is not intrusively described." Edgerton goes on to say, however, that overwriting in other scenes bogs the story down, as does inappropriately placed

If you enjoy the works of Sharyn Mc-Crumb, you may also want to check out the following books and films:

Arthur Conan Doyle, *The Sign of the Four,* 1890.
Lee Smith, *Oral History,* 1983.
Phyllis A. Whitney, *The Singing Stones,* 1990.
Christy, a film based on the novel by Catherine Marshall, 1994.

literary references. He concluded that the novel is "an interesting story, but distractions limit its effect."

The Ballad of Frankie Silver and *The Rosewood Casket* continue the "Ballad" series. *The Ballad of Frankie Silver* is an examination of capital punishment. Sheriff Spencer Arrowood, haunted by his role in the case of death row inmate "Fate" Harkryder, delves once more into the case, as well as the 1833 hanging of Frankie Silver, the first woman hanged for murder in North Carolina. In a review of *The Rosewood Casket,* Emily Melton of *Booklist* wrote that what is most notable about this story is "the aptness of McCrumb's observations about people and life." The novel focuses on Old Man Stargill, who is dying, and his four sons who are called to his bedside to fulfill his wish that they build him a rosewood casket. As the sons come together, long-simmering family tensions and long-forgotten tragedies surface. "In an earlier life, McCrumb must have been a balladeer, singing of restless spirits, star-crossed loves, and the consoling beauty of nature," Maureen Corrigan noted in the *Washington Post Book World.*

McCrumb, who lives in a Virginia Blue Ridge farmhouse with her husband, David, and their children, Spencer and Laura, also wrote *Foggy Mountain Breakdown and Other Stories,* her first collection. In the introduction to the work, McCrumb tells readers that spending her childhood in the mountains gave her a colorful outlook on life. It was, she said, "a wild, exciting place," adding that, "the quiet tales of suburban angst so popular in modern fiction are Martian to me." McCrumb explained in the *Armchair Detective* interview that she hoped to change how people feel about Appalachia, which is often stereotyped as culturally backward, with the "Bal-

lad" series: "I think if people know more about the culture of the mountains, perhaps, I could do something to change that stereotype," adding, "I want to show them how much history we have and what real connections there are within the culture."

■ Works Cited

Blackman, Ira Hale, review of *Missing Susan, Armchair Detective,* Spring, 1992, p. 234.

Blackman, Ira Hale, review of *Zombies of the Gene Pool, Armchair Detective,* Fall, 1992, p. 500.

Bryant, Edward, review of *Zombies of the Gene Pool, Locus,* June, 1992, p. 21.

Carroll, Mary, review of *She Walks These Hills, Booklist,* August, 1994, p. 1989.

Champlin, Charles, review of *The Windsor Knot, Los Angeles Times Book Review,* September 9, 1990, p. 10.

Champlin, Charles, review of *The Hangman's Beautiful Daughter, Los Angeles Times Book Review,* April 12, 1992, p. 12.

Corrigan, Maureen, review of *The Rosewood Casket, Washington Post Book World,* April 21, 1996, p. 7.

Dowell, Pat, review of *If I'd Killed Him When I Met Him . . . , Washington Post Book World,* June 18, 1995, p. 11.

Edgerton, Clyde, review of *She Walks These Hills, New York Times,* January 8, 1995.

Maio, Kathleen, review of *If Ever I Return, Pretty Peggy-O, Wilson Library Bulletin,* September, 1990.

McCrumb, Sharyn, interview in *Armchair Detective,* Fall, 1995.

Melton, Emily, review of *The Rosewood Casket, Booklist,* March 15, 1996, p. 1219.

Robertson, Peter, "The *Booklist* Interview: Sharyn McCrumb," *Booklist,* March 15, 1992, p. 1340.

Review of *She Walks These Hills, Publishers Weekly,* August 29, 1994, p. 63.

Stasio, Marilyn, review of *If Ever I Return, Pretty Peggy-O, New York Times Book Review,* May 20, 1990.

Stasio, Marilyn, review of *Missing Susan, New York Times Book Review,* September 15, 1991.

Stasio, Marilyn, review of *The Hangman's Beautiful Daughter, New York Times Book Review,* April 19, 1992.

Review of *Zombies of the Gene Pool, Analog: Science Fiction/Science Fact,* June, 1993, p. 166.

Review of *Zombies of the Gene Pool, Kirkus Reviews,* January 1, 1992, p. 22.

■ **For More Information See**

PERIODICALS

Booklist, September 1, 1991, p. 34.
Library Journal, September 1, 1997, p. 222.
Los Angeles Times, June 11, 1995, p. 7.
New York Times Book Review, May 20, 1990, p. 53;
    October 14, 1990; January 18, 1998.
Publishers Weekly, March 27, 1995, p. 78.
Tribune Books (Chicago), May 5, 1996.

—Sketch by Diane Andreassi

James A. Michener

■ Personal

Birth date believed to be February 3, 1907; birthplace unknown; died of renal failure, October 16, 1997, in Austin TX; foster son of Mabel (Haddock) Michener; married Patti Koon, July 27, 1935 (divorced, 1948); married Vange Nord, September 2, 1948 (divorced, 1955); married Mari Yoriko Sabusawa (died, 1994), October 23, 1955. *Education:* Swarthmore College, A.B. (summa cum laude), 1929; Colorado State College of Education (now University of Northern Colorado), A.M., 1936; research study at University of Pennsylvania, University of Virginia, Ohio State University, Harvard University, St. Andrews University, and University of Siena. *Politics:* Democrat. *Religion:* Society of Friends (Quakers).

■ Career

Worked variously as an actor in a traveling show and as a sports columnist, c. 1923; Hill School, PA, teacher, 1932; George School, PA, teacher, 1933-36; Colorado State College of Education (now University of Northern Colorado), Greeley, associ-

ate professor, 1936-41; Macmillan Co., New York City, associate editor, 1941-42, 1946-49; freelance writer, 1949—. Creator of *Adventures in Paradise* television series, 1959. Visiting professor, Harvard University, 1940-41, and University of Texas at Austin, 1983. Chairman, President Kennedy's Food for Peace Program, 1961; congressional candidate to Pennsylvania's Eighth District, 1962; secretary, Pennsylvania Constitutional Convention, 1967-68. Member, U.S. State Department advisory committee on the arts, 1957; U.S. Information Agency advisory committee, 1970-76; committee to reorganize U.S. I S, 1976; U.S. Postal Service advisory committee, 1978-87; National Aeronautics and Space Administration (NASA) advisory council, 1979-83; and U.S. International Broadcasting Board, 1983-89. *Military service:* U.S. Naval Reserve, 1942-45; became lieutenant commander; naval historian in the South Pacific. *Member:* Phi Beta Kappa.

■ Awards, Honors

Pulitzer Prize for fiction, 1948, for *Tales of the South Pacific*; D.H.L., Rider College, 1950, and Swarthmore College, 1954; National Association of Independent Schools Award, 1954, 1958; LL.D., Temple University, 1957; Litt.D., American International College, 1957, and Washington University, St. Louis, 1967; Einstein Award, 1967; Bestsellers Paperback of the Year Award, 1968, for *The Source*; George Washington Award, Hungarian Studies Foundation, 1970; U.S. Medal of Freedom, 1977;

D.Sc., Jefferson Medical College, 1979; Franklin Award for distinguished service, Printing Industries of Metropolitan New York, 1980; cited by the President's committee on the arts and the humanities, 1983, for long-standing support of the Iowa Workshop writer's project at the University of Iowa; Lippincott Travelling fellowship, British Museum; U.S. Medal of Freedom; Distinguished Service Medal, NASA; Golden Badge of Order of Merit, 1988.

■ Writings

NOVELS

Tales of the South Pacific, Macmillan, 1947.
The Fires of Spring, Random House, 1949.
The Bridges at Toko-Ri (originally published in *Life,* July 6, 1953), Random House, 1953.
Sayonara, Random House, 1954.
Hawaii (first section originally published in *Life*), Random House, 1959.
Caravans, Random House, 1963.
The Source, illustrated by Richard Sparks, Random House, 1965.
The Drifters, Random House, 1971.
Centennial, Random House, 1974.
Chesapeake, illustrated by Alan Philips, Random House, 1978, selections published as *The Watermen,* Random House, 1979.
The Covenant, Random House, 1980.
Space, Random House, 1982.
Poland, Random House, 1983.
Texas, Random House, 1985, published in two volumes, University of Texas Press, 1986, selection published as *The Eagle and the Raven,* illustrations by Charles Shaw, State House Press, 1990.
Legacy, Random House, 1987.
Alaska, Random House, 1988.
Journey, Random House, 1989.
Caribbean, Random House, 1989.
The Novel, Random House, 1991.
Mexico, Random House, 1992.
Creatures of the Kingdom, Random House, 1993.
Recessional, Random House, 1994.

NONFICTION

Voice of Asia, Random House, 1951.
The Floating World, Random House, 1954.
(With A. Grove Day) *Rascals in Paradise* (biography), Random House, 1957.

The Bridge at Andau, Random House, 1957.
Japanese Prints: From the Early Masters to the Modern, Tuttle, 1959.
Report of the County Chairman, Random House, 1961.
The Modern Japanese Print: An Appreciation, Tuttle, 1968.
Iberia: Spanish Travels and Reflections, Random House, 1968.
America vs. America: The Revolution in Middle-Class Values, New American Library, 1969.
Presidential Lottery: The Reckless Gamble in Our Electoral System, Random House, 1969.
The Quality of Life (essays), Random House, 1969, published with *Presidential Lottery,* Transworld, 1980.
Facing East: A Study of the Art of Jack Levine, Random House, 1970.
Kent State: What Happened and Why, Random House, 1971.
About "Centennial": Some Notes on the Novel, Random House, 1974.
Sports in America, Random House, 1976, revised as *Michener on Sport,* Transworld, 1977.
(With John Kings) *Six Days in Havana,* University of Texas Press, 1989.
Pilgrimage: A Memoir of Poland and Rome, Rodale, 1990.
James A. Michener's Writer's Handbook: Explorations in Writing and Publishing, Random House, 1992.
My Lost Mexico, illustrated with photographs by Michener, State House Press, 1992.
The World Is My Home: A Memoir, Random House, 1992.
Literary Reflections: Michener on Michener, Hemingway, Capote, and Others, State House Press, 1993.
Miracle in Seville, Random House, 1995.
This Noble Land: My Vision for America, Random House, 1996.

OTHER

(Editor) *The Future of the Social Studies,* National Council for the Social Studies, 1939.
(With Harold Long) *The Unit in the Social Studies,* Harvard University Press, 1940.
Return to Paradise, Random House, 1951.
Selected Writings, Modern Library, 1957.
(Editor) *Hokusai Sketchbooks,* Tuttle, 1958.
A Michener Miscellany: 1950-1970, Random House, 1973.
(Editor) *Firstfruits: A Harvest of Twenty-five Years of Israeli Writing,* Jewish Publication Society of America, 1973.

(Contributor and author of foreword) *James Michener's U.S.A.*, edited by Peter Chaitin, Crown, 1981.

A Century of Sonnets (poetry), State House Press (Austin, TX), 1997.

Contributor of introductory essays to numerous books, including John W. Grafton, *America: A History of the First Five Hundred Years*, Crescent, 1992; Henryk Sienkiewicz, *With Fire and Sword*, Macmillan, 1993; Robert Bansemer, *Mountains in the Mist: Impressions of the Great Smokies*, Taylor, 1993; Steven Goldsberry, *Over Hawaii*, Weldon Owen, 1995; Jake Rajs, *America*, Universe Publishing, 1996; and Michi Nishiura Weglyn, *Years of Infamy: The Untold Story of America's Concentration Camps*, University of Washington Press, 1996.

Michener's works have been translated into over fifty foreign languages. Collections of his books and manuscripts are kept at the Swarthmore College and University of Hawaii libraries; the Library of Congress also has a large collection of his papers.

■ Adaptations

Tales of the South Pacific was adapted for the stage by Richard Rodgers and Oscar Hammerstein II as the musical *South Pacific*, and a film was adapted from the play in 1958. *Return to Paradise, The Bridges of Toko-Ri*, and *Sayonara* were all adapted as motion pictures, as were *Until They Sail* and *Mr. Morgan*, both from *Return to Paradise*; "Forgotten Heroes of Korea" was adapted as the film *Men of the Fighting Lady*, 1954; *Hawaii* was adapted as the films *Hawaii*, United Artists (UA), 1966, and *The Hawaiians*, UA, 1970; *Centennial* was adapted for television, 1978-79; *Space* was adapted as a television mini-series, 1985; *Texas* was adapted by ABC-TV, 1995. Many of Michener's works have been recorded on audio tape, including *Space* and *Journey*, Books on Tape, 1994-95; *Miracle in Seville*, Random AudioBooks, 1995; *This Noble Land*, Books on Tape, 1996; and *The Eagle and the Raven*, Media Books, 1996.

■ Sidelights

As Harrison Salisbury wrote in the *Chicago Tribune*, "James Michener is as much an American institution as the Fourth of July or apple pie."

Michener wrote short stories, essays, poems, and art histories, but he was best known as the author of lengthy novels (replete with factual information) often published to mark times of national turmoil or celebration. Herbert Mitgang explained in *Saturday Review* that "Michener presents what he conceives would help the reading public to understand a subject, a lifestyle, or a country" in his novels. Very often Michener's novels follow a handful of fictional families as their bloodlines stretch through the ages and family members affect the course of history; historical figures make appearances as well. Some critics, uncomfortable labeling Michener's large tomes "novels" or "historical fiction," have searched for other ways to characterize his work. Pearl K. Bell of *Commentary* wrote in a review of *The Covenant* that Michener's works are "printed docudramas," deeming them "a new genre of the information age."

Many of Michener's novels have been best-sellers. By the time of his death in late 1997, there were more than seventy-five million copies of his books in print. And those who had not actually read one of his novels may have been exposed to Michener's work through various adaptations, from plays and films to television mini-series. But, while Michener's novels have been popular among readers, they did not always receive praise from critics. The length of the books was a problem, as was the quality of Michener's prose. Some reviewers commented that his character portrayals were shallow and lacking in credibility. Others complained about Michener's tendency to write about animals as if they had human traits. Frequently, the novelist's moral stance, clearly delineated in his work, was often a cause for dismay. Finally, not everyone approved of Michener's presentation of the facts of history. "No man has done more to corrupt the historical perspective of Americans than Michener," exclaimed D. Keith Mano in *National Review*.

Given such complaints about Michener's novels, many critics continued to express puzzlement over the writer's success with the reading public. As Nicholas Lemann noted in the *Washington Post Book World*, "Everyone is entitled to a theory as to why of all American writers Michener is the most popular." Lemann, for one, thought it was because Michener's mixture of appealing "melodrama" and factual information made readers "feel that the long hours spent reading" a Michener book "qualify as self-improvement." Peter C. Newman, in the Chicago *Tribune Books*, speculated that perhaps the "real point of Michener's books" is that "[t]hey are truly awful, but you can't stop reading them."

Some of the same critics who pointed out the flaws in Michener's works argued that Michener did not attempt literary perfection, and that his work should be analyzed on its own terms. They noted Michener's incredible memory and his presentation of interesting facts. They praised his ability to write engagingly about a wide variety of topics, and to keep the reader turning pages. Some critics applauded his efforts to teach readers about history inside and outside the United States. In a review of *Chesapeake* for the *New York Times Book Review*, for example, critic Jonathan Yardley defended Michener for his "entirely serious" intent "to instruct."

Other critics remarked on Michener's progressive messages. Pearl K. Bell noted in *Commentary* that "in many of his books" Michener "tries to improve" the hearts of his readers "by exposing . . . the torment and destruction caused by racial intolerance and religious bigotry." According to Yardley in the *New York Times Book Review*, Michener "has been a passionate and outspoken advocate of racial and religious tolerance," and "assign[ed] important roles to women . . . long before feminism became fashionable." Writing about *Centennial*, A. Grove Day commented in *Dictionary of Literary Biography* that, "As in earlier novels, progress is the result of ethnic intermingling, and in Michener's simple Quaker creed, all men and women are brothers and sisters." No matter what critics wrote, readers have continued to buy Michener's books, and the novelist received encouragement from the countless letters he received from fans.

Up until his death Michener wrote and published numerous works of both fiction and nonfiction. Despite the hours he devoted to writing and research, he was more than a writer. Michener nurtured a love of the fine arts—he established the James A. Michener Art Museum in his childhood hometown of Doylestown, Pennsylvania—and a passion for opera. He was a "citizen" in the true sense of the word, active in civic and government affairs on several levels and pondering the problems of his country. He was an adventurer who traveled throughout the United States and the

world. Michener was also an educator: living modestly despite the millions of dollars he earned, he gave much of his money to educational institutions, contributing $39 million to the University of Texas alone. Part of this generous gift was to establish the Texas Center for Writers; additional gifts—totalling over $117 million in the author's lifetime—went to Swarthmore College and the Honolulu Academy of Arts.

Michener Grows up Tough

Unsure of the date or place of his birth, Michener was adopted and raised by Mabel Michener, a widow who worked as a laundress to support the children she took in. Michener worked from the time he was nine years old to help support the family, but at times, he had to stay in a poor house; the fact that he was adopted was not revealed to him until he was a teen. Michener believed that his difficult childhood made him stronger. "I'm not glad it happened," he told Jenny Andrews Harwell in the *Saturday Evening Post*. "I would rather have had it the other way." Michener left his difficult childhood behind him when he discovered athletics. In high school he applied himself academically, earning excellent grades and becoming an outstanding basketball player. He did all of this while working a variety of jobs and traveling occasionally. (He hitchhiked through almost all of the U.S. states when he was just fourteen years old).

As high school valedictorian and sports star, Michener earned a scholarship to attend Swarthmore College. There, he studied English, philosophy, and history, and, as he told Jim Shahin in the *Saturday Evening Post*, he "led the fight to ban fraternities" which he considered "so unfair to young people who wanted to make something of themselves." Michener also developed a love for drama at Swarthmore. He graduated with highest honors from the college in 1929 and became a member of Phi Beta Kappa. At first, he taught school, and then he earned a scholarship which he used to travel to Scotland, where he studied at St. Andrew's University. He also traveled to England and Greece, returning to the United States in the early 1930s. He returned to a teaching career and married Patti Koon in 1935.

While continuing to teach, Michener earned a masters degree from Colorado State College of

Education; after receiving his degree he stayed to teach and write social studies articles until 1939. The next year he found a post as a visiting professor at Harvard University, where he taught post-graduate students. He left Boston for New York City in 1941 to work in publishing at Macmillan. This career move was interrupted by World War II and Michener's decision to serve in the U.S. Navy. He was assigned to serve as an aviation secretary, and later, as a historian for the navy in the South Pacific. There, he traveled to numerous islands, observed his surroundings carefully, and eventually began to write the stories that would become *Tales of the South Pacific*. Michener was some forty years old.

#1 BESTSELLER
JAMES A. MICHENER
Author of MEXICO
Centennial

"A hell of a book...While he fascinates and engrosses, Michener also educates."—*Los Angeles Times*

Michener traces the history of Colorado from prehistoric times to the Old West in this 1974 novel.

Michener was discharged from the navy in 1946, and his first book was published by Macmillan the following year. *Tales of the South Pacific*, a novel comprised of related stories, was lauded by critics. *Dictionary of Literary Biography* essayist Day hailed Michener's debut as "one of the best novels about Americans in the Pacific theatre in World War II." In 1948 *Tales of the South Pacific* won the Pulitzer Prize for fiction.

Although *Tales of the South Pacific* was not popular with readers, it was adapted as a musical by Richard Rodgers and Oscar Hammerstein II in 1949 as *South Pacific*. The musical had a run of almost two thousand performances on Broadway, causing Michener to later tell Jolee Edmondson in a *Writer's Digest* interview, "I have had a fantastic chain of good luck." Royalties from the musical adaptation of *Tales of the South Pacific* provided Michener with a modest annual income. Although not large, to Michener this income "made a heck of a difference. It gave me the priceless luxury of freedom." Michener was now able to devote all of his time to writing.

During the late 1940s Michener divorced his first wife and married Vange Nord. He also went to work for Macmillan in New York City. Disappointed when that publisher rejected his second book, he took the manuscript for *The Fires of Spring* to Random House, which published this novel, as well as most of his subsequent works of fiction. Critical reaction to Michener's second effort—a quasi-biography that recalls his youth in Pennsylvania—was not altogether positive. Walter Havighurst wrote in *College English* that "there was little in *The Fires of Spring* to suggest the balance, restraint, and controlled intensity of *Tales of the South Pacific*."

Hawaii and Other "Super-Novels"

Although this second novel did not fare as well as *Tales of the South Pacific*, Michener continued to write. In the early 1950s he focused once again on the South Pacific and Asia, publishing *Return to Paradise*, a book containing essays about various places in Asia paired with short stories set in the same locale. As well as writing two works of nonfiction during these years—*The Voice of Asia* contained interviews with Asians, while *The Floating World* focused on Japanese art—Michener wrote two more novels. *The Bridges at Toko-Ri*

(1953) and *Sayonara* (1954) are both about Americans in the Korean War (the latter book features a love affair between a U.S. officer and a Japanese woman); both novels were adapted for film. In 1954 Michener met his third wife, Mari Yoriko Sabusawa, a Japanese-American editor for the American Library Association. The following year, he divorced his second wife and married Sabusawa, who would be his almost constant companion until her death in 1994.

Michener spent the mid-1950s writing nonfiction; he worked in Hawaii with A. Grove Day to write *Rascals in Paradise*, about historical figures of the Pacific. He also worked on *Hawaii*, a novel published in 1959 (the same year Hawaii was granted statehood). With this novel, Michener first presented his famous mix of detailed information about a region and a family saga that traces the interactions of fictional individuals through that region's history. Beginning with the origins of the islands, *Hawaii* explains how they were populated, first by the people of Bora Bora, and then by people from the New World and Asia. According to Day, *Hawaii* is "not a historical novel in the usual sense," but "a pageant of the coming of settlers from many regions." While *Hawaii* did not garner overwhelming praise from critics, it was a big hit with readers and was adapted into two films produced by United Artists.

After the publication of *Hawaii*, Michener continued writing nonfiction. He also became more active in U.S. politics, working for John F. Kennedy's presidential campaign and unsuccessfully campaigning for a seat in the House of Representatives from Pennsylvania himself in 1962. In 1963 he published *Caravans*, a book set in Afghanistan in 1946; two years later his phenomenal best-seller *The Source* appeared.

The Source takes the reader on a journey in and around the land that eventually became Israel, and also travels through time, from the distant past to the modern-day Jewish state. The focus of the work is the archaeological excavation of Makor Tell, a mound that contains the remnants of various settlements built over the course of many centuries. The origins of Judaism, as well as Christianity and Islam, are explored. In the opinion of *New York Times Book Review* contributor Robert Payne, "one reads the book for the occasional light it throws on Biblical history, as seen through the eyes of a professor who is puzzled, appalled, de-

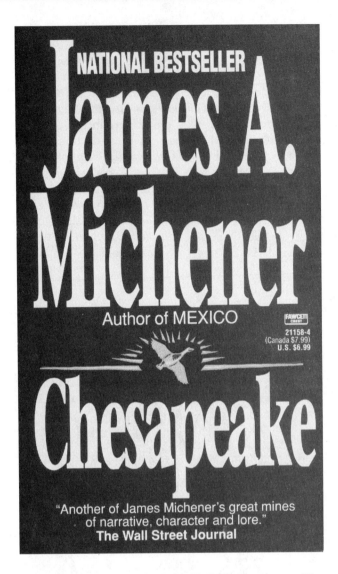

Beginning with Captain John Smith's journey to Virginia, this novel follows one family whose lives reflect the four-hundred-year saga of the Chesapeake Bay.

lighted, enriched and impoverished by the spectacle." This "amazing super-novel," as Samuel Irving Bellman described it in *Congress Bi-Weekly*, presents "an invaluable examination of the circumstances surrounding the origin and development of Judaism." "*The Source* is one of the longest of Michener's books, and the best in the opinion of many readers," commented Day in *Dictionary of Literary Biography*.

In the late 1960s and early 1970s, Michener published books about politics in the United States, an account of his travels through Spain, a collection of essays, and a discussion of the killing of students at an American college, *Kent State: What Happened and Why*. A novel published during this period, *Centennial*, explored the history of Colorado and its people. Michener, who went to school and taught in Colorado, fastidiously crafted this novel as he had *Hawaii* and *The Source*.

Centennial is narrated by a fictional professor who has been presented with the task of documenting the history of Centennial, a village. The novel, as Jean Stafford of the *Washington Post Book World* noted, begins "at the beginning when the North American continent is still under water." After discussions of the prehistoric animals and plants that lived in Colorado, (in which animals from dinosaurs to bison are anthropomorphized), the reader is then led to more recent times when Native Americans lived in Colorado, and when colonists fought with Native Americans, panned for gold, and drove cattle. Arthur Cooper of *Newsweek* noted that the novel's "underlying concerns are the relationships of men to the land—and to each other." Yet more than one critic lamented the length of *Centennial*. In the opinion of *National Review* contributor Rene Kuhn Bryant, the "surging torrent of information and instruction . . . ultimately drowns the interest of even the most determined and sympathetic of readers."

Michener's next large novel, *Chesapeake* (1978), features the people living on the eastern shore of Maryland, on Chesapeake Bay. Michener portrayed the Native Americans who first lived there, as well as colonists and their ancestors. He also, as Garry Wills of the *New York Review of Books* pointed out, portrayed geese and crabs. The novel "is an interesting and ambitious quilt of history," commented Boyd Gibbons in the *Washington Post Book World*. Nevertheless, concluded Gibbons, "overall there is a shallowness about this book and the people in it." D. Keith Mano sharply criticized the book in the *National Review*, stating that "Michener is more interested in hardware than people: ships particularly."

Taking on Texas, South Africa, and Space

During the 1980s Michener continued to travel, research, and write at a fast pace. He also continued to tackle controversial issues, grand topics, and large places with complex histories in his novels. *The Covenant*, published in 1980, relates the history of South Africa "set against the backdrop of history from the formation of the earth's crust to the present day," according to Andre Brink of the *Washington Post Book World*. The book's "narrative proper commences somewhere between the 15th and 17th centuries," and weaves together lives of three families, one Black, one Dutch, and another English. Some critics noted Michener's objectivity in his presentation of the struggle among the three groups in South Africa. Yet after "the horror of apartheid" that Michener reflected in his novel, the fact that he attempted "to portray the Afrikaners as basically honorable albeit misguided" did not sit well with critic Thomas M. Gannon of *America*. John F. Burns of *New York Times Book Review* noted that Michener's "characterizations are sometimes flat, his sentiments naive, his dialogue unreal."

Space, published just two years later, is set in the post-World-War II era, and examines the U.S. space program by tracing the paths of a German family and three American families. According to Ben Bova of the *Washington Post Book World*, Michener's *Space* reveals "the central issue of modern American society": the tension between "an incredibly rich and powerful scientific technology that can transform our world" and "a deep-rooted fear of the new, the unknown." Michener "comes down heavily on those who allow the hostility toward space exploration to spread," noted *New York Times Book Review* contributor John Noble Wilford. *Space* attained bestseller status.

In the early 1980s Michener lived in Texas, working as a visiting scholar at the University of Texas in Austin, in order to learn more about the area, and he grew to love life in the Lone Star state. In *Writer's Digest*, Jolee Edmondson reported on Michener's daily routine: "At 7:30 every morning, he applies two fingers to the keyboard and pecks out an average of 2,400 words in five hours." In the afternoon, "he shifts into exploratory gear. Cattle ranches, desolate outposts and booming metropolises are out there, waiting for his deft scrutiny." Andrea Chambers commented in *People* on Michener's "avuncular style," which, she noted, "encourages people to tell him everything about themselves. The novelist absorbs it all, occasionally jotting down a number or date."

Texas, the result of Michener's research received mixed reviews. *New York Times* critic Michiko

Kakutani lamented that, in *Texas,* Michener treats a multitude of characters without thoroughly developing them, "rushing them on stage and off, before we have time to get to know them or care." Hughes Rudd, referring to *Texas* as "history in a hurry," commented in the *New York Times Book Review* that Michener "has bitten off too much." However, Peter Applebome of *Wall Street Journal* appreciated Michener's "sharp critical intelligence," maintaining that the author "very acutely homes in on the tensions between Hispanics and Anglos and whites and blacks that have been at the heart of the Texas history."

Octagenarian Keeps Writing

Michener often insisted that he didn't read reviews of his work. Yet he also revealed that letters from fans—especially those that describe how his books have affected or inspired them—were important to him. "If I get two or three of those a week . . . I can absorb some hard knocks," he told Lynn Rosellini in *U.S. News and World Report.* Indeed, during the late 1980s and into the 1990s, Michener wrote nonfiction, novels, and short essays, seemingly without consideration either of critics' jibes or his advancing age. He produced three more of the long, historical novels that his fans so approved of: *Alaska, Caribbean,* and *Mexico.* Other books written during this period, among them *The Novel* and *Recessional,* are not typical Michener fare; *The Novel* (1991) is about writing and publishing, and *Recessional* features elderly characters coping with the challenges of aging. In addition, Michener also wrote a memoir and published a volume of poems.

Michener published *Alaska* in 1988. This novel once again portrays the diverse people who, throughout the ages, have lived in one place. In this novel, however, Michener placed a great deal of emphasis on conservation efforts. According to Christopher Lehmann-Haupt of the *New York Times,* the theme of *Alaska* is that "if nature and Russia have been magnificently cruel to Alaska, it is as nothing compared to the way America . . . has kicked the place and its people around." While *Los Angeles Times Book Review* contributor Tom Bodett commented that *Alaska* "is colorful, informative, and historically accurate," the critic added that it also "reads more like a history of the United States' largest member than an epic novel." Tom Vines of the *Wall Street Journal* criti-

cized Michener's "insensitivity toward the frontier culture" as evidenced by "his anthropomorphic portrayal of wild animals."

After the completion of *Texas,* Michener and his wife had moved to Coral Gables, Florida, where he could conduct research for his book, *Caribbean.* The resulting work, another best-seller, opens in 1310 and tells the story of the native people as well as explorers, colonists, and more contemporary inhabitants of the Caribbean. Herbert Mitgang of the *New York Times* noted that Michener "permits himself a little more editorializing" in *Caribbean* than in his other works. *New York Times Book*

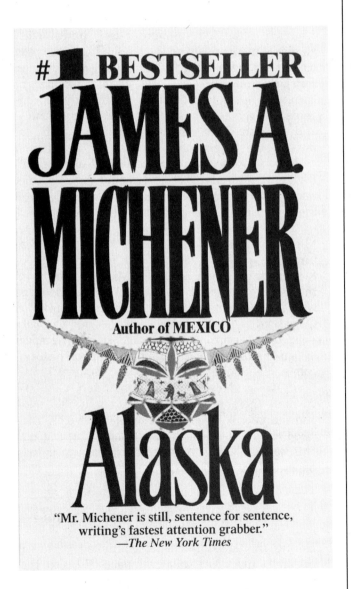

In this historical novel, the author tells the story of Alaska through characters and events.

Review critic Robert Houston commented that Michener is "an insistent puppet master," and that his characters are "tools for the author's plot-related or didactic purposes." John Hearne of the *Washington Post Book World* commented on the historical accuracy of the book: "*Caribbean* is a work which anybody strange to the islands and wanting to know something about them could read with confidence." Moreover, according to Hearne, the work is "a deeply felt, highly responsible tale."

In 1992 Michener published *Mexico,* a novel he had begun several decades previous. Considered among the novelist's "finest efforts" by Charles Michaud in *Library Journal,* the novel opens as a photographer returns to his hometown in Mexico to watch a bullfight. The same year *Mexico* was published, Michener published an explanation of the work, *My Lost Mexico.* According to Clifford Irving of *New York Times,* "*My Lost Mexico* on its own is a treat." He continued, "Mr. Michener is a brave man. By arranging the publication of these books simultaneously, he gives us an opportunity to second-guess him."

Michener also published his memoir, *The World Is My Home,* in 1992. The book, according to Bill Barich in the *Los Angeles Times Book Review,* contains "no drunken brawls, no brilliant seductions, no drugs, and precious little animosity." The work is organized by subject, and Michener "jumps backward and forward in time," opening "gaps in the narrative that leave a reader scratching his head over the missing parts of the puzzle." In addition to shedding light on Michener's childhood, *The World Is My Home* describes its author's study of writing and provides helpful advice to would-be novelists. Doris Grumbach of *New York Times* commented that the work is "always intriguing." She concluded, "there is every chance that he [Michener] will be remembered as well for being . . . a highly unusual fellow, almost a Renaissance man, adventurous, inquisitive, energetic, unpretentious and unassuming, with an encyclopedic mind and a generous heart."

This Noble Land: My Vision for America, published in 1996, discusses the problems Michener saw with the United States and describes potential solutions. According to Fritz Buckallew of *Library Journal,* the "moving book will serve as a starting point for many a discussion group and term paper." According to a *Publishers Weekly* critic,

---

If you enjoy the works of James A. Michener, you may also want to check out the following books and films:

Louis Bromfield, *The Farm,* 1974.
Elizabeth Crook, *Promised Lands: A Novel of the Texas Rebellion,* 1994.
Larry Watson, *Justice,* 1995.
Roots, a miniseries based on the work by Alex Haley, 1977.

Michener's text is "energized by the passion of his hopes and fears for his beloved country."

During the late 1980s Michener suffered from several health problems, and in 1994 his beloved wife Mari died of cancer. Three years after her death, the novelist decided to end the dialysis that now kept him alive. He died on October 16, 1997, and was buried in Austin, Texas. At a celebration of Michener's life, Random House announced the establishment of the Michener Memorial prize, a ten thousand dollar award to a writer over the age of forty publishing his or her first work. Although Michener's literary contribution continues to be debated, there is a consensus that he made a lasting mark on U.S. popular culture, and that his books will continue to entertain and inform readers. As A. Grove Day wrote in *James A. Michener,* "So long as modern Americans need to know who they are . . . so long will Michener's books be read."

■ Works Cited

Applebome, Peter, "Wait for the Miniseries," *Wall Street Journal,* November 12, 1985, p. 26.

Barich, Bill, "Sing along with Michener," *Los Angeles Times Book Review,* January 12, 1992, p. 488.

Bell, Pearl K., "James Michener's Docudramas," *Commentary,* April, 1981, pp. 71-73.

Bellman, Samuel Irving, "Tales of Ancient Israel," *Congress Bi-Weekly,* June 14, 1965, p. 18.

Bodett, Tom, "Texas Was Too Small," *Los Angeles Times Book Review,* July 3, 1988, pp. 1-7.

Bova, Ben, "James Michener Blasts Off," *Washington Post Book World,* September 12, 1982.

Brink, Andre, "Skimming over South Africa," *Washington Post Book World,* November 2, 1980, p. 3.

Bryant, Rene Kuhn, "Michener's Deluge," *National Review*, November 22, 1974, p. 1365.

Buckallew, Fritz, review of *This Noble Land: My Vision for America*, *Library Journal*, October 15, 1996, pp. 79-80.

Burns, John F., "Michener: The Novelist as Teacher," *New York Times Book Review*, November 23, 1980, pp. 3, 27.

Chambers, Andrea, "After Space and Poland, James Michener Stalks Deep in the Heart of Texas," *People*, March 28, 1983, pp. 42-44, 47.

Cooper, Arthur, "Eohippus Opera," *Newsweek*, September 16, 1974, pp. 82-86.

Day, A. Grove, *James A. Michener*, Twayne, 1964.

Day, A. Grove, *Dictionary of Literary Biography*, Volume 6: *American Novelists since World War II, Second Series*, Gale, 1980.

Edmondson, Jolee, "Michener," *Writer's Digest*, February, 1985, pp. 28-32.

Gannon, Thomas M., review of *The Covenant*, *America*, January 24, 1981, pp. 66-67.

Gibbons, Boyd, "James Michener Bridges the Bay," *Washington Post Book World*, July 9, 1978.

Grumbach, Doris, review of *The World Is My Home*, *New York Times*, January 19, 1992.

Harwell, Jenny Andrews, "At Home with James A. Michener," *Saturday Evening Post*, September, 1985, pp. 30, 32, 34.

Havighurst, Walter, "Michener of the South Pacific," *College English*, October, 1952, pp. 1-6.

Hearne, John, "The Middle Sea of the Americas," *Washington Post Book World*, November 12, 1989, p. 4.

Houston, Robert, "Paradise Tales," *New York Times Book Review*, November 5, 1989, p. 22.

Irving, Clifford, review of *My Lost Mexico* and *Mexico*, *New York Times*, December 20, 1992.

Kakutani, Michiko, review of *Texas*, *New York Times*, October 9, 1985, p. C20.

Lehmann, Nicholas, "James Michener's Ten-Gallon Epic," *Washington Post Book World*, September 29, 1985, pp. 1, 13.

Lehmann-Haupt, Christopher, "Michener's Cautionary Tale of the 49th State," *New York Times*, June 23, 1988, p. C21.

Mano, D. Keith, "Poop Poop!" *National Review*, September 15, 1978, pp. 1153-54.

Michaud, Charles, review of *Mexico*, *Library Journal*, November 1, 1992, p. 118.

Mitgang, Herbert, "The Caribbean as Lead Character in a Michener Novel," *New York Times*, November 2, 1989, p. C23.

Mitgang, Herbert, "Why Michener Never Misses," *Saturday Review*, November, 1980, pp. 20-24.

Newman, Peter C., "A Stagey, Readable Leftover from Michener's 'Alaska,'" *Tribune Books* (Chicago), July 2, 1989, p. 4.

Payne, Robert, review of *The Source*, *New York Times Book Review*, May 23, 1965, p. 45.

Rosellini, Lynn, "The Man Who Loves Facts," *U.S. News and World Report*, June 17, 1991, pp. 58-59.

Rudd, Hughes, "Four Centuries of Tex Arcana," *New York Times Book Review*, October 13, 1985, p. 9.

Salisbury, Harrison, review of *The World Is My Home*, *Chicago Tribune*, December 29, 1991, p. 4.

Shahin, Jim, "The Continuing Sagas of James A. Michener," *Saturday Evening Post*, March, 1990, pp. 66-70, 106.

Stafford, Jean, "How the West Was Lost," *Washington Post Book World*, September 1, 1974, pp. 1-2.

Review of *This Noble Land: My Vision for America*, *Publishers Weekly*, September 2, 1996, p. 102.

Vines, Tom, "Michener on the Northern Frontier," *Wall Street Journal*, August 5, 1988, p. 15.

Wilford, John Noble, "A Novel of Very High Adventure," *New York Times Book Review*, September 19, 1982, pp. 3, 26.

Wills, Garry, "Typhoon on the Bay," *New York Review of Books*, August 17, 1978, pp. 31-32.

Yardley, Jonathan, "An American Vision," *New York Times Book Review*, July 23, 1978, p. 11.

■ For More Information See

BOOKS

Authors in the News, Volume 1, Gale, 1976.

Becker, G. J., *James A. Michener*, Ungar, 1983.

Contemporary Literary Criticism, Gale, Volume 1, 1973, Volume 5, 1976, Volume 11, 1979, Volume 29, 1984; Volume 60, 1990.

Conversations with Writers, Gale, 1978.

Dybwad, G. L., and Joy V. Bliss, *James A. Michener: The Beginning Teacher and His Textbooks*, The Book Stops Here, 1995.

Groseclose, David A., *James A. Michener: A Bibliography*, State House Press, 1995.

Hayes, J. P., *James A. Michener*, Bobbs-Merrill, 1984.

Kings, J., *In Search of Centennial*, Random House, 1978.

Murrow, Edward Roscoe, *This I Believe*, Volume 2, Simon & Schuster, 1954.

Newquist, Roy, *Conversations*, Rand McNally, 1967.

Prescott, Orville, *In My Opinion: An Inquiry into the Contemporary Novel*, Bobbs-Merrill, 1952.

Severson, Marilyn S., *James A. Michener: A Critical Companion*, Greenwood Press, 1996.

Stuckey, W. J., *The Pulitzer Prize Novels*, University of Oklahoma Press, 1966.

Warfel, Harry Redcay, *American Novelists of Today*, American Book, 1951.

PERIODICALS

America, August 31, 1963; September 23, 1978.

Antioch Review, fall-winter, 1970-71.

Art America, November, 1969.

Atlantic, March, 1949; July, 1951; September, 1953; April, 1957; October, 1958; September, 1963; May, 1968; June, 1971; November, 1974.

Best Sellers, September 1, 1963; June 15, 1965; July 1, 1968; December 15, 1970; June 15, 1971; November, 1976; September, 1978.

Booklist, December 1, 1993, p. 671; September 1, 1996, pp. 3-4.

Bookmark, June, 1951.

Books, October, 1971; January, 1995, p. 12.

Books and Bookmen, December, 1971.

Book Week, May 30, 1965.

Catholic World, June, 1960.

Chicago Sun, February 9, 1949.

Chicago Sunday Tribune, May 6, 1951; November 25, 1951; July 12, 1953; January 31, 1954; December 26, 1954; March 3, 1957; November 22, 1959; May 7, 1961.

Chicago Tribune, January 17, 1982; September 29, 1983; June 27, 1985; October 17, 1985.

Children's Book World, November 5, 1967.

Christian Science Monitor, February 5, 1949; May 1, 1951; July 9, 1953; December 23, 1954; February 28, 1957; September 11, 1958; June 3, 1965; May 9, 1968; June 17, 1970; September 18, 1978; November 10, 1980; October 6, 1982.

Commonweal, April 27, 1951; February 12, 1953; July 31, 1953; April 12, 1957.

Esquire, December, 1970; June, 1971.

Good Housekeeping, February, 1960.

Guardian, November 10, 1961.

Harper's, January, 1961.

History Today, August, 1997, p. 25.

Insight, September 1, 1986.

Kirkus Reviews, August 1, 1995, p. 1051.

Library Journal, October 7, 1970; November 15, 1993, p. 79.

Life, November 7, 1955; June 4, 1971.

Los Angeles Times, November 21, 1985.

Los Angeles Times Book Review, December 7, 1980; October 3, 1982; July 31, 1983; September 4, 1983; April 7, 1991.

Nation, February 12, 1949; May 12, 1951; April 20, 1957; January 31, 1959; December 12, 1959; July 19, 1971; March 5, 1983.

National Observer, May 27, 1968; June 7, 1971.

National Review, June 29, 1971; June 29, 1974; August 7 and 14, 1976; May 27, 1983; November 11, 1983, pp. 1418, 1420.

New Republic, May 14, 1951; August 17, 1953; May 29, 1961; September 21, 1974; August 7-14, 1976.

New Statesman, June 25, 1960; November 29, 1974.

Newsweek, January 25, 1954; May 14, 1962; August 12, 1963; May 24, 1965; May 6, 1968; July 24, 1978; November 24, 1980; January 16, 1984; September 23, 1985.

New York, September 2, 1974, p. 62.

New Yorker, February 19, 1949; May 3, 1951; January 23, 1954; March 16, 1957; August 14, 1978.

New York Herald Tribune, May 28, 1961.

New York Herald Tribune Book Review, February 2, 1947; February 13, 1949; April 22, 1951; May 20, 1951; October 7, 1951; July 12, 1953; July 19, 1953; January 24, 1954; December 12, 1954; March 3, 1957; August 10, 1958; November 22, 1959; December 20, 1959; August 11, 1963.

New York Review of Books, December 19, 1968.

New York Times, February 2, 1947; February 3, 1947; February 6, 1949; February 7, 1949; April 22, 1951; October 30, 1951; July 12, 1953; January 24, 1954; December 12, 1954; March 3, 1957; August 3, 1958; May 1, 1968; June 10, 1971; September 27, 1974; July 1, 1976; August 1, 1978; November 14, 1980; September 29, 1982; September 3, 1983; February 20, 1984; September 25, 1984; October 31, 1985.

New York Times Book Review, May 16, 1948; May 22, 1949; July 12, 1953; March 3, 1957; November 8, 1959; November 22, 1959; June 18, 1961; August 11, 1963; July 24, 1966; May 12, 1968; May 25, 1969; June 6, 1971; June 27, 1971; September 30, 1973; February 10, 1974; September 8, 1974; June 27, 1976; November 26, 1978; July 15, 1979; June 12, 1983; September 4, 1983; November 20, 1983; September 6, 1987; June 26, 1988; July 9, 1989; November 12, 1989; September 30, 1990; March 31, 1991; November 28, 1993, p. 26; October 16, 1994, p. 20; January 7, 1996, p. 20, November 17, 1996.

New York Times Magazine, September 8, 1985.

Palm Springs Life, October, 1974.

Paradise of the Pacific, September-October, 1963.

People, November 3, 1997, p. 67.

Philadelphia Bulletin, September 13, 1974.

Publishers Weekly, October 18, 1993, p. 54; August 21, 1995, p. 46.

Reader's Digest, April, 1954.

San Francisco Chronicle, February 4, 1949; May 6, 1951; July 12, 1953; January 29, 1954; December 19, 1954; February 28, 1957; August 17, 1958; November 24, 1959; November 25, 1959; May 3, 1961.

Saturday Evening Post, January, 1976.

Saturday Review, July 1, 1953; February 6, 1954; January 1, 1955; March 2, 1957; November 21, 1959; June 10, 1961; September 7, 1963; May 29, 1965; May 4, 1968; April 12, 1969; May 1, 1971; September 18, 1971; June 26, 1976; June, 1980.

Saturday Review of Literature, February 12, 1949; April 28, 1951.

School Library Journal, May, 1994, p. 143.

Spectator, June 25, 1954; September 15, 1955; November 10, 1961.

Sports Illustrated, May 12, 1980.

This Week, December 4, 1966.

Time, February 4, 1949; April 23, 1951; July 13, 1953; January 25, 1954; March 4, 1957; November 23, 1959; August 9, 1963; May 28, 1965; May 17, 1968; May 3, 1971; September 23, 1974; June 28, 1976; July 10, 1978; February 9, 1981; October 3, 1983; October 28, 1985.

Times Literary Supplement, October 26, 1951; July 9, 1954; May 17, 1957; February 19, 1960; June 17, 1960; November 17, 1961; October 14, 1965; November 7, 1968; July 23, 1971; November 22, 1974; July 22, 1977.

Tribune Books (Chicago), October 3, 1982; September 4, 1983; October 13, 1985.

U.S. News & World Report, February 4, 1980, pp. 39-42.

U.S. Quarterly Book Review, June, 1947; September, 1951; September, 1955.

Variety, June 22, 1970; November 8, 1972; November 7, 1994.

Vital Speeches, July 15, 1979.

Vogue, November 1, 1966.

Washington Post, September 2, 1983.

Washington Post Book World, May 5, 1968; June 1, 1969; November 9, 1969; July 4, 1971; July 18, 1971; June 4, 1972; September 30, 1979; December 6, 1981; September 12, 1982; September 29, 1985; July 3, 1988; March 2, 1991; December 8, 1991; October 16, 1994, p. 1.

Writer's Digest, April 1972; May, 1972.

Yale Review, spring, 1947; spring, 1949.

■ Obituaries

PERIODICALS

Economist, November 1, 1997, p. 92.

Forbes, December 1, 1997, p. 28.

Maclean's, October 27, 1997, p. 11.

Time, October 27, 1997, p. 31.

U.S. News and World Report, October 27, 1997, p. 18.*

—Sketch by R. Garcia-Johnson

Lensey Namioka

American Mathematical Society, translator, 1958-66. *Member:* Authors Guild, Authors League of America, Mystery Writers of America, Society of Children's Book Writers and Illustrators, PEN (USA West), Seattle Free Lances.

■ Personal

Born June 14, 1929, in Peking, China; daughter of Yuen Ren (a linguist) and Buwei (a physician and writer; maiden name, Yang) Chao; married Isaac Namioka (a mathematician), September 9, 1957; children: Aki, Michi. *Education:* Attended Radcliffe College, 1947-49; University of California, Berkeley, B.A., 1951, M.A., 1952. *Hobbies and other interests:* Music ("I prefer to make it myself badly than to hear it performed superbly").

■ Addresses

Home—2047 23rd Avenue E., Seattle, WA 98112. *Agent*—Ruth Cohen, Box 7626, Menlo Park, CA 94025.

■ Career

Wells College, Aurora, NY, instructor in mathematics, 1957-58; Cornell University, Ithaca, NY, instructor in mathematics, 1958-61; Japan Broadcasting Corporation, broadcasting monitor, 1969—.

■ Awards, Honors

Washington State Governor's Award, 1976, for *White Serpent Castle*, 1996, for *April and the Dragon Lady;* runner-up, Edgar Allan Poe award, 1982, for *Village of the Vampire Cat;* Certificate of Merit, *Parenting* magazine, 1994, for *The Coming of the Bear;* Parents' Choice recognition, 1995, for *Yang the Third and Her Impossible Family.*

■ Writings

FICTION FOR YOUNG ADULTS

The Samurai and the Long-Nosed Devils, McKay (New York City), 1976.
White Serpent Castle, McKay, 1976.
Valley of the Broken Cherry Trees, Delacorte (New York City), 1981.
Village of the Vampire Cat, Delacorte, 1981.
Who's Hu?, Vanguard (New York City), 1981.
The Phantom of Tiger Mountain, Vanguard, 1986.
Island of Ogres, Harper (New York City), 1989.
The Coming of the Bear, HarperCollins (New York City), 1992.

Yang the Youngest and his Terrible Ear, illustrated by Kees de Kiefte, Joy Street (Boston), 1992.

April and the Dragon Lady, Browndeer (San Diego), 1994.

The Loyal Cat, illustrated by Aki Sogabe, Browndeer, 1995.

Yang the Third and Her Impossible Family, illustrated by Kees de Kiefte, Little, Brown (Boston), 1995.

Den of the White Fox, Harcourt, 1997.

The Laziest Boy in the World, illustrated by YongSheng Xuan, Holiday House, 1998.

OTHER

(Translator) Buwei Y. Chao, *How to Order and Eat in Chinese*, Vintage (New York City), 1974.

Japan: A Traveler's Companion, Vanguard, 1979.

China: A Traveler's Companion, Vanguard, 1985.

Also contributor of plays to *Center Stage*, edited by Donald Gallo. Contributor of travel and humor articles to magazines and newspapers.

■ Sidelights

Lensey Namioka worked primarily as a mathematics instructor before beginning her career as a published writer in the mid-1970s. As she once told *Something about the Author*, her works "draw heavily" on her "Chinese cultural heritage and on [her] husband's Japanese cultural heritage." Namioka is best known for her series of exciting, adventure-mystery books about two sixteenth-century Japanese samurai warriors and for her humorous, juvenile novels about young Chinese immigrants living in Seattle: *Yang the Youngest and His Terrible Ear* and *Yang the Third and Her Impossible Family*.

Namioka was born in China in 1929 to Yuen Ren, a linguist, and Buwei Yang Chao, a working mother who pursued dual careers as a physician and writer. Her parents instilled in her a love for music, making it a constant in their household—likely the reason music figures in a number of Namioka's books. As a young adult, she came to the United States for schooling, attending Radcliffe and earning degrees from the University of California at Berkeley. It was there that she met her husband, Isaac, a mathematician of Japanese and French descent who grew up in Japan. They were married in 1957.

Namioka began her career as an mathematics instructor, first at Wells College and then Cornell. While math was an important part of her life, Namioka wrote in *Something about the Author Autobiography Series* (*SAAS*), it also held a stigma. When she began attending school in America she learned "girls weren't supposed to be good in math. When I got good grades in math, I found out the other kids thought I was weird." These feelings of being an outsider would become a lifetime challenge and ultimately influenced many of her books.

Namioka explained that her preoccupation with outsiders may have sprung from her childhood. Both of her parents came from families of officials in China, and it was the policy of the government to move their officials around constantly to lessen the likelihood that they might accept favors from local factions and lose their impartiality. "My parents continued their roving lives after they got married," Namioka wrote in *SAAS*. Her two older sisters were born in Boston; the family didn't stay there long, however, moving to Washington, D.C., and then back to China. Her father eventually landed a job at an American university, and the family immigrated to the United States. Because of the constant moving about, Namioka "never felt like I really belonged" to any one place.

Career Path Changes

Forsaking mathematics, Namioka took a different career path when she turned to translating work for the American Mathematical Society, as well as her mother's book, *How to Order and Eat in Chinese*. This became Namioka's launching pad for her own writing career. Her debut novel, *The Samurai and the Long-Nosed Devils*, is set in sixteenth-century Japan and introduces Konishi Zenta and Ishihara Matsuzo, who would become the protagonists in a series of her books. They are unemployed samurai warriors, or *ronin*, who wander the countryside to find work. Zenta, the wise mentor, stands in contrast to his protege, the brash young Matsuzo. When they gain employment as the bodyguards of Portuguese missionaries, they must solve a murder mystery to save their employers. As their investigation progresses, the two ronin find themselves enmeshed in a web of political intrigue. Namioka explained to interviewer Suzanne Rahn in *The*

April feels caught between her grandmother's traditional Chinese ways and her American school life in this novel inspired by the author's immigrant experiences.

Lion and the Unicorn that Zenta and Matsuzo were patterned after Sherlock Holmes and Dr. Watson. Zena Sutherland in *Bulletin of the Center for Children's Books* commented that the book "has a lively plot with an abundance of derringdo." In a sequel, *White Serpent Castle*, Zenta and Matsuzo must confront the ghost of a white serpent as they investigate another mystery. According to Sada Fretz in *Kirkus Reviews*, the "solution . . . folds in on itself like . . . origami." Namioka includes historical notes and bibliographies in both *The Samurai and the Long-Nosed Devils* and *White Serpent Castle*.

Zenta and Matsuzo continue their adventures in *Valley of the Broken Cherry Trees*. Expecting to see the beautiful cherry trees of the famed valley, the two currently unemployed samurai are shocked to find destruction: a number of trees have been mutilated. As they investigate to determine who has harmed the trees, they once again find themselves in the middle of a power struggle. A critic in *Bulletin of the Center for Children's Books* reported that the author "evokes the place and period vividly." Paul Heins of *Horn Book* noted that the "narrative, which develops an elaborate plot, is threaded with mystery, intrigue, action, and suspense." A contributor in *Kirkus Reviews* wrote that the many characters "have distinct personalities and motives, that the whole imbroglio accurately reflects the internal turmoil of the period, adds substance and continuous interest to what is also spanking entertainment."

When Zenta and Matsuzo arrive at a familiar village to visit an old tea master in *Village of the Vampire Cat*, they discover another mystery: a Vampire Cat seems to be killing young women. Zenta and Matsuzo investigate the murders and prove that the Vampire Cat is neither a vampire nor a cat. They also participate in the Japanese tea ceremony. As Betsy Fuller McGuckin in *School Library Journal* noted, Namioka's characters "offer all the mystery and contradiction of human nature." According to Zena Sutherland in *Bulletin for the Center of Children's Books*, "the period details, the mores, and the customs are smoothly integrated."

In *Island of Ogres*, another samurai, Kajiro, is sent to an island to spy on its commander. Kajiro is mistakenly identified as Zenta, who is already hiding on the island, having fallen in love with the commander's wife. Matsuzo's challenge in this story is to help Zenta. As Christine Behrmann in *School Library Journal* wrote, the plot in this book is "byzantine" and "appearance versus reality permeates the plot." According to Behrmann, readers who follow the shifting perspectives and "elliptical style" so appreciated by Namioka's fans "will be rewarded." Reviewer Mary M. Burns of *Horn Book* praised *Island of Ogres* as an "unusual mystery-adventure for the more demanding lovers of the genre."

In *The Coming of the Bear,* Zenta and Matsuzo are taken prisoner on the island of the Ainu, a race of round-eyed people that still live on the

Lensey Namioka

Yang the Third and Her Impossible Family

The companion to
Yang the Youngest
and His Terrible Ear

Illustrated by **Kees de Kiefte**

In a desperate attempt to break free of her Chinese heritage and befriend a popular American girl, Yingmei Yang adopts a kitten and must keep it a secret from her family.

island of Hokkaido. They nevertheless manage to solve the mystery of a killer bear *and* stop a war between the Ainu and Japanese settlers. According to Lola H. Teubert in *Voice of Youth Advocates*, this book will "bring to the reader romance, adventure, cunning, mystery . . . and insight into a vanishing culture," and John Philbrook in *School Library Journal* wrote, "it's a real page-turner." A critic in *Kirkus Reviews* noted that the "author throws up a few red herrings to complicate the otherwise simple, quickly paced plot."

In *Den of the White Fox* the legend of a white fox takes the *ronin* to a small village under an occupying force. There they search for answers to whether the fox is an evasive wild animal, a

supernatural being, the creation of masquerading pranksters, or a criminal mind. Fans of the earlier books about the pair will enjoy the story's "strong characters into its rousing period mystery," according to Ellen Mandel in *Booklist*. Reviewer Roger Sutton of *Horn Book* wrote that "Zenta and Matsuzo are approachable variants on Batman and Robin who could pleasurably surprise more than a few reluctant readers." Robyn Ryan Vandenbroek wrote in *School Library Journal* that *Den of the White Fox* is an "intriguing blend of historical fiction and mystery that will be appreciated by fans of the genre."

Moves to Contemporary Fiction

Namioka's first book of young adult fiction set in contemporary times, *Who's Hu?*, was published in 1981. This novel follows Emma, a Chinese teenager who must decide whether to adhere to Chinese ways or those of the Americans she meets in the Boston area, her new home. Emma is led to believe that appearances, and fitting in, are more important in this culture than academic excellence; she must discover what she herself values. Malinda Sinaiko in *School Library Journal* noted that "an entertaining education in Chinese customs and culture vs. the American way of life" is included in the plot.

Similar to *Who's Hu?*, Namioka's *April and the Dragon Lady* is a novel about a girl coming to terms with the differences between her Chinese cultural heritage and contemporary American expectations. April Chen must balance her plans to go away to college with her responsibilities to her grandmother, the "dragon lady." She must also weigh the respect she has for her family with her decision to see a white boyfriend. "This is a well told story, believable and engaging," wrote Linda Palter in *Voice of Youth Advocates*. "Sparked by Namioka's own experiences as an Asian-American, April's first person narrative rings true," concluded Sharon Korbeck in *School Library Journal*.

A Musical Family

Yang the Youngest and His Terrible Ear and *Yang the Third and Her Impossible Family* are humorous novels about a family of Chinese musicians who have just immigrated to Seattle. In *Yang the*

Zenta and Matsuzo attempt to learn the secret behind the white fox who leads the political rebellion in this story of sixteenth-century feudal Japan.

Youngest and His Terrible Ear, tone-deaf Yang Yingtao has a difficult time performing in the family quartet and prefers to exercise his natural athletic talent in baseball games. He develops a friendship with a boy at school, and they introduce each other to their different norms, customs, and prejudices. A *Publishers Weekly* reviewer wrote that Namioka's "comic timing and deadpan delivery are reminiscent of Betsy Byars, and her book will leave readers begging for more." According to Nancy Vasilakis in *Horn Book*, Namioka "explores issues of diversity, self-realization, friendship, and duty with sensitivity and a great deal of humor."

In *Yang the Third and Her Impossible Family*, Yingmei, or Mary, wants desperately to be liked by Holly, a popular girl at school; her parents' social awkwardness, though, makes things difficult. Mary gradually comes to terms with the embarrassment cultural differences bring her. Hazel Rochman in *Booklist* remarked upon the book's "uproarious scenes of cross-cultural awkwardness," and concluded that children will understand its message "that we are all 'ethnic.' " Namioka explained in *SAAS* that her stories about immigrants "describe outsiders trying to fit into a new country and a new society." In *Yang the Third*, she stated, "the hero is an outsider even in his own family."

If you enjoy the works of Lensey Namioka, you may also want to check out the following books and films:

Frank Chin, *Donald Duk*, 1991.
Erik Christian Haugaard, *The Boy and the Samurai*, 1991.
Laurence Yep, *Mountain Light*, 1985.
The Joy Luck Club, a film based on the novel by Amy Tan, 1993.

Many of Namioka's themes hone in on feelings of fitting in and being an outcast, an emotion many young adult readers find themselves facing regarding different issues including, but not limited to, race. Namioka stated in *SAAS* that at first she was unhappy "always to be an outsider." But this later proved a benefit. She knew firsthand the experiences of her books' protagonists, especially in *Who's Hu* and *Yang the Third and Her Impossible Family*, stories in which characters gain a gradual understanding of their differences and come to terms with being an outsider. Another benefit of her ethnicity was that her books were sought out. "More and more publishers asked for books about ethnic minority groups, including Asians," she said in *SAAS*. "I was certainly standing in the right place at the right time." Namioka also noted that her books contain themes that are important to her, like women in mathematics and science, but she doesn't write books "because I have a crusade or a wish to right a social wrong. I write books because it's fun. There's nothing else I enjoy more."

■ Works Cited

Behrmann, Christine, review of *Island of Ogres, School Library Journal*, March, 1989, p. 200.

Burns, Mary M., review of *Island of Ogres, Horn Book*, September-October, 1989, pp. 647-48.

Review of *The Coming of the Bear, Kirkus Reviews*, May 1, 1992, p. 615.

Fretz, Sada, review of *White Serpent Castle, Kirkus Reviews*, October 15, 1976, p. 1146.

Heins, Paul, review of *Valley of the Broken Cherry Trees, Horn Book*, June, 1980, pp. 307-8.

Korbeck, Sharon, review of *April and the Dragon Lady, School Library Journal*, April, 1994, p. 152.

Mandel, Ellen, review of *Den of the White Fox, Booklist*, June 1 & 15, 1997, p. 1686.

McGuckin, Betsy Fuller, review of *Village of the Vampire Cat, School Library Journal*, May, 1981, p. 76.

Namioka, Lensey, comments in *Something about the Author*, Volume 89, Gale, 1997, pp. 149-52.

Namioka, Lensey, "Outsider," *Something about the Author Autobiography Series*, Volume 24, Gale, 1997, pp. 181-96.

Palter, Linda, review of *April and the Dragon Lady, Voice of Youth Advocates*, June, 1994, pp. 87-88.

Philbrook, John, review of *The Coming of the Bear, School Library Journal*, March, 1992, p. 240.

Rahn, Suzanne, "An Interview with Lensey Namioka," *The Lion and the Unicorn*, Volume 13, Number 1, 1989, pp. 74-81.

Rochman, Hazel, review of *Yang the Third and Her Impossible Family, Booklist*, April 15, 1995, p. 1500.

Sinaiko, Malinda, review of *Who's Hu?, School Library Journal*, February, 1982, p. 79.

Sutherland, Zena, review of *The Samurai and the Long-Nosed Devils, Bulletin of the Center for Children's Books*, January, 1977, pp. 78-79.

Sutherland, Zena, review of *Village of the Vampire Cat, Bulletin of the Center for Children's Books*, June, 1981, p. 200.

Sutton, Roger, review of *Den of the White Fox, Horn Book*, March-April, 1997, pp. 203-4.

Teubert, Lola H., review of *The Coming of the Bear, Voice of Youth Advocates*, October, 1992, p. 227.

Review of *Valley of the Broken Cherry Trees, Bulletin of the Center for Children's Books*, June, 1980, p. 197.

Review of *Valley of the Broken Cherry Trees, Kirkus Reviews*, September 15, 1980, p. 1236.

Vandenbroek, Robyn Ryan, review of *Den of the White Fox, School Library Journal*, June, 1997, p. 122.

Vasilakis, Nancy, review of *Yang the Youngest and His Terrible Ear, Horn Book*, July-August, 1992, pp. 452-53.

Review of *Yang the Youngest and His Terrible Ear, Publishers Weekly*, May 18, 1992, pp. 70-71.

■ For More Information See

BOOKS

Twentieth-Century Young Adult Writers, 1st Edition, St. James Press, 1994, pp. 480-81.

PERIODICALS

ALAN Review, Spring, 1998.

Booklist, November 15, 1976, p. 468; May 1, 1981, p. 1191; March 1, 1992, p. 1272; June 1 & 15, 1997, p. 1686.

Bulletin of the Center for Children's Books, June, 1992, p. 272; April, 1994, p. 267.

Horn Book, May-June, 1995, p. 350.

Kirkus Reviews, May 1, 1997, p. 725.

New York Times Book Review, September 20, 1998, p. 33.

Publishers Weekly, October 12, 1998, p. 76.

Quill and Quire, April, 1995, p.43.

School Library Journal, January, 1977, p. 104; July, 1992, p. 74; August, 1998, p. 164; October, 1998, p. 109.

Voice of Youth Advocates, June, 1998, pp. 104-5.*

—Sketch by Diane Andreassi

Larry Niven

■ Personal

Born Lawrence Van Cott Niven, April 30, 1938, in Los Angeles, CA; son of Waldemar Van Cott (a lawyer) and Lucy Estelle (Doheny) Niven; married Marilyn Joyce Wisowaty, September 6, 1969. *Education:* Attended California Institute of Technology, 1956-58; Washburn University of Topeka, A.B., 1962; attended graduate courses at University of California, Los Angeles, 1962-63. *Politics:* Republican. *Hobbies and other interests:* Science fiction conventions, computer games, folksinging.

■ Addresses

Home and office—136 El Camino Dr., Beverly Hills, CA 90620.

■ Career

Writer, 1964—. Co-founder, Citizen's Advisory Council for a National Space Policy. *Member:* Science Fiction Writers of America, Los Angeles Science Fantasy Society.

■ Awards, Honors

Hugo Award, World Science Fiction Convention, 1967, for story "Neutron Star," 1971, for novel *Ringworld*, 1972, for story "Inconstant Moon," 1975, for story "The Hole Man," and 1976, for novelette "The Borderland of Sol"; Nebula Award, Science Fiction Writers of America, 1970, and Ditmar Award, 1972, both for *Ringworld*; E. E. Smith Memorial Award, 1978; Japanese fiction awards for *Ringworld* and "Inconstant Moon," both 1979; Inkpot Award, San Diego Comic Convention, 1979; LL.D. (honorary), Washburn University of Topeka, 1984.

■ Writings

NOVELS

World of Ptavvs (see also below), Ballantine, 1966.
A Gift from Earth (see also below), Ballantine, 1968.
Ringworld, Ballantine, 1970.
(With David Gerrold) *The Flying Sorcerers,* Ballantine, 1971.
Protector, Ballantine, 1973.
(With Jerry Pournelle) *The Mote in God's Eye,* Simon and Schuster, 1974.
(With Jerry Pournelle) *Inferno,* Pocket Books, 1976.
A World Out of Time, Holt, 1976.
(With Jerry Pournelle) *Lucifer's Hammer,* Playboy Press, 1977.
The Magic Goes Away, Ace Books, 1978.

The Patchwork Girl, Ace Books, 1980.

The Ringworld Engineers, Holt, 1980.

(With Steven Barnes) *Dream Park,* Ace Books, 1981.

(With Jerry Pournelle) *Oath of Fealty,* Simon and Schuster, 1981.

(With Steven Barnes) *The Descent of Anansi,* Pinnacle Books, 1982.

The Integral Trees, Ballantine, 1984.

(With Jerry Pournelle) *Footfall,* Ballantine, 1985.

The Smoke Ring, Ballantine, 1987.

(With Steven Barnes and Jerry Pournelle) *The Legacy of Heorot,* Simon and Schuster, 1987.

(With Poul Anderson and Dean Ing) *The Man-Kzin Wars,* Baen Books, 1988.

(With Steven Barnes) *Dream Park II: The Barsoom Project,* Ace Books, 1989.

(With Dean Ing and S. M. Stirling) *Man-Kzin Wars II,* Baen Books, 1989.

(With Steven Barnes) *Achilles' Choice,* illustrated by Boris Vallejo, Tor Books, 1991.

(With Jerry Pournelle and Michael Flynn) *Fallen Angels,* Baen Books, 1991.

(With Steven Barnes) *The California Voodoo Game,* Ballantine, 1992.

(With Jerry Pournelle) *The Gripping Hand* (sequel to *The Mote in God's Eye*), Pocket Books, 1993.

Crashlander, Ballantine, 1994.

(With Steven Barnes and Jerry Pournelle) *Beowulf's Children* (sequel to *The Legacy of Heorot*), Tor Books, 1995.

The Ringworld Throne, Ballantine, 1996.

Three Books of Known Space (includes the previously published *World of Ptavvs* and *A Gift from Earth,* plus short stories), Ballantine, 1996.

Destiny's Road, Tor Books, 1997.

Also coauthor of *Man-Kzin Wars III* and creator of *Man-Kzin Wars VI* and *Man-Kzin Wars VII.*

STORY COLLECTIONS

Neutron Star, Ballantine, 1968.

The Shape of Space, Ballantine, 1969.

All the Myriad Ways, Ballantine, 1971.

The Flight of the Horse, Ballantine, 1973.

Inconstant Moon, Gollancz, 1973.

A Hole in Space, Ballantine, 1974.

Tales of Known Space, Ballantine, 1975.

The Long ARM of Gil Hamilton, Ballantine, 1976.

Convergent Series, Ballantine, 1979.

Niven's Laws, Owlswick Press, 1984.

The Time of the Warlock, SteelDragon, 1984.

Limits, Ballantine, 1985.

N-Space, Tor Books, 1990.

Playgrounds of the Mind, Tor Books, 1991.

Green Lantern: Ganthet's Tale, DC Comics, 1992.

Flatlander: The Collected Tales of Gil "The Arm" Hamilton, Ballantine, 1995.

OTHER

(Contributor) Harlan Ellison, editor, *Dangerous Visions: 33 Original Stories,* Doubleday, 1967.

(Contributor) Reginald Bretnor, editor, *The Craft of Science Fiction,* Harper, 1976.

(Editor) *The Magic May Return,* Ace Books, 1981.

(Editor) *More Magic,* Berkley Publishing, 1984.

(Contributor) Ellen Datlow, editor, *Alien Sex: Nineteen Tales by the Masters of Science Fiction and Dark Fantasy,* NAL/Dutton, 1992.

Work appears in anthologies and has been translated in German, Spanish, and Polish. Contributor of short stories to *Magazine of Fantasy and Science Fiction, Galaxy, Playboy,* and other magazines.

■ Adaptations

Ringworld, The Integral Trees, and *The Smoke Ring* were adapted for audio cassette by Blackstone Audio, 1996; *The Gripping Hand* was adapted for audio cassette by Simon and Schuster, 1993.

■ Sidelights

Larry Niven writes science fiction with an emphasis on hard science. In his Hugo and Nebula award-winning book *Ringworld,* Niven constructed an enormous hoop-shaped artificial planet a million miles wide and with a diameter of 190 million miles. All the scientific questions about such a mega-planet were answered by the author, who stated in an interview with Jeffrey Elliot in *Science Fiction Review* that he attempts to make his stories "as technically accurate as possible." Niven created in his *Ringworld* the "greatest of fictional artifacts," according to Bud Foote in *Detroit News.* In further award-winning stories and in novels, Niven has written no less than a future history of Known Space, a timeline and mythos within which his stories would piece together like a puzzle finely cut. In his writings, he explores themes from first contact with alien civilizations to the ethics of organ transplant; from psychic power to the benefits of technology. In fact, according to Raymond J. Wilson in *Dictionary of Lit-*

erary Biography, "much of Larry Niven's fiction reveals a love affair with technology." Niven also writes a hybrid of science fiction and fantasy, as in books such as *The Magic Goes Away,* and in collaboration both individually and as a group with Jerry Pournelle and Stephen Barnes has created classic series and novels such as *Dream Park* and *The Legacy of Heorot.* As comfortable in the short story format as he is in novels, and in collaboration as he is in solo works, Niven and his work can be categorized only by one of the author's own personal "laws," as he stated in *Contemporary Authors Autobiography Series (CAAS).* "The only universal message in science fiction:

There exist minds that think as well as you do, but differently."

Born in Los Angeles, Niven was raised in Beverly Hills and attended school both there and at the Cate School in Carpinteria. He flunked out of California Institute of Technology after, as he reported in *CAAS,* "discovering a bookstore jammed with used science fiction magazines." He subsequently graduated in mathematics from Washburn University in Kansas and did a year of graduate work in math at the University of California at Los Angeles before he finally decided to devote full time to writing. By 1964 he had sold his first story, "The Coldest Place," to *Worlds of If.* Two years later he turned another short story into his first published novel, *World of Ptavvs,* the book which initiated his "Known Space" series. With this novel, Niven also introduced one of his major themes—contact with an alien civilization by humans. The planet Thrintun wants to enslave all other races through their power of mind control. The "ptavv" in the title is their word for slave, and that is the plan for planet Earth: to create a world of slaves. Kzanol is the alien representative marooned on Earth and his human opposite is Larry Greenberg, who executes a memory transfer with the Thrintun alien. According to Wilson in *Dictionary of Literary Biography,* "The novel's success lies in its differentiation of human and alien perspectives." Niven continued his Known Space series with *A Gift from Earth,* a book which deals with the ethics of organ transplant. The colonists on the planet Plateau finally revolt against the tyrannical masters known as the "crew"—descendants of the space crew which brought the first colonizers to the planet. The crew use the colonists as a source for organ transplants, leading to the revolt which is aided by one Matthew Keller who is developing psychic power.

Niven creates a habitable planet based on actual scientific theory in this Hugo and Nebula Award winning novel.

Ringworld

Niven's third novel was the award-winning *Ringworld,* depicting a planet he subsequently returned to in *Ringworld Engineers* and in *Ringworld Throne.* Inspired by the speculative theories of the physicist Freeman Dyson, Ringworld is a planet constructed by humans by converting gaseous planets into much heavier elements and then subsequently using this material to construct a habitable environment. In the first of the series, a human expedition is forced to journey across vast spaces after it crash-lands on the planet. In such a vast space, a myriad of independent races and cultures have developed, and Niven delights in describing them. And in back of it all is the secret of who built Ringworld, a secret not divulged until the novel *Protector.*

A sequel, *Ringworld Engineers,* appeared a decade after the first in the series, inspired by fan interest in the first. Niven, in fact, incorporated new ideas suggested by some of his readers. Now the barbarian descendants of the original builders of Ringworld are in trouble. They no longer understand the technology that built their planet, and when stabilizer rockets used to keep the planet in orbit are removed, it is left to an earthling and

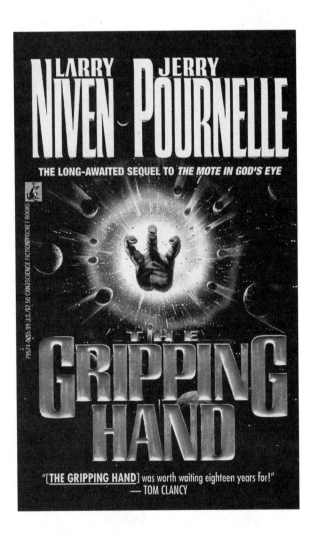

In this sequel to a popular science fiction novel cowritten by Niven and Jerry Pournelle, humans find it difficult to quarantine the alien race that poses a deadly threat to earth.

an alien to fix the problem before it is too late. Again, the search takes these two through more of the cultures of the planet. Writing in *Times Literary Supplement,* Galen Strawson noted that "the book is alive with detail. . . . Faults of construction cease to matter in the steady stream of invention." K. Sue Hurwitz, writing in *School Library Journal,* commented that "Niven's alien beings are believable and surprisingly likable," but for her, the real star of this "rousing good adventure" was the massive planet of Ringworld itself. A reviewer for *Voice of Youth Advocates* concluded that "the plot moves along nicely to a rousing conclusion, which could lead to a third novel." It took another sixteen years for that to happen, however.

Told in episodic form, this third novel in the series, *Ringworld Throne,* tells the story of the power-hungry alien puppeteer, Hindmost, trapped on Ringworld. Also making an appearance is a super-vampire named Bram, after the creator of the original Dracula stories, Bram Stoker. *Booklist's* Carl Hays, while commenting that this third book was not equal to the earlier two, noted that "any addition to Niven's famous series should attract plenty of attention." *Publishers Weekly* concurred, stating that "Niven still ranks near the top of the SF field, but this outing is likely to satisfy determined Ringworld fans more than other readers."

Niven is also the author of such popular SF novels as *A World out of Time* and the fantasy, *The Magic Goes Away.* The former, a story about cryogenics, in which Jaybee Corbell awakens in the twenty-second century after being frozen for two hundred years, is a mixture of "hard science with mind-boggling concepts of time and space," according to *Publishers Weekly.* A departure from hard science is *The Magic Goes Away,* in which four magicians team up to attempt to replenish the supply of mana, the source of magic in the world. Algis Budrys of *Booklist* noted that Niven, though prominent for his "excellent science fiction," is "equally deft with fantasy." Niven has also put one of his short story personas, police detective Gil Hamilton, into service in his novel-length *The Patchwork Girl.* A *Publishers Weekly* reviewer concluded that Hamilton "is an interesting character and works well in the novel format."

A duet of hard science novels are *Integral Trees* and its sequel *The Smoke Ring.* A ring of breathable air surrounds a neutron star, and it is here that a group of mutineering space adventurers

A new generation must battle a beast more terrible than the Grendels in this sequel to *The Legacy of Heorot*.

have set up a new civilization. Again evident in both volumes is Niven's inventiveness. Reviewing the first novel in the series, *The Integral Trees*, Roland Green of *Booklist* noted that the "world described here is almost too rich" for a book of this size and concluded: "A major sf novel, likely to be in demand almost everywhere." *Publishers Weekly* described the first novel as "marvelous, sense-of-wonder, hardcore SF." With the sequel, *The Smoke Ring*, Niven produced a more character-oriented book, relying less on raw adventure than usual. Reviewing that book, *Booklist*'s Green commented that "this solid, well-paced story, featuring a richness of scientific concepts" was bound

to be welcome in all public libraries. Niven has also written almost a score of short story collections, with tales that introduced well-known Niven characters such as Gil Hamilton and Beowulf Shaeffer, as well as stories that deal with time travel, warlocks, and hard science. His award-winning stories appear both in individual volumes as well as in anthologies such as *N-Space* and *Playgrounds of the Mind*.

Writing In Tandem

Niven, who has not shied away from incorporating reader suggestions in his novels, has also teamed up on collaborations, most often with Jerry Pournelle, especially in their popular *The Mote in God's Eye* and its sequel, *The Gripping Hand*, and with Steven Barnes in the "Dreamland" series. He has also teamed up with the both of them on companion books, *The Legacy of Heorot* and *Beowulf's Children*. Set in the thirty-first century when Earth reigns supreme, *The Mote in God's Eye* is an alien encounter novel. Moties, furry creatures possessed of superior intelligence, send an emissary to Earth who is killed accidentally. More aliens appear in this "long, involved and busy novel," as *Publishers Weekly* characterized the book, and there are adventures galore. "This absorbing treatment of communication with an alien race is a must for sci fi collections," concluded Joni Bodari in *School Library Journal*. Of the long-awaited sequel, *The Gripping Hand*, Carl Hays in *Booklist* commented that "it is a pleasure to return to the company of what is surely one of the most intriguing, endearingly quirky alien races of all of science fiction." Set some quarter of a century later than the first book, *The Gripping Hand* is a "good bet to make the Hugo ballot, as well as the bestseller lists," according to *Kirkus Reviews*, though *Publishers Weekly* felt that the book was no more than a "perfectly adequate, largely irrelevant sequel." Niven has also collaborated with Pournelle on *Inferno*, a take-off on Dante, *Lucifer's Hammer*, a best-seller about a comet striking Earth, *Oath of Fealty*, and the highly acclaimed *Footfall*, in which an alien invasion forces old enemies—the United States and Russia—to join forces to battle a new foe.

With Steven Barnes, Niven has written most significantly *Dream Park*, *Dream Park II: The Barsoom Project*, and the third book in the series, *The California Voodoo Game*. Set in California in the twenty-

If you enjoy the works of Larry Niven, you may also want to check out the following books and films:

Orson Scott Card, *The Ships of Earth,* 1994.
Anne McCaffrey and Elizabeth Ann Scarborough, *Power Play,* 1995.
Jack McDevitt, *The Engines of God,* 1994.
Dune, a film based on the novel by Frank Herbert, 1984.

first century, *Dream Park* is the ultimate virtual reality: a computerized holographic theme park. It is a fantasy world into which murder as well as industrial espionage suddenly appear in the first book of the series, a "good inventive SF with the makings of an excellent mystery," according to *Publishers Weekly.* About its sequel, *The Barsoom Project,* a reviewer for *Kliatt* noted that YA readers would enjoy "the skillful and fast-paced blend of fantasy, SF, and mystery elements in this novel." In addition to the "Dream Park" series, Niven and Barnes have also collaborated on *The Descent of Anansi* and *Achilles' Choice.*

Additionally, the trio of Niven, Pournelle, and Barnes joined forces on *The Legacy of Heorot* and its sequel, *Beowulf's Children.* Based loosely on the Beowulf legend, the books employ a monstrous Grendel to mix up the action. Earth colonists are settling the planet Avalon, still in its prehistoric age. Things are idyllic on this untouched Eden, until entrance of the beast. A reviewer for *Kliatt* noted that characters and action in the first of the Beowulf books "involve the reader totally in this fast-moving, tension-filled story." The storyline progresses two decades for the second installment of the tale, *Beowulf's Children,* "an example of panoramic sf at its best," according to *Library Journal.*

Niven has created worlds within worlds with his novels and short stories. His percolating imagination has lent reality to fantasy for legions of readers. Combining a quirky blend of action, punning humor, and hard science, he has carved out new ground in the science fiction genre, a sort of Niven-land, instantly recognizable to readers. As he stated in *CAAS,* "I'm a compulsive teacher, but I can't teach. I lack at least two of the essential qualifications. I cannot 'suffer fools gladly.' The smartest of my pupils would get all my atten-

tion, and the rest would have to fend for themselves. And I can't handle being interrupted. Writing is the answer. Whatever I have to teach, my students will select themselves by buying the book. And nobody interrupts a printed page. I knew what I wanted when I started writing. I've daydreamed all my life, and told stories, too. One day the daydreams began shaping themselves into stories. I wanted to share them. Astrophysical discoveries made peculiar implications, worlds stranger than any found in fantasy. I longed to touch the minds of strangers and show them wonders."

■ Works Cited

Review of *Beowulf's Children, Library Journal,* September 15, 1995, p. 97.

Bodari, Joni, review of *The Mote in God's Eye, School Library Journal,* March, 1975, p. 112.

Budrys, Algis, review of *The Magic Goes Away, Booklist,* February 1, 1979, p. 856.

Review of *Dream Park, Publishers Weekly,* March 13, 1981, pp. 86-87.

Review of *Dream Park II: The Barsoom Project, Kliatt,* January, 1990, pp. 20-21.

Elliot, Jeffrey, "An Interview with Larry Niven," *Science Fiction Review,* July, 1978, pp. 24-27.

Foote, Bud, review of *Ringworld, Detroit News,* April 20, 1980.

Green, Roland, review of *The Integral Trees, Booklist,* February 1, 1984, p. 770.

Green, Roland, review of *The Smoke Ring, Booklist,* March 1, 1987, p. 948.

Review of *The Gripping Hand, Kirkus Reviews,* December 1, 1992, p. 1472.

Review of *The Gripping Hand, Publishers Weekly,* December 28, 1992, p. 70.

Hays, Carl, review of *The Gripping Hand, Booklist,* December 15, 1992, p. 699.

Hays, Carl, review of *Ringworld Throne, Booklist,* May 1, 1996, p. 1492.

Hurwitz, K. Sue, review of *Ringworld Engineers, School Library Journal,* March, 1980, p. 147.

Review of *The Integral Trees, Publishers Weekly,* January 4, 1985, p. 68.

Review of *The Legacy of the Heorot, Kliatt,* January, 1989, pp. 22-23.

Review of *The Mote in God's Eye, Publishers Weekly,* September 16, 1974, p. 54.

Niven, Larry, comments in *Contemporary Authors Autobiography Series,* Volume 12, Gale, 1990, pp. 211-24.

Review of *The Patchwork Girl, Publishers Weekly,* February 22, 1980, p. 107.

Review of *Ringworld Engineers, Voice of Youth Advocates,* June, 1981, p. 38-39.

Review of *Ringworld Throne, Publishers Weekly,* May 13, 1996, p. 60.

Strawson, Galen, review of *Ringworld Engineers, Times Literary Supplement,* November 7, 1980, p. 1265.

Wilson, Raymond J., "Larry Niven," *Dictionary of Literary Biography, Volume 8: Twentieth-Century American Science Fiction Writers,* Gale, 1981, pp. 37-48.

Review of *A World Out of Time, Publishers Weekly,* August 23, 1976, p. 61.

■ For More Information See

BOOKS

Contemporary Literary Criticism, Volume 8, Gale, 1978.

Reginald, Robert, *Science Fiction and Fantasy Literature, 1975-1991,* Gale, 1992.

Stein, Kevin, *The Guide to Larry Niven's Ringworld,* illustrated by Todd Hamilton and James Clouse, Baen, 1994.

Twentieth-Century Science-Fiction Writers, 3rd Edition, St. James Press, 1991.

PERIODICALS

Kliatt, July, 1998, p. 20.

Los Angeles Times Book Review, March 25, 1984, p. 2; August 2, 1987, p. 11; April 21, 1996, p. 8.

New York Times Book Review, January 12, 1975, p. 32; October 17, 1976, p. 43; November 13, 1977, p. 26; November 25, 1984, p. 2; September 8, 1985, p. 28; January 31, 1993, p. 25.

School Library Journal, December, 1976, p. 74; January, 1982, p. 92; December, 1985, pp. 113-14; January, 1988, p. 97.

Voice of Youth Advocates, April, 1982, p. 40; April, 1983, p. 46; August, 1984, pp. 147-48; December, 1984, p. 268; February, 1986, p. 396; April, 1990, p. 18; December, 1991, p. 324; August, 1992, p. 178; April, 1993, p. 14; August, 1993, p. 169.*

—*Sketch by J. Sydney Jones*

Garth Nix

Personal

Born 1963, in Melbourne, Australia. *Education:* University of Canberra, B.A., 1986. *Hobbies and other interests:* Traveling, fishing, bodysurfing, book collecting, reading, films.

Addresses

Home—Sydney, Australia. *Electronic mail*—garth nix@ozemail.com.au.

Career

Author and publisher. Gotley Nix Evans Pty. Ltd., Sydney, Australia, marketing communications consultant. Worked for the Australian government; worked also in a bookstore and as a sales representative, publicist, and senior editor in the publishing industry. *Military service:* Served four years in the Australian Army Reserve.

Awards, Honors

Notable Book citation, Children's Book Council, for *The Ragwitch;* Notable Book citation and Best Books for Young Adults citation, American Library Association (ALA), Best Fantasy Novel and Best Young Adult Novel, Aurealis Awards for excellence in Australian Speculative Fiction, 1995, "Books in the Middle: Outstanding Titles" selection, *Voice of Youth Advocates,* 1996, all for *Sabriel;* Best Books for Young Adults citation, ALA, and "Books in the Middle: Outstanding Titles" selection, *Voice of Youth Advocates,* 1997, both for *Shade's Children.*

Writings

Very Clever Baby's Ben Hur: Starring Freddy the Fish as Charlton Heston, Nix Books (Sydney), 1988.
Very Clever Baby's First Reader: A Simple Reader for Your Child Featuring Freddy the Fish and Easy Words, Nix Books, 1988.
Very Clever Baby's Guide to the Greenhouse Effect, Nix Books, 1992.
Bill the Inventor, Koala Books, 1998.

FANTASY NOVELS

The Ragwitch, Pan Books (Sydney), 1990, Tor, 1995.
Sabriel, HarperCollins, 1995.

Shade's Children, Allen & Unwin (St. Leonard's, New South Wales), 1997, HarperCollins, 1997.

OTHER

The Calusari (novelization of *The X-Files* series), HarperCollins, 1997.

Also author of short stories and coauthor of shows for dinner theater.

■ Work in Progress

Lirael: Daughter of the Clayr, a related book to *Sabriel,* set twenty-two years after the events of that book, expected 1999.

■ Sidelights

Australian writer Garth Nix was weaned on fantasy novels; it is no coincidence he grew up to write such popular titles as *Sabriel* and *Shade's Children.* "My mother was reading *The Lord of the Rings* when she was pregnant with me," Nix told J. Sydney Jones in an interview for *Authors and Artists for Young Adults* (*AAYA*). "So I absorbed this master work of fantasy *in utero,* as it were. Later on I became a great fan of Tolkien's stories." Nix's explanation of this early influence is partly tongue-in-cheek, but it is clear from his writings that there is nothing fanciful about his dedication to his craft. "One of the best fantasies of this or any other year," is how a reviewer in *Voice of Youth Advocates* described *Sabriel.* A contributor in *Publishers Weekly* called that same novel "excellent high fantasy."

With only a handful of novels to his credit, Nix has already made a name for himself as a fantasy and science fiction writer of note in his native Australia, and increasingly in the United States as well. Nix's lighter side can be witnessed in a trio of books in the "Very Clever Baby" series, parodies of easy readers which are intended for parents. Written for two sets of parents who had babies on the way, these books exemplify the Nix philosophy of writing: "Essentially written for me. . . . It was what I wanted to read." Nix has made a cottage industry of writing books that he himself wants to read. The serendipity to this equation is that such books please a larger audience, too.

Youth in Canberra

Though born in Melbourne in 1963, Nix was raised in Canberra, Australia's national capital. "It was (and is) an unusual city," Nix noted in his interview, "having a population then of only about 200,000 people, but all the amenities of a capital." A completely planned city, most of it was built from the 1950s on; a fitting background for the future fantasy writer to have a city growing around him as he came of age. Books formed a baseline of interest for Nix from his early youth, both inside and outside the home. "Probably the most important influence on me becoming a writer was my parents, who both read voraciously and who both write. My father is a scientist with hundreds or even thousands of publications to his name, and my mother an artist who works in paper and incorporates her writing into her work. Our house was always full of books, and there was a culture of reading."

This "culture of reading" carried over to the outside world, as well. A loyal patron of the Canberra Public Library Service, Nix visited the children's library section daily. Located between his home and school, this children's library introduced Nix to the works of Ursula Le Guin, Robert Heinlein, John Masefield, Robert Louis Stevenson, Mary Stewart, Madeleine L'Engle, Isaac Asimov, and a host of other writers. Nix recalled that this children's library "was very much the best place of my six-to-ten-year-old life, other than my home." A self-declared "bookworm," Nix would generally rather read a novel than do school homework. "But I wasn't the solitary type. I had a good bunch of friends and was OK at playing sport, though it never really interested me. The only sport that captured my imagination at school was fencing, which I did for a year, till it was discontinued after a foil broke and nearly skewered a student."

At age seventeen, Nix joined the Australian Army Reserve, serving one weekend a month and about one month a year out in the bush. "This provided an outlet for energy that might otherwise have been misapplied," Nix commented in his interview, adding that it gave him a place to dispose of a vague sort of anger he was feeling as a teenager. "I didn't know what I was angry about, but I was definitely confused about life in general." His time in the reserves not only focussed his energies and gave him some self-discipline, but taught him an essential lesson: "removing the vague notion I had that life was supposed to be fair." Additionally, this time provided Nix with valuable information for later use when writing about anything military.

Following his final two months in the reserves, Nix worked as a salaries clerk in the Department of Aviation, saving money in order to travel. He intended to hang on at the job for a year; he lasted just over eleven months. "It was a soul-destroying bureaucracy, too much for me to cope with." Clearing out his savings account, he went off to travel for six months.

When an evil doll takes over a girl's spirit, her brother must follow them into another dimension to save her in this 1990 work.

Writer in Training

Most of his traveling was done out of an old Morris 1200, traveling the byways of England—something of a required pilgrimage for those born down under. Books were his companion, and also a typewriter, "a metal Silver-Reed which was a delight to work on. I had to sell it before I left, because I was so broke I couldn't afford the bus fare to Heathrow." But not before he had typed out his first published story on it. However, he only found out about that sale months later in Australia when he was contacted for reprint rights to his "Sam, Cars and the Cuckoo" for the magazine *Warlock.* This early sale confirmed for Nix that he could build a career as a writer.

Common sense, however, also came into play: he enrolled in a professional writing program at Canberra College of Advanced Education (now the University of Canberra) and ultimately earned his bachelor's degree in the discipline. "This proved to be a good course," Nix told *AAYA,* "and I benefited from being in the company of the many other writers who were doing the degree. Perhaps the main benefit of the course was in being forced to write a lot. During my three years there I wrote half of my first published novel, *The Ragwitch,* two feature-length screenplays, and numerous articles and short stories." He also collaborated with other students in scriptwriting for local theater restaurants, creating audience-participation murder mysteries.

Continuing his methodical apprenticeship, Nix took a job in a bookshop upon graduation from college. "I now believe that anyone who works in publishing should spend at least three months in a bookshop, where the final product ends up meeting the customer." After six months of such work, he joined up in the other end of the book business, working as a sales representative, publicist, and then editor for Australian publishers, including HarperCollins. This work took Nix to Sydney, where he still resides. During his six years in publishing, he became a published writer, first with the "Very Clever Baby" books, and then with his novel, *Ragwitch,* begun when he was twenty-one and published six years later. Of the former books, which feature Freddy the Fish and deal variously with the greenhouse effect and the movie *Ben Hur,* Nix noted on his web page that the "basic idea . . . is, of course, a joke. But it is ideal to give as a card to expectant parents. If anyone has a 3-6 month old baby who actually can read at all, let alone words like ICHTHYOL-OGY and TETRAODONTIDAE, they should be congratulated."

The Ragwitch, however, was no joke; it has been the slowest developing of any of Nix's books thus far. "It was written from a desire to write a C. S. Lewis style book that was more gritty and real," Nix explained to *AAYA*. "I wanted to get across more real fear, more discomfort and so on, without being disgusting or off-putting."

Another example of his writing-what-he-wants-to-read philosophy, Nix's first novel tells the story of Paul and his sister Julia who are exploring an aboriginal midden—literally a prehistoric garbage dump. There they find a nest and inside the nest a ball of feathers containing a rag doll. From deep within himself, Paul hears an urgent warning, but too late. The rag doll transforms itself into the Ragwitch and captures Julia in its power, thus initiating "a horrific series of adventures," according to Laurie Copping who reviewed the book in the *Canberra Times*. "Paul enters a strange fantasy land where he searches for his sister," Copping continued, which involves "strange creatures, magical animals and communication from one world to another. . . . An engrossing novel which should be enjoyed by true lovers of high fantasy." Pam Brown, writing in the *West Australian*, concluded that Nix "has created a complex and exciting story in the tradition of C. S. Lewis and the Tales of Narnia." Paul's adventures in the land of Gwarulch, Angarling, and Meepers also enthused Ann Tolman, reviewing the book in *Australian Bookseller and Publisher*: "Nix skillfully relates a magical tale which begins in a nice and easy way, but soon develops into a compelling and involving story of a journey through evil times. . . . Good adult mystic escapism with considerable imaginative experiences for the reader."

Inspirations for this first novel range from images from Nix's childhood to his experiences in the reserves. The midden itself comes from one such place on the coast near his family's holiday home. Paul's adventures in turn were enhanced by details gained from "night-time exercises in the Army Reserve where I once had to play the part of an escaping prisoner, pursued through the bush like a hunted animal." The adrenalin rush of that experience found its way into Nix's writing. "*The Ragwitch* did reasonably well," Nix told *AAYA*,

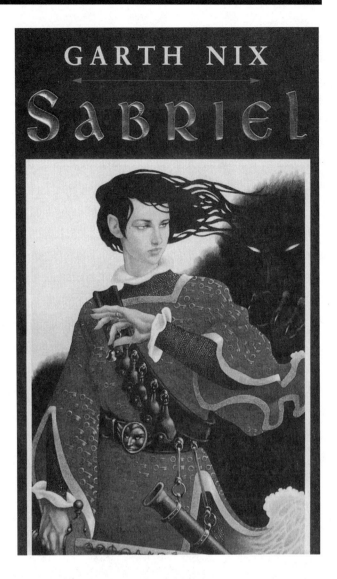

In this 1995 work Sabriel must travel to the mysterious Old Kingdom to rescue her father, the necromancer Abhorsen.

"selling out its print run in Australia in over a year, but not well enough to get reprinted." After many attempts, Nix also found a U.S. publisher for the book. However, when finally published as a paperback, "it was labeled as horror, thus bypassing most of its intended audience." Nonetheless, these early publications gave Nix encouragement to attempt something more in his life. After a long overland trip from London to Pakistan in 1992, he left publishing and went to work in public relations and marketing, forming his own company with two other partners, a position he maintained until 1998 when he left public relations to become a full-time writer.

Sabriel

Nix's next publication, *Sabriel,* was an important book for him. "It didn't disappear into the obscurity of my first book," Nix observed. "It wasn't an instant success either, but it has steadily grown more popular and has picked up important listings, nominations, and awards." Nix's intent with this second published novel was to create "an interesting, well-crafted fantasy that wasn't just a copy of Tolkien." Partly inspired by his recent journey from London to Pakistan, as well as by locations in his native Australia, *Sabriel* tells the story of a young woman trained by her necromancer-father, Abhorsen. He, unlike other necromancers, puts souls at ease rather than raising them, and Sabriel takes his lessons to heart. Attending the proper Wyverly College in Ancelstierre, Sabriel is busy learning other things than magic: music, fighting arts, English, and etiquette. Soon, however, she is involved in an attempt to save her father, protector of the magical Old Kingdom, to rescue him from the world beyond the Land of the Living. She is aided in her quest by Mogget, a powerful being in the form of a cat, and by the young prince, Touchstone, whom she has brought back from the dead. Battling her way past all forms of monsters and beasts, Sabriel finally reaches her father, only to lose him. But Sabriel learns in the process that she is truly her father's successor and that the Old Kingdom needs her protection, just as it did her father's.

Critics both in Australia and the United States applauded the publication of Nix's second novel. Colin Steele, writing in the *Canberra Times,* called Nix "a rising star in the fantasy world" and noted that *Sabriel* "fuses traditional quest and use of magic in split worlds with characterization far beyond its young adult market." *Horn Book,* among others, greeted the novel's U.S. publication with high praise. Reviewer Ann A. Flowers called *Sabriel* a "compelling fantasy," and noted that "the story is remarkable for the level of originality of the fantastic elements." *Booklist*'s Sally Estes observed that the "action charges along at a gallop, imbued with an encompassing sense of looming disaster," and that Sabriel herself "proves to be a stalwart heroine, who, in the end, finds and accepts her destiny." Alix Madrigal, reviewing the novel in the *San Francisco Chronicle,* also noted Sabriel's strength as a character, remarking that the book "cheerfully turns the tables on sexual role models." Madrigal concluded that *Sabriel* "is an engaging tale that slays sexual stereotypes along with its monsters." John Peters, in *School Library Journal,* concluded that "This book is guaranteed to keep readers up way past their bedtimes."

All this was music to Nix's ears, for his primary goal with his books is that "they are read and enjoyed," as he explained to *AAYA.* "Ideally they will transport the reader to my invented worlds completely while they read. If they have any greater effect than entertainment, I hope it is positive, and they will perhaps make people think about things they might otherwise not." Nix, who writes his first drafts into handbound notebooks with a Waterman fountain pen, still loves the portability of such writing tools. "I wrote a chapter [of *Sabriel*] longhand sitting on the wall of a

This work of science fiction depicts a terrifying future and the children who fight to make their city safe for humans again.

Crusader castle in Syria." These longhand chapters are then keyed into a word processor for a second draft. Final revisions are done on subsequent printouts. Since devoting himself full time to writing, Nix is able to work on his books up to six hours a day, and often seven days a week when deadlines are tight.

Shade's Children **and Beyond**

"*Shade's Children* [Nix's third novel] was an example of the 'writing for me' philosophy carried to its limit," Nix told *AAYA*. "While my publishers and many readers wanted another *Sabriel*, I had a much grimmer book inside me that wanted to come out. So I chose to write a science fiction novel rather than fantasy (though it is really very soft SF), and much more a straight-out thriller. . . . A bleak, violent vision of a near-future world." Essentially another quest tale, *Shade's Children* features a young psychic, Gold-Eye, who runs away from the cruel Overlords who harvest children's brains to transplant into their evil minions. The aliens that have taken over Earth have destroyed everyone over fourteen; Shade, a computer-generated hologram, is the only nurturing adult presence. Gold-Eye, along with a band of other teenagers—Drum, Ella, and Ninde—fight the new Overlords from their sanctuary at Shade's base. Sacrifice is demanded of them, and they must learn to deal with betrayal and their own special talents.

A reviewer for *Publishers Weekly* invited readers to "Plunge directly into a nightmare" with the opening sequence of *Shade's Children* in which "a scrawny boy flees monstrous trackers in an urban wasteland." *Horn Book*'s Flowers called Nix's second book a "slick, engrossing science fiction novel. . . . Grim, unusual, and fascinating." Janice Del Negro observed in *Bulletin of the Center for Children's Books* that the "plot has a little of everything—a post-apocalyptic setting, the perfect YA cast (no adults except the bad guys), and short bursts of chapters that hint at horrors, violence, and betrayal." Donna L. Scanlon, writing in *Voice of Youth Advocates,* noted that through "a fast-paced combination of narrative, transcripts, chilling statistical reports, and shifting points of view, Nix depicts a chilling future." But Scanlon also pointed out that Nix's grim vision of the future "is laced with hope . . . and it is this hope that sustains the reader through the nail-biting plot to

f you enjoy the works of Garth Nix, you may also want to check out the following books and films:

John Christopher's "Tripods" trilogy, 1967-68.
Gary Crew, *Strange Objects,* 1990.
Tamora Pierce, *Wolf-Speaker,* 1994.
Invasion of the Body Snatchers, a film based on the novel by Jack Finney, 1956.

the satisfying conclusion." A reviewer for *Reading Time* called *Shade's Children* "Deeply involving and exciting," and concluded that it was "one of the best adolescent reads of the year."

Nix followed this work with a young adult novelization of an episode from the popular television series, *The X-Files.* Nix's contribution to the six-part series was *The Calusari.* Hard upon this, Nix began a near-sequel to *Sabriel,* entitled *Lirael: Daughter of the Clayr.* This book returns to the world of Ancelstierre and the Old Kingdom, twenty-two years after the events related in *Sabriel* but with a new cast of characters. The main characters include Lirael, one of the Clayr; Sameth, Sabriel's son; and Nicholas Sayre, an Ancelstierran and school chum of Sameth's. Nick's fate lies in the hands of both Prince Sameth and Lirael when he crosses into the Old Kingdom from Ancelstierre. "In some ways *Lirael* is more complex than *Sabriel,*" Nix told *AAYA*. "It is told for a large part from two different viewpoints, and it also brings in more of the underlying story of the world. It doesn't necessarily explain anything (didactic passages in fantasy books are one of my pet hates), but it does make some things from *Sabriel* more clear, while muddying the waters about new things."

The lack of "didactic passages" is another Nix hallmark. "I never intentionally start with a theme or a message, or try to put one in," Nix explained to *AAYA* in his interview. "I believe in writing stories, not didactic tracts. However themes do seem to creep in from my subconscious, and . . . there does seem to be some basic philosophy that runs through all my books. One theme seems to be an emphasis on assuming responsibility—not only for yourself, but for others or even for whole societies. Another is that even though you might get what you want, there will be a cost of some kind involved somewhere. This includes happy endings. They are possible, but generally at a cost to someone, somewhere."

Nix is far from personal endings, happy or otherwise. Early successes in fantasy and science fiction bode well for his writing future. He is, as reviewers have noted, a writer to watch. "My future plans for writing are to keep doing it," Nix concluded to *AAYA*. "I will probably tend to write more fantasy than science fiction, because I think I'm better at the former. I also have some plans to write a contemporary thriller or two. But who knows? Like most writers I know, my notebooks are full of ideas and concepts. It's the execution of them that's difficult."

■ Works Cited

Brown, Pam, review of *The Ragwitch, West Australian*, June 15, 1991.

Copping, Laurie, review of *The Ragwitch, Canberra Times*, June 2, 1991.

Del Negro, Janice, review of *Shade's Children, Bulletin of the Center for Children's Books*, November, 1997, p. 94.

Estes, Sally, review of *Sabriel, Booklist*, October 1, 1996, p. 350.

Flowers, Ann A., review of *Sabriel, Horn Book*, January-February, 1997, pp. 64-65.

Flowers, Ann A., review of *Shade's Children, Horn Book*, September-October, 1997, pp. 576-77.

Madrigal, Alix, review of *Sabriel, San Francisco Chronicle*, December 1, 1996.

Nix, Garth, comments in *www.ozemail.com/~garthnix/garthnix.html*.

Nix, Garth, interview with J. Sydney Jones for *Authors and Artists for Young Adults*, conducted July, 1998.

Peters, John, review of *Sabriel, School Library Journal*, September, 1996, p. 228.

Review of *Sabriel, Publishers Weekly*, October 21, 1996, p. 84.

Review of *Sabriel, Voice of Youth Advocates*, June, 1997.

Scanlon, Donna L., review of *Shade's Children, Voice of Youth Advocates*, June, 1998, p. 132.

Review of *Shade's Children, Publishers Weekly*, June 16, 1997, p. 60.

Review of *Shade's Children, Reading Time*, November, 1997, p. 35.

Steele, Colin, review of *Sabriel, Canberra Times*, January 30, 1996.

Tolman, Ann, review of *The Ragwitch, Australian Bookseller and Publisher*, November, 1990.

■ For More Information See

PERIODICALS

Australian Book Review, September, 1996, p. 63.

Booklist, October 1, 1997, p. 320.

Bulletin of the Center for Children's Books, December, 1996, p. 146.

Chicago Tribune, November 10, 1996.

Kirkus Reviews, August 15, 1997, pp. 1309-10.

Locus, July, 1995; January, 1997.

Magpies, September, 1997, p. 39.

Reading Time Supplement, Volume 42, number 2.

School Library Journal, August, 1997, p. 158.

Viewpoint, Spring, 1995.

—Sketch by J. Sydney Jones

Naomi Shihab Nye

■ Personal

Maiden name is pronounced "*shee*-hab"; born March 12, 1952, in St. Louis, MO; daughter of Aziz (a journalist) and Miriam (a Montessori teacher; maiden name, Allwardt) Shihab; married Michael Nye (a photographer and lawyer), September 2, 1978; children: Madison Cloudfeather (son). *Education:* Trinity University, B.A. (summa cum laude) in English and World Religions, 1974. *Politics:* Independent. *Religion:* Independent. *Hobbies and other interests:* Reading, cooking, exercising, bicycling, traveling, collecting old postcards, "walking around staring at things."

■ Addresses

Home and office—806 South Main Ave., San Antonio, TX 78204. *Electronic mail*—nshihab@aol.com.

■ Career

Poet, editor, and writer of children's books. Worked full time in the Texas Commission on the Arts Writers in the Schools project, 1974-86; has been a visiting writer or writer in residence through numerous arts programs and schools in Texas, Wyoming, Maine, California, and Alaska; has taught at the University of California, Berkeley, the University of Hawaii at Manoa, and the University of Texas at both Austin and San Antonio. Member of the Friends of the Library in San Antonio and the King William Downtown Neighborhood Association. *Member:* American-Arab Anti-Discrimination Committee, Radius of Arab-American Writers (RAWI), Texas Institute of Letters, Phi Beta Kappa, Academy of American Poets.

■ Awards, Honors

Voertman Poetry Prize, Texas Institute of Letters, 1980, for *Different Ways to Pray*; four Pushcart Prizes; Voertman Prize, Texas Institute of Letters, and Notable Book, American Library Association (ALA), both 1982, and National Poetry Series selection, all for *Hugging the Jukebox*; Lavan Award, Academy of American Poets, and co-winner, Charity Randall Citation for Spoken Poetry, International Poetry Forum, both 1988; Jane Addams Children's Book Award, and Honorary Book for Christians and Jews, National Association for Christians and Jews, both 1992, both for *This Same Sky: A Collection of Poems from around the World*; Best Book citation, *School Library Journal*, 1994, Pick of the List citation, American Booksellers Association, 1994, Notable Children's Trade Book in the

Field of Social Studies citation, National Council for Social Studies and Children's Book Council (NCSS/CBC), 1995, and Jane Addams Children's Book Award for picture book, 1995, all for *Sitti's Secrets*; Paterson Prize for Books for Young People, Paterson Poetry Center, Children's Book of Distinction, *Hungry Mind Review*, Best Books for Young Adults, ALA, and Notable Children's Book in the Field of Social Studies, NCSS/CBC, all 1996, all for *The Tree Is Older Than You Are: Bilingual Poems and Stories from Mexico*; Jane Addams Children's Book Award, Judy Lopez Memorial Award for Children's Literature, National Women's Book Association, Best Book for Young People, Texas Institute of Letters, Best Books for Young Adults, and Notable Book for Young Readers, ALA, Best Books for the Teen Age, New York Public Library, and Dorothy Canfield Fisher Children's Book Award Master List, all 1998, all for *Habibi*; Best Books for Young Adults, and Notable Book for Young Readers, ALA, 1998, for *The Space between Our Footsteps: Poems and Paintings from the Middle East*; Guggenheim Fellowship, 1997-98.

■ Writings

FOR JUVENILES

(Editor) *This Same Sky: A Collection of Poems from around the World*, Four Winds Press, 1992.

Sitti's Secrets (picture book), illustrated by Nancy Carpenter, Four Winds Press, 1994.

Benito's Dream Bottle (picture book), illustrated by Yu Cha Pak, Simon & Schuster, 1995.

(Editor) *The Tree Is Older Than You Are: Bilingual Poems and Stories from Mexico*, Simon & Schuster, 1995.

Lullaby Raft (picture book), illustrated by Vivienne Flesher, Simon and Schuster, 1996.

(Editor with Paul B. Janeczko) *I Feel a Little Jumpy around You: A Book of Her Poems and His Poems Collected in Pairs*, Simon and Schuster, 1996.

Habibi (young adult novel), Simon and Schuster, 1997.

(Editor) *The Space between Our Footsteps: Poems and Paintings from the Middle East*, Simon and Schuster, 1998.

POETRY FOR ADULTS

Tattooed Feet, Texas Portfolio, 1977.

Eye-to-Eye, Texas Portfolio, 1978.

Different Ways to Pray, Breitenbush, 1980.

On the Edge of the Sky, Iguana, 1981.

Hugging the Jukebox, Dutton, 1982.

Yellow Glove, Breitenbush, 1987.

Invisible, Trilobite, 1987.

Mint, State Street Press, 1992.

Red Suitcase, BOA Editions Ltd., 1994.

Words under the Words: Selected Poems, Far Corner Books/Eighth Mountain, 1995.

Fuel, BOA Editions Ltd., 1998.

Also author of "Twenty Other Worlds," in *Texas Poets in Concert: A Quartet*, edited by Richard B. Sale, University of North Texas Press, 1990, and *Never in a Hurry: Essays on People and Places*, University of South Carolina Press, 1996.

RECORDINGS

Rutabaga-Roo (children's songs), Flying Cat, 1979.

Lullaby Raft (folk songs), Flying Cat, 1981.

The Spoken Page (poetry), International Poetry Forum, 1988.

■ Adaptations

Several of Nye's poems have been set to music and recorded by Bill Mackechnie on his CD, *Famous*.

■ Work in Progress

A young adult novel for Greenwillow; poems for adults; two poetry anthologies for teens, *What Have You Lost* and a second as yet untitled compilation of one hundred poems written by young writers; *Come with Me*, a book of poems for young readers with illustrations by Dan Yaccarino.

■ Sidelights

Naomi Shihab Nye is an award-winning poet who has turned her hand to children's books—poetry anthologies, picture books, and young adult novels—which in one way or another deal with the idea of connections. In award-winning anthologies such as *This Same Sky: A Collection of Poems from around the World*, *The Tree Is Older Than You Are: Bilingual Poems and Stories from Mexico*, and *The Space between Our Footsteps: Poems and Paintings from the Middle East*, Nye has not only made poetry accessible to a younger audience, but has also introduced young readers to a bigger world than that encompassed by the walls of their schools. Compiling poems, short stories, and artwork from creative people around the world, she has attempted to open windows on the world, to build bridges between "us" and "them."

More than a simple tip of the hat toward fashionable multiculturalism, Nye's work has been built on a bedrock of such simple connections as the everyday lives of people around the world, or of ancestry played out in primary daily tasks. Never one to write with a thesaurus rather than her heart, Nye employs a "direct, unadorned vocabulary," according to Pat Monaghan in a *Booklist* review of *Red Suitcase,* that conveys both depth and mystery. "I write poems and stories out of daily life," Nye told *Authors and Artists for Young Adults* (*AAYA*) in an interview, "with lots of invention thrown in." Reviewing *Fuel,* her 1998 collection of poems, a *Publishers Weekly* critic hit on a core attribute to all of Nye's writing. Noting that much of her work deals with the quotidian around the world, the reviewer wrote that such "small-scale multi-ethnic negotiations . . . convey a delicate sense of moral concern and a necessary sense of urgency."

Nye's works often tell the human stories behind the headlines, as with her young adult novel, *Habibi,* which deals with the problems of the Middle East on a very personal level. Her anthology *The Space between Our Footsteps* is also an attempt to show young readers that there is more than just conflict in the Middle East, more than simple politics at work. Both Israelis and Arabs are included in this collection, a celebration of life and diversity. Throughout Nye's work for both young readers and adults is an optimism, a quiet belief in variety and the possibility of change. "I believe we can revise our lives by writing," Nye told *AAYA*. "We can invent and explore new connections through language. Writing is contagious; it promotes other writing. And with writing we can help to invite people into their own lives. To be connected in a deeper sense with themselves."

St. Louis to Jerusalem to Texas

The idea of connections between peoples is fundamental to Nye's own personal life. The daughter of a Palestinian immigrant and an American,

Nye was brought up in two worlds. "I felt I had an ideal childhood," Nye once told *Something about the Author* (*SATA*) in an interview. "I grew up in a mixed neighborhood in St. Louis, in a home very nurturing for self-expression. I had the sense of people speaking up for themselves very early on. My father was a spectacular teller of Middle Eastern folktales. My brother and I always went to sleep with my father's folktales and my mother's lullabies." Nye's father was a journalist and her mother a fine arts graduate in painting, so there was never any lack of verbal or visual stimuli. "But I don't remember books being an obsession in our home like they are for me now," Nye told *SATA*. "I have twenty books stacked up by my bed at all times and I get very nervous when I enter someone's house and no books are visible. I read incessantly, sometimes many things at once."

At about age five Nye encountered the poet Carl Sandburg, first on TV and then a bit later, when she learned to read, through his poems. "I began writing as a child of six, fascinated by the power of words on the page to make us look differently at our lives, to help us see and connect," Nye observed to *SATA*. "Early on I was introduced to the works not only of Sandburg, but also Margaret Wise Brown, Emily Dickinson, William Blake in his *Songs of Innocence,* and Louisa May Alcott. Reading gave me the passionate urge to write." By the age of seven, Nye had published her first poem in the publication *Wee Wisdom*. "I had a second grade teacher who was a strong advocate of memorizing poetry and writing it ourselves. She nurtured the seed that was already growing. I also remember that the library was my great friend as a child. It still is. But then it was truly the heart of my life and I was always searching out new places to submit my poetry." Throughout her school years Nye continued publishing her works, first in children's magazines and then later in publications such as *Seventeen*.

Her childhood was not all books, though, as she described to *SATA*. "I guess I was a fairly normal kid and did the usual things with friends: baseball, dolls, skating in the winter, Girl Scouts, playing the violin and piano, movies. But I always knew I had a private place to go, an interior haven that was all mine, partly as a Palestinian American and partly as an interested observer of the world. I never felt prejudice; my father was a respected man in the community—a charismatic, handsome type. People were naturally drawn to him. But still I felt I had a choice: I could be in the middle of the circle of our neighborhood, so to speak, or step back and watch the circle and wonder about it. The writer's ability to detach and witness. I do remember how troubled I was as a child that there were no black students in my school. St. Louis was a mixed community, but the lines were drawn. Black students went to their schools and we went to ours. I always wondered about that. Why was my father acceptable, yet black kids wouldn't be? Now, of course, that neighborhood is thoroughly integrated. But back then I wondered how different you could be and still be accepted."

In high school Nye moved with her family to Jerusalem, and for the first time she met her father's family. The move was a revelation for her, a confirmation of what she had long suspected: that though separated by space and time, there is a real connection between all peoples. She attended high school first in Ramallah, and then at St. Tarkmanchatz in the old city of Jerusalem. "The lessons were taught in Arabic, Armenian, and English," Nye recalled for SATA, "so I just sat back and waited for the teachers' English lessons to come on." Her father was editing the *Jerusalem Times* and Nye wrote a column on teen matters for that same daily's English-language newspaper. The Six-Day War cut short the family's stay, and they returned to the United States, settling in San Antonio, Texas, where Nye still resides.

Various male/female twosomes offer their perspectives on gender, relationships, love, and other subjects in this 1996 collection of poems.

Itinerant Writer

"I finished high school in Texas," Nye told SATA. "And I was always proud of the fact that I did so without ever having attended a football game. The football players themselves even bought me a mum to celebrate it. I guess you have to be from Texas to understand what an accomplishment that is." Known as something of a renegade in high school, Nye was still devoted to reading and writing. "I passionately consumed the writings of Thoreau in high school," she recalled. "In college I was very attracted to the Beat writers like [Jack] Kerouac, [Gregory] Corso, and [Gary] Snyder. The writers of the Twenties were very appealing, too, especially Gertrude Stein. But my strongest influence was and is William Stafford. I started reading him in high school, but never formally stud-

ied under him. In fact, I didn't meet him until the late 1970s, but his work and life remain a powerful inspiration for me today." Nye attended Trinity University in San Antonio, living at home all four years. She continued writing and publishing throughout her college years, "but I never called myself a writer until I graduated from college," she told SATA.

Upon graduation, Nye found work in the Texas Writers in the Schools project, under whose auspices writers would go into the schools to work directly with the children. "For the next dozen years or so," Nye explained to SATA, "I was the most active visiting writer around. I worked full time at it, every day of the week in different schools all around the state." Meanwhile she was also establishing a name for herself as a poet with a distinctive voice, publishing chapbooks and collections of poetry. In 1982, her second full-length collection, *Hugging the Jukebox*, was chosen for the National Poetry Series, and Nye gained national publication. Her poems deal with the everyday aspects of life and with the harsh realities as well: death and missed opportunities. "Nye observes the business of living and the continuity among all the world's inhabitants, whether separated by oceans or time," wrote Jane L. Tanner in *Dictionary of Literary Biography*. "She lives in Texas but is regional only insofar as she has a strong sense of place wherever she happens to be." Nye also garnered prestigious awards and was invited as a visiting instructor to colleges and schools around the country. "Basically," Nye told *SATA*, "I have made a permanent job out of being an itinerant visitor. I've never had benefits and so forth, and don't expect them. I feel more free this way."

Changing Focus

Nye was married in 1978 to a lawyer and budding photographer who has since become a photographer and sometime-lawyer, and in 1986 their son Madison was born. "It was then I really began to look around for other ways to make a living so that I would not be in the schools full time," Nye told *SATA*, She turned her hand to a wide variety of writing styles, but it was not until the early 1990s that she got into children's writing. "I had done an earlier album of children's songs," Nye explained to *SATA*, "now out of print. And I always felt that my poetry was for all ages. In fact some of my collections are used in high schools around the country. I've always been attracted to texts for children, whether poetry or prose. I think adults need them as much as children do sometimes, for clarity and focus. One of the delights of having our son was that it was now legitimate for me to return to that part of the library I so loved when I was young. I never felt there had to be a huge division between adult and children's literature. We often underestimate what kids can understand. Working with so many students in schools over the years, that is one thing I learned—don't underestimate."

So when editor Virginia Duncan contacted Nye for possible children's book ideas, Nye found the offer appealing. Having a child herself as well as having worked with children for so many years made it seem like a natural next step to create her own children's books. "I was always looking for crossover texts," Nye told *SATA*, "for the books that would appeal to fifth graders as well as college-age readers. Finally I had the opportunity to try to make some myself. In my own writing, I did not see it as such a stretch to be understood by both audiences. My style is both simple and understandable. I always felt revulsion for the cutesie sorts of children's books. I had no desire to be condescending." But the first several ideas Nye came up with were rejected. Finally an idea for an anthology of poems grew quite naturally out of her work in the schools. "It was during the Gulf War," Nye recalled for *SATA*, "and the country was pulsing with 'hatred' for Arabs. It was a deeply depressing time for me, and I wanted to bring the war down to the human level for the children I was working with. So I found some poems by Iraqi poets and had the kids read them and let them see that these people were no different than we were. They had the same daily needs, the same inner lives: Moms talking about worries and kids, poems about choosing a personal path in life. It was a very powerful experience and the teachers wanted more. They wanted an international anthology to share with their students. That's when I got the idea for *This Same Sky*."

Nye's itinerant life served her well in compiling this collection, for she had contacts with writers all around the world. "I basically sat down and wrote letters all over the place requesting submissions," Nye told *SATA*. "What resulted was an international anthology that has gone through several printings and has been used in schools around the country. That makes me very happy." Nye gathered together 129 poets from sixty-eight countries to celebrate the natural world and its human and animal inhabitants in *This Same Sky: A Collection of Poems from around the World*. "The book as a whole reflects the universality of human concerns across cultures," commented Jim Morgan in *Voice of Youth Advocates*. According to Morgan, "the most striking aspect of this collection, and the book's greatest potential appeal to adolescents, is the sense of real human life behind the words." The poets speak directly, not in some idealized manner, and the work "would definitely be a strong multicultural contribution" to a school's poetry collection, Morgan concluded. Mary M. Burns in *Horn Book* thought *This Same Sky* "should prove invaluable for intercultural education as well as for pure pleasure." *This Same Sky* won for Nye a batch of awards and set her on a new course for her writing.

Sitti's Secrets, also written during the Gulf War, was Nye's second children's offering, this time a picture book. "I always felt close to my paternal grandmother, despite the fact that she lived so far away," Nye explained to *SATA*. "I was intrigued that when you have a loved one on the other side of the world, it is hard to look at that world as divided. There is a link between people, between all people, and that's what I wanted to write about when I began this story of a 'sitti' or grandmother." "The author writes a compassionate story in poetic, rich language," noted Maeve Visser Knoth in *Horn Book*. This is a book, concluded Knoth, "about the love of a family separated by space but united in spirit." Betsy Hearne, in *Bulletin of the Center for Children's Books*, thought that "the setting is unusual and the details vividly realized," and Luann Toth, in *School Library Journal*, wrote that *Sitti's Secrets* "serves as a thoughtful, loving affirmation of the bonds that transcend language barriers, time zones, and national borders."

"What pleases me most about the book," Nye said to *SATA*, "is how universally it seems to have worked for children. When I am with kids in the schools after reading the book, they talk about their own relatives who are far away. They'll say they have a grandmother in another country. She's actually in Montana, but the concept of country is relative. What's important is that the story has translated the emotion of missing someone, acknowledging their own details, and feeling connected despite distance."

From Picture Books to Young Adult Novels

Nye's son Madison was the inspiration for her next picture book, *Benito's Dream Bottle*. "When Madison was two," Nye explained to *SATA*, "he began telling about a bottle he carried inside his body that stretched from his stomach up to his chest. It held his dreams. He really believed in that bottle and would talk about it every morning. I loved the idea of dreams being something we carry around with us and that we fill up and empty, fill up and empty." *Booklist*'s Hazel Rochman noted in a review of the work that "Nye is a fine poet, and the words here have a nice

rhythm and a joy in the domestic and the imaginary."

For her next children's book, Nye returned to anthologies, compiling poems, stories, and paintings from Mexico in the bilingual *The Tree Is Older Than You Are: Bilingual Poems and Stories from Mexico*. "I've travelled in Mexico quite a lot and love the culture," Nye reported to *SATA*. "And living in San Antonio I am in the midst of Mexican American culture. I've noticed there are quite a few books dealing with latino or latina culture in the U.S. but too few that represent Mexican culture on its own terms. That's what I hoped to do with *The Tree Is Older Than You Are*." Readers and reviewers alike found the attempt successful. Delia A. Culbertson, writing in *Voice of Youth Ad-*

In this highly lauded novel, the Arab-Israeli conflict is viewed from a young person's perspective when fourteen-year-old Liyana moves from the U.S. to her father's homeland in Jerusalem.

vocates, noted that this "bilingual anthology . . . brims over with a sense of wonder and playful exuberance, its themes as varied and inventive as a child's imagination." Writing in *Bulletin of the Center for Children's Books,* Deborah Stevenson called Nye "a gifted poet and anthologist," and observed that the poems selected "are generally elegant and eloquent, often richly imaged and dreamy," while *Horn Book's* Nancy Vasilakis concluded that "this bountiful, joyous collection offers much to appreciate."

A picture book and an anthology were Nye's next two projects for young readers. With *Lullaby Raft,* Nye returned to a song which she recorded in 1981 to create an illustrated bedtime book in which a child imagines various animals drifting off to sleep at the end of a busy day. The anthology, which she co-edited with Paul Janeczko, is a book of gender poems, *I Feel a Little Jumpy around You.* "The poems are arranged thematically," Nye explained to *SATA,* "with a male and a female viewpoint, either parallel or contrasting, on the same subject or theme on facing pages. It's an attempt at showing the connections and contrasts we have across gender much as the earlier anthologies show it across cultures." Dubbed "a wonder" by a *Kirkus Reviews* contributor, and described as "a rich source for thought and discussion" in by a reviewer in *School Library Journal. I Feel a Little Jumpy around You* gathers some two hundred "rich, subtle poems," according to a critic in *Booklist,* which detail the feelings of both genders on topics from politics to parenting. The anthology includes poets such as Robert Bly, W. S. Merwin, and Rita Dove and supplies "visceral proof of how men and women perceive the world differently and what dreams and memories we hold in common," according to a reviewer in *Horn Book.*

With *Habibi,* Nye turned her hand to novel writing—a first for her. "This was extremely challenging for me," Nye told *AAYA* in her interview. "I usually have a one- to ten-page attention span with my poems and essays. So this was a stretch putting together several hundred manuscript pages. But I used poetry quite a lot in the book, not only with the chapter headings, but also with the organization. I had a sense of the book from the beginning as a series of poems. While I was writing the book, I kept saying that it would be my first and last novel, but when I finished, I was hooked on novel-writing. I missed the daily

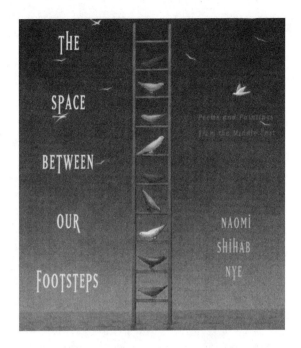

More than a hundred poets and artists from nineteen Middle Eastern countries explore both universal and everyday themes in this collection selected by Nye.

contact with my characters, so I guess I'm a convert. I'm at work now on another YA novel, this time set in San Antonio."

On the surface, *Habibi* seems to be an autobiographical novel, reminiscent of *Sitti's Secrets.* A young Arab American leaves her home in St. Louis to move to Jerusalem where her father was born, much as Nye herself did. "The book is based on facts in my life," Nye told *AAYA,* "but the story is pure fiction. I wanted to give the story behind the story that we see on the evening news. I keep hoping kids might be invested with a greater fervor to somehow solve the problems that exist than adults are. So many times with things political, it's a matter of adults betraying children." The title comes from the Arab word for "darling," which is what Liyana Abboud's father calls her. She is fourteen and would much rather stay in St. Louis. Once in Jerusalem, the Abbouds face racial prejudice and suspicion. Not only must the family deal with cultural differences between America and the Middle East, but also with the daily strife between Arabs and Jews. Israeli soldiers ransack her Arab grandmother's house; her doctor father is briefly arrested when he tries to

If you enjoy the works of Naomi Shihab Nye, you may also want to check out the following books:

Tamar Bergman, *The Boy from Over There*, 1988.
Uri Orlev, *The Lady with the Hat*, 1995.
Suzanne Fisher Staples, *Shabanu: Daughter of the Wind*, 1989, and *Haveli*, 1993.

protect a Palestinian youth shot by soldiers. When Liyana befriends a Jewish boy, Omer, she tests her family's espoused beliefs in tolerance. A reviewer in *Publishers Weekly* called the novel "soul-stirring," and concluded that "Nye's climactic ending will leave readers pondering, long after the last page is turned, why Arabs, Jews, Greeks and Armenians can no longer live in harmony the way they once did." *Horn Book*'s Jennifer M. Brabander noted that the "leisurely progression of the narrative matches the slow and stately pace of daily life in this ancient land, and the text's poetic turns of phrase accurately reflect Liyana's passion for words and language." Writing in the *New York Times Book Review*, Karen Leggett concluded that *Habibi* "gives a reader all the sweet richness of a Mediterranean dessert, while leaving some of the historical complexities open to interpretation."

A Writer of Many Parts

Nye further explored the "story behind the story" of the Middle East with her 1998 anthology, *The Space between Our Footsteps*. "Speaking at schools and with librarians I discovered there was really no collection of poems about the Middle East that was accessible to young readers," Nye told *AAYA*. "As with *This Same Sky*, I wanted to introduce them to the incredible variety of voices that exist elsewhere and to put a human face on regions that are often looked at simply as headlines. I also decided I would like to showcase artwork from the region, and there was a tremendous response to requests for such works. We had to choose from hundreds of submissions." The anthology contains over a hundred poets and artists from nineteen countries, "a potluck of Middle Eastern tastes, and every dish is full of flavorful surprises," according to Angela J. Reynolds in *School Library Journal*. A reviewer for *Horn Book* compared

the work with the author's earlier *This Same Sky*, observing that "Nye sets herself a smaller geographic landscape but as daunting a task—to capture in art and poetry the 'secrets [which] live in the spaces between our footsteps' in the multifarious cultures of the Middle East," a task which *Publishers Weekly* declared Nye "amply achieves," providing "a type of 'hors d'oeuvre' to stimulate further interest." *Kirkus Reviews* called the anthology a "nourishing feast" and concluded that the "diversity of viewpoint and universality of feeling will open the eyes of readers whose picture of this part of the world has been shaped by museum exhibits, the Arabian Nights, and the nightly news."

Nye maintains a busy if not hectic schedule. She spends less time in the schools now, but has at least three or four projects going at once. She is at work on poetry for both young readers and adults, anthologies, a young adult novel, and increasingly finds herself a spokesperson for all of the above. Additionally, Nye has taken part in two television series aired by PBS: a Bill Moyers production, *Language of Life,* and another about poets around the country, *United States of Poetry.* Nye's is an energetic life and to squeeze all the projects in she gets up at four in the morning to start her work day. "Those are the best hours," she told *SATA*, "the early morning sweet silence when everyone else is still asleep. I believe in abundance: write a lot and if you're lucky, you'll like *something.* I never work to a real schedule unless I have a deadline to make. Usually I just let whatever needs to come, come, whether it is poetry or children's stories. I keep notebooks and refer to them for images or opening lines, but writing is an ongoing process. You're doing it even when you're not sitting down with pen and paper in front of you. You're thinking it, seeing it, hearing it in your mind. Recently I've been experimenting with William Stafford's technique of lying down on the couch to write poems. Just writing as freely as possible and letting directions evolve."

Nye's years of working with children in the schools have given her a natural sense of audience. "I don't really think of audience when I write," she explained to *SATA*. "But I do know instinctively what appeals to students of different ages, what works with them. And it is so rewarding writing for children. They are still linked to that essential world of childhood where everything is possible. It is the most exquisite world if one is favored with good circumstances. If not, writing may still be a crucial tool for expression. Words have magic for children. They are less tired of things. I hope for a certain receptivity in younger readers that is sometimes harder to find in adults. And the amazing thing is that it is still there, in spite of television.

"Ultimately I look at writing as a form of discovery," Nye told *SATA*. "I hope my words reach out to the reader and welcome them. 'Yes, I have felt that way before.' I personally feel close to what other people are saying all the time. Their words broaden my life. They give comfort that we are not, and never have been, alone out here. I always tell young writers how important the link is between reading and writing. You just cannot be a good writer without reading, reading. It's a way of sharing. I didn't set out to publish to prove something. It was simply a way to connect with unseen friends out there. I felt the writers I read were my personal friends, and I still feel that way. That's the effect I'm trying to achieve with my own work. To connect."

■ Works Cited

Brabander, Jennifer M., review of *Habibi*, *Horn Book*, November-December, 1997, pp. 683-84.

Burns, Mary M., review of *This Same Sky: A Collection of Poems from around the World*, *Horn Book*, March-April, 1993, p. 215.

Culbertson, Delia A., review of *The Tree Is Older Than You Are*, *Voice of Youth Advocates*, December, 1995, pp. 333-34.

Review of *Fuel*, *Publishers Weekly*, April 27, 1998, p. 62.

Review of *Habibi*, *Publishers Weekly*, September 8, 1997, p. 77.

Hearne, Betsy, review of *Sitti's Secrets*, *Bulletin of the Center for Children's Books*, March, 1994.

Review of *I Feel a Little Jumpy around You*, *Booklist*, April 1, 1996, p. 131.

Review of *I Feel a Little Jumpy around You*, *Horn Book*, November-December, 1996, p. 755.

Review of *I Feel a Little Jumpy around You*, *Kirkus Reviews*, April 1, 1996, p. 534.

Review of *I Feel a Little Jumpy around You*, *School Library Journal*, May, 1996, p. 143.

Knoth, Maeve Visser, review of *Sitti's Secrets*, *Horn Book*, May-June, 1994, pp. 317-18.

Leggett, Karen, "Where Rage Lives," *New York Times Book Review*, November 16, 1997.

Monaghan, Pat, review of *Red Suitcase*, *Booklist*, October 15, 1994, p. 395.

Morgan, Jim, review of *This Same Sky: A Collection of Poems from around the World*, *Voice of Youth Advocates*, April, 1993, p. 59.

Nye, Naomi Shihab, *Sitti's Secrets*, Four Winds Press, 1994.

Nye, Naomi Shihab, *Benito's Dream Bottle*, Simon & Schuster, 1995.

Nye, Naomi Shihab, interview with J. Sydney Jones for *Something about the Author*, Volume 86, Gale, 1996, pp. 170-75.

Nye, Naomi Shihab, interview with J. Sydney Jones for *Authors and Artists for Young Adults*, conducted July 10, 1998.

Reynolds, Angela J., review of *The Space between Our Footsteps*, *School Library Journal*, May, 1998, p. 159.

Rochman, Hazel, review of *Benito's Dream Bottle*, *Booklist*, May 1, 1995, p. 1580.

Review of *The Space between Our Footsteps*, *Horn Book*, March-April, 1998, pp. 229-30.

Review of *The Space between Our Footsteps*, *Kirkus Reviews*, April 1, 1998, p. 499.

Review of *The Space between Our Footsteps*, *Publishers Weekly*, March 2, 1998, p. 69.

Stevenson, Deborah, review of *The Tree Is Older Than You Are*, *Bulletin of the Center for Children's Books*, November, 1995, p. 101.

Tanner, Jane L., "Naomi Shihab Nye," *Dictionary of Literary Biography*, Volume 120: *American Poets Since World War II*, Gale, 1992, p. 223.

Toth, Luann, review of *Sitti's Secrets*, *School Library Journal*, June, 1994, p. 112.

Vasilakis, Nancy, review of *The Tree Is Older Than You Are*, *Horn Book*, March-April, 1996, p. 218.

■ For More Information See

BOOKS

Contemporary Poets, 6th edition, St. James Press, 1996.

Spaar, Lisa Russ, introduction to *Texas Poets in Concert: A Quartet*, University of North Texas Press, 1990, p. 2.

PERIODICALS

Booklist, March 15, 1993, p. 1338; March 15, 1994, p. 1374.

Bulletin of the Center for Children's Books, November, 1995, p. 101; May, 1998, pp. 332-33.

Kirkus Reviews, February 15, 1994, p. 231; August 15, 1997, p. 1310; July 1, 1998, p. 930.

New York Times Book Review, April 11, 1993, p. 30.

Publishers Weekly, April 24, 1995, p. 71; June 23, 1997, p. 90.

School Library Journal, December, 1992, p. 139; October, 1995, p. 150; May, 1996, p. 143; November, 1996, p. 142; July, 1997, p. 35.

Swamp Root, spring, 1989, pp. 83-93.

Voice of Youth Advocates, December, 1995, p. 333; August, 1996, p. 178; August, 1998, p. 228.

—Sketch by J. Sydney Jones

Trey Parker and Matt Stone

Matt Stone (left) and Trey Parker, co-creators of the controversial, irreverent, and sometimes raunchy animated hit *South Park.*

■ Personal

Trey Parker: Born in 1969, in Conifer, CO; son of a United States Geological Service geologist. *Education:* Attended University of Colorado, Boulder. *Hobbies and other interests:* Tae Kwon Do, playing piano.

Matt Stone: Full name, Matthew Stone; born in 1971 in Houston, TX. *Education:* University of Colorado, Boulder, B.S. (mathematics). *Hobbies and other interests:* Playing guitar, bass, and drums.

■ Addresses

Trey Parker: *Home*—Bel Air, CA.

Matt Stone: *Home*—Southern California.

■ Career

Co-creators, executive producers (with Brian Graden and Anne Garefino), and writers of animated television series, *South Park*, Comedy Central, 1997—. Co-directors and creators of animated short, *The Spirit of Christmas*, 1995. Parker and Stone operate a production studio in Marina del Rey, California.

Trey Parker: Director of films *The Giant Beaver of Sri Lanka* (short), 1989, *First Date* (short), 1990, *American History* (short), 1992, *Cannibal! The Musical* (also known as *Alferd Packer: The Musical*), Avenging Conscience Inc./Cannibal Films Ltd., 1996, and *Orgazmo*, 1997. Also producer, sound designer, and composer for *Cannibal!* Editor for *Orgazmo*. Provided voices for *The Spirit of Christmas* (also known as *Jesus vs. Frosty*) and provides voices for Stan Marsh, Eric Cartman, Mr. Garrison, Officer Barbrady, and others in *South Park*. Actor in films *Cannibal!* (as Alferd Packer), *Orgazmo* (as Joe Young), and *BASEketball* (as Joseph "Coop" Cooper), Universal, 1998.

Matt Stone: Co-producer of films *Cannibal! The Musical* (also known as *Alferd Parker: The Musical*), Avenging Conscience Inc./Cannibal Films Ltd., 1996, and *Orgazmo*, 1997. Music composer for soundtrack of animated series *South Park*, 1997—. Actor, providing various voices for *The Spirit of Christmas*, 1995, and *South Park* (voices of Kyle Broslofski, Kenny McCormick, Pip, Jesus, Jimbo Marsh, and others), and actor in films *Orgazmo*, 1997, and *BASEketball*, Universal, 1998.

■ Awards, Honors

Cable Ace Award for Best Animated Programming Special or Series, 1997, to both Parker and Stone, for *South Park*.

■ Writings

Trey Parker: Author of scripts for animated short *The Spirit of Christmas* (also known as *Jesus vs. Frosty*), 1995, and feature films *Cannibal! The Musical* (also known as *Alferd Packer: The Musical*), 1996, and *Orgazmo*, 1997.

■ Adaptations

A feature-length film of *South Park* is scheduled to be made by Paramount, as well as video and PC game versions of the cartoon.

■ Work in Progress

A prequel to the film *Dumb and Dumber*; a sound recording of Isaac Hayes as "Chef" from *South Park* singing with Fiona Apple, Ozzy Osborne, and others.

■ Sidelights

"Oh, my God, they killed Kenny!" Anyone unfamiliar with this line by now has never heard of the outrageous, scandalously scatological animated television series *South Park*. Created by "twenty-somethings" Trey Parker and Matt Stone, the show has only been on the air on Comedy Central since 1997, but it has already made a big splash, becoming the highest rated show in the cable television network's history. *South Park*, with its crude animation and even cruder humor, is an unlikely success story, but its doe-eyed, foul-mouthed stars Kyle, Stan, Cartman, and Kenny have already found their way onto all kinds of merchandising and dozen of Internet fan Web sites.

Many *South Park* fans are familiar with the story of how the smash hit started off as a short animated video "greeting card" entitled *The Spirit of Christmas* that was commissioned by an executive at the Fox network. The video then gained wider notice when actors George Clooney and other Hollywood celebrities began making copies and distributing them to friends. But there is more to the tale than this.

College Days

Trey Parker and Matt Stone met as film students at the University of Colorado, where they discovered they liked making the same kinds of films. They "were the only ones who didn't want to make black-and-white films about lesbians," Parker said in a *Newsweek* interview with Rick Marin. But even though they didn't try to make any art nouveau pictures, their talent was evident. In fact, Parker won a Student Academy Award. Unlike his future partner, Stone (who has sometimes been called the more practical of the two), Parker never graduated from the university; he was too wrapped up in his own filmmaking to attend classes.

The film that ended Parker's college days was entitled *Alferd Packer, Cannibal: The Musical,* and was later renamed simply *Cannibal: The Musical.* The problem with making any feature-length film—even a mere student project—is money. Parker and Stone managed to pull together $300, which they used to make a preview of the film to show potential financial backers. As Parker recalled during an appearance at the 1998 U.S. Comedy Arts Festival in Aspen, Colorado, a transcript of which was published on the Comedy Central Web site, "[We] went around to rich people and said, 'We need finishing money.' Like this movie is almost done, we're so close, here's the preview. And they saw the preview and go, oh, that's really funny, here's some finishing money. And all of a sudden, like, two months later, we had $125,000. And it was the same with the 'South Park' phenomenon."

Cannibal is based on the real story of a nineteenth-century gold-seeking expedition in which five of the six men died, their bodies bearing evidence of cannibalism. Alfred Packer, the only one to survive, was convicted of the crime. Leave it to Parker to turn such a grim story into a gay musical featuring such songs as "Shpadoinkle," "That's All I'm Asking For," and "Let's Build a Snowman." The bizarre humor in the film has been compared to that of England's Monty Python troupe (Parker and Stone are fans), and it has since been shown at film festivals in Europe and the United States.

South Park and *The Spirit of Christmas*

Parker and Stone, along with fellow students Jason McHugh and Ian Hardin, formed a small production company called The Avenging Conscience to make the film; that was their introduction to the business side of the industry. When people in entertainment circles began taking notice of Parker and Stone's nutty brand of humor, they were invited to do an animated short for then Fox executive Brian Graden, who now heads programming at MTV. Parker used the same animation technique he used for the first animated short he did at college called *American History* and another short called *The Spirit of Christmas.* He and Stone used cutouts of construction paper, which they then repositioned, frame by frame, using the stop-motion technique to make the figures look as if they were moving. *The Spirit of Christmas* is the story of what happens when four children put a magic hat on a snowman, who then goes on a rampage and fights with baby Jesus (the film is sometimes also called "Frosty" for the obvious liberties it takes with the classic Christmas song and animated feature "Frosty the Snowman.")

In the 1995 short Parker and Stone made for the executive, which they also entitled *The Spirit of Christmas,* Jesus fights Santa Claus at the mall and the children—who at this point look very similar to the *South Park* characters—stop the fight. The moral of the story is that Christmas is really all about presents. Parker and Stone were given $2,000 to make the film, but they only spent $750 of it. It was a small beginning to something big. Copies of the short were soon made and sent to friends and associates all around Hollywood. Soon, Parker and Stone were being approached by executive producers offering to let them do a show, but when Parker said he wanted to make a cartoon featuring a talking piece of cartoon poo many backed off. However, the executives at the Comedy Central cable television company were not turned off. Although the idea of doing an entire show starring talking feces was rejected, the character of Mr. Hanky did eventually become a part of *South Park.*

There are quite a few elements in *South Park* that come from the creators' childhoods. South Park itself is a real place in Colorado, the state where Parker and Stone both grew up. Although it is a county and not a city, South Park, Colorado, has a reputation for having a lot of strange goings-on such as UFO and Bigfoot sightings. The characters in the show are also based somewhat on reality. For example, Mr. Hanky, who wears a jaunty Christmas cap on his head and can sing and dance, was inspired by Parker's potty training. When his mother told Parker's father to talk to the young Trey because the boy wouldn't flush after going to the bathroom, he told his son that if the boy didn't flush the poo would come alive and eat him. (Fortunately, Mr. Hanky isn't so mean.) Mr. Garrison, the depressed teacher who talks to his students through a hand puppet called

Mr. Hat, is based on two people. Parker's kindergarten teacher used to also put a Mr. Hat puppet on her hand, and later, while in college, Parker had a British literature teacher who talked like Mr. Garrison, calling everyone a "big silly."

As for Stan, Kyle, Cartman, and Kenny, only Stan has much basis in reality. Stan is Parker's alter ego in a way. Both Stan and Parker have a father who is a geologist and a mother who likes to bake cookies for any occasion; Parker does Stan's voice for the show. Stone, who is the voice of Kyle, has nothing in common with that character: Kyle is Jewish, and Stone's mother is not the reactionary Kyle's mother is. Kenny, the ill-fated boy who is killed horribly in almost every episode, is voiced by Stone and represents the poor boy in the neighborhood that many children meet at one

Kenny, Cartman, Kyle, and Stan are among the cast of the popular television show *South Park*.

time or another in their lives. Cartman (voiced by Parker), on the other hand, represents "the garbage in everyone's soul," as Stone told Stef McDonald of *TV Guide*.

Big Stars in *South Park*

If Parker and Stone couldn't believe their luck at getting their own show, they were even more surprised when they got their favorite band, Primus, to perform the theme song. Then Isaac Hayes, famous for writing the music to the film *Shaft*, for which he became the first African American to win an Academy Award for original score, agreed to do the voice of Chef, the singing school cook. Asked at the Comedy Arts Festival about how they got a major band to do the opening song, Parker replied, "That was actually . . . one of the coolest parts, because we got approached to do the show. . . . But . . . we need[ed] a theme song. And Matt and I were just huge Primus fans in college. And we said, maybe we could get them to do the theme song?"

Parker and Stone sent a copy of *The Spirit of Christmas* to the group, and it wasn't long before they got a call saying that the band, indeed, wanted to do the song. It was one of the biggest thrills of their lives. The next thrill came when they had another seemingly impossible idea, which was to have Hayes do the voice for Chef. The character is a kindly cook at the school who likes to give the boys advice, which often leads him to break into inappropriate songs about making love to a woman. "When my agent first called to tell me about it," Hayes recalled in a *TV Guide* article by Peter Marks, "he didn't even know how to explain it." But Hayes thought it would be fun and agreed to do the bit. "I thought, 'I wonder what's going to happen when these things come out. . . . Am I stupid, or are other people going to get this?'"

The show's creators planted a couple of inside jokes about Chef. For one thing, he does not fit at all with the gold-chain wearing, militant image Hayes cultivated in his early 1970s heyday; the other joke is that the songs Chef sings parody the type of soulful music that is Hayes's trademark. But Hayes enjoys the irony, as well as the recognition he now gets from a younger generation. "I went to Michael Jordan's party during the All-Star Game weekend," Hayes told Peter Marks. "All the

---

If you enjoy the works of Trey Parker and Matt Stone, you may also want to check out the following:

The films of Peter and Bobby Farrelly, including *Dumb & Dumber*, 1994.
The animation of Matt Groening, best known as the creator of *The Simpsons*.

---

kids kept coming up to me, going, 'It's Chef!' Talk about cool. I felt like the hit of the party."

Other stars have done guest voices on *South Park*, but they have to agree to Parker and Stone's twisted sense of irony: the bigger the star, the smaller the part. George Clooney, to whom they owe some of their success when the actor spread copies of the original short throughout Hollywood, did the voice of Stan's gay dog Sparky in the episode "Big Gay Al's Big Gay Boat Ride." Jay Leno is the voice of Kitty in the "Cliffhanger" episode in which Cartman tries to find out who his father is. "We knew we didn't want to do what 'The Simpsons' does, which was like, 'Oh, look who did a voice this week,'" Parker told Yahoo! editor Stevan Keane in an interview. "And there they are being glorified. . . . If we really do a celebrity's voice, it's going to be totally minimal, because that's the joke." One star, Jerry Seinfeld, turned down a role on the show because the creators wouldn't let him have a big part.

The cartoon's creators also like to make fun of famous people, such as Bob Saget, who is spoofed as the extremely unfunny host of a "funniest videos" show, and Barbra Streisand, who turns into a robotic monster who threatens the world in "Mecha Streisand." (The show's creators aren't fans of Streisand because she boycotted Colorado on one of her tours.)

Is *South Park* Too Crude?

While *South Park* has some big star voices behind it, the animation might be considered less than stellar. The drawings, which were originally created out of cut-out paper but are now done with computer animation, are extremely crude. At first, this was out of necessity, since Parker and Stone had a small budget, but even now with a staff of thirty-five animators and support personnel at their Marina del Rey studio, they haven't tried to make the animation any better. Part of this is because of the speed at which they have to produce shows (four or five episodes are in various stages of production at any one time), but another possible reason is that the animation has a certain innocent charm that belies its overt crudity. The plus side of this technique is that it is ideal for use on the Internet. Hundreds of unofficial Web sites can now be found, many of them offering downloadable video clips. Unlike live video, the stop-motion animation takes up less memory, and thus takes less time to download. There are even episodes of *South Park* available on the Web that haven't been aired on Comedy Central, which runs the official site.

Comedy Central allows what other copyright holders would consider bootlegging because many areas of the country can't get *South Park* on cable. Even Parker and Stone's home state didn't have a cable company that carried the show until very recently, and Parker's hometown still does not receive the show. News of the show spread via the Internet as well as by videotapes passed between friends. And, of course, there is a good deal of merchandising being done for the show. However, its creators have not reaped many of the benefits from the sale of T-shirts and other products. "Thirty million in T-shirt sales, and I got a check for $7,000," Parker revealed to Marin. (He did manage to buy a house for 1.2 million dollars, though.)

Many parents are concerned about how the bad language and bizarre situations (in one episode, for example, a bookmobile librarian has sex with chickens) could affect their children. The show, of course, is geared not for children but for adults ages eighteen to the early thirties, but because it is a cartoon it appeals to audiences who are younger, too. While Comedy Central airs the program late at night, that doesn't stop children from watching. But Marin defends the show. "Saying that the show corrupts young minds is selling short the show and the young minds," he wrote. "Underage fans grasp that the selfish racist fat kid Cartman is not a role model." And even Parker and Stone have their limits to what they will do. For example, they cut a scene in which one character throws matches at another when Comedy Central producers feared it would give some chil-

dren bad ideas. In a *USA Today* article, Elizabeth Weise noted that some parents have come to realize that there is more to *South Park* than just flaming fart jokes. Weise talked to Donna Heap, a mother who used to forbid her son to watch the show but who now "likes the show as well: 'It's pretty hysterical, and it touches on a lot of things that people think but don't say.'"

For whatever the reason, *South Park*'s popularity is undeniable. Inevitably, people have tried to pinpoint just what the secret to that success is. "I think one reason Park has such enthusiastic word of mouth . . . ," speculated *Entertainment Weekly* writer Ken Tucker, "is that, because the show is tucked away on a still relatively obscure channel, each viewer thinks it's his or her own private discovery, and seeks to share it with the world." And according to Bob Strauss's "Surf Park" site on Yahoo!, Comedy Central vice-president Larry Lieberman concluded that the "enormous cyber-popularity [can be attributed] to its dead-on demographics—the bulk of the show's audience is constituted of Internet-savvy 18- to 29-year-olds, the same folks who helped make 'Beavis and Butt-Head' and 'The Simpsons' such huge hits."

With the show now going full steam ahead, one might think Parker and Stone would have their hands full making episodes of *South Park*, but the two are involved in several other projects as well. Parker and Stone are writing a prequel to the 1994 film *Dumb and Dumber*, and they starred in the 1998 comedy *BASEketball* as well as *Orgazmo*, a spoof of the porno industry. A feature-length *South Park* is also a possibility in the near future. Asked by *USA Today* reporter Ann Oldenburg whether success has changed them, Parker replied sardonically, "Only in that we don't have lives anymore. . . . We're really depressed."

■ Works Cited

Keane, Stevan, Yahoo! Internet Life interview with Trey Parker, http://www.everwonder.com/david/southpark/spinterview.html.

Marin, Rick, "The Rude Tube," *Newsweek*, March 23, 1998, pp. 56-62.

Marks, Peter, "Compliments of the Chef," *TV Guide*, March 28, 1998, pp. 26-27.

McDonald, Stef, "25 Shocking Secrets You Need to Know about *South Park*," *TV Guide*, March 28, 1998, pp. 23-27.

Oldenburg, Ann, "In the Company of Comedy," *USA Today*, March 9, 1998, pp. D1, 2D.

"'South Park' Comes Home," http://www.comedycentral.com/southpark.

Strauss, Bob, "Surf Park," http://www.zdnet.com/.yil/content/mag/9802/south1.html.

Tucker, Ken, "Frat's Entertainment at Comedy Central, Home of the Vulgar South Park and Smut-mouthed Daily Host Craig Kilborn," *Entertainment Weekly*, January 16, 1998, p. 53.

Weise, Elizabeth, "'South Park' Kids Find Home on Web," *USA Today*, February 27, 1998, p. D-1.

■ For More Information See

PERIODICALS

Detroit Free Press, February 4, 1998, p. C-6.
Newsweek, July 21, 1997, p. 69.
People Weekly, August 11, 1997, p. 17.
Time, August 18, 1997, p. 74.
USA Today, March 18, 1998, p. 3D.*

—Sketch by Kevin S. Hile

Erich Maria Remarque

■ Personal

Born June 22, 1898, in Osnabrück, Germany; immigrated to Switzerland, 1931; immigrated to the United States, 1939, naturalized citizen, 1947; died September 25, 1970, in Locarno, Switzerland; son of Peter Maria (a bookbinder) and Anna Maria Remark; married first wife, 1923 (divorced, 1932); married Jutta Ilse Zambona, 1938 (divorced); married Paulette Goddard (an actress), February 25, 1958. *Education:* Attended University of Munster.

■ Career

Novelist and playwright. Worked as substitute teacher in and around Osnabrück, Germany; editor of *Sport im Bild* (sports magazine), Berlin, Germany; worked variously as a stonecutter, drama critic, salesman for a tombstone company, test driver for a Berlin tire company, advertising copywriter for an automobile company, and organist at an insane asylum. *Military service:* German Army, served on Western front during World War I; wounded. *Member:* German Academy of Speech and Poetry.

■ Awards, Honors

Great Order of Merit, Federal Republic of Germany, 1967.

■ Writings

NOVELS

Die Traumbude: Ein Kuenstlerroman (title means "The Dream Room" or "Dream Den"), Schoenheit, 1920.

Im Westen nichts Neues, Kiepenheuer & Witsch, 1928, reprinted, 1968, translation by A. W. Wheen published as *All Quiet on the Western Front,* Little, Brown, 1929, reprinted, Fawcett, 1987.

Der Weg zurueck, Im Propylaen-verlag, 1931, translation by Wheen published as *The Road Back,* Little, Brown, 1931.

Drei Kameraden, Querido Verlag, 1937, abridged edition, American Book Co., 1941, complete original edition reprinted, Desch, 1969, original edition translated by Wheen published as *Three Comrades,* Little, Brown, 1937.

Liebe deinen Naechsten, Querido Verlag, 1941, translation by Denver Lindley published as *Flotsam,* Little, Brown, 1941.

Arc de Triomphe, F. G. Micha, 1946, translation by Walter Sorell and Lindley published as *Arch of Triumph,* Appleton-Century, 1945, reprinted, New American Library, 1985.

Der Funke Leben, Kiepenheuer & Witsch, 1952, 6th edition, 1972, original edition translated by James Stern and published as *Spark of Life*, Appleton-Century, 1952, reprinted, Granada, 1981.

Zeit zu Leben und Zeit zu Sterben, Kiepenheuer & Witsch, 1954, translation by Lindley published as *A Time to Love and a Time to Die*, Harcourt, 1954.

Der Schwarze Obelisk: Geschichte einer verspaeteten Jugend, Kiepenheuer & Witsch, 1956, translation by Lindley published as *The Black Obelisk*, Harcourt, 1957.

Der Himmel kennt keine Guenstlinge, Kiepenheuer & Witsch, 1961, translation by Richard Winston and Clara Winston published as *Heaven Has No Favorites*, Harcourt, 1961, published as *Bobby Deerfield*, Fawcett, 1961.

Die Nacht von Lissabon, Robin Productions, 1961, translation by Ralph Manheim published as *The Night in Lisbon*, Harcourt, 1964.

Schatten im Paradies, Droemer Knaur, 1971, translation by Manheim published as *Shadows in Paradise*, Harcourt, 1972.

OTHER

Die lezte Station (play; title means "The Last Station"; first produced in 1956), adaptation by Peter Stone published as *Full Circle*, Harcourt, 1974.

Also author of film script *The Last Act*, 1955.

■ Adaptations

Three film adaptations of *All Quiet on the Western Front* have been produced, one of which, Universal's 1929 version, won an Academy Award for best picture; an audio cassette edition of *All Quiet on the Western Front* was produced by Cram Cassettes, 1988; *The Road Back* was adapted for a movie by Universal, 1937; *Three Comrades* was adapted for a 1938 MGM film with a screenplay by F. Scott Fitzgerald; *Flotsam* was adapted for a movie under the title *So Ends Our Night*, 1941; *Arch of Triumph* was adapted for a film by Universal Artists in 1948, starring Charles Boyer and Ingrid Bergman; *A Time to Love and a Time to Die* was adapted for a film by Universal in 1958.

■ Sidelights

In the first chapter of the classic World War I novel *All Quiet on the Western Front*, four German soldiers at the front are disconsolate after having visited one of their friends, who is dying in a field hospital. They have had to bribe an orderly with cigarettes—the currency of the trenches—to give their comrade morphine. Now, one of the soldiers receives a letter from their former school master, Kantorek, who persuaded the four to join up to fight for their fatherland. The teacher, who is safe at home, refers to them in his letter as the "young men of iron." Hearing this, Paul Bäumer, the narrator, reflects for all young soldiers: "Young men of iron. Young? None of us is more than twenty. But young? Young men? That was long ago. We are old now."

With this, the German author Erich Maria Remarque stated a theme that would recur throughout his most famous novel, as well as his ten subsequent novels: the dislocations caused by the political and military events of the turbulent twentieth century. Remarque wrote of young men who formed a lost generation that had lost not only its youth, but also its connection to society as a whole. In *All Quiet on the Western Front*, the comradeship of the trench soldier is the one affirmative human quality left. However, in Remarque's later novels, including the sequel, *The Road Back*, and in the final volume of his World War I trilogy, *The Three Comrades*, even this connection is lost in the trauma of the post-war world.

Remarque knew all about such dislocations. As a child, his working-class family moved eleven times by 1916, when he was drafted into the army as an eighteen-year-old. After serving in World War I, he returned to civilian life a changed man, out of place in a changed society. With the publication in 1929 of *All Quiet on the Western Front*, Remarque won international fame and fortune, but he was reviled in his native Germany for the book's pacifist sentiments. When the Nazis came to power in 1933, the author fled the country. He lived in Switzerland and the United States for the rest of his life. Although he was a successful author and was a celebrity because of a long-term relationship with actress Marlene Dietrich and a marriage to actress Paulette Goddard, Remarque remained acutely aware of the fragility of security and the impermanence of life; in one way or another, all his writings speak of the transitory nature of happiness and love.

This transitory quality was mirrored in Remarque's own life. As Charles W. Hoffmann has pointed out in *Dictionary of Literary Biography*, "It is sometimes claimed that next to the Bible . . . *All Quiet on the Western Front* has sold more copies than any other book in history" and that Remarque's name "is recognized by more readers around the world than that of any other modern German writer. . . . [and] it is difficult to find a literate person anywhere who has not read [*All Quiet on the Western Front*]." Yet it is generally forgotten that Remarque wrote ten more novels and several works for the stage and screen. Many of his novels were best-sellers and were adapted for movies. *Arch of Triumph*, for example, is considered one of his best works, and other books blend his use of first-person, present-tense narrative and realistic style in the same compelling manner as *All Quiet on the Western Front*. Even so, for most readers, Remarque is a one-novel author, and most critics in his homeland regard him as being too popular to be taken seriously or to be ranked with great German writers such as Thomas Mann or Hermann Hesse. Although Remarque spent much of his later life working to refute this one-book image, he was largely unsuccessful.

A Young Man from Osnabrück

Born in Osnabrück, Lower Saxony, Germany, on June 22, 1898, as Erich Paul Remark, the author later changed both his middle name and the spelling of his last name. Maria he took from his mother, Anna Maria Remark, and the spelling of his last name was, as Hoffmann pointed out in *Dictionary of Literary Biography*, from that of his French ancestors. His father, Peter Franz Remark, was a bookbinder. Father and son were never close. Remarque also had two sisters; an older brother died at age six. The author's youth was lived in near poverty and in what Julie Gilbert termed in her dual biography, *Opposite Attraction: The Lives of Erich Maria Remarque and Paulette Goddard*, a "dour and rigid atmosphere at home," yet it was apparently a happy childhood. Remarque loved his mother, who gave him freedom to roam the streets of Osnabrück as well as the surrounding countryside. As a youth, he collected butterflies, kept a homemade aquarium, and became involved in gymnastics. Remarque also demonstrated a distinct inclination to daydream, a tendency little appreciated by teachers or parents. His first passion was music, and he played both the organ and piano. Next in line was writing; by age

sixteen he was composing poems, essays, and the beginnings of a novel, which he completed and published after the war. Educated in Catholic schools, Remarque was not admitted to college-preparatory courses such as those attended by upper-middle class youths. Instead, he took courses that would allow him to enter a Catholic teachers' training college. Remarque was not challenged academically at school, and so he read voraciously on his own; the works of Hesse, Mann, Proust, Goethe, Schopenhauer, and Nietzsche were among his favorites.

In 1916, while Remarque was preparing for a career as an elementary school teacher, he met up with a group of kindred spirits who formed what they called the Dream Circle. These young men and women, led by an eccentric older painter, Fritz Hörstemeier, got together to discuss art and culture. Such a circle provided Remarque with his first intellectual home, and Hörstemeier became his artistic mentor. All this only made Remarque's next transition—being drafted and sent off to war—more wrenching. Two other connections also made the parting painful: his mother had been diagnosed with cancer, and he had fallen in love with Erika Haase, another young member of the Dream Circle.

Unlike his main character in *All Quiet on the Western Front*, Remarque did not go off in a flurry of patriotic sentiment to the recruiters, but waited until he was called up in November 1916. As his mother was seriously ill, he was given frequent leaves to be at her side, and was not posted to France until the summer of 1917. Though Remarque was in the army for three years and was often close to the front, he never actually fought. In July 1917, one of Remarque's comrades, Troske, was injured by shell fragments and Remarque carried the man back to safety. Despite these efforts, Troske died, and this is one of many personal experiences that Remarque later incorporated into *All Quiet on the Western Front*. Not long afterward, Remarque himself was wounded in three places by shrapnel from long-range artillery shells.

In September 1916, while recuperating he was allowed leave to Osnabrück. It was a sad homecoming, for he attended his mother's funeral. The following June, while Remarque was still in the hospital, he received word of another death in Osnabrück: that of his Dream Circle mentor Fritz Hörstemeier. Remarque spent most of the rest of the war recuperating from his wounds in a Duisburg hospital. He was deemed fit to return to active duty on October 31, 1918, but with the signing of the Armistice on November 11, 1918, he never got near the front again.

It was during his enforced convalescence that the persona of Erich Maria Remarque appeared from that of Erich Paul Remark. In the hospital, he wrote regularly and worked on his music. However, his injuries forced him to give up all hopes of a professional career as a pianist. Now he gave lessons and composed. Remarque also painted, and he began to see how he could fuse music, painting, and poetry into a writer's art, applying these lessons to what would become his first novel, *The Dream Room*. Most important, he was developing a vision of himself as the outsider and a pacifist, a difficult role in German society. A soldier's disillusionment with the politicians who had allowed the war to happen is noticeable in his diaries of the period.

Upon his return to Osnabrück, Remarque began exhibiting what friends thought to be odd behavior. Discharged from the army as a private, he nonetheless took to parading the streets of his hometown in the uniform of a lieutenant, bedecked with war medals, including the Iron Cross. Though Remarque claimed the latter was awarded to him for carrying his wounded friend to safety, it is unclear whether or not he actually was awarded the medal. In fact, Remarque felt guilty about not fighting in the war, even though he had been near the front so often. In his second novel he would vicariously experience the events he escaped in reality.

By 1919, Remarque was back in the Catholic Seminary for Teachers, preparing for a teaching career. Meanwhile, he was also putting the finishing touches on his first novel, *The Dream Room*. He sold his piano to help defray the costs of self-publishing it. It is best that the book has been forgotten, for as Hoffmann noted in *Dictionary of Literary Biography*, it was "written in a flowery art nouveau style and was an embarrassment to Remarque after he turned seriously to literature." His teaching career did not fare much better, lasting little more than a year. Working as a substitute teacher in several small towns around Osnabrück, Remarque managed to antagonize administrators with his loner attitude and lack of cooperation. He was also falsely accused—according to Remarque—of involvement in a left-wing, pro-Bolshevik revolutionary movement called the Spartacists, and finally decided that a career in education was not for him.

Im Westen nichts Neues

For the next several years Remarque worked variously as a peddler, a gravestone salesman, an organist in an asylum for the mentally ill, and as an advertising copywriter. It was in this latter position that he began to refine his writing skills. By 1925, he was working in Berlin as editor of the magazine *Sport im Bild*. It was during this period that Remarque earned a reputation for loving fast cars and hard living. He married the actress Jutta Zambona in 1925, and started his literary rebirth with publication of the racing car story "Stations on the Horizon" in the magazine he edited. Yet there seemed little in his background to foreshadow the novel he wrote in a few months in 1927, *Im Westen nichts Neues*, or as it is known in English translation, *All Quiet on the Western Front*.

Initially, Remarque could find no publisher for his book, and it came out in serial form in 1928. When Ullstein Publishers brought it out in early 1929 as a book, it was an instant success, selling more than half a million copies in just three months. Foreign-language editions soon appeared—twenty-five in all—and by 1931 worldwide sales totalled 3.5 million copies. Ullstein boosted the phenomenal sales with a promotional campaign that was quite unusual for the staid publishing world in the 1920s, and the book has remained in print and continued to sell for more than seventy years, inspiring three film versions and influencing several generations of young men and women who were faced with the prospect of going to war.

All Quiet on the Western Front is less a novel than a series of episodes in the lives of eight ordinary young men. These eight men can be divided into two groups—four schoolmates who volunteer, and the older, less educated men they meet in the army. Originally numbering twenty young scholar-soldiers at the beginning of the novel, only four of the students survive: Kropp, Muller, Leer and Paul Bäumer, the book's narrator. These four are balanced by the others: the mechanic Tjaden, the turf-cutter Westhus, the farmer Detering, and the oldest of the group at forty, Katczinsky—"Kat," as he is called by the others. As Christine R. Barker and R. W. Last pointed out in their 1979 biography *Erich Maria Remarque*, this juxtaposing of an educated elite with a less-educated but more worldly-wise quartet "points to a strong sense of organization on the part of the author which . . . is fundamental to the entire work and has been studiously ignored by most critics."

In their analysis, Barker and Last divide the book into three parts, plus a short interlude. In the first section, Remarque explores the experiences of a private soldier at the front via flashbacks and

THE GREATEST WAR NOVEL OF ALL TIME

ERICH MARIA REMARQUE

All Quiet on the Western Front

On the threshold of life,
they faced an abyss of death....

FAWCETT
CREST
0-449-21394-3

Remarque's classic, highly realistic depiction of war may have sold more copies than any other book in history, except for the Bible.

memories of life before the war. The novel opens with the company numbering eighty men out of an original one hundred fifty, and closes with that number down to thirty-two. The middle section of the book recounts the mens' experiences with women, dreams of what the future might bring after the war, and with Bäumer's disastrous leave at home with a dying mother and a father from whom he is estranged. He feels totally alien in "the civilian world."

In an interlude between the novel's second and third sections, Bäumer begins to see humanity in the face of the enemy while guarding some Russian prisoners of war. When he and his friends discuss the meaning of the war, the older, more mature Kat wonders aloud why a "French locksmith or a French shoemaker" would want to attack them. "No, it's just the governments. I'd never seen a Frenchman before I came here, and most of the Frenchmen won't have seen one of us. Nobody asked them any more than they did us," he says. When one of his comrades asks why there is a war, Kat shrugs and adds, "There must be some people who find the war worthwhile."

Shortly after this exchange, Bäumer kills a French soldier, his first. He cannot leave the shell hole where his victim lies dying of knife wounds, and must listen to the man's death throes for hours. Bäumer subsequently muses about the meaning of this war and of war in general. It was these contemplations that later became the focal point for debate and vituperation, especially among German right-wing militarists and Nazis.

The action is more intense in the book's third section. Short vignettes describe the fate of Bäumer's fellow soldiers, each of whom dies. In a short epilogue, Bäumer, too, is killed. Remarque writes, "He fell in October 1918, on a day that was so quiet and still along the entire front line that the army despatches restricted themselves to the single sentence: that there was nothing new to report on the western front."

These final lines of the book in fact supplied the ironic title for the German original: *Im Westen nichts Neues*. Bäumer's death is thus made insignificant; just another casualty, but nothing new or important. English editions whose title resonates with the one-time popular song, "All Quiet along the Potomac," lost the irony of the German-language title.

Richard Thomas starred in the 1979 television adaptation of Remarque's *All Quiet on the Western Front.*

Remarque's work is impressionistic as well as realistic. Food, bodily functions, and women are the mainstays of morale and discussion. There is little sense of history in the novel, and no mention of which battles the men are fighting—all battles are the same. Officers, such as Corporal Himmelstoss, are martinets or sadists, and when the men beat the cruel Himmelstoss, there is a sense of justice in the action. Comrades, friends in the trenches, die and are mourned for a time. But their goods are quickly shared; a fine pair of English boots are passed down from the dying man at the beginning of the book to Muller, and then at his death to Bäumer, who dies in turn.

The men are cast into a timeless round of battle and waiting for battle, of trying to survive in the trenches and in no-man's land. As Barker and Last explained, "one might all too readily gain the impression that the novel is a succession of nightmarish situations and unrelieved gloom, but this is not so. Remarque skilfully paces the development of the action, interposing scenes of real happiness and contentment, some of which contain episodes that are extremely funny." The soldiers' unrelenting search for food as well as their comradely discussions behind the lines serve as a foil to the scenes of barbarous warfare, making the latter all the more powerful. Remarque also employs symbolism: earth is a regenerative force; a butterfly becomes an ironic insertion of bucolic nature in the midst of carnage as well as a metaphor for the fleeting quality of life. And throughout the novel, Remarque writes in a matter-of-fact prose style which minutely describes the lives and experiences of men at the front in mankind's first mechanized war.

Remarque and the Critics

The critical reception for *All Quiet on the Western Front* followed a pattern that would become the norm for Remarque's later books: praise from the foreign press and mixed reviews in his native Germany. Writing in the *New York Herald Tribune*, Frank Ernest Hill noted that the novel "will give any sensitive reader a terrific impact," while Joseph Wood Krutch observed in the *Nation* that "Remarque tells his plain tale with a sort of naivete which is the result, not of too little experience, but of too much." Henry Seidel Canby, in the *Saturday Review*, called *All Quiet on the Western Front* "the greatest book about the war that I have seen," and in England, Herbert Read of the *Manchester Guardian Weekly* termed it "the greatest of all war books."

In Germany, however, Remarque landed in the middle of a political battle despite huge sales. His book was anathema to the right for its supposed pacifist sentiments and it was equally criticized by the left for being too soft on the industrialists who had brought about the war. This furor actually helped sales of the novel, but when the Nazis came to power in 1939, Remarque was on their hate list of writers and *In Westen nichts Neues* was one of the books publicly burned by the new regime. German critics also tried to prove that Remarque was fudging on his own war experience, grossly misrepresenting the realities of World War I. To this day in Germany, Remarque's writing is not considered worthy of serious study.

Retreats into Exile

In 1930, the same year Remarque and his wife divorced, he brought out a sequel to *All Quiet on the Western Front*. *The Road Back* recounts the trials and tribulations of soldiers trying to readjust to life in the civilian world. Once again, Remarque had hit the pulse of the times and the book sold well. Writing in the *New Republic*, the novelist William Faulkner commented that it was "missing significance," yet it was "a moving book." The premier of the film version of *All Quiet on the Western Front* that same year brought protests in Germany, and as a result, Remarque began spending more time in Switzerland, where he had purchased a villa near Lago Maggiore. By the end of 1933, he and his former wife—whom he would remarry in 1938—moved permanently to Switzerland.

Three Comrades, the final installment in Remarque's trilogy about World War I and its aftermath, was published in 1937. Reviewing that novel in *Satur-*

If you enjoy the works of Erich Maria Remarque, you may also want to check out the following books and films:

Philip Caputo, *A Rumor of War*, 1977.
Stephen Crane, *The Red Badge of Courage*, 1895.
Tim O'Brien, *The Things They Carried*, 1990.
Platoon, a film by Oliver Stone, 1986.

---

day Review, the critic Bernard DeVoto favorably compared Remarque to Ernest Hemingway, noting that he had "an ability to make the commonplaces evoke the profoundest emotion, to focus immensities through the smallest and simplest details." DeVoto concluded that *Three Comrades* "is a memorable love story; it is also a novel about the tortured spirit of man." Indeed, by now Remarque was writing about female characters, too.

In 1938, the Nazis revoked Remarque's German citizenship, and he became stateless. Partly through the personal intercession of President Franklin D. Roosevelt, Remarque was allowed to enter the United States the following year. He lived and worked in Hollywood until 1942. In Hollywood, Remarque became a celebrity, maintaining a gossip-column relationship with Marlene Dietrich, another high-profile German expatriate, and associating with the likes of Cole Porter, Charlie Chaplin, Ernest Hemingway, and F. Scott Fitzgerald, who wrote the screenplay for the film version of *Three Comrades*. Remarque's fourth novel appeared while he was living in California. *Flotsam* employs more material from the author's own life in a story that details the fate of political refugees who make their way from Germany to Austria and then to Switzerland. This somewhat melodramatic love story ends tragically with the protagonist captured by the SS when he returns to Berlin to be with his dying wife.

Remarque moved from California to New York in 1943 (the same year his sister Elfriede was executed by the Nazis for her part in the White Rose resistance group). Remarque now began painting, and he exhibited his work in New York galleries. He was also working on a new book set in Paris just before the fall of France and the German occupation. First published in English in

1945, *Arch of Triumph* was an instant best-seller and according to Charles W. Hoffmann in *Dictionary of Literary Biography* is a novel worthy of the author of *All Quiet on the Western Front.* "In *Arch of Triumph* the surface story takes on a metaphoric quality that Remarque's work had not had since *Im Westen nichts Neues*", wrote Hoffmann. The critic also pointed out that the protagonist of this novel, Ravic, "is the most complex, least one-dimensional hero that Remarque had created to this point."

After Another War

Remarque became a naturalized U.S. citizen in 1947, and thereafter he divided his time between his adopted country and Switzerland. Remarque had large-canvas material to deal with throughout his career: the political tragedies of the twentieth century, which led to two world wars. But he always dealt with this material from the point of view of a small, well-defined cast of characters caught in the maw of history. With the end of World War II, he continued to detail the costs of war. His 1952 novel *Spark of Life* describes life in the concentration camps, while *A Time to Live and a Time to Die* is about a soldier who falls in love while on leave from the Russian front toward the end of World War II, and who dies on the battlefield upon his return to the front. Remarque's other books include the autobiographical *The Black Obelisk* and the poorly received *Heaven Has No Favorites.*

In 1957 Remarque and Jutta Zambona divorced for the second time, and the next year he married film actress Paulette Goddard. Following his marriage, he and Goddard spent most of their time at Remarque's Swiss villa. In 1963, he published his last complete novel, *The Night in Lisbon,* which reviewers praised highly for its compelling story of those who fled Nazi persecution. He was at work on another book, *Shadows in Paradise,* when he died in a hospital in Locarno, Switzerland, on September 25, 1970. That book, which was published posthumously a year later, chronicles the lives of political refugees in America; it was intended as a companion volume to *Flotsam* and *The Night in Lisbon.*

Remarque's death made headlines around the world. Posterity did little to enhance his literary stature, though being remembered as the author of *All Quiet on the Western Front* is no small praise. Harley U. Taylor, Jr. observed in his *Erich Maria Remarque: A Literary and Film Biography* that "Not even Hesse or Mann had a single novel with the international impact of *Im Westen nichts Neues.*" And as Brian Murdoch noted in his afterword to his 1994 translation of that novel, Remarque has left a lasting picture of the horrors of war. "[It] is not about heroism, but about terror," Murdoch wrote, ". . . about losing all human dignity and values, about becoming an automaton; it is not about falling bravely and nobly for one's country . . . but about soiling oneself in terror under heavy shellfire." As an anti-war testament, *All Quiet on the Western Front* takes its place alongside other classics such as Bertha von Suttner's *Lay Down Your Arms,* Jaroslav Hasek's *The Good Soldier Schweik,* and Hemingway's *A Farewell to Arms.*

However, Remarque's literary legacy goes well beyond his best-known novel; in the entirety of his work, he became a chronicler of the fate of Germany between 1917 and 1945. His constant underlying theme, as Hoffmann noted, of the "breakdown of Western civilization and order that World War I brought to the surface of European consciousness" is an important one. Yet Remarque's enduring achievement, as Barker and Last concluded, "is the way in which he has charted the history of a generation of young men alienated not only from the past and the present but also from their own true selves."

■ Works Cited

Barker, Christine R., and R. W. Last, *Erich Maria Remarque,* Oswald Wolff, 1979, pp. 32-68, 51.

Canby, Henry Seidel, "Modern War," *Saturday Review,* June 8, 1929, p. 1087.

DeVoto, Bernard, "Germany in the Vortex," *Saturday Review,* May 1, 1937, pp. 3-4.

Faulkner, William, "Beyond the Talking," *New Republic,* May 20, 1931, pp. 23-24.

Gilbert, Julie, *Opposite Attraction: The Lives of Erich Maria Remarque and Paulette Goddard,* Pantheon, 1995, p. 4.

Hill, Frank Ernest, "Destroyed by the War," *New York Herald Tribune,* June 2, 1929, pp. 1-2.

Hoffmann, Charles W., "Erich Maria Remarque," *Dictionary of Literary Biography.* Volume 56: *German Fiction Writers, 1914-1945,* Gale, 1987, pp. 222-41.

Krutch, Joseph Wood, "Glorious War," *Nation*, July 10, 1929, p. 43.

Read, Herbert, "German War Books," *Manchester Guardian Weekly*, April 26, 1929, p. 335.

Remarque, Erich Maria, *All Quiet on the Western Front*, translated by Brian Murdoch, Cape, 1994, pp. 13, 145, 207, 215.

Taylor, Harley U., Jr., *Erich Maria Remarque: A Literary and Film Biography*, Peter Lang, 1989.

■ **For More Information See**

BOOKS

Baumer, Franz, *E. M. Remarque*, Colloquium, 1976.

Contemporary Literary Criticism, Volume 21, Gale, 1982.

Elfe, Wolfgang, et al., editors, *The Fortunes of German Writers in America: Studies in Literary Reception*, University of South Carolina Press, 1992, pp. 211-30.

Firda, Richard Arthur, *Erich Maria Remarque: A Thematic Analysis of His Novels*, Peter Lang, 1988.

Firda, Richard Arthur, *All Quiet on the Western Front: Literary Analysis and Cultural Context*, Twayne, 1993.

Gelder, Robert Van, *Writers and Writing*, Scribner, 1946, pp. 377-81.

Genno, Charles H., and Heinz Wetzel, editors, *The First World War in German Narrative Prose*, University of Toronto Press, 1980, pp. 71-92.

Owen, C. R., *Erich Maria Remarque: A Critical Bio-Bibliography*, Rodopi, 1984.

Spalek, John M., and Robert F. Bell, editors, *Exile: The Writer's Experience*, North Carolina Press, 1982, pp. 247-57.

Wagener, Hans, and James Hardin, editors, *Understanding Erich Maria Remarque*, University of South Carolina Press, 1991.

PERIODICALS

Boston Transcript, June 1, 1929.

Bulletin of Bibliography, December, 1982, pp. 207-10.

Catholic World, November, 1929.

Comparative Literature Studies, winter, 1984, pp. 409-33.

Forum for Modern Language Studies, January, 1992, pp. 56-74.

German Life and Letters, October, 1989, pp. 49-62.

Modern Language Review, April, 1977, pp. 359-73.

Nation and Atheneum, April 27, 1929.

Newsweek, April 1, 1957.

New Yorker, May 12, 1945.

New York Times Book Review, January 27, 1946, p. 3.

Outlook, July 31, 1929.

Perspectives on Contemporary Literature, Number 1, 1977, pp. 15-22.

Saturday Review, May 22, 1954, p. 15.*

—*Sketch by J. Sydney Jones*

Shelley Stoehr

■ **Writings**

Crosses, Delacorte, 1991.
Weird on the Outside, Delacorte, 1995.
Wannabe, Delacorte, 1997.
Tomorrow Wendy: A Love Story, Delacorte, 1998.

■ **Personal**

Born Michelle Stoehr in Pennsylvania; married Mark Buhler, a photographer. *Education:* Graduated from Connecticut College, New London, Connecticut.

■ **Addresses**

Home—San Francisco, CA.

■ **Career**

Writer; modern dance choreographer and teacher; massage therapist. Has performed with a modern dance troupe and as a street entertainer, and has worked as a bartender.

■ **Awards, Honors**

Honor book citation, Eighth Annual Delacorte Press Prize for Best First Young Adult Novel, 1990, for *Crosses*.

■ **Sidelights**

Shelley Stoehr's books are about the hard journeys that take some young women deep into themselves. *Wannabe*'s Catherine is a good student who daydreams about a writing career, but in her hurry to escape a troubled family life and the social confines of her traditional, working-class Italian neighborhood, she launches herself on an alcohol and cocaine-powered trajectory that lands her dangerously off the mark. Tracey, in *Weird on the Outside*, flees school and the conflicted relationships she has with her divorced parents for a precarious independence as a topless dancer in a New York City strip club. And in *Crosses*, punked-out Nancy and her friend Katie deal with "everything awful" in their lives by compulsively cutting themselves. When they aren't having sex with their more straight-laced boyfriends or chugging vodka secreted out of the house in a shampoo bottle, they are carving crosses into their skin with any sharp object they can find. "When we cut, we're in control—we make our own pain, and we can stop it whenever we want," Nancy explains. "Physical pain relieves mental anguish. For a brief moment, the pain of the cutting is the only thing in the cutter's mind, and when that stops and the other comes back, it's weaker. Drugs do that too, and sex, but not like cutting. Nothing is like cutting."

Filled as they are with sex, cigarettes, alcohol and drugs, profanity, and domestic violence, Stoehr's first four novels built for her a reputation as a spinner of teen-angst tales whose characters hang from the threads she winds for them out of unhappy means and undesirable ends. Some critics see her work as bold and honest. Others find that its shock value belies a lack of literary depth. Regardless, hers is a contemporary handling of the difficult subject matter out of which some young adult lives are made. Patty Campbell, writing in *Horn Book*, called Stoehr "one of the new young breed of truth-telling young-adult writers."

Born in Pennsylvania, Stoehr grew up on Long Island, New York. She graduated from Connecticut College in New London, where she studied modern dance. She and her husband, a photographer, later moved to New York City, where she was a member of a modern dance troupe, worked as a street performer and a bartender, and took training in message therapy. She and her husband now make their home in San Francisco.

The First Time Is a Charm

An avid reader (among her young adult favorites were books by Judy Blume, S. E. Hinton, and Lois Duncan), Stoehr began writing at a young age, and was encouraged by her father, who, she told Campbell, was "a very good editor and critic." Stoehr believes that college students should write books for young adults, since they still have a hold on the emotional reality of teenage life. In fact, she wrote her first novel, *Crosses*, while a college student. After thorough rewriting, and then another reworking of its ending, it was accepted by Delacorte Press, published in 1991, and received a Delacorte honor citation for Best First Young Adult Novel.

Crosses is "not a book to 'like' exactly," according to Teri S. Lesesne, describing it in the *ALAN Review* as an "uncompromising examination of the dark world of adolescents with emotional problems compounded by drug dependencies." In it, two friends, Nancy and Katie, are drawn together by their need to cut designs into their skin when

they feel bored or overwhelmed. Their family life is virtually nonexistent: Katie's single mother is promiscuous and mouthy and she mostly overlooks her daughter's misdemeanors, while Nancy's parents are alcoholics who spend their time at home watching television and fighting, sometimes violently. In the story's beginning, Nancy is a good student, but her grades and self-worth suffer as she and Katie get caught in a downward spiral of delinquency. They skip class at every opportunity to get high or drunk, and they sneak out at night to party with their boyfriends or less desirable acquaintances who have access to more drugs.

When the two hit bottom and tragedy strikes, Nancy finds herself in a mental ward faced with some hard decisions about how to take hold of the second chance tenuously held out in her direction by newly sober parents intent on recovery. Graphic and unrelenting, as one drug-using, drunken, hung-over scene is followed by another and then another, *Crosses* is not without its critics. "Nancy's first-person narration is believably angry and self-absorbed, but the book is superficial, lacking any distance or perspective on her problems that would allow them more effect than the thrill of titillation," wrote Roger Sutton in the *Bulletin of the Center for Children's Books*. A *Publishers Weekly* reviewer called it "more a journal than a story."

Keeping Secrets

The main characters in Stoehr's books, each in her own way, explore the appeal and power (usually illusory) of an out-of-bounds secret life, one carried on beyond the knowledge and approval of parents and teachers, or, even further afar, outside of society's expectations of what is appropriate for teenaged women. In Stoehr's second novel, *Weird on the Outside*, Tracey Bascombe is a determined young woman with her sights set on medical school, yet she runs away to New York City, finds housing in a seedy hotel, and becomes a topless dancer—all because she's fed up with her neglectful parents, an MIT biochemist father and a North Carolina manicurist mother who takes too much Valium.

Smart and pretty, "Tracey is one of the most interesting female characters in recent YA fiction," according to Campbell, since she is emotionally

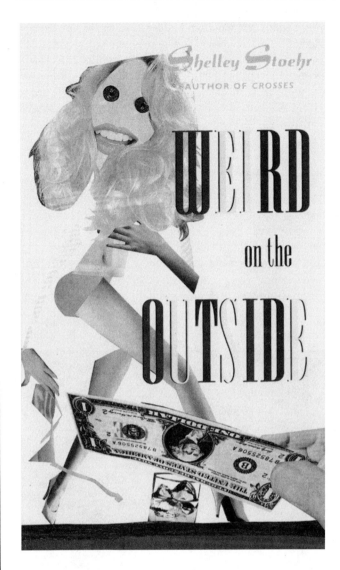

A sixteen-year-old runaway in New York makes ends meet by taking on a new persona and working as a topless dancer.

immature yet also a self-reliant survivor. She learns about sexual power play as she picks up the tricks of her sordid trade, and she taps into the sweaty wisdom of her newfound backstage sisterhood, so that when she winds up in the hospital after being assaulted, she is able to see that she has made the passage into womanhood and is at last ready to go home. *Weird on the Outside* "contains some of the grubbiest scenes of sexual exploitation ever to appear in adolescent literature," according to Campbell, who goes on to say that it is Stoehr's use of demeaning and violent experiences to bring her young character to self-awareness "that in the final analysis is most

controversial—the idea that a young girl can grow and mature from a stint as a sex worker."

The message earned the novel mixed reviews. "Tracey's descent into booze, cocaine and ever-riskier business counterpoints a murkily developed theme that has something to do with gaining independence or female power; the irony here is never certain," a *Publishers Weekly* reviewer wrote. And though Deborah Stevenson concluded in the *Bulletin of the Center for Children's Books* that *Weird on the Outside* is "quite readable, and kids will relish the danger of Tracey's razor's edge existence and thrill to the earthy dialogue," she also described it as "the ultimate made-for-cable rebellion fantasy" and found that "Tracey herself is more interesting for where she is than who she is."

Stoehr crafted the vivid particulars of her strip bar scenes out of personal experience—not as a topless dancer but from time spent with strippers on the job. Campbell described how a friend of Stoehr's invited her to do the opening-night choreography for dancers in his club, which led to some massage therapy work with dancers in their dressing room: "Listening to their shop talk and gossip and watching them at work, [Stoehr] absorbed the sights and sounds and smells of their world: the humiliation and also the feminine power of sexual display, their ribald talk about the categories of male customers, their fierce code of ethics which drew an uncrossable line between topless and bottomless. A story began to shape itself in her mind: a novel about a young girl who desperately needs to prove that she can make it on her own."

In Stoehr's 1995 novel *Wannabe*, young Catherine Tavarelli creates a secret life out of a similar need to prove herself. Catherine's story, however, plays itself out close to home and takes its shape as much from family troubles as it does outside forces. Unlike Nancy and Tracey, "Cat" has meaningful family ties. She shows consistent concern for her older brother Mickey with whom she is close, and she feels the influence of a mother who is always bone-tired and largely ineffective but persistent nonetheless in her efforts to keep the fractious family together. One night when Catherine complains about having to help with the dishes while Mickey gets to do as he pleases, her mother suggests that having her daughter's help is one of her few parental joys:

"Catherine, your brother is pretty much lost to me. If I asked him to help, he might even laugh in my face. So I don't ask. You're a good girl, Catherine. Can't you just let me enjoy it? One Mickey is enough in this house. Don't defy me. I've got enough to worry about already."

Yeah, don't we all, I thought. But I took the plates as she handed them to me and started drying.

This simple, brief kitchen scene displays a mother-daughter connection that is rare in Stoehr's novels—most of her parents are drawn as background characters whose influences on their children are minimal or negative—and the scene's irony makes a direct, if unacknowledged, hit to Catherine's conscience, for she is not such a "good girl."

Catherine's parents think she has a job in a late-night cafe, but she really works as a cocktail waitress in a Mafia club, where she wears a wig and crotch-high red leather "hooker boots" that get her lots of pinches and ogling, but good tips as well. Catherine is often tired and sick because she and her friend Erica regularly get drunk and do drugs. She has worries, too: What can she do about Mickey, who has quit college in favor of gophering for drug-dealing mobster wannabes in the neighborhood? How can she save enough money for college and the computer she wants so that she can begin her hoped-for writing career? How can she continue to make good grades and still keep up the nightlife that helps her feel like she fits in somewhere? She starts dating a neighborhood mobster, Joey (in reality an undercover cop), and uses more and more drugs to avoid her problems. Soon Catherine finds herself in dangerous situations in her pursuit of cocaine, all climaxing in a hold-up scene in which Mickey gets shot in the leg.

Again, the book's reviews were mixed, citing lively characters and provocative, action-oriented scenes, but also a sensational plot, a "too happy and too quick" ending, as reviewer Joel Shoemaker described it in *School Library Journal*, and unsuccessful use of chapters written in Mickey's voice spliced in between those narrated by Catherine. "Cat doesn't plummet as far as the characters in Stoehr's previous books (she's into drugs but not sex, for one thing), so her last-minute redemption isn't as absurd as theirs, though it's still tacked on abruptly with no fictional logic for it," Stevenson wrote in *Bulletin of*

the *Center for Children's Books*. A critic in *Kirkus Reviews* added that "The characters aren't likable, even when they are believable, while the lurid world they inhabit is offered in admiring glimpses. It wouldn't matter if Stoehr didn't show such promise, but she does, and here it goes largely unfulfilled."

Sex, Drugs, and Rock and Roll

For Stoehr, criticism comes with the writing territory she has chosen, and she seems to take any controversy over her novels' subject matter in stride. "In many ways, I believe, the issues for contemporary young adults are not so different now than they have always been for young people—the main concerns still being sex, drugs,

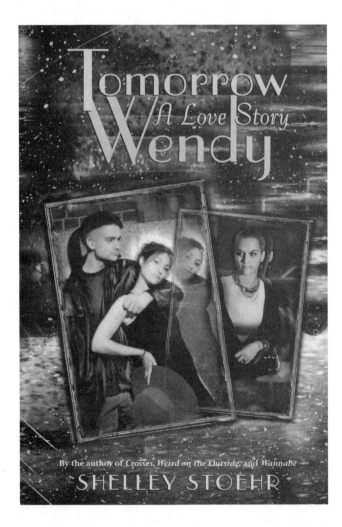

Cary faces a sexual identify crisis when she finds herself attracted to her boyfriend's twin sister.

and rock and roll. What's changed more than the issues themselves is how they are dealt with by the media, and the arts, including literature," Stoehr said in a 1995 workshop presentation published in the *ALAN Review*. In it, she defended her fictional portrayals of teenage sex, casual drug use, and profane language by saying that she hadn't "invented any new words" or behaviors, but was simply being honest about teenage life.

"I'm not saying it's impossible to write a young adult novel that speaks to teen-agers without using foul language in the work. Many authors don't use foul language and still create beautiful, meaningful young adult novels. It happens not to be the way I write, and more importantly, it's not the way my characters talk," she added.

She also spoke doubtfully about any potential influence her books might have over young readers. "Don't get me wrong, I'm not pro-drug use. In my books, it's clear that, although there is some casual drug use, wherein my characters don't seem to suffer repercussions, in the end there certainly are some very serious repercussions."

Ultimately, young readers may identify as much with how Stoehr's young characters feel as with what they do. She told Campbell that most young adults experience anger: "They don't fit in anywhere yet. They're not children but they still have to listen to their parents. I certainly thought, as a young adult, that I knew exactly where everything was at, and it wasn't until much later that I realized I didn't know everything."

Love's Ambiguities

Such self-discovery doesn't come easily for Cary, the heroine of *Tomorrow Wendy: A Love Story*, Stoehr's 1998 novel about a high school girl's sexual identity crisis. Cary is an Audrey Hepburn wannabe who is disconnected from her country-clubbing parents. She has a boyfriend, Danny, but she is more attracted to his twin sister, Wendy. She uses drugs and sex with Danny as distractions from the possibility that she might be gay, and relies on the advice of her imaginary friend Rad, who communicates only through pop music lyrics. The plot is further complicated when Raven, a new girl at school who is an open lesbian, falls for Cary and challenges her denial. Slowly Cary comes to see herself as she really is

If you enjoy the works of Shelley Stoehr, you may also want to check out the following books and films:

M. E. Kerr, *Deliver Us from Evie*, 1994.
Joyce Sweeney, *Right behind the Rain*, 1985.
Virginia Euwer Wolff, *Make Lemondade*, 1993.
Foxfire, a film based on the novel by Joyce Carol Oates, 1996.

and begins summoning up the strength for self-acceptance. "Stoehr gives her young narrator a saving sense of irony, and displays a keen appreciation for love's ambiguities and complexities," a critic in *Kirkus Reviews* observed. *School Library Journal* reviewer Miriam Lang Budin, however, wrote that "considering that this book is subtitled 'A Love Story,' there is precious little tenderness." Indeed, *Tomorrow Wendy* features all the sex, drugs, and profane language that Stoehr's readers expect. A *Publishers Weekly* contributor found that in this case, though, the sometimes contrived-sounding but "grittier elements of the story are in clearer service of a theme and message, and when the strands of the plot come together, the impact has force and vigor."

While not necessarily condoning the casual sex and drug use that her characters engage in, Stoehr does believe it's appropriate for young people to read about them. "The most important thing about reading is that they read, anything . . . ," Stoehr said in the *ALAN Review*. "The fact is, reading is good, it's important, and for young adults it doesn't always have to be *The Great Gatsby*." She added, "We need to worry less about the inevitable sex, drugs and rock and roll, and more about whether young adults are reading. Once they're reading, and choosing to read because they like it, the other issues become easier to address and conquer."

■ Works Cited

Budin, Miriam Lang, review of *Tomorrow Wendy: A Love Story*, *School Library Journal*, March, 1998, p. 224.

Campbell, Patty, "The Sand in the Oyster," *Horn Book*, July-August, 1995, pp. 495-98.

Review of *Crosses, Publishers Weekly*, November 15, 1991, p. 74.

Lesesne, Teri S., "Forget-Me-Nots: Books Worth a Second Look," *ALAN Review,* Winter, 1998, p. 52.

Shoemaker, Joel, review of *Wannabe, School Library Journal,* January, 1997.

Stevenson, Deborah, review of *Weird on the Outside, Bulletin of the Center for Children's Books,* March, 1995, p. 252.

Stevenson, Deborah, review of *Wannabe, Bulletin of the Center for Children's Books,* March, 1997, p. 258.

Stoehr, Shelley, *Crosses,* Delacorte, 1991.

Stoehr, Shelley, *Wannabe,* Delacorte, 1997.

Stoehr, Shelley, "Controversial Issues in the Lives of Contemporary Young Adults," *ALAN Review,* Winter, 1997, pp. 3-5.

Sutton, Roger, review of *Crosses, Bulletin of the Center for Children's Books,* November, 1991, p. 77.

Review of *Tomorrow Wendy: A Love Story, Kirkus Reviews,* December 1, 1997, p. 1780.

Review of *Tomorrow Wendy: A Love Story, Publishers Weekly,* December 1, 1997, p. 54.

Review of *Wannabe, Kirkus Reviews,* November 1, 1996.

Review of *Weird on the Outside, Publishers Weekly,* December 12, 1994, p. 63.

■ **For More Information See**

PERIODICALS

Bulletin of the Center for Children's Books, May, 1998, pp. 340-41.

Kirkus Reviews, December 1, 1997.

Voice of Youth Advocates, October, 1991, p. 232; February, 1995, p. 342; April, 1998, p. 50.

Wilson Library Bulletin, February, 1992, p. 86.*

—Sketch by Tracy J. Sukraw

Margaret Willey

■ Personal

Born November 5, 1950, in Chicago, IL; daughter of Foster (an artist) and Barbara (Pistorius) Willey; married Richard Joanisse, 1980; children: one daughter. *Education:* Grand Valley State College, B.Ph., B.A., 1975; Bowling Green State University, M.F.A., 1979.

■ Addresses

Home—431 Grant, Grand Haven, MI 49417.

■ Career

Writer.

■ Awards, Honors

American Library Association Best Books for Young Adults listings, 1983, for *The Bigger Book of Lydia*, 1986, for *Finding David Dolores*, 1988, for *If Not for You*, and 1990, for *Saving Lenny*; Creative

Artist Grant, Michigan Arts Council, 1984, 1988, and 1995; Recommended Books for Reluctant YA Readers selection, Young Adult Services Division, 1989, for *If Not For You*; Best of the Best for Children listing, American Library Association, 1993, for *David Dolores*; Paterson Prize for Books for Young People, and American Library Association Quick Pick, both 1997, both for *Facing the Music*.

■ Writings

The Bigger Book of Lydia, Harper, 1983.
Finding David Dolores, Harper, 1986.
If Not for You, Harper, 1988.
Saving Lenny, Bantam, 1990.
The Melinda Zone, Bantam, 1993.
Facing the Music, Delacorte, 1996.
Thanksgiving with Me, illustrated by Lloyd Bloom, HarperCollins, 1998.

Also author of short stories published in *Redbook*, *Good Housekeeping*, and literary journals.

■ Sidelights

Margaret Willey published her first young adult novel, *The Bigger Book of Lydia*, to critical acclaim in 1983. Since then she has become one of the foremost authors of books about teenage issues and problems. *Twentieth-Century Young Adult Writers* contributor Jan Tyler echoed the praise that has consistently greeted Willey's work: "Hers are distinctly drawn personalities with a range of conflicts: problems with parents; troubles with boyfriends; breeches of loyalty between best friends; school woes; and particularly, always, the struggle to find and to be oneself." Willey is the winner of numerous literary awards, including several honors from the American Library Association.

During an interview with *Authors and Artists for Young Adults* (*AAYA*) Willey talked about her goals as a writer. Born in Chicago, Illinois, she grew up in St. Joseph, Michigan, which was the model for the town of St. Martin's in her early novels. The author is the oldest daughter in a family of eleven children, a fact that has directly influenced her work. Willey commented to *AAYA*: "My role in my family of origin played an enormous part in my development as a writer and a creative person. As the eldest daughter I was a kind of premature adult and very much involved in taking care of others, watching them and observing them and in some ways identifying with them. It was my boot camp for writing, especially for writing about teenagers. I was surrounded by adolescent turmoil. All the things I observed about the different ways of coping with adolescence stayed with me. I also had a need to re-enact a less chaotic and more orderly adolescence than the one I had, which I have been able to do through my novels."

Between Two Worlds

Reflecting on the differences between her own adolescent self and teenagers today, Willey pointed out that "Some aspects of adolescence are the same. The concept of a teenager as a person who is somewhere between childhood and adulthood is a fairly modern phenomenon. It was in full bloom when I was a teenager, and I think there is still a holding-tank time for teenagers before they become adults. Ideally it would be a time of safety and learning, but it's not." Instead, Willey observed, "[Adolescence has] become a time of conflict. In some ways teenagers have more challenges today. They have a more constant battle with sexuality issues, with health issues." Complicating the problem is a lack of adult understanding or awareness of teenagers' needs, she asserted. "Many adults don't want teenagers to have the information [about those issues]. They want to protect them. I grew up before there was

a drug culture. It was coming, but it hadn't really hit yet, and that was a huge difference. Today there is no way to protect teenagers from exposure to the social issue of drug abuse."

Willey's experiences as a teenager provided a model for several of the female characters in her books. She recalled, "Because I was a classically artistic girl I had a lot of qualities that I've given to my characters. One was a kind of radar for other people's expectations and feelings, another was a strong need for a creative outlet." Willey said her own adolescent years were difficult, primarily because her role within her family did not

Margaret Willey

Success could ultimately lead to disappointment when a girl becomes a singer for her brother's band in this 1993 novel.

prepare her for the isolation she felt at school. "In my family I was very powerful," the author said, "and I had a strong sense of belonging because of my role; I was essential to the survival of the family. So, there was a real dichotomy between the power I felt in my family as opposed to the invisibility that I felt at school. It was almost like having a split personality. There's still a lot of creative energy for me in focusing on that dichotomy, which continues to inspire me to write."

Similarly, Willey remembers struggling with the fact of being female: "I had some concerns about being female because of what being female had meant for my mom." Another gender problem she confronted was body image: "The body issue for adolescent girls is one I'm fascinated with because I struggled with it myself." Yet, she observed, "Finding a comfortable body image and making peace with a diversity of body types is much more difficult for teenagers today." The challenge to find a comfortable body image eventually led Willey to write *The Bigger Book of Lydia.*

Feeling Like a Writer

The author told *AAYA* how she became a writer of novels for young adults. "I wrote all through my adolescence and into college," Willey recalled. "I kept a journal and I wrote poetry, but it was a very private process. It wasn't until I was in my late twenties, after having a variety of jobs, that I decided that what I really wanted to do was write professionally. I entered an MFA program in writing at Bowling Green State University. For the first time I really felt like a writer. I wrote every day, and I had never done that. I started calling myself a writer in the midst of other people who called themselves writers."

Nevertheless, Willey encountered some difficulties. "I was writing in the voice of a young girl at that point," she said, "and I didn't get a lot of encouragement. My first publications were for adults. Then I started writing a story about a girl who had a fear of being small, who felt like she was in constant danger because she was small. That was Lydia. The story just got longer and longer, and it eventually became *The Bigger Book of Lydia.*"

The Bigger Book of Lydia is the story of fifteen-year-old Lydia Bitte. Since the death of her father when she was ten, she has been keeping a journal called the "Bigger Book," in which she records her feelings and fears about being small. Lydia is obsessed with her size, but she receives no support from family members who are locked into their own problems. Making matters even worse, she is picked on by her classmates and she wants to drop out of school. Soon she turns to her mother's friend Claudine, who helps her find perspective on her situation. Lydia's life is changed when Claudine's teenage niece, Michelle, stays with the Bittes for a few months. Michelle is anorexic and must undergo treatment at a nearby clinic. As the two girls grow closer, Michelle begins eating again and Lydia learns to accept herself. Then Michelle's father steps in and demands that Michelle return home, claiming she is cured and needs no further care. Although everyone realizes Michelle still has anorexic tendencies, she has gained strength from the loving environment provided by the Bittes, Lydia, and Claudine. In turn bolstered by the friendship with Michelle, Lydia makes a significant step by deciding she will finish her high school education.

A contributor in *Bulletin of the Center for Children's Books* called *The Bigger Book of Lydia* "a remarkably good first novel, written with intelligence, wit, and insight; the characterizations and relationships are strong, the development believable, and the writing style fluent." Audrey B. Eaglen observed in *School Library Journal* that the novel is "a story of mutually strengthening friendship between two interesting young women and, incidentally, is informative about the problems of anorexia. . . ." *Voice of Youth Advocates* reviewer Ellen Gulick found the characters to be "well-defined" in this "excellent first novel."

After the success of *The Bigger Book of Lydia,* Willey became a full-time author of books for adolescent readers. Her second novel, *Finding David Dolores,* explores the challenges of friendship as well as the difficulties of young romance. The main character is thirteen-year-old Arly, who has isolated herself from family and friends. One day, while taking a walk alone, she sees David Dolores, a tall, handsome older boy, and begins having romantic fantasies about him. Following David at a distance, Arly collects magazines he has thrown away and secretly listens while he practices his oboe. Then Arly meets Regina, a seemingly glamorous and sophisticated new girl in town, who encourages Arly's solitariness and her infatuation with David. The girls' friendship becomes complicated, however, when Regina decides she needs a new mother and she chooses David's mother, Althea. Arly prefers to admire David from a distance, so she feels uncomfortable with Regina's intense pursuit of Althea. Eventually Regina's neurotic behavior causes problems: Arly loses her illusions about David while Regina hurts her own mother and damages the relationship between David and Althea. In the end Arly rescues Regina by refusing to compromise her own values.

Critics praised *Finding David Dolores* as a believable portrayal of the way people simultaneously need and misuse one another. A *Bulletin of the Center for Children's Books* contributor stated that "the multiple tensions between characters are remarkably well-played in a deceptively simple and compelling story." In the *New York Times Book Review* Ann Turner noted that the work would appeal to teenagers because it is "briskly written with a lot of emotional content. What Arly and Regina have to tell us about friendship is important and needs hearing." Turner also pointed out that plot and characterization sometimes could be clarified. Yet she added that these minor concerns are outweighed by the fact that Willey "knows adolescents and is not afraid to explore complicated questions. . . ."

Exploring Relationships

The topic of Willey's next novel, *If Not For You*, is teenage marriage. The story unfolds through the eyes of Bonnie, who is intrigued by Linda, the older sister of her best friend Jenny. Linda became pregnant, ran away from home, and married the boy she loved. After she comes back to town to have her baby she hires Bonnie as a babysitter. This move causes a rift between Bonnie and Jenny, who feels slighted by her sister. Over time Bonnie is drawn into Linda's world, watching the teenage mother and father trying to cope with adult responsibilities. Increasingly, Linda relies on Bonnie as a confidante and a connection with the carefree life she has lost. Finally the brief marriage ends and Bonnie gains valuable insight into her own relationship with Robert, her first boyfriend, who is shy and emotionally stable. *Horn Book* reviewer Nancy Vasilakas commented that Willey's primary purpose in writing the novel clearly was to "warn against the pitfalls of teenage marriage."

But, she continued, the author skillfully "raises the story above the level of formula fiction." A *Publishers Weekly* contributor found the novel to be "riveting, as [Willey] penetrates and reveals the ways in which friendships flow and the ways in which they falter."

Teenage romance is also the focus of *Saving Lenny*. The novel depicts the dilemma of Jesse, a pretty and popular high school senior who falls in love with a mysterious boy named Lenny. When she meets Lenny at a football game, her best friend Kay urges her to write him a note asking for a date. Soon Lenny is in love with Jesse and becomes increasingly dependent upon her—he quits the tennis team, lets his homework slide, and even talks Jesse into skipping school with him. When Jesse discovers that Lenny suffers from deep depression, she decides not to go to college because he needs her help. In spite of protests from Kay and her parents, Jesse moves with Lenny to a cottage on a lake. She then takes a job as a waitress and spends her spare time trying to save Lenny from his mental illness. Before long Jesse feels smothered by his possessiveness and becomes ill herself. As their relationship falls apart she alerts Lenny's parents to the seriousness of his problems. By this time Jesse realizes she has pushed her parents and Kay aside in her exhausting efforts to support Lenny. *Voice of Youth Advocates* critic Susan Rosenkoetter welcomed *Saving Lenny* as an "appealing problem novel [that] can be enjoyed, booktalked, and discussed on many levels." She commends Willey's "skillful device" of employing a first-person narrative that alternates chapters between Jesse and Kay, giving the reader "both involvement and objectivity."

Revisiting Misery

As Willey continued her career, she began to draw increasingly upon her own adolescence experiences. Willey told *AAYA*, "In order to go on being an author in this area, to keep growing, I had to look at my own misery as a teenager and try to come to a better understanding, to revisit that place—it's almost like a geographic place. Not only do you revisit misery but you also reclaim the strength that got you through. Everybody develops coping strategies in childhood." Coping strategies are essential to fourteen-year-old Melinda, the central character in Willey's third novel, *The Melinda Zone.* Melinda is constantly

The Melinda Zone

MARGARET WILLEY

author of **Saving Lenny**

Melinda's summer with relatives gives her the courage to confront her divorced parents about the way they treat her.

being forced to split her loyalties—and her sense of self—between her divorced parents. Known as Mindy when she visits her mother's apartment in Milwaukee, she is called Linda while visiting her father's farm.

During Melinda's fifteenth summer she is excluded from her parents' plans, so she goes to stay with her aunt, uncle, and cousin Sharon in St. Joseph, Michigan. Melinda had hoped to spend time with Sharon, but Sharon has become involved with her boyfriend, Evan, which causes tension in the family. Melinda then turns to a new friend, Paul, and finds what he calls her "Melinda Zone."

She also reclaims her real name, and when she returns home at the end of the summer she confronts her parents with the problems they have caused her. *Voice of Youth Advocates* reviewer Joyce Hamilton described *The Melinda Zone* as "an upbeat[,] oftentimes humorous story" that gives "a very refreshing look at a fifteen-year-old girl from a broken home who tries to bring some normalcy to her life and does a lot of growing up in the process." Carolyn Phelan noted in *Booklist* that Willey "writes with keen perception," producing "well-drawn characters."

In the interview with *AAYA* Willey described her method for developing characters and stories. "An idea sits with me for a long time," the author said, "sometimes over a year, and gradually it starts to take its place in my imagination. Usually it's through a character whose voice I start to hear, until the personality of that character gains clarity. That can happen for a long time before I actually start to write the novel or story around that character. The next step then comes gradually: What are the circumstances of this character's life? What is the challenge? What's the problem? In what way have things broken down for this character? What is the task the character has to face?" She recalled that this process was particularly important when she wrote *The Melinda Zone* and created the character of Lisa Franklin in *Facing the Music.*

In *Facing the Music* fifteen-year-old Lisa Franklin has to confront several tasks: recovering from her mother's death, struggling with her dependence on her brother Mark, dealing with her first romance, and recognizing an emerging sense of self. As the story opens Mark has joined a band called Crawl Space in an effort to break away from Lisa. He is therefore upset when Danny Fabiano, the leader of the band, asks Lisa to be the vocalist. Soon Lisa also becomes Danny's girlfriend, but they keep their relationship a secret because Mark knows about Danny's reputation as a heartbreaker. The band is a success and Lisa is catapulted from her withdrawn world into the spotlight as a local celebrity. Before long the band is beset by internal conflict and breaks up. Danny also drops Lisa and she must painfully come to terms with rejection. At the same time, however, she discovers she has genuine musical talent.

Reviewers praised Willey's technique of interspersing Lisa and Mark's accounts of the action

If you enjoy the works of Margaret Willey, you may also want to check out the following books and films:

Pamela Conrad, *What I Did for Roman*, 1987.
Caroline B. Cooney, *Don't Blame the Music*, 1986.
Norma Klein, *No More Saturday Nights*, 1988.
The Man in the Moon, a film starring Reese Witherspoon, 1991.

throughout the narrative, and again the author was commended for her ability to create believable characters. Carolyn Noah stated in *School Library Journal* that "Lisa is convincingly drawn" and predicted that this "fast-paced read" will "keep kids turning pages and leave them with something to think about as well." *Booklist* critic Anne O'Malley called the novel a "realistic portrayal of the adolescent psyche," and a *Publishers Weekly* contributor observed that the characters in *Facing the Music* "seem to acquire a life off the page, too."

Childhood Memories

Willey recently published her first verse work, an illustrated book for children. Titled *Thanksgiving with Me*, it is a dialogue between a six-year-old girl and her mother as they wait for the girl's six uncles to arrive for Thanksgiving dinner. The mother reminisces about the rollicking, joyful times she had with these brothers on past Thanksgivings. Willey, who has six brothers herself, told *AAYA* that she wrote the story for her daughter and drew upon her own childhood experiences. The author enjoys writing poetry: "It is the closest I'll ever come to making music."

Willey has several forthcoming projects. Among them is a collection of essays for young readers on women's issues and a collection of short stories for adults, which focuses on adults and teenagers in confrontation. The author mentioned that her sixteen-year-old daughter volunteered to be a "consultant" for the essays. Willey elaborated: "Sometimes I miss the mark, so now I feel that I have a great resource for checking my accuracy and information. Not only my daughter but also

her friends. My house is full of teenagers now, so it's like a bonus. I've never been more inspired and fascinated by teenagers than I am now." With the short-story collection Willey hopes to achieve better adult awareness of teenage problems. "Adults are willing to remember their childhoods," she commented to *AAYA*, "but very few adults will revisit their adolescence. There's a huge resistance to it because it represents so many things that adults fear of—being powerless, having no control, experiencing loneliness, confronting sexual confusion. They put it behind them and that's where they want it to stay, and that's why there's an ongoing generation gap."

Although Willey has had a successful career, she told *AAYA* that she confronts rejection daily. "The fact that I didn't have to deal with it as a younger writer somewhat spoiled me. I have times of discouragement." Nevertheless, like her characters, Willey has discovered coping strategies: "I've developed some techniques for working through discouragement. I've learned how to find a sense of accomplishment in doing household tasks or having a brief conversation with my daughter, which can outweigh the disappointments of a few discouraging phone calls." The writer attributes her resilience to experiences she had as a teenager. "I've always felt like I'm on my own, a strength I developed at an early age," she remarked to *AAYA*. She also finds a direct connection between being an artist and being a teenager. "One is that you really are alone," Willey observed, "and you have to face the music—if I can quote my own book title—of that loneliness. There are some things that require you to find your own inner strength in order to cope. That is one of the similarities between the creative life and the challenge of adolescence." Describing both the role of the artist and the dilemma of the teenager who must develop a sense of self, Willey concluded, "It's a matter of achieving a balance between isolation and connection."

■ Works Cited

Review of *The Bigger Book of Lydia*, *Bulletin of the Center for Children's Books*, January, 1984, p. 99.
Eaglen, Audrey B., review of *The Bigger Book of Lydia*, *School Library Journal*, December, 1983, p. 78.
Review of *Facing the Music*, *Publishers Weekly*, February 26, 1996.

Review of *Finding David Dolores, Bulletin of the Center for Children's Books,* May, 1986.

Gulick, Ellen, review of *The Bigger Book of Lydia, Voice of Youth Advocates,* April, 1984, p. 36.

Hamilton, Joyce, review of *The Melinda Zone, Voice of Youth Advocates,* April, 1993, p. 32.

Review of *If Not for You, Publishers Weekly,* August, 1988, p. 91.

Noah, Carolyn, review of *Facing the Music, School Library Journal,* February, 1996.

O'Malley, Anne, review of *Facing the Music, Booklist,* April, 1996.

Phelan, Carolyn, review of *The Melinda Zone, Booklist,* January 15, 1993, p. 892.

Rosenkoetter, Susan, review of *Saving Lenny, Voice of Youth Advocates,* October, 1990, p. 223.

Turner, Ann, review of *Finding David Dolores, New York Times Book Review,* October 12, 1986, p. 37.

Tyler, Jan, "Margaret Willey," *Twentieth-Century Young Adult Writers,* St. James Press, 1994, pp. 708-9.

Vasilakas, Nancy, review of *If Not for You, Horn Book,* November/December, 1988, pp. 793-94.

Willey, Margaret, interview with Peggy Saari for *Authors and Artists for Young Adults,* June, 1998.

■ For More Information See

BOOKS

Something About the Author, Volume 86, Gale, pp. 235-37.

PERIODICALS

Booklist, January 15, 1993; April, 1996.
Booktalker, January, 1991, p. 13.
Bulletin of the Center for Children's Books, March, 1993, p. 229; April, 1996, p. 281; November, 1998, p. 115.
Kirkus Reviews, November 1, 1983, p. 210; January 1, 1993, p. 69; April, 1996; September 1, 1998, p. 1295.
Publishers Weekly, December 9, 1983, p. 50; January 18, 1993; September 28, 1998, p. 50.
School Library Journal, December, 1983, p. 78; March, 1993, p. 224.
Voice of Youth Advocates, April, 1984, p. 36; August/October, 1986, p. 131; April, 1996.

—Sketch by Peggy Saari

Acknowledgments

Acknowledgments

Grateful acknowledgment is made to the following publishers, authors, and artists for their kind permission to reproduce copyrighted material.

NATHAN AASENG. Aaseng, Nathan, photograph. Reproduced by permission./ From a jacket of *Navajo Code Talkers* by Nathan Aaseng. National Archives (127-MN-69889-B)./ From a cover of *You Are the President* by Nathan Aaseng. The Oliver Press, Inc., 1994. Copyright © 1994 by The Oliver Press, Inc. Reproduced by permission of the publisher./ From a jacket of *The Locker Room Mirror: How Sports Reflect Society* by Nathan Aaseng. Walker and Company, 1993. Reproduced by permission of the publisher./ King, Martin Luther (being congratulated by King Olav of Norway), 1964, photograph. National Archives (286-MP-NOR-1306).

SCOTT ADAMS. Adams, Scott (holding ink drawing of Dilbert with Dogbert), photograph. AP/Wide World Photos. Reproduced by permission./ From a cover of *The Dilbert Principle: A Cubicle's-Eye View of Bosses, Meetings, Management Fads, & Other Workplace Afflictions* by Scott Adams. HarperBusiness, 1996. Copyright © 1996 by United Feature Syndicate, Inc. All rights Reserved. Reproduced by permission of United Media Enterprises.

LLOYD ALEXANDER. Alexander, Lloyd, photograph by Alexander Limont. Reproduced by permission of Lloyd Alexander./ From a cover of *The Beggar Queen* by Lloyd Alexander. Laurel-Leaf Books, 1984. Copyright © 1984 by Lloyd Alexander. Used by permission of Bantam Doubleday Dell Books for Young Readers./ From a cover of *The High King* by Lloyd Alexander. Yearling, 1968. Copyright © 1968 by Lloyd Alexander. Used by permission of Bantam Doubleday Dell Books for Young Readers./ From a cover of *The Black Cauldron* by Lloyd Alexander. Yearling, 1965. Copyright © 1965 by Lloyd Alexander. Used by permission of Bantam Doubleday Dell Books for Young Readers./ Zelinsky, Paul O., illustrator. From a jacket of *The Remarkable Journey of Prince Jen* by Lloyd Alexander. Dutton Children's Books, 1991. Copyright © 1991 by Paul O. Zelinsky. Used by permission of Dutton Children's Books, a division of Penguin Putnam Inc.

JAMES CAMERON. Cameron, James, directing *True Lies*, photograph by Zade Rosenthal. The Kobal Collection. Reproduced by permission./ Winslet, Kate with Leonardo DiCaprio, starring in the film *Titanic*, photograph by Merie W. Wallace. The Kobal Collection. Reproduced by permission./ Schwarzenegger, Arnold, in a scene from *Terminator*, photograph. The Kobal Collection. Reproduced by permission./ Weaver, Sigourney in the film *Aliens*, photograph. The Kobal Collection. Reproduced by permission./ Scene from *Terminator 2: Judgement Day*, movie still. The Kobal Collection. Reproduced by permission./ Schwarzenegger, Arnold, with Jamie Lee Curtis and Art Malik, in the film *True Lies*, photograph by Zade Rosenthal. The Kobal Collection. Reproduced by permission.

AIDAN CHAMBERS. Chambers, Aidan, photograph by Lydia van der Meer. Reproduced by permission of Aidan Chambers./ Jacket of *Dance on My Grave* by Aidan Chambers. Harper & Row, 1982. Jacket © 1982 by Harper & Row, Publishers, Inc. Reproduced by permission of HarperCollins Publishers, Inc.

DANIEL DEFOE. DeFoe, Daniel, drawing. The Library of Congress./ Quinn, Aidan, in the film *Crusoe*, photograph. The Kobal Collection. Reproduced by permission./ Illustration from *Robinson Crusoe* by Daniel DeFoe. David McKay, Publisher, n.d.

LOREN D. ESTLEMAN. Estleman, Loren D., photograph by Deborah Morgan. Reproduced by permission./ Hall, Tom, illustrator. From a cover of *Bloody Season* by Loren D. Estleman. Bantam Books, 1988. Cover Art © 1988 by Tom Hall. Used by permission of Bantam Books, a division of Bantam Doubleday Dell Publishing Group, Inc./ Lurin, Larry, illustrator. From a cover of *Whiskey River* by Loren D. Estleman. Bantam Books, 1990. Jacket design © 1990 Larry Lurin. Used by permission of Bantam Books, a division of Bantam Doubleday Dell Publishing Group, Inc./ From a cover of *Stress* by Loren D. Estleman. Warner Books, 1996. Copyright © 1996 by Loren D. Estleman. Reproduced by permission./ From a cover of *Never Street* by Loren D. Estleman. Warner Books, 1997. Copyright © 1997 by Loren D. Estleman. Reproduced by permission.

TERRY GOODKIND. Goodkind, Terry, photograph by Jeri Goodkind. Reproduced by permission./ From a cover of *Wizard's First Rule* by Terry Goodkind. Tom Doherty Associates, Inc., 1994. Copyright © 1994 by Terry Goodkind. Reproduced by permission./ From a cover of *Stone of Tears* by Terry Goodkind. Tom Doherty Associates, Inc., 1995. Copyright © 1995 by Terry Goodkind. Reproduced by permission./ From a cover of *Blood of the Fold* by Terry Goodkind. Tom Doherty Associates, Inc., 1996. Copyright © 1996 by Terry Goodkind. Reproduced by permission.

KAREN HESSE. Hesse, Karen, (standing outside, leaning on balcony), photograph. AP/Wide World Photos. Reproduced by permission. From a cover of *Out of the Dust* by Karen Hesse. AP/Wide World Photos. Reproduced by permission./ Harlin, Greg, illustrator. From a cover of *The Music of Dolphins* by Karen Hesse. Scholastic Press, 1996. Illustration copyright © 1996 by Greg Harlin. Reprinted by permission of Scholastic Inc.

1997 by HarperCollins Publishers. Used by permission of HarperCollins Publishers./ From a cover of *The Ragwitch* by Garth Nix. Tom Doherty Associates Books, 1990. Copyright © 1990 Garth Nix. Reproduced by permission of St. Martin's Press.

NAOMI SHIHAB NYE. Nye, Naomi Shihab, photograph. Reproduced by permission./ Colón, Raúl, illustrator. From a cover of *Habibi* by Naomi Shihab Nye. Simon & Schuster Books For Young Readers, 1997. Jacket illustration copyright © 1997 by Raúl Colón. Reproduced by permission./ Russo, Anthony, illustrator. From a cover of *I Feel A Little Jumpy Around You* by Naomi Shihab Nye and Paul B. Janeczko. Simon & Schuster Books For Young Readers, 1996. Front jacket copyright © 1996 by Anthony Russo. Reproduced by permission./ Eksjoglu, Gürbüz D., illustrator. From a cover of *The Space Between Our Footsteps* by Naomi Shihab Nye. Simon & Schuster Books For Young Readers, 1998. Jacket illustration copyright © 1998 by Gürbüz D. Eksjoglu. Reproduced by permission.

TREY PARKER AND MATT STONE. Stone, Matt with Trey Parker, photograph. AP/Wide World Photos. Reproduced by permission./ Scene from the show, *South Park*, photograph. AP/Wide World Photos. Reproduced by permission.

ERICH MARIA REMARQUE. Remarque, Erich Maria, with dog, photograph. AP/Wide World Photos. Reproduced by permission./ From a cover of *All Quiet on the Western Front* by Erich Maria Remarque. Fawcett Crest Books, 1992. Copyright 1929, 1930 by Little, Brown and Company; copyright renewed 1957, 1958 by Erich Maria Remarque. Reproduced by permission of Random House, Inc./ Thomas, Richard starring in the television movie *All Quiet on the Western Front*, 1979, photograph. The Kobal Collection. Reproduced by permission.

SHELLEY STOEHR. From a cover of *Weird on the Outside* by Shelley Stoehr. Laurel-Leaf Books, 1995. Copyright © 1995 by Michelle Stoehr. Used by permission of Bantam Doubleday Dell Books for Young Readers. Stabin, Victor, illustrator./ From a cover of *Tomorrow Wendy: A Love Story* by Shelley Stoehr. Delacorte Press, 1998. Jacket illustration © 1998 by Victor Stabin. Used by permission of Bantam Doubleday Dell Books for Young Readers./ Stoehr, Shelley, photograph by Mark Buhler. Reproduced by permission.

MARGARET WILLEY. Willey, Margaret, photograph by Marc Hoeksema. Reproduced by permission./ Leon, Jana, illustrator. From a cover of *Facing the Music* by Margaret Willey. Laurel-Leaf Books, 1997. Reproduced by permission of Bantam Doubleday Dell Books for Young Readers./ From a cover of *The Melinda Zone* by Margaret Willey. Dell Books, 1994. Reproduced by permission of Dell Books, a division of Bantam Doubleday Dell Publishing Group, Inc.

Cumulative Index

Author/Artist Index

The following index gives the number of the volume in which an author/artist's biographical sketch appears.